Thus saith the Lord...

Thus saith the Lord...

The Role of Prophets
and Revelation
in the Kingdom of God

DUANE S. CROWTHER

INTERNATIONAL STANDARD BOOK NUMBER
0-88290-168-0

LIBRARY OF CONGRESS CATALOG CARD NUMBER
80-83862

Printed and Distributed in the
United States of America
by

**Horizon
Publishers &
Distributors**

―――――――――

P.O. Box 490
50 South 500 West
Bountiful, Utah 84010

Dedication

To my family—

Jean,

Don,

Scott,

Laura,

Lisa,

David,

William,

Sharon, and

Bethany

May they say, as did the prophet Nephi,

"Behold, my soul delighteth in the things of the Lord, and my heart pondereth continually upon the things which I have seen and heard."

Salvation cannot come without revelation; it is in vain for anyone to minister without it. No man is a minister of Jesus Christ without being a Prophet. No man can be a minister of Jesus Christ except he has the testimony of Jesus; and this is the spirit of prophecy.

Joseph Smith
History of the Church
Volume III, page 389

Contents

CONTENTS   13

Key to Abbreviations
Used in the Footnotes

Ibid., — (For the Latin *ibidem,* "in the same place") means that the quotation is taken from the same source as the reference which preceded it.

Op. Cit., — (For the Latin *opere citato,* "In the work cited") means that the quotation is taken from the same book which has previously been quoted by that author.

HC 5:265 — means Joseph Smith, *History of the Church of Jesus Christ of Latter-day Saints,* (Salt Lake City, Utah: The Deseret Book Company for the Church, Second Edition revised, 1959), volume five, page 265.

CHC 1:362 — means Brigham H. Roberts, *A Comprehensive History of The Church of Jesus Christ of Latter-day Saints* (Salt Lake City, Utah: Deseret News Press for the Church, 1930), volume one, page 362.

JD 12:127 — means *Journal of Discourses* (Liverpool: F. D. and S. W. Richards; photo lithographic reprint of exact original edition by General Printing & Lithograph Co., Los Angeles, California, 1961), volume twelve, page 127.

D&C 1:14 — means *The Doctrine and Covenants of The Church of Jesus Christ of Latter-day Saints* (Salt Lake City, Utah: The Church of Jesus Christ of Latter-day Saints, 1952), section one, verse fourteen.

CR — means Conference Report of the annual or semi-annual conference of The Church of Jesus Christ of Latter-day Saints, published by the Church at Salt Lake City, Utah.

Standard abbreviations are used for scriptural references.

Prologue

Believe in the Lord your God, so shall ye be established; believe his prophets, so shall ye prosper.[1]

These were the words of Jehoshaphat, king of Judah, spoken early in the morning to Judah's army in the wilderness of Tekoa. They were preparing to resist the onslaught of an overwhelming attack mounted against them by an alliance of three nations: the Ammonites, the Moabites, and the Edomites. The attacking force was huge, and so strong that there was little hope that Judah's small host could resist them.

Several days earlier, as the opposing army formed and began to advance upon Judah, Jehoshaphat called a national fast,[2] and then prayed to the Lord in the temple for succor to prevent the fall of his nation.[3] As all Judah "stood before the Lord,"[4] the Spirit of the Lord came upon Jahaziel, a Levite who stood in the midst of the congregation.[5] Jahaziel revealed the Lord's reply to the fervent prayer uttered by Jehoshaphat:

> Thus saith the Lord unto you, *Be not afraid nor dismayed by reason of this great multitude, for the battle is not yours, but God's.* . . .
> *Ye shall not need to fight in this battle:* set yourselves, stand ye still, and see the salvation of the Lord with you, O Judah and Jerusalem: fear not, nor be dismayed, tomorrow go out against them: for the Lord will be with you.[6]

---

1. II Chron. 20:20.
2. II Chron. 20:3.
3. II Chron. 20:5-12. Verse 9, a portion of his prayer, shows what it means to stand in holy places at a time of trial:

> *If when evil cometh upon us, as the sword, judgment, or pestilence, or famine, we stand before this house, and in thy presence, (for thy name is in this house,) and cry unto thee in our affliction, then thou wilt hear and help.*

For allusions to a future period when the saints will again have to stand in holy places see D&C 45:30-33; 87:4-8; 101:17-23.
4. II Chron. 20:13.
5. Note that Jahaziel was neither the head of the church nor the king's agent in political affairs. Those posts were held by Amariah, the "chief priest," and Zebadiah. (II Chron. 19:11.) Jahaziel was only a priest who was a member of the choir (one of the "sons of Asaph").
6. II Chron. 20:15, 17.

15

As the Lord directed through Jahaziel, Jehoshaphat led his army to the revealed battle site. There Judah's singers raised a song of praise to the Lord as they watched the approaching army suddenly turn on one another and fight to the death, so that none of the attacking horde escaped.[7] Jehoshaphat's army stripped the corpses of their booty, and the riches were so great it took three days for them to gather the spoils before they returned to Jerusalem with joy.

What was the process by which the Lord revealed His will to the people of Judah in their hour of impending tragedy? How does God reveal His will to man? To whom, and through whom, does He speak? And how can people know if a prophecy will truly come to pass? How can they know who to trust and who to follow? Will we really prosper if we follow the prophets, as Jehoshaphat admonished? This book is written to answer these and many other related queries.

The Troublesome Question: "When Is a Prophet a Prophet?"

The doctrines of "revelation" and "prophecy," with their many ramifications, are frequently misunderstood by Latter-day Saints today. Indeed, this author has found that more questions are asked on this subject than on any other doctrinal theme. Over the years, confusion concerning how God speaks to man has led to serious breaches and disagreements within the Church, resulting in apostasy, bitterness, persecution, and the disaffection even of members of the highest councils of Church leadership.

President Harold B. Lee was deeply aware of the tremendous need for the saints to understand how God speaks to man, and of the danger of disaffection that can arise when the doctrines of "revelation" and "prophecy" are misunderstood. In the priesthood session of General Conference of April, 1970, he spoke these words:

> *You brethren of the priesthood should be well advised that the principle of revelation through proper channels has been at issue in every persecution of the Latter-day Saints in this dispensation, whether it be on the subject of priesthood, marriage, the gathering of Zion, or succession of the priesthood.*[8]

His observation is valid. Cries of "Fallen prophet!" brought the great apostasy of 1837-1838, in which a third of the Church and almost half of its leaders fell away. The question of who was the proper successor to Joseph Smith ultimately led to the formation of several "break-off" churches, some of which are still in existence today. The question of

---

7. II Chron. 20:20-27.
8. Harold B. Lee, *Conference Report,* April 1970, p. 56.

whether or not God actually instructed the saints to stop living the principle of plural marriage, through the manifesto released by President Wilford Woodruff, brought the loss of other members and general authorities of the Church, and led to the formation of various fundamentalist cults. And recent issues cannot be ignored. Many faithful saints have sought answers to queries such as "Did God actually reveal that the Negro was not to hold the priesthood in Joseph Smith's day, or was that merely a policy adopted by early Church leaders to avoid social pressures and conflict with the slavery issue? And has God now revealed that negroes may hold the priesthood today? And what about the ERA—are we dealing with a policy set by men, or with servants of God responding to revealed instruction as we observe the stand taken by Church leaders on the Equal Rights Amendment?" There's no doubt about it: "when is a prophet a prophet," and "how and to whom does God speak" are questions that have troubled the saints for over 150 years, and which persist to this day.

Two Contending Beliefs

A "tug-of-war" situation seems to exist, which usually functions below the level of obvious perception most of the time, but rises to more obvious levels as issues become the center of controversy.

Apostate and anti-Mormon challengers have raised challenges concerning the legitimacy of authority of past and present Church leaders, and deny that those men were actually the authorized spokesmen for God in these latter days. Others assert that theories expressed by early leaders, which were never canonized as doctrine by the Church, are actually revealed truths which one must accept to be able to gain salvation and exaltation. And others assert that items such as the manifesto were not revelations at all, but rather a yielding by the Church to the intense social pressure exerted against the practice of plural marriage and the political "kingdom of God" which held strong temporal power in the Utah Territory. They claim that revealed principles were abandoned for the sake of popularity, and that by abandoning those principles the prophets have led the Church members astray. Other apostates have challenged the "form" and "style" of recorded revelations, asserting that God does not speak to man in that manner.

Critics of the Church are very vocal, and raise a variety of challenges intended to spread doubt and distrust among the members of the Church. They mix in falsehoods and half truths, inserting their own theories and ill-founded "logic"—but their central thrust is almost always the same: to challenge the legitimacy of the vital Latter-day Saint doctrine that God is still revealing His will to man through modern Prophets and Revelators.

But the pendulum swings both ways. "In the other corner," zealous Church members have sought to generate loyalty and unity by a continual outpouring of preachments on the themes of "living prophets" and "follow the brethren." Sunday School manuals for the youth, with year-long curricula, are devoted to the subject, as are semester courses at the Brigham Young University and in the Church Institute system.

But problems exist, which are of increasing concern to Church members. Some saints are overzealous, jealously "protecting the prophet," and attempting to expand the scope of the role he plays. There is a definite move, which some regard as dangerous, towards the concept of infallibility, with an increasing call to accept as "inspired," and as "doctrine," all the comments, addresses and writings of general authorities, without question or analysis. Some saints hold the view that doctrinal books written by general authorities are the only ones that should be read and studied by Church members. Impassioned statements that the "prophet will never lead the Church astray," that "we should obey the prophet—even if he tells us to do something wrong we'll be blessed for our obedience," that we "should sustain calls made by Church leaders to show our obedience to those leaders," and that "living prophets take precedence over dead prophets" are becoming more frequent.

Some assert that it is no longer necessary for a prophet to identify revelations from God to the Church as being actual revelations, and insist that members should regard *all* the prophet's statements as being revelations. Indeed, those who insist on the necessity of using "Thus saith the Lord" or similar revelation-identifying phrases are considered suspect in some circles. Monthly magazine articles containing counsel and advice by members of the First Presidency and other authorities are frequently represented as being the "latest revelation" to the Church.

Hosts on temple square emphasize to visitors that the Church has living prophets who are receiving revelations on a day-to-day basis, but the hosts, like the rest of the Church, lack access to those specific revelations and are left without definitive answers when non-members ask, "What are some of the revelations that have been sent by God recently?" "Last Thursday," the usual meeting day for the general authorities, is offered as the reply to the question, "When was revelation last received by the Church?" rather than furnishing details and documentation.

Those who share personal manifestations are regarded by some as usurpers—individuals who need to be carefully watched and regarded as suspect—while spiritual gifts being experienced and reported by the members increasingly have become a rarity. Few living Latter-day Saints have witnessed others prophesy, speak in tongues, or receive the more visible gifts of the spirit, and such experiences have somehow become items to be kept secret, rather than to be openly reported and discussed in the meetings of the Church as they were in earlier times.

For a Latter-day Saint to raise some of the above concerns in a Church class is considered "murmuring," yet the concerns are widespread, and this author would not be honest if he did not acknowledge their existence. The saints have faith in their leaders, but in this day of graduate degrees and in-depth media reporting, they also want *facts* about God's present communication with man. Where revelation is concerned, they want to know who, where, when, and why, and they want to know the exact wording. And a public-relations program is no substitute for details and facts.

The Lord's Systems of Checks and Balances

Latter-day Saints accept the Constitution of the United States as being an inspired document. Indeed, the Lord has revealed that *"I established the Constitution* of this land, by the hands of wise men whom I raised up unto this very purpose, . . ."[9]

There is an important lesson we need to learn from that great document: that God controls men in positions of power through an intricate system of checks and balances. In the United States Government three branches exist, each with power to restrain the actions of another branch. The Executive branch has the presidential power to veto legislation passed by the Legislative Branch. The Judicial Branch has the Supreme Court power to negate presidential and congressional decisions, yet the president has the power to select the men who will sit in that court. And the Legislative Branch has power to pass laws which affect the judgments of the Judicial machinations. In one way or another, each branch has the ability to correct the excesses of the other branches. Thus, a system of checks and balances exists which holds the nation to a valid course without allowing it to engage itself for long in extreme or unwise policies.

A revealed system of checks and balances exists within the Church also. Relationships between the First Presidency, the Quorum of the Twelve, and the First Quorum of the Seventy are defined,[10] and "in case that any decision of these quorums is made in unrighteousness," the matter "may be brought before a general assembly of the several quorums, which constitute the spiritual authorities of the Church."[11] In matters not involving those quorums, a higher judicial system is established to provide "a final decision upon controversies in spiritual matters."[12] The Lord has even provided for the trial of the President of the Church if he should transgress.[13]

---

9. D&C 101:80. See also verse 77.
10. D&C 107:21-31.
11. D&C 107:32.
12. D&C 107:78-80.
13. D&C 107:81-84.

But the Lord's system of checks and balances extends beyond the relationships of the presiding quorums and the higher judicial system. It also defines, in clear and undisputable terms, the responsibilities of the President of the Church as he functions in the roles of Prophet, Seer and Revelator. With equal clarity, the scriptures define the responsibilities of the individual members of the Church pertaining to revealed instructions given through the Revelator. The mortal head of the Church has scriptural mandates he is required to fulfill to the saints, and the members have commandments they must fulfill pertaining to the Prophet. These inter-woven commandments serve as an effective set of revealed checks and balances which, if fulfilled, chart the course of the Church in righteousness.

It appears that some of the saints are unaware of this revealed "checks and balances" relationship between the saints and God's spokesman. Because of its great importance, two chapters of this book will be devoted to that relationship—one reviewing what the Lord requires of His prophets, the other considering the instructions given to the saints.

As will be seen in the chapters of this book, the Lord has revealed in careful detail the many facets of His methodology for revealing His words to His people. It is far broader and more complex than can be effectively discussed in a typical Sunday School or Priesthood class, or in a ward Sacrament Meeting.

Much of what the Lord has set forth is not common knowledge among the saints—indeed, many appear to be lacking in the knowledge of some of the key principles concerning revelation which He has established, and actively espouse beliefs which conflict with the revealed patterns.

The Future Danger—False Prophets Shall Arise

Danger lies ahead! The scriptures speak in great detail of a rapidly-approaching time of "great tribulation," in which false prophets will take a heavy toll among the saints, "Insomuch that, *if it were possible,* they shall *deceive* the very elect."[14] What would make such deception possible? *Lack of knowledge of how and to whom God's word is revealed, and a break-down of the system of checks and balances by which the integrity of God's word is protected!*

The Lord revealed that during that critical period,

> . . . There shall arise *false Christs*, and *false prophets, and shall shew great signs and wonders; . . .*[15]

---

14. Mt. 24:24. Some of the scriptural predictions concerning the influence of false prophets in the last days are considered in chapter 9. For a more detailed treatment, see the author's book, *Prophetic Warnings to Modern America* (Bountiful, Utah: Horizon Publishers, 1977), pp. 227-258 and other related portions.

15. *Ibid.*

John the Revelator warned of a false prophet in the last days who will have world-wide influence:

> . . . I saw three unclean spirits like frogs come out of the mouth of the dragon, and out of the mouth of the beast, and out of the mouth of the *false prophet.*
> *For they are the spirits of devils, working miracles, which go forth unto the kings of the earth and of the whole world,* to gather them to the battle of that great day of God Almighty.[16]

The prophet Zechariah told of how false prophets would be functioning among the people of Israel in the last days, just prior to the coming of the Savior:

> And it shall come to pass in that day, saith the Lord of hosts, that I will cut off the names of the idols out of the land, and they shall no more be remembered: and also *I will cause the prophets and the unclean spirit to pass out of the land.*
> And it shall come to pass, that *when any shall yet prophesy, then his father and his mother that begat him shall say unto him, Thou shalt not live; for thou speakest lies in the name of the Lord: and his father and his mother that begat him shall thrust him through when he prophesieth.*
> And it shall come to pass in that day, that *the prophets shall be ashamed every one of his vision, when he hath prophesied; neither shall they wear a rough garment to deceive:*
> But he shall say, I am no prophet, I am an husbandman; for man taught me to keep cattle from my youth.[17]

When that period of great tribulation comes, it is expected that Satan will wage his war of cunning deception on many levels and in many places. Numerous passages of scripture, and statements by prophets since the restoration, warn that the saints will have to contend with false prophets within their midst, and that much of the challenge they will face will come from among their own ranks. As Heber C. Kimball prophesied,

> . . . *It will be difficult to tell the face of a Saint from the face of an enemy to the people of God.* Then, brethren, lookout for the great sieve, for *there will be a great sifting time, and many will fall;* . . .[18]

As deception, conflict and persecution take their toll, *"No man nor woman will be able to endure on borrowed light. Each will have to be guided by the light within himself."*[19]

A firm, complete knowledge of how God speaks to man will be the essential basis required to provide each saint with much of the stability and discernment he will need.

---

16. Rev. 16:13-14. See also Rev. 13.

17. Zech. 13:2-5.

18. Orson F. Whitney, *Life of Heber C. Kimball* (Salt Lake City, Utah: Bookcraft, Inc., 1967), p. 446.

19. *Ibid.*, p. 450.

Remember well, and heed, the Savior's parable from the Sermon on the Mount in this context:

> . . . *whosoever heareth these sayings of mine, and doeth them*, I will liken him unto a *wise man*, which *built his house upon a rock:*
> And the rain descended, and the floods came, and the winds blew, and beat upon that house; and it fell not: for it was founded upon a rock.
> And everyone that heareth these sayings of mine, and *doeth them not,* shall be *likened unto a foolish man*, which built his house upon the sand:
> And the rain descended, and the floods came, and the winds blew, and beat upon that house; and it fell: and great was the fall of it.[20]

My Role in Writing This Book

This book is a personal effort on my part, privately undertaken, and is not a publication of The Church of Jesus Christ of Latter-day Saints. I write, in part, to render obedience to the Lord's commandment that it is the duty of the Elders of the Church *"to teach, expound, exhort,* baptize, and *watch over the church; . . .*[21]

Contained within this book are expositions of broad scriptural patterns, some of which will perhaps provide new understandings to a number of Latter-day Saints. The scriptures have not changed, and these insights are not new, yet many of the patterns drawn herein are not common knowledge to some Church members. I preach no new doctrines—I merely say, "Observe carefully that revealed doctrines already exist in many areas," and assemble sufficient passages of scripture as evidence so these patterns are readily apparent and clearly substantiated.

As will soon be obvious to the reader, I document carefully and thoroughly. I am careful to quote passages with proper regard to their context. I don't make doctrinal statements without providing careful substantiation for what I have said. I am a reporter and commentator, not a creator of doctrine, and I do my best to be carefully and squarely based in the scriptures. I rejoice in the word of God, and count myself blessed when I have sufficient of that precious quantity—time—to be able to study and contemplate God's word.

Let there be no confusion on the matter—I am not *a* prophet; and certainly I am not *the* prophet. My role as author of this book is that of student and reporter, rather than that of revealer of inspired truths. Several chapters treat in considerable detail how God reveals His will through His designated spokesman here on the earth. Certainly it is neither my desire nor my intention to either "counsel the brethren" or to "steady the ark."

---

20. Mt. 7:24-27.
21. D&C 20:42.

It is not my place to instruct the Prophet. It is appropriate, however, to assemble this collection of doctrinal insights, for the saints and all who choose to read it. In thousands of passages of scripture, the Lord has set forth a clear and unmistakable pattern which shows how He intends to reveal His word to mankind. The nature of revelation is one of the most prominent doctrines revealed in scripture, and is fully deserving of careful study and exposition. Certainly it comes within the scope of the admonition found in Doctrine and Covenants 88:77—an instruction to all the Church: "I give unto you *a commandment* that you shall *teach one another the doctrine of the kingdom."* And it is equally appropriate to strive for the realization of the goal set forth in the verse that follows: "be instructed more perfectly in theory, in principle, in doctrine, in the law of the gospel, in all things that pertain unto the kingdom of God, . . ."

The documentation for this book is drawn almost entirely from the scriptures. Since my objective has been to write a definitive work on this important subject, I choose to use scriptural statements as my primary source, thus reporting teachings which have been canonized and accepted as the actual doctrine of the Church. I sought to avoid controversy by supporting the conclusions drawn with evidence which was not subject to question in any way. The reader will note that I have cited passage upon passage as supporting evidence, drawing doctrinal patterns which are clearly set forth in the scriptures and which are not subject to other meanings or interpretations. I have written no new doctrine—I have merely sought to expound and reassert that which God has already revealed.

It is the duty of priesthood holders *"to watch over the church always,* and be with and *strengthen them;* And *see that there is no iniquity in the church, . . ."*[22] I seek to properly discharge those responsibilities in this book. I seek to strengthen the saints, and I also seek to warn of dangerous unscriptural trends and teachings which I see surfacing within the Church. In some cases I am judgmental. Using the scriptures as my guide and standard, I sometimes express concern about various philosophies and practices, and suggest the need for caution and reappraisal. I remember well the Lord's instruction that "the thing which will be of the most worth unto you will be to *declare repentance unto this people,* that you may bring souls unto me."[23] With that instruction as my guide, I do not feel it amiss to do so.

The "Watchman Upon the Tower" Responsibility

One other concern should be mentioned. A continual theme in the scriptures is the responsibility placed on the individual saints to be knowledgeable concerning gospel principles and particularly concerning the

22. D&C 20:53-54.
23. D&C 16:6.

events prophesied to transpire in the last days. That oft-quoted passage from D&C 88:81, that "it becometh every man who hath been warned to warn his neighbor," is applicable in this situation. I have devoted twenty years of intensive study to the nature of God's communication to man. I have written six major books on that subject,[24] and have a graduate degree in Old and New Testament from BYU, which represents somewhat of a level of background and devotion to the subject. Over the years, I've been blessed with an understanding of gospel themes. I have come to understand, however, that "of him unto whom much is given much is required."[25] My study and writing has obligated me to function in the role of "watchman upon the tower,"[26] alerting others to the enemy which surely must come. It is neither a pleasant role nor a self-appointed one. I would be free of it if I could, but the Spirit continues to whisper, and my lot remains my lot.

Though I do not seek the responsibility, I have been compelled to recognize and acknowledge, for the present at least, that it is mine. I thank God that many others appear to hold the same responsibility within the Church. More and more I perceive that "this is a day of warning, and not a day of many words"[27]—and the era is dawning to which the Lord referred when He said,

> . . . I will . . . that *every man* should take righteousness in his hands and faithfulness upon his loins, and *lift a warning voice unto the inhabitants of the earth;* and *declare both by word and by flight that desolation shall come upon the wicked.*[28]

In this book, as in others I have written, I raise the warning voice, and again warn the saints of grave difficulties which lie ahead—in this instance they may be difficulties from a source they "think not of."[29]

---

24. My master's thesis, known by the popular title *Prophecy—Key to the Future*, details prophecies pertaining to future events of the last days. *The Prophecies of Joseph Smith* documents almost 150 prophecies made by Joseph Smith and shows how each one received literal fulfillment. *Life Everlasting* deals with hundreds of communications from departed spirits in the Spirit World, and examines their validity. *Gifts of the Spirit* treats each of the spiritual gifts outlined in the scriptures, with considerable emphasis on personal revelation. *Prophets and Prophecies of the Old Testament* treats hundreds of passages on the nature of God's communication to man in its doctrinal analysis section, as well as compiling the Old Testament prophecies of the last days. And *Prophetic Warnings to Modern America* deals once again with future events, raising the warning voice concerning the future of America and detailing many of the difficult events which the saints must eventually endure and overcome.

25. D&C 82:3. See Lk. 12:48.

26. See D&C 101:43-62.

27. D&C 63:58.

28. D&C 63:37.

29. This is an allusion to Joseph Smith's prophecy of June 24, 1844. See the author's book, *The Prophecies of Joseph Smith*, pp. 384-385.

Well do I remember the Lord's warning to the prophet Ezekiel,

> Son of man, *I have made thee a watchman* unto the house of Israel: therefore hear the word at my mouth, and *give them warning from me.*
>
> When I say unto the wicked, thou shalt surely die; and thou givest him not warning, nor speakest to warn the wicked from his wicked way, to save his life; the same wicked man shall die in his iniquity; but *his blood will I require at their hand.*
>
> *Yet if thou warn the wicked, and he turn not from his wickedness, nor from his wicked way, he shall die in his iniquity; but thou hast delivered thy soul.*[30]

This is the way the Lord places responsibility upon His servants—upon every Latter-day Saint—there is no alternative but to obey.

Sincerely,

Duane S. Crowther

---

30. Ezek. 3:17-19. See also 33:1-9.

1

What is a 'Prophet', a 'Seer', and a 'Revelator'?

To understand the role of revelation within the Church, three terms must first receive careful definition. These terms are "prophet," "seer," and "revelator." Like many words, these terms are subject to varying definitions, which differ in their nature according to the viewpoint of the individual or organization offering the definition.

For instance, a Protestant church which believes the Bible to be the only revealed word of God would define the term "prophet" in a far different manner from a Pentecostal church which accepts some aspects of modern revelation. And certainly, both their definitions would be distinctly different from the Catholic view which designates many former prophets as "saints."

For terms such as "prophet," "seer," and "revelator," recourse to a dictionary is of little value, since a dictionary is primarily a recording of what dictionary-makers consider to be "current usage." By no means is a definition set forth in a dictionary absolute. It may change radically in the next decade.[1] And looking in a modern dictionary of Hebrew or Greek will lend no new insight of value either, for such dictionaries give definitions of ancient scriptural terms as they are presently perceived by modern Bible scholars, who usually are giving definitions from a typical Protestant or Catholic perspective.

The Term "Prophet" Defined

Certainly an objective of any careful student of religion should be to define theological terms in the sense which the servants of God have used them in the scriptures. This will insure a continuity of understanding over the centuries.

In the Bible, the term "prophet" is applied internally to twenty-two men who are specified by name.[2] The Book of Mormon also refers to five

---

1. Sydney J. Harris, in his syndicated column which appeared in the *Deseret News* on July 21, 1968, commented forcefully on the role of a dictionary. In his article entitled "Dictionary Is No 'Last Word' On Words," he wrote:

> It is interesting—to me, at least—that most of the letters I receive about my columns on the use of words refer me to some dictionary or other as evidence that I am 'wrong' in my definitions and distinctions.
>
> *But a dictionary is no more a guide to good usage than a telephone directory is a guide to good addresses.* The Yellow Pages can tell you where to shop, but not which shop is better than any other.
>
> *Most dictionaries (especially in America) follow the current of contemporary speech;* if most people say 'disinterested' when they mean 'uninterested,' the dictionary will list 'disinterested' as a secondary form of 'uninterested,' even though they are quite opposite words in their original meanings.
>
> *A dictionary, on the whole, is a scoreboard, not an umpire.* It follows the 'election returns' on the usage of words, and when enough people confuse 'masterly' and 'masterful,' most dictionaries will give up the fight against the distinction and list them as synonyms—though, again, their original meanings were quite different.
>
> *It is of no use to cite a dictionary for anything but the most obvious and elementary spellings and definitions; it is a reflection of public taste and tendencies, not a bastion of good or proper usage.*

2. These men are Abraham (Gen. 20:7), Aaron, the brother of Moses (Ex. 7:1), Gad (I Sam. 22:5, II Sam. 24:11), Nathan (I Ki. 1:32, 44), Ahijah (I Ki. 11:29), Jehu (I Ki. 16:7, 12), Elijah (I Ki. 18:22, 36; II Chron. 21:12; Mal. 4:5), Elisha (II Ki. 5:3, 13; 6:12; Lk. 4:27), Isaiah (II Ki. 20:11; 32:20; Mt. 1:22; 2:15; 3:3; 4:14; 8:17; 21:4; Lk. 3:4; 4:17; Jn. 1:23; 12:38; Acts 8:28, 30; 28:25), Shemaiah (II Chron. 12:5), Iddo (II Chron. 12:22), Oded (II Chron. 15:8), Samuel (II Chron. 35:18; Acts 13:20), Jeremiah (II Chron. 36:12; Jer. 28:6; 36:26; 37:2; 38:10; Mt. 2:17; 27:9), Haggai (Ezra 5:1; 6:14), Zechariah (Ezra 5:1; 6:14), Habakkuk (Hab. 3:1), Jonah (Mt. 12:39; Lk. 11:29), Jesus (Mt. 21:11), Daniel (Mt. 24:15; Mk. 13:14), John the Baptist (Lk. 7:28), and Joel (Acts 2:16).

of these same men as prophets,[3] and specifies nine others as being prophets in addition to the five.[4] Those who wish to understand the function of a prophet would do well to study the recorded words of these men in the scriptures.[5] These men are depicted in many circumstances in the scriptures, yet one unifying factor relates them: they foretell future events.

The major prophetic function is to foretell the future. This is the message of the scriptures. A study of the recorded life of the thirty-one men specifically mentioned as being prophets in the Bible and Book of Mormon shows that actual prophecies are recorded in the scriptures for thirty of them.[6] For many of these men, nothing else but their prophecies are recorded. Their inspired foretelling of future events is what caused them to be cited in scripture, and what caused them to be identified as prophets.

Certainly no definition of the term "prophet" which excludes the predicting of future events, or minimizes such inspired foresight as a prophet's major role, can be considered valid in the light of the scriptures. As Nephi wrote, "By the Spirit are *all things made known* unto the prophets, *which shall come upon the children of men* according to the flesh."[7] Ammon defined the term "prophet" as meaning "*a chosen man of God*, who told them of their wickedness and abominations, and *prophesied of many things which are to come*, yea, even the coming of Christ."[8] When Alma described his role as a prophet,[9] he said, "I have been called to preach the word of God among all this people, *according to the spirit of revelation and prophecy*."[10] That same spirit moved upon Ether, "a prophet of the Lord," and caused him to predict future events to the degree that when he "*began to prophesy* unto the people, . . . *he could not be restrained because of the Spirit of the Lord* which was in him."[11]

---

3. These men are Jesus (1 Ne. 10:4; 22:20-21; 3 Ne. 20:23), John the Baptist (1 Ne. 10:7-10; 11:27; 2 Ne. 31:4), Isaiah (1 Ne. 19:23-24; 2 Ne. 6:12; 3 Ne. 16:17), Jeremiah (Hel. 8:20), and Elijah (3 Ne. 25:5).

4. These men are Zenos (1 Ne. 19:10-12; Jac. 5:1-2; 6:1; Al. 33:3; Hel. 8:20; 15:11; 3 Ne. 10:16), Abinadi (Al. 5:11), Alma (Al. 8:20; 10:7), Ammon (Al. 19:4), Zenock (Al. 33:15-17), Nephi (Hel. 8:9; 11:18), Samuel (3 Ne. 1:9; 8:3; Mor. 2:10), Gidgiddoni (3 Ne. 3:19), and Ether (Eth. 12:2).

5. The author's book, *Prophets and Prophecies of the Old Testament* analyzes and records the functions of the prophetic office in detail as it considers the prophetic books of the Old Testament and the historical books pertinent to the era they span.

6. The one for whom no prophetic message is on record is Iddo. However, the scriptures make specific reference to him as being a seer (II Chron. 9:29; 12:15).

7. 1 Ne. 22:2.

8. Mos. 7:26.

9. See Al. 8:20.

10. Al. 8:24.

11. Eth. 12:2.

Key passages from the Old Testament clearly define the major role of prophets as foretellers of the future events and insist that fulfillment of his prophecies is the proof that a man is truly called of God to be a prophet. The prophet Jeremiah said, for instance,

> . . . *When the word of the prophet shall come to pass, then shall the prophet be known, that the Lord hath truly sent him.* [12]

Ezekiel, after foretelling events to transpire in the land of Israel, concluded his prophecy with these words, which again show that fulfillment of prophecy was regarded as proof of one's God-inspired prophetic calling:

> *And when this cometh to pass*, (lo, it will come,) *then shall they know that a prophet hath been among them.* [13]

The Lord revealed to Moses that fulfillment of prophecy was to be the test by which people could know if a man was truly a prophet, speaking in behalf of the Lord, and if that prophet's utterance was inspired:

> And if thou say in thine heart, How shall we know the word which the Lord hath not spoken?
> When a prophet speaketh in the name of the Lord, *if the thing follow not, nor come to pass, that is the thing which the Lord hath not spoken, but the prophet hath spoken it presumptuously*: thou shalt not be afraid of him. [14]

The New Testament also emphasizes that fulfilled prophecy is the identifying characteristic of God's prophets. The writer of Acts, for instance, asserted that

> . . . *All the prophets* from Samuel and those that follow after, *as many as have spoken, have likewise foretold of these days.* [15]

And he explained that

> . . . *Those things, which God had shewed by the mouth of all his prophets*, that Christ should suffer, *he hath so fulfilled.* [16]

Literally hundreds of passages, throughout the Old and New Testament, [17] are devoted to showing that prophecy was literally fulfilled, constantly revealing prophetic fulfillment to be the sign that the ancient prophets were truly prophets of the Lord.

---

12. Jer. 28:9.
13. Ezek. 33:33.
14. Deut. 18:21-22.
15. Acts 3:24.
16. Acts 3:18.
17. These passages are so numerous that they are not cited here, though many will be referred to throughout this book. Reading the gospel of Matthew would help the reader locate many typical passages of this type.

As the great apostacy caused prophets to cease foretelling future events in the name of the Lord, the common definition of a prophet began to change. The definition expanded to such breadth that Catholics and Protestants, functioning without prophets who were receiving current revelation, could still be comfortable with the term "prophet." In their view, a prophet came to be a great "teacher" or "expounder and interpreter of scripture."

This author has observed with alarm that the same tendency to soften the definition has begun to be manifested among the Latter-day Saints. No, the term prophet does not mean "teacher"—it means *foreteller of future events*. We do ourselves a severe disservice to define it otherwise.

Though a prophet may fill many other functions in his roles[18] as a seer, a revelator, a preacher, a teacher, an organizer, a messenger, a spokesman, an interpreter, an expounder of gospel principles, etc., yet that which makes him a "prophet of God" is the foretelling of future events under divine inspiration. That is basic! To assert otherwise is to contradict an overwhelming mass of scriptural evidence.

The Term "Seer" Defined

A "seer" is an individual who can receive revelation through sacred instruments such as a Urim and Thummim or a seer stone. The Book of Mormon gives considerable light concerning the meaning of the term. In the encounter between King Limhi and Ammon, the latter is asked by Limhi if he can translate a group of records which have been discovered. While Ammon is unable to translate the records, he knows that Mosiah can, because Mosiah is a seer. Ammon's explanation to King Limhi is as follows:

> I can assuredly tell thee, O king, of a man that can translate the records; for *he has wherewith that he can look*, and translate all records that are of ancient date; and *it is a gift from God*. And the things are called interpreters, and no man can look in them except he be commanded, lest he should look for that he ought not and he should perish. *And whosoever is commanded to look in them, the same is called seer.*
>
> And behold, the king of the people who are in the land of Zarahemla is the man that is commanded to do these things, and who has this *high gift from God.*
>
> And the king said that a seer is greater than a prophet.
>
> And Ammon said that *a seer is a revelator and a prophet also; and a gift which is greater can no man have*, except he should possess the power of God, which no man can; yet a man may have great power given him from God.

---

18. Many of these roles are also to be filled by others as holders of the priesthood. (See D&C 20:38-59; 88:76-81; etc.) They do not originate with the prophetic calling, neither are they restricted to prophets for their performance.

But a seer can know of things which are past, and also of things which are to come, and by them shall all things be revealed, or, rather, shall secret things be made manifest, and hidden things shall come to light, and things which are not known shall be made known by them, and also things shall be made known by them which otherwise could not be known.

Thus God has provided a means that man, through faith, might work mighty miracles; therefore he becometh a great benefit to his fellow beings.[19]

While telling of translations made by King Mosiah, the Book of Mormon records:

And now he translated them by the means of these two stones which were fastened into the two rims of a bow.

Now these things were *prepared from the beginning,* and were handed down from generation to generation, *for the purpose of interpreting languages:*

And they have been kept and preserved by the hand of the Lord, that he should discover to every creature who should possess the land the iniquities and abominations of his people;

And whosoever has these things is called seer, after the manner of old times.[20]

---

19. Mos. 8:13-18. See also Omni 20; Mos. 21:28; 28:13-16; Al. 37:23-25.

20. Mos. 28:13-16. Other Book of Mormon passages speak of special instruments being prepared so that revelation could be received. For instance, as Alma turned his records and materials over to his son, Helaman, he said,

And the Lord said: *I will prepare unto my servant Gazelem, a stone, which shall shine forth in darkness unto light, that I may discover unto them the works of their brethren, yea, their secret works, their works of darkness, and their wickedness and abominations.*

And now, my son, these interpreters were prepared that the word of God might be fulfilled, which he spake, saying:

I will bring forth out of darkness unto light all their secret works and their abominations; and except they repent I will destroy them from off the face of the earth; and I will bring to light all their secrets and abominations, unto every nation that shall hereafter possess the land. (Al. 37:23-25.)

And the Lord said unto the Brother of Jared,

And behold, these two stones will I give unto thee, and ye shall seal them up also with the things which ye shall write.

For behold, the language which ye shall write I have confounded; wherefore I will cause in my own due time that these stones shall magnify to the eyes of men these things which ye shall write. . . .

And it came to pass that the Lord commanded him that he should seal up the two stones which he had received, and show them not, until the Lord should show them unto the children of men. (Eth. 3:23-24, 28. See also 4:5.)

The angel Moroni, in his visits to Joseph Smith, told him of the plates of the Book of Mormon. He also told of the instrument that was buried with them:

> There were two stones in silver bows—and these stones, fastened to a breastplate, constituted what is called the *Urim and Thummim*—deposited with the plates; and *the possession and use of these stones were what constituted 'seers' in ancient or former times; and that God had prepared them for the purpose of translating the book.*[21]

Thus, *a seer is one who possesses, uses, and is commanded to look in certain instruments for receiving revelation.* According to Ammon, the privilege of seership is greater than that of being either a prophet or a revelator. A seer is one who sees things revealed, as contrasted with a prophet, who sometimes only repeats a message given by voice or inspiration from the Lord. This was emphasized by Isaiah, who told how the rebellious people of Judah would "say to the Seers, *See not;* and to the prophets, *Prophesy not* unto us right things, speak unto us smooth things, prophesy deceits."[22]

While the passages which tell of the nature of the seer's calling emphasize the use of revelatory instruments for the purpose of translation, Ammon also stressed that a seer can know of all things past, of things which are to come, of secret things to be made manifest, and of things which otherwise could not be known. Thus God has provided that a seer may be of "great benefit to his fellow beings."[23]

Many ancient prophets had the use of revelatory instruments and were, therefore, seers. Among these were Abraham,[24] Aaron,[25] Joshua,[26] and Abiathar.[27] In the early days of Old Testament history, those of whom men would inquire of God were called seers. Though some may later have referred to them only as prophets,[28] yet differentiation was still made

---

21. JS 2:35.

22. Is. 30:10.

23. Mos. 8:17-18. Certainly the necessity of sharing his visions with others by a seer is implied in this passage. How else could he be of benefit to others in this calling?

24. Abra. 3:1.

25. Ex. 28:30. See also Lev. 8:8; Deut. 33:8; I Sam. 28:6; Ez. 2:61-63; Neh. 7:63-65.

26. Num. 27:18-23.

27. I Sam. 23:9-12. The ephod was a richly-made garment in the shape of a waistcoat, to which the breastplate was fastened in which the Urim and Thummim was kept. (See Ex. 28:1-35.) Thus to call for the ephod was to call for the Urim and Thummim.

28. See I Sam. 9:9.

between the role of prophet and seer.[29] Various individuals were designated as seers, including Samuel,[30] Zadok,[31] Gad,[32] Heman,[33] Iddo,[34] Hanani,[35] Asaph,[36] Jeduthun,[37] and Amos,[38] and others whose names were not recorded.[39]

In the days of the restored Church, many individuals have functioned as seers through the use of revelatory instruments known as seer stones. Just as Joseph Smith frequently used a seer stone[40] in addition to the Urim and Thummim, others also possessed seer stones and used them, with varying degrees of success. These included Church stalwarts who were not Church leaders such as Philo Dibble and Edwin Rushton, among others.[41] Presumably some individuals still possess the ability to receive revelation through revelatory instruments.

According to Brigham Young, the prophet Joseph said that every man was entitled to have and use a seer stone:

> Dec. 27, 1841:
> I met with the Twelve at Brother Joseph's. He conversed with us in a familiar manner on a variety of subjects, and explained to us the Urim and Thummim which he found with the plates, called in the Book of Mormon the Interpreters. *He said that every man who lived on the earth was entitled to a seer stone, and should have one, but they are kept from them in consequence of their wickedness, and most of those who do find one make an evil use of it;* he showed us his seer stone.[42]

Neither the gift of seership, nor the ability to function as a prophet or revelator, entitle one to claim the right to leadership of the Church, as was stressed by President Young:

---

29. See II Sam. 24:11; II Ki. 17:13; II Chron. 29:25; Is. 29:10.
30. I Sam. 9:10-19; I Chron. 9:22; 26:28; 29:29.
31. II Sam. 15:27.
32. II Sam. 24:11; I Chron. 21:9; 29:29; II Chron. 29:25.
33. I Chron. 25:5.
34. II Chron. 9:29; 12:15.
35. II Chron. 16:7, 10; 19:2.
36. II Chron. 29:30.
37. II Chron. 35:15.
38. Amos 7:12.
39. See II Chron. 33:18-19; Is. 30:10.
40. See CHC 1:127-130, in which the manner in which Joseph received revelation through the revelatory instruments is discussed. Joseph's seer stone is still in the possession of the Church and was consecrated on the altar of the Manti Temple at the temple dedication. (See CHC 6:230.)
41. A comprehensive gathering of data concerning past and present Latter-day Saints who have functioned with revelatory instruments would make an interesting and valuable study and contribution to Church literature and scholarship.
42. *Millennial Star* 26:118.

Does a man's being a Prophet in this Church prove that he shall be the President of it? I answer, no! A man may be a Prophet, Seer, and Revelator, and it may have nothing to do with his being the President of the Church.[43]

In summary, a seer is one who receives revelation from God through revelatory instruments. Possession of seership ability does not constitute claim upon the leadership of the Church. The President of the Church, however, is sustained as a seer. To sustain him as such is to pledge one's faith and confidence that he does receive revelation in this manner from time to time as did the seers of old.

The Term "Revelator" Defined

This term is peculiar to Mormondom and is generally not found in dictionaries, Bible commentaries, and other non-Mormon works. The meaning of the word is somewhat difficult to document because it is infrequently used in the scriptures and is not employed in a definitive manner. The Bible does not use it, nor does the Pearl of Great Price. It is used only once in the Book of Mormon, where Ammon stated that "a seer is a revelator and a prophet also."[44] The term appears six times in the Doctrine and Covenants. Three times it is found in allusions to a Church leader as "a prophet, and a seer, and a revelator unto my church."[45] Two more of the references are allusions to the apostle John, who is designated as "the Revelator."[46] The best key to understanding the term is found in Doctrine and Covenants 100:11. In this passage, the Lord is telling Sidney Rigdon the relationship the prophet Joseph would have to Sidney. Concerning Joseph, the Lord revealed:

He shall be a *revelator* unto thee, *that thou mayest know the certainty of all things pertaining to the things of my kingdom on the earth.*

From the limited evidence available, we see that *a revelator reveals to the Church*[47] *the Lord's will* concerning the things of His temporal kingdom. The role of revelator would seem to be the role of spokesman for God to the people of the Church and, in a larger sense, to the people of the world. His calling is to direct the Church through divine revelation.

It should be observed that the Presidents of the Church, for many years, have functioned in this aspect of their calling to a far greater degree

---

43. JD, 1:133. Apr. 6, 1853. It is expected that seership ability will be granted to all inhabitants of the celestial kingdom. (See Rev. 2:17; D&C 130:8-11.)

44. Mos. 8:16.

45. D&C 124:94. See also D&C 124:125; 107:92.

46. D&C 77:2; 128:6.

47. See again D&C 124:94, 125.

than as "prophets" or "seers." Indeed, General Authorities and other intimate acquaintances of the President of the Church frequently bear witness that revelation is coming to him concerning the daily affairs of the kingdom. In contrast, evidence and testimonies concerning the "prophetic" and "seership" aspects of the labors of Church Presidents are relatively rare, and have been for many years.[48]

The President of the Church Is Sustained as "Prophet, Seer, and Revelator"

As commanded by the Lord, the President of the Church is sustained by Church members as "Prophet, Seer, and Revelator, and President of the Church of Jesus Christ of Latter-day Saints."[49] This pattern was established from the very day the Church was restored, for during the first meeting of the Church the Lord revealed to Joseph Smith,

> There shall be a record kept among you; and in it *thou shalt be called a seer, a translator, a prophet, an apostle of Jesus Christ, an elder of the church* through the will of God the Father, and the grace of your Lord Jesus Christ.[50]

Five years later, in 1835, the Lord again gave this terminology by revelation in setting forth the role of the President of the Church, who is actually the President of the High Priesthood:

> The duty of the President of the office of the High Priesthood is to preside over the whole church, and to be like unto Moses—
> Behold, here is wisdom; yea, *to be a seer, a revelator, a translator, and a prophet, having all the gifts of God which he bestows upon the head of the church.*[51]

In 1841, the Lord once more asserted the importance of this title as He said, "I give unto you my servant Joseph to be a presiding elder over all my church, to be *a translator, a revelator, a seer, and prophet.*"[52]

---

48. A careful reading of conference reports for decades past will bear this out. The speakers, with few exceptions, bear witness that guidance in the daily affairs of the Church is what is being received. Though terminology may be confused, the reporting of revealed prophecies concerning future events, and especially allusions to revelations received through revelatory instruments, is infrequent.

49. Widtsoe, John A., "What Is the Meaning of the Title, 'Prophet, Seer, and Revelator?'," *Evidences and Reconciliations* (Salt Lake City, Utah: Bookcraft, Inc., 1960), p. 25. This terminology is used in each general conference as the President of the Church is sustained.

50. D&C 21:1. This revelation was given at the Peter Whitmer home in Fayette, New York, on April 6, 1830.

51. D&C 107:91-92. See also verses 64-67.

52. D&C 124:125.

Joseph Smith used this terminology in reference to himself. For instance, he concluded a message to the saints at Nauvoo with the words, "I subscribe myself your servant in the Lord, prophet and seer of the Church of Jesus Christ of Latter-day Saints."[53] Others also used the terms in reference to him. The account of his death, for instance, calls him "Joseph Smith, the Prophet and Seer of the Lord."[54]

The varied forms of reference concerning the sustaining of the President of the Church have become standardized in the conferences of the Church. Now reference is made to the spiritual leader of the saints as the "Prophet, Seer, and Revelator." In his treatment of these terms, Elder John A. Widtsoe made this explanation concerning the omission of the word "translator:"

> In current practice, the word "translator" is omitted, since should records appear needing translation, the President of the Church may at any time be called, through revelation, to the special labor of translation.[55]

It should be understood that the sustaining vote of the Church membership does not *make* their leader a prophet, a seer, or a revelator. Their vote is an expression of acceptance, confidence and loyalty, not a delegation of divine power. Only God can make a man a prophet, seer, and revelator of God, by extending to him the necessary guidance and revelation.

A man may hold the title and authorization for these powers continually, yet he becomes a prophet only when he prophesies the word of God, a seer when he actually uses the revelatory instruments, and a revelator when he reveals messages from on high to the Church. These privileges are God's powers delegated to man, not the powers of man himself.

The sustaining vote of the membership, however, does give the head of the Church the privilege of being President of the Church. As Brigham Young explained,

> Suffice it to say, that Joseph was the President of the Church, as long as he lived; the people chose to have it so. *He always filled that responsible station, by the voice of the people.* Can you find any revelation appointing him the President of the Church? The keys of the Priesthood were committed to Joseph, to build up the Kingdom of God on the earth, and were not to be taken from him in time or in eternity; but *when he was called to preside over the Church, it was by the voice of the people; though he held the keys of the Priesthood, independent of their voice.*[56]

---

53. D&C 127:12.

54. D&C 135:3.

55. Widtsoe, *Ibid.*, p. 256. Information concerning the gift of translation is found in the author's book, *Gifts of the Spirit* (Salt Lake City, Utah: Bookcraft, Inc., 1965), pp. 258-260.

56. JD, 1:133. Apr. 6, 1853. See the discussion of the principle of common consent found on pp. 82-89.

Other General Authorities Also Are
Sustained as "Prophets, Seers, and Revelators"

The practice of sustaining others of the general authorities besides the Presidency as prophets, seers, and revelators was introduced by Joseph Smith at the dedication of the Kirtland Temple on March 27, 1836. During that meeting, Sidney Rigdon, after a lengthy discourse, called on the quorums to rise in turn and signify their willingness to acknowledge Joseph "as a Prophet and Seer, and uphold [him] as such by their prayers of faith."[57] Hymns were sung, there was a short intermission, and then Joseph

> Made a short address, and called upon the several quorums, and all the congregation of Saints, *to acknowledge the Presidency as Prophets and Seers*, and uphold them by their prayers. They all covenanted to do so, by rising.
>
> I [Joseph] then called upon the quorums and congregations of Saints to *acknowledge the Twelve Apostles, who were present, as Prophets, Seers, and Revelators, and special witnesses* to all the nations of the earth, holding the keys of the kingdom, to unlock it, or cause it to be done, among them, and uphold them by their prayers, which they assented to by rising.[58]

In general conferences of the Church today, in addition to sustaining the President of the Church, the saints sustain "The Counselors in the First Presidency, the Apostles and the Patriarch to the Church as Prophets, Seers, and Revelators."[59] Even this practice is undergoing change, as the Patriarch to the Church has recently been assigned "Emeritus" status.

What is the relationship of the other general authorities sustained as prophets, seers, and revelators to the calling held by the President of the Church? Do they also function as spokesmen through which the Lord reveals His commandments to the Church? Do they stand equal in authority and responsibility with the President of the Church before the Lord and before the saints? The answer to this question lies in understanding the principle of priesthood "keys," and procedures used in the transmittal of authority on the highest level within the Church.

Elder Joseph Fielding Smith, while president of the Quorum of the Twelve, commented on this matter in detail.[60] He has explained, "Only

---

57. HC, 2:416.

58. HC, 2:417.

59. CR, Sept. 29, 1967, p. 25.

60. It should be noted that in these important areas of keys and the exact nature of the authority of the President of the Church, few other definitive statements by general authorities other than President Joseph Fielding Smith are readily available to the membership of the Church. The level of his explanations, however, extends far beyond that which is defined in the scriptures.

one man at a time on the earth holds the *keys*[61] of the priesthood, only one man at a time has the power to receive revelations *for the Church.*"[62] On another occasion he stated,

> *The President of the Church holds the keys over all the Church.* In him is concentrated the power of the priesthood. He holds all the keys of every nature, pertaining to the dispensation of the fulness of times. All the keys of former dispensations which have been revealed are vested in him.
> We are taught that the new and everlasting covenant of the gospel embraces the fulness of the gospel—every covenant, contract, bond, obligation, vow, authority— and that *the keys of this authority are held by the President of the Church, who is president of the High Priesthood, 'and there is never but one on the earth at a time on whom this power and the keys of this priesthood are conferred.'*[63]

It is understood that the Quorum of the Twelve collectively hold the keys which are held individually by the President of the Church.[64] Thus, at the death of a President of the Church, the Twelve are able to confer the keys upon a new President of the High Priesthood and reorganize the First Presidency. As Joseph Fielding Smith explained:

------

61. This term is defined in *A Light Unto The World*, the 1967-68 Melchizedek Priesthood Course of Study, as follows:

> Keys are the right of presidency and are conferred upon and held by the presiding officer of a quorum or other organization. (p. 23.)

> Concerning the keys of the priesthood President Joseph F. Smith said,

> The Priesthood in general is the authority given to man to act for God. Every man ordained to any degree of the Priesthood, has this authority delegated to him.
> But it is necessary that every act performed under this authority shall be done at the proper time and place, in the proper way, and after the proper order. The power of directing these labors constitutes the keys of the Priesthood. *In their fulness, the keys are held by only one person at a time, the prophet and president of the Church. He may delegate any portion of this power to another, in which case that person holds the keys of that particular labor.* (Smith, Joseph F., *Gospel Doctrine* (Salt Lake City, Utah: Deseret Book Co., 8th ed., 1949), p. 136.

62. McConkie, Bruce R. [comp.], *Doctrines of Salvation* (Salt Lake City, Utah: Bookcraft, 1956), vol. 3, p. 132. See, however, D&C 81:1-2, which sets forth the teaching that the keys belong to the *Presidency* of the High Priesthood. See also D&C 124:126; 107:9-10; 112:15-16; 124:128.

63. McConkie, *Ibid.*, vol. 3, p. 135. President Smith is commenting on D&C 132:7 in this passage.

64. For statements of testimony indicating that these keys were held by the Quorum of the Twelve at the martyrdom of Joseph Smith see Smith, Joseph Fielding, *Succession in the Presidency of the Church of Jesus Christ of Latter-day Saints* (Salt Lake City, Utah: Deseret News Press, n.d.), pp. 18-20.

The Prophet, in anticipation of his death, conferred upon the Twelve all the keys and authorities which he held. He did not bestow the keys on any one member, but upon them all, so that each held the keys and authorities. *All members of the Council of the Twelve since that day have also been given all of these keys and powers. But these powers cannot be exercised by any one of them until, if the occasion arises, he is called to be the presiding officer of the Church. The Twelve, therefore, in the setting apart of the President, do not give him any additional priesthood, but confirm upon him that which he has already received; they set him apart to the office, which it is their right to do.*

On the death of the President, the Council of the Twelve becomes the presiding quorum in the Church until by their action they organize again the First Presidency. This is a consistent order. *If only one man held this binding and loosing power, then the Lord would be under the necessity of restoring it each time a new President of the Church was called.*[65]

---

65. McConkie, *Ibid.*, vol. 3 pp. 155-156. His commentary is an explanation of the meaning of D&C 107:21-26. The Prophet Joseph Smith, in a meeting of the Twelve on January 16, 1836, explained their relationship to the First Presidency, saying:

The Twelve are not subject to any other than the first Presidency, viz., 'myself,' said the Prophet, 'Sidney Rigdon, and Frederick G. Williams, who are now my Counselors; and *where I am not, there is no First Presidency over the Twelve.*' (HC, 2:374. Jan. 16, 1836.)

In explaining the succession of authority set forth in D&C 107:21-26, President Joseph Fielding Smith stated:

There has been a slight misunderstanding on the part of some because of the statement that the twelve are equal in authority and power to the three members of the First Presidency. The fact that it is also stated that the seventies hold equal authority has also caused some misunderstanding. It is impossible, of course, for two, much less three, councils, to have equal authority and power at the same time. If that were the case, there could be no head. The interpretation of these statements is that *the twelve apostles hold all the authority and power that is vested in the First Presidency, but it cannot be exercised as long as the First Presidency is intact.* On the death of the President of the Church, the First Presidency is dissolved, and then the Council of the Twelve Apostles exercises all the authority that was vested in the Presidency, and this continues until the First Presidency is organized again and becomes the presiding council in the Church. If the time should ever come, which is improbable, when both the First Presidency and the entire quorum of the apostles should be destroyed, then, and only then, would the First Council of the Seventy have the power and authority mentioned in the revelation. *In no other way are these three councils equal in authority, and the First Presidency holds the keys of authority while the President of the Church is living.* (Smith, Joseph Fielding, "History and Authority of Apostleship," *Answers to Gospel Questions* (Salt Lake City, Utah: Deseret Book Company, 1966), vol. 5, pp. 178-179.)

While other general authorities besides the President of the Church are sustained as prophets, seers, and revelators, their role is to preserve these keys, rather than to function in them, according to Joseph Fielding Smith, who defined the relationship in this manner:

> The Twelve Apostles have been sustained as prophets, seers, and revelators ever since the time of the dedication of the Kirtland Temple. *There is only one man at a time who holds the keys of revelation for the Church. The Twelve Apostles may receive revelation to guide them in their labors and to assist them in setting in order the priesthood and organizations of the Church.* When they are sent out into a stake by authority, they have all the power to receive revelation, to make changes, and to conduct the affairs according to the will of the Lord. *But they do not receive revelations for the guidance of the whole Church, only wherein one of them may succeed to the Presidency.* In other words the right to receive revelation and guidance for the whole Church is vested in each one of the Twelve which he could exercise should he succeed to the Presidency. *But this power is dormant while the President of the Church is living.*[66]

President Smith defined these relationships in a concise manner, and his comments on the subject have therefore been quoted frequently, and have sometimes been held up as being the official position of the Church. Unfortunately, his clearly-defined lines as to who may and may not receive particular types of revelation do not reflect, without exception, the manner in which God has revealed His will to His people, as recorded in numerous LDS historical sources. There are far too many exceptions to the above guidelines set down by President Smith for them to be regarded as anything more than a general summation. Certainly they are not an infallible rule. The evidence is overwhelming that God has not confined Himself to the strict outline set forth above as He has poured out His revelations upon the saints. Many examples to be cited will show that his outline does not fully reflect the manner in which past revelations have been granted, and thus that it cannot be regarded as more than a generalization.

One cannot safely deduce, from Doctrine and Covenants 132:7 and the quotations above, for instance, that revelation in the Church is granted *only* to the President because all the keys of presidency are conferred upon him. He holds the keys of missionary work, yet many serve as missionaries and receive guidance which is ultimately used Church-wide; he holds the keys of temple work, yet many perform ordinances in the temples and receive insights which eventually become part of the general temple program; he holds the keys of Church administration, yet many serve as administrators in the Church and develop inspired programs which finally bless all the

---

66. McConkie, *Doctrines of Salvation, op. cit.,* vol. 3, pp. 156-157. See HC, 2:477.

Saints: The keys are widely delegated throughout the Church. Just as many serve as missionaries, temple workers, administrators, etc., many receive revelation and prophesy through the same delegated keys and/or through the gifts and manifestations of God.

Neither is one able to assume that every new Church-wide program and idea in the Church had its origin with revelation to the President of the Church. That has been neither the claim nor the practice of the Church. Many Church programs and activities have had their origins in the inspired insights and labors of members and leaders in lower levels of responsibility.

The relationship of the revelation given to other members and that which is given to the President of the Church will be considered in detail in the chapters which follow.

Summary

1. Dictionary definitions of theological terms are often invalid. They may represent the "current usage" employed in various sects and churches rather than the original meanings of terms used in the scriptures.

2. A prophet, by definition, is one who foretells future events. A prophet may perform other tasks and have other abilities, but it is the foretelling of future events which makes him a prophet. The term prophet is often misused within the Church, being used where the term "revelator" would be more applicable.

3. A seer, by definition, is an individual who can receive revelation through sacred instruments such as a Urim and Thummim or a seer stone. A seer can know of things past, present, and future, and of secret things to be made manifest. The privilege of seership is greater than that of being either a prophet or a revelator.

4. A revelator is one who reveals the will of the Lord concerning His temporal kingdom. The role of revelator seems to be that of spokesman for God to the people of the Church and of the earth. Little of a definitive nature is found concerning this office in the scriptures.

5. In recent decades, most of the inspired functioning of the President of the Church which has been made known to the general Church membership has been in his role of revelator. Testimonies of general authorities and other intimate acquaintances of Church Presidents are frequently borne of their personal knowledge that Church Presidents receive revelations concerning the daily affairs of the Church. Evidence and testimonies concerning the "prophetic" and "seership" aspects of the labors of recent Church Presidents, however, are relatively rare.

6. The First Presidency, the Quorum of the Twelve, and the Patriarch to the Church, are sustained as "Prophets, Seers, and Revelators" by the membership of the Church. To sustain a leader means to accept him as a

duly constituted authority, to uphold him as such by prayers and faith, to render obedience to counsel and direction which he gives when speaking under inspiration from God, and to accept on faith that he will be an instrument used by God for the accomplishment of the divine will.

7. Little is revealed in the scriptures concerning the proper relationship between the President of the Church and other general Authorities. The few definitive statements available on the subject by modern LDS authors and expounders of scripture tend to over simplify and to disregard the lessons of history. There is need for further clarifying information from a variety of qualified witnesses and historical sources pertaining to the matter.

8. The term "keys" is understood to mean "the right of presidency."

9. The keys of the presidency of the High Priesthood are understood to be held by the President of the Church. It is understood that the members of the Quorum of the Twelve collectively hold these keys as a quorum, but their keys remain dormant until a President dies, when the Twelve then set apart a new President of the Church.

10. There is a tendency to confuse the holding of keys of presidency with the privilege of receiving revelation and prophecy. Certain erroneous assumptions seemingly stem from this confusion.

2

What Does God Require of His Prophets as He Reveals His Will?

Of major interest and concern to Latter-day Saints is the manner in which God speaks to His people in the latter days. Church members want to understand how God communicates with man, to whom His revealed word will come, and exactly how they can know when the Lord has spoken to the Church.

It is essential that the Church be able to recognize when its leaders are speaking the will of the Lord under divine inspiration, as opposed to instances when they are acting on the basis of their own educated judgment and experience. Prophecies of a future crisis and period of apostasy[1] the Church must endure should alert the saints to the need and importance of correct understanding in this regard. Dissension on the question of "when is a prophet a prophet?" or "when is he speaking only as a man?" has taken a heavy toll on previous occasions in the Church's history; it must not be allowed to happen again.

A Lesson from History—The Apostasy of 1837

In the mid 1830's, converts were joining the Church and gathering in rapidly-increasing numbers to Kirtland, Ohio. Many who came to be near the Church leaders had given up their homes and possessions in other areas at great sacrifice, and were in an impoverished condition. Gentile land speculators had sought to reap an exhorbitant profit from the Mormons gathering at Kirtland and had raised the price on available lands to the point that few could afford to purchase building lots for new homes. Those saints who already resided in Kirtland had spent much of their meager funds to aid in the construction of the Kirtland Temple. In an effort to meet the economic crisis which confronted them, the saints undertook to establish a bank. Application was made for a charter from the Ohio State legislature

---

1. See chapter 9. The previously-quoted statement of President Harold B. Lee should be recalled in this context:

> You brethren of the priesthood should be well advised that the principle of revelation through proper channels has been at issue in every persecution of the Latter-day Saints in this dispensation, whether it be on the subject of priesthood, marriage, the gathering of Zion, or succession of the priesthood. (*Conference Report,* April 1970, p. 56.)

but the charter was denied.² The saints then chose to establish the bank as a "Stock Industrial Company" without state approval, and did so, naming it the "Kirtland Safety Society, Anti-Banking Company." A meeting held January 2, 1837, formally established the rules by which the banking society was to be governed.³ The organization was to be directed by a group of thirty-two managers which were to be elected from the Society's membership. A person gained membership by purchasing one or more shares at $50 a share. The Society could then loan money to the saints for the purchase of land, implements, and the supplies which were needed by its members. The managers agreed to hold their personal goods as bond for the redemption of any loans made by the society to the amount of $100,000 each. The organization functioned under the guidance of a number of the Church leaders who had been elected to the managerial offices. Sidney Rigdon was named secretary and Joseph Smith was named treasurer.⁴

At this time, Martin Van Buren had just assumed the presidency of the United States. Soon after he became president the country plunged into a great commercial crisis. Reckless financial speculation had been increasing for several years across the country.

Suddenly, in April, 1837, financial panic erupted. Many hundreds of banks throughout the country closed their doors. The Kirtland Safety Society, not yet a year old, was unable to withstand the extreme financial problems created by the nationwide panic, and it also collapsed, with tragic consequences for the Church. Joseph Smith later wrote the following concerning this period:

> At this time the spirit of speculation in lands and property of all kinds, which was so prevalent throughout the whole nation, was taking deep root in the Church. As the fruits of this spirit, evil surmisings, fault-finding, disunion, dissention, and apostasy followed in quick succession, and it seemed as though all the powers of earth and hell were combining their influence in an especial manner to overthrow the Church at once, and make a final end. Other banking institutions refused the "Kirtland Safety Society's" notes. The enemy abroad, and apostates in our midst, united in their schemes, flour and provisions were turned toward other markets, and *many became disaffected toward me as though I were the sole cause of those very evils I was most strenuously striving against, and which were actually brought upon us by the brethren not giving heed to my counsel.*
>
> No quorum of the Church was entirely exempt from the influence of those false spirits who are striving against me for the mastery; even some of the Twelve were so far lost to their high and responsible calling, as to begin to take sides, secretly, with the enemy.⁵

2. HC 2:467-68.
3. HC 2:470-73. This meeting annulled the previous constitution of the group which had been adopted two months earlier.
4. CHC 1:403.
5. HC 2:487-88.

It appears that the Adversary chose this moment to exert his greatest efforts against the Church. At this same time a great controversy broke out among the saints in Missouri concerning matters of doctrine and the authority of the High Council there.[6] Similar disputes soon broke out in Kirtland.[7] At this time the Prophet was taken sick and the apostate element spread the rumor that the illness was an indication that Joseph was "in transgression, and had taught the Church things contrary to godliness."[8] Though his recovery was rapid, the seeds of distrust had been effectively sown. One of those most filled with the spirit of apostasy was Warren Parish, of the Kirtland Safety Society, who embezzled over $25,000 of the Society's funds. As Society treasurer, Joseph had previously counseled against the unwise decisions of the bank managers,[9] but his warnings went unheeded. The saints were defeating the purpose of the Society by joining in the land speculation. More and more of them were borrowing from the Society to buy land, then holding the land for the price to raise so they could sell it at a profit. This land speculation, of course, which was causing prices to be seriously inflated, was the very problem the Society had been formed to combat. Finally, because of the speculative course being followed by the Society, Joseph resigned his position as treasurer and withdrew his membership in the organization. Of this he wrote,

> I resigned my office in the "Kirtland Safety Society," disposed of my interest therein, and withdrew from the institution; being fully aware, after so long an experiment, that no institution of the kind, established upon just and righteous principles for a blessing not only to the Church but the whole nation, would be suffered to continue its operations in such an age of darkness, speculation and wickedness. Almost all banks throughout the country, one after the other, have suspended specie payment, and gold and silver have risen in value in direct ratio with the depreciation of paper currency.[10]

Shortly after his withdrawal, the Kirtland Safety Society met its disastrous end. The financial panic then sweeping the nation engulfed it and the struggling enterprise, still in its infancy, crumbled. Since it had no bank charter, the Society's bank notes had no legal standing as currency and were rejected by its creditors in New York, Pittsburg, and Cleveland. Large tracts of land purchased by members had to be sold at a loss as real estate prices rapidly declined.

The failure of the Society left many of the Church members in great distress. Many of the Church leaders, who had given their personal goods as bond, were among the hardest hit, and suffered severe personal losses as

---

6. HC 2:481-84.
7. HC 2:485-86.
8. HC 2:493.
9. HC 2:488.
10. HC 2:497.

they attempted to repay the losses incurred by Society members from their personal funds. However, since Joseph Smith had resigned from the Society just before its collapse, he escaped the financial ruin which came to the others. He reaped, instead, a bitter hatred which caused many of the Church leaders and members to apostatize during the months that followed.

As the Church struggled to understand the great crisis which engulfed it, many members faltered in their testimonies. Since the Kirtland Safety Society had been formed at the suggestion of the prophet Joseph, some believed this automatically meant that "the bank was instituted by the will of God"[11] and that "it should never fail, let men do what they would."[12] On the contrary, Joseph, as a prominent citizen in the community, had merely seen a need and suggested that a society could be formed to fill that need. In a council held in September, 1837, the Prophet refuted the idea that the Society was divinely inspired, and "stated that if this had been declared no one had authority from him for so doing, for he had always said that unless the institution was conducted on righteous principles it would not stand."[13]

The apostasy of Kirtland resulted in a loss of almost half the Quorum of the Twelve and almost a third of the total Church membership. Two elements, linked together, seemed to be the cause of the apostasy: (1) severe financial loss and (2) uncertainty as to whether the Prophet was truly receiving revelations from God.

To a great extent, the apostasy which rocked the Church in Kirtland and soon spread to Missouri took place because the saints failed to recognize that the Kirtland Safety Society was a secular activity in which Joseph was just another participant, rather than a God-given panacea for all their temporal problems. Joseph Smith neither claimed, nor taught, that the Kirtland Safety Society was established because God had revealed that it should be, but the *people assumed that God had spoken* because their leader, whom they trusted as a prophet of God, had suggested that it be organized. There is danger in a blind, unknowing faith which fails to make such distinctions.

This situation posed the question which still has vital implications for the membership of the Church: Is every action—every word—of a man holding the calling of President or general authority in the Church to be considered the will and word of God? Does The Church of Jesus Christ of Latter-day Saints hold to the doctrine of infallibility taught by some other denominations, such as the Catholic Church? Does it believe that its prophet can speak no error—that his every word is the expression of God's revealed

---

11. HC 2:509-10.
12. HC 2:510.
13. HC 2:510.

will? Joseph Smith gave his answer to this important doctrinal question when he wrote that he

> . . . visited with a brother and sister from Michigan, who thought that "a prophet is always a prophet;" but *I told them that a prophet was a prophet only when he was acting as such.*[14]

The Church makes no claim to a doctrine of infallibility, and that belief has been specifically rejected by the President of the Church.[15] To the contrary, dozens of passages of scripture show that prophets and Church leaders can err even as they function in their religious callings.

God's System of Checks and Balances

God works with, and directs with care, the affairs of the earth. Because he knows the frailties of men who wield power, he places systems of checks and balances which will control those who rule. The Constitution of the United States, which Latter-day Saints hold to be inspired of God, is an example of these checks and balances. It calls for executive, legislative, and judicial branches of government, each of which exercises various control functions over the others. Thus, a balance of power is preserved, and a protection against extreme error is maintained.

Within His Church, God has also established a set of checks and balances. He has revealed guidelines and safeguards which direct and also limit both the prophets and the membership of the Church. Each has responsibilities to fulfill in order to insure that the proper channels of communication are open.

It will be seen that the Lord, through a broad pattern of scriptural injunctions, carefully restricts the role of His prophets. He places strict

---

14. HC 5:265. Feb. 8, 1843.

15. See President Spencer W. Kimball's comment that no claim of infallibility is made for the prophet of the Church, recorded in the April, 1970, *Conference Report*, p. 120. It was at this conference that Joseph Fielding Smith first presided as President of the Church.

The doctrine of infallibility within the Roman Catholic Church has been defined by one Catholic author as follows:

> The doctrine of infallibility was defined by Vatican Council I and promulgated on July 18, 1870.
>
> *The doctrine that the pope is free from error insofar as he is head of the Church on earth and when he speaks in that capacity to define a doctrine of faith or morals. Such statements are irreformable by nature, not by reason of the Church's consent.* Infallibility of the pope is neither impeccability nor inspiration. Infallibility refers only to the pope's ex cathedra statements, not to his every doctrinal act. Infallibility resides primarily in the Church. (Nevins, Albert J., *The Maryknoll Catholic Dictionary,* (New York: Grosset & Dunlap) p. 293.

limitations upon what the Church membership should regard as the revealed word of God. He also places responsibility upon the Church members to give diligent heed and obedience to His word when it is revealed.

There is need for clarifications to be made concerning the checks and balances within the Church, based upon careful consideration of all the scriptural passages pertinent to the subject. That system provides effective safeguards against the possibility of error, and it is important that it be thoroughly understood and carefully implemented.

There has been a tendency among some Latter-day Saints to overstate and to draw meanings and interpretations on this subject not supported by scripture, nor by the history of God's dealings with His Church. There is a need to call attention to these explanatory passages and historical examples. It is also important for the saints to recognize what the scriptures do *not* say, as well as what they *do* say.

Two chapters have been devoted to a discussion of this system of revealed checks and balances. This chapter will consider the guidelines and restrictions the Lord has revealed concerning His revelations to the prophets, while the next chapter will deal with responsibilities and requirements the Lord has placed upon the membership of the Church pertaining to the revelations and manifestations He grants unto man.

Basic Passages Define the Role of the Church President in Receiving Commandments

When the President of the Church receives commandments and instructions of God for the Church, he is usually functioning in the role of "revelator," rather than in the role of "prophet" or "seer." He is receiving the will of the Lord through revelation. He then has the responsibility to serve as spokesman for God and to clearly communicate God's will to the entire membership of the Church, and, in some instances, to the entire world. In cases where the revelation pertains to administrative or organizational matters, the President is also responsible for the implementation of the instruction, by bringing to pass action which will accomplish the Lord's will.

A series of three basic passages in the Doctrine and Covenants sets forth the manner in which the President of the Church is to receive commandments for the Church. These passages are frequently quoted, and form the basis for almost all discourses attempting to define the nature of revelation to the Church.[16]

16. It should be noted that these passages were revealed before the structure of Church government was established—before the position of President of the Church and the title "Prophet, Seer, and Revelator" came into usage. They do not fully define the relationships which exist between the presiding quorums and between

In the first passage, received in 1830 on the day the Church was restored, the Lord revealed to Joseph Smith these words:

Wherefore, meaning the church, *thou shalt give heed unto all his words and commandments which he shall give unto you as he receiveth them, walking in all holiness before me;*
For his word ye shall receive, as if from mine own mouth, in all patience and faith.
For by doing these things the gates of hell shall not prevail against you; yea, and the Lord God will disperse the powers of darkness from before you, and cause the heavens to shake for your good, and his name's glory.
For thus saith the Lord God: Him have I inspired to move the cause of Zion in mighty power for good, and his diligence I know, and his prayers I have heard.
Yea, his weeping for Zion I have seen, and I will cause that he shall mourn for her no longer; for his days of rejoicing are come unto the remission of his sins, and the manifestations of my blessings upon his works.
For, behold, I will bless all those who labor in my vineyard with a mighty blessing, and *they shall believe on his words, which are given him through me by the Comforter.* [17]

Second, in September of 1830, in a revelation given through the prophet Joseph Smith to Oliver Cowdery, the Lord revealed,

I say unto thee, *no one shall be appointed to receive commandments and revelations in this church excepting my servant Joseph Smith, Jun., for he receiveth them even as Moses.*
And thou shalt be obedient unto the things which I shall give unto him, even as Aaron, *to declare faithfully the commandments and the revelations, with power and authority unto the church.*
And if thou art led at any time by the Comforter to speak or teach, or at all times by the way of commandment unto the church, thou mayest do it.
But thou shalt not write by way of commandment, but by wisdom;
And thou shalt not command him who is at thy head, and at the head of the church;
For I have given him the keys of the mysteries, and the revelations which are sealed, until I shall appoint unto them another in his stead.
And now, behold, I say unto you that you shall go unto the Lamanites and preach my gospel unto them; and inasmuch as they receive thy teachings thou shalt cause my church to be established among them; and *thou shalt have revelations, but write them not by way of commandment. . . .*
And again, thou shalt take thy brother, Hiram Page, between him and thee alone, and tell him that those things which he hath written from that stone are not of me, and that Satan deceiveth him;
For, behold, these things have not been appointed unto him, *neither shall anything be appointed unto any of this church contrary to the church covenants.*

the general authorities and the Church membership. Yet they do provide a basis for partial understanding of how the Lord reveals His will to His people.

17. D&C 21:4-9. April 6, 1830.

> *For all things must be done in order, and by common consent in the church, by the prayer of faith.* [18]

Third, in February of 1831, the Lord revealed,

> O hearken, ye elders of my church, and give ear to the words which I shall speak unto you.
>
> For behold, verily, verily, I say unto you, that ye have received a *commandment for a law* unto my church, *through him whom I have appointed unto you to receive commandments and revelations from my hand.*
>
> *And this ye shall know assuredly—that there is none other appointed unto you to receive commandments and revelations until he be taken, if he abide in me.*
>
> But verily, verily, I say unto you, that *none else shall be appointed unto this gift except it be through him;* for if it be taken from him he shall not have power except to appoint another in his stead.
>
> And this shall be a law unto you, that *ye receive not the teachings of any that shall come before you as revelations or commandments;*
>
> *And this I give unto you that you may not be deceived, that you may know they are not of me.*
>
> For verily I say unto you, that he that is ordained of me shall come in at the gate and be ordained as I have told you before, to teach those revelations which you have received through him whom I have appointed. [19]

These basic passages are detailed and complex. They deserve careful study and analysis. They have a four-fold message, for they (1) define the responsibilities of a revelator, (2) state the blessings of revelators who fulfill those responsibilities, (3) define the responsibilities of Church members toward God-appointed revelators and the commandments revealed through them, and (4) state the blessings of Church members who fulfill those responsibilities. A brief outline of the basic passages might be made as follows:

Responsibilities of the Revelator

1. Give commandments unto the Church when he receives them. (D&C 21:4)

2. Communicate to the Church the words of Christ given through the Comforter. (D&C 21:9)

3. Represent his words as being from the mouth of God. (D&C 21:5)

Responsibilities of Church Members

1. Give heed to the words and commandments of the revelator (D&C 21:4) when he

   A. gives commandments unto the Church as he receives them

   B. communicates to the Church the words of Christ given through the Comforter

---

18. D&C 28:2-8, 11-13.
19. D&C 43:1-7.

4. Abide in Christ, so he may retain his gift to receive revelations and commandments. (D&C 43:3)

5. Appoint nothing contrary to the church covenants. (D&C 28:12)

6. All things must be done in order. (D&C 28:13)

7. All things must be done by common consent in the Church. (D&C 28:13)

8. All things must be done by the prayer of faith. (D&C 28:13)

C. represents his words as being from the mouth of God.

D. abides in Christ, so he may retain his gift to receive revelations and commandments

E. appoints nothing contrary to the church covenants

F. does all things in order

G. does all things by common consent in the church, and

H. does all things by the prayer of faith.

2. Receive the revealed words of God in all patience and faith. (D&C 21:5)

3. Believe on the revelator's inspired words. (D&C 21:9)

4. Appoint none else to have the gift of receiving revelations or commandments except it be through the revelator. (D&C 28:2)

5. Receive not the teachings of others as revelations or commandments. (D&C 43:5)

6. When led by the Comforter to speak or teach to the Church, they may do it. (D&C 28:4)

7. They shall not write by way of commandment, but by wisdom. (D&C 28:5)

8. They shall not command the head of the Church. (D&C 28:6)

9. They shall have revelations and write them, but are not to write them by way of commandment. (D&C 28:8)

10. Come in at the gate and be ordained if they are to teach
the revelations. (D&C 43:7)

11. Walk in holiness before the
Lord. (D&C 21:4)

Blessings of Revelator Who
Fulfills the Above Responsibilities

1. He is inspired to move the cause
of Zion in mighty power for
good. (D&C 21:7)

2. His diligence is known by God.
(D&C 21:7)

3. His prayers are heard by God.
(D&C 21:7)

4. He gains the remission of his sins.
(D&C 21:8)

5. The Lord's blessings are manifested upon his works. (D&C 21:8)

Blessings of Church Members Who
Fulfill the Above Responsibilities

1. The gates of hell shall not prevail against you. (D&C 21:6)

2. The Lord will disperse the
powers of darkness from before
you. (D&C 21:6)

3. The Lord God will cause the
heavens to shake for your good,
and his name's glory. (D&C
21:6)

4. The Lord God will bless all
those who labor in his vineyard
with a mighty blessing. (D&C
21:9)

Again, this chapter will consider the duties and blessings of a revelator; the next chapter will consider the duties and blessings of Church members pertaining to new revelation. Emphasis will be placed upon the specific requirements the Lord has established, both upon His revelators and upon the Church membership.

The Revelator Is to Give Commandments Unto the Church When He Receives Them—A "Time" Requirement

The Lord has revealed a series of important guidelines to enable the Church to properly receive the words of the Prophet, Seer, and Revelator. He has set up checks and balances, and has placed restrictions upon both the Revelator and the Church. As in all the commandments and counsel for righteous living revealed by the Lord, problems are avoided when these instructions or limitations are observed. Conversely, difficulties arise when the Lord's counsel is disobeyed by men.

One important guideline revealed by the Lord is the instruction concerning *when* revelations are to be given to the Church. Said the Lord, "Wherefore, meaning the Church, thou shalt give heed unto all his words and commandments *which he shall give unto you as he receiveth them. . . .*"[20]

Certainly those through whom the Lord reveals His words are expected to be diligent servants who hasten to deliver His words unto His people. They are not to delay the word of God, neither are they to refuse to deliver His revelations unto those for whom the message is intended. Two historical events provide more than adequate evidence that the Lord expects His Revelators to deliver their messages promptly. The prophet Jonah was commanded to "go to Nineveh, that great city, and cry against it,"[21] yet he feared to deliver God's revealed words, and instead fled to Tarshish. God chastened him with a storm, allowed him to be cast into the sea, and left him in "the belly of the fish three days and three nights." Only then, when Jonah was ready to deliver the message God had revealed through him, was he released.

The second example which shows the Lord's displeasure when His Revelators withhold His words is found in Latter-day Saint Church history. The prophet Joseph Smith apparently withheld the revelation on marriage (Doctrine and Covenants 132) from the Church until

> An angel with a flaming sword descended from the courts of glory and, confronting the Prophet, commanded him in the name of the Lord to establish the principle so long concealed from the knowledge of the Saints and of the world. . . .[22]

Both of these instances indicate that it is God's intention that his revealed words be delivered promptly to their intended audience, and that the Lord does not tolerate delays on the part of His Revelators and Prophets. For a Revelator to fail to deliver the Lord's message is to bring condemnation upon himself. Recall the Lord's warning to a former Revelator, Ezekiel. The Lord told him that if a revelator fails to deliver the warning

---

20. D&C 21:4.

21. Jon. 1:2.

22. Whitney, Orson F., *Life of Heber C. Kimball,* (Salt Lake City, Utah: Bookcraft, Inc., third edition, 1967), p. 321. Benjamin F. Johnson also left record of this incident:

> "Benjamin heard the prophet explain that an angel appeared unto him with a drawn sword, threatening to slay him [Joseph] if he did not proceed to fulfill the law that had been given to him [Joseph]."

LeBaron, E. Dale, *Benjamin Franklin Johnson: Colonizer, Public Servant, and Church Leader,* (Provo, Utah: Thesis, August, 1966), p. 83, as cited from Johnson, "Benjamin F. Johnson's Testimony," affidavit in *The Historical Record,* compiled by Andrew Jensen (Salt Lake City, Utah, 1882-1890), VI (May, 1887), pp. 221-222.

God has revealed through him, God will hold the Revelator responsible for his failure, and make him responsible for the wicked one's failure to repent:

> Son of man, I have made thee a watchman unto the house of Israel: therefore hear the word at my mouth, and give them warning from me.
>
> *When I say unto the wicked, Thou shalt surely die; and thou givest him not warning, nor speakest to warn the wicked from his wicked way, to save his life; the same wicked man shall die in his iniquity; but his blood will I require at thine hand.*
>
> Yet if thou warn the wicked, and he turn not from his wickedness, nor from his wicked way, he shall die in his iniquity; but thou hast delivered thy soul.
>
> Again, when a righteous man doth turn from his righteousness, and commit iniquity, and I lay a stumblingblock before him, he shall die: *because thou hast not given him warning, he shall die in his sin, and his righteousness which he hath done shall not be remembered; but his blood will I require at thine hand.*
>
> Nevertheless if thou warn the righteous man, that the righteous sin not, and he doth not sin, he shall surely live, because he is warned; also thou hast delivered thy soul.[23]

The Revelator Is to Communicate the Words of Christ Given Through the Comforter—An "Inspiration" Requirement

Speaking of the relationship of the Church to the Revelator, the Lord commanded, "They shall believe on his words, *which are given him through me by the Comforter.*"[24] Here the Lord emphasizes that the words of the Revelator which are binding upon the Church as commandments are only those which he has received from God through revelation or inspiration. This is also set forth in His statement, "Thou shalt be obedient *unto the things which I shall give unto him.* "[25] In his role as Revelator, the President of the Church is to convey new instructions from God to the saints. It is these instructions, which are actually revealed by God and received by the Revelator, which the Lord makes the Church responsible to observe. Note that the Lord is very specific about it—He limits the responsibility of the saints to giving obedience to that which is actually revealed, rather than to all that is said by Church leaders.

It is obvious that this responsibility upon Church members is cumulative—it includes direct revelations given to former Revelators as well as those given to the current President of the Church, for man's responsibility is to live by all the revealed word of God.

As will be seen from the example continually set forth in the scriptures, the Lord's Revelators have carefully recorded the words of the revelations they have received. Thus we see that the saints are entitled to know the exact

---

23. Ezek. 3:17-21.
24. D&C 21:9.
25. D&C 28:3.

words of a revelation, not receive only a paraphrase of it or an allusion to it. They should be given all God's words in their original form. They are also entitled to information as to the date, place, and circumstances of the revealed message. That is the pattern the Lord has established in the scriptures, particularly in the revelations granted in this dispensation. Those exact details increase the understanding and faith of the saints.

Controversy and sorrow have been the result when the exact wording and the pertinent circumstances are not given, as the history of the saints clearly shows. Probably the most controversial of all issues within the Church have related to plural marriage and to the Negro being denied the priesthood—both practices being plagued with problems, from beginning to end, because this inspired requirement was not fulfilled. A careful recording of the revelations which began these policies was not made, nor has a proper and thorough record of the Church formally adopting these practices ever been available to the saints. In like manner, the saints never received the specific wording and background detail and documentation of the revelations which caused these practices and policies to cease. Perhaps that is why they both were controversial doctrines, and continue to be so for some individuals even today.

It should be noted that the Lord does not extend the responsibility of the saints to accept as doctrine the general statements, writings, commentaries, and other expressions of opinion voiced or penned by the President of the Church. The Lord expressly limits the responsibility of the saints to actual revelations from God which the Revelator conveys to the Church. This by no means should be understood to mean that the other statements made by the President of the Church are of no value—only that they are not binding upon the Church as being the revealed word of God and should be so regarded. The insights on doctrine, the order of the Church, and of the nature of the eternal plan which the Presidents of the Church have frequently given, are of great value and interest. They are worthy of diligent study and consideration. As Elder John A. Widtsoe wrote,

> . . .His unofficial expressions carry greater weight than the opinions of other men of equal or greater gifts and experience but *without the power of the prophetic office.* It would be wisdom on all occasions and with respect to all subjects in any field of human activity, to hearken to the prophet's voice. *There is safety and ultimate happiness in following the counsel that may be received from the prophet.*[26]

Yet the distinction between the word of God revealed through the Revelator and the President's personal counsel and wisdom must still be made, for the former is from God while the latter is from man. There is danger in failure

---

26. Widtsoe, John A., "When Does A Prophet Speak as a Prophet?", *Evidences and Reconciliations,* (Salt Lake City, Utah: Bookcraft, Inc., 1960), p. 237.

to make with exactness this distinction which the Lord has commanded. The failure of the Saints to do so is what occasioned the tragic apostasy of 1837. For the Church to forget the lesson of that painful experience would be tragic.

Elder Brigham H. Roberts, in an article entitled "Relation of Inspiration and Revelation to Church Government," wrote the following concerning the need for the saints to properly understand the degree and quantity of revelation manifested in leading the Church:

> *We should recognize the fact that we do many things by our own uninspired intelligence for the issues of which we are ourselves responsible. Moreover, the Lord desired that we should seek to do good things on our own account* as indicated in the revelation quoted. [D&C 58:27-28] We are prompted by our native intelligence to perform most of the ordinary actions of life. But for the accomplishment of extraordinary duties, for the achievement of high purposes, the soul, conscious of its own limitations, reaches out for help, deep calls unto deep, the infinite in man seeks union with the infinite in God, and *when necessary for the achievement of God's purposes, we believe that the Lord deigns to communicate his will to man.* He will help men at need, but *I think it improper to assign every word and every act of a man to an inspiration from the Lord.* Were that the case, we would have to acknowledge ourselves as being wholly taken possession of by the Lord, being neither permitted to go to the right nor the left only as he guided us. There could then be no error made, nor blunder in judgment; free agency would be taken away, and the development of human intelligence prevented. Hence, *I think it a reasonable conclusion to say that constant, never-varying inspiration is not a factor in the administration of the affairs of the Church; not even good men, no, not even though they be prophets or other high officials of the Church, are at all times and in all things inspired of God. It is only occasionally, and at need, that God comes to their aid.*
>
> That *there have been unwise things done in the Church* by good men, men susceptible at times to the inspiration of the Spirit of God, we may not question. Many instances in the history of the Church, through three quarters of a century, prove it, and it would be a solecism to say that God was the author of those unwise, not to say positively foolish, things that have been done. For these things men must stand responsible, not God.
>
> *It is well nigh as dangerous to claim too much for the inspiration of God, in the affairs of men, as it is to claim too little. By the first, men are led into superstition, and into blasphemously accrediting their own imperfect actions, their blunders, and possibly even their sins, to God; and by the second, they are apt to altogether eliminate the influence of God from human affairs; I pause in doubt as to which conclusion would be the worse.*[27]

27. Roberts, B. H., "Relation of Inspiration and Revelation to Church Government," *Improvement Era,* (Salt Lake City, Utah: Young Men's Mutual Improvement Association, Church of Jesus Christ of Latter-day Saints,) Vol. 8, pp. 366-367.
28. D&C 21:5.
29. D&C 28:3.
30. Moses 6:27.
31. 2 Ne. 3:7.

The Revelator Is to Designate Revelations as Being from God—An "Identification" Requirement

The Lord has commanded that the Revelator is to identify when the messages he delivers to the Church are revelations from God, in order that Church members can receive his words *"as if from mine own mouth."* [28] He is to "declare faithfully the commandments and the revelations, with power *and authority* unto the church."[29] The entire pattern of scripture shows that the Lord intends that His prophets clearly indicate when they are conveying a revelation from God to the people. Throughout history the prophets have so identified their words as being the revealed word of God when functioning as His spokesmen. When God spoke through Enoch His words were identified by the phrase, "Thus saith the Lord."[30] So were the messages revealed through Joseph, who was sold into Egypt,[31] Moses,[32] Joshua,[33] Samuel,[34] Nathan,[35] Gad,[36] Ahijah,[37] Shemaiah,[38] Elijah,[39] Elisha,[40] Zechariah, the son of Jehoiada,[41] Isaiah,[42] Huldah, the prophetess,[43] Jahaziel,[44] Jeremiah,[45] Ezekiel,[46] Amos,[47] Obadiah,[48] Micah,[49]

32. Ex. 4:22; 5:1; 7:17; 8:1, 20; 9:1, 13; 10:3; 11:4; 32:27; Num. 14:28.
33. Josh. 7:13; 24:2.
34. I Sam. 10:18; 15:2.
35. II Sam. 7:5, 8; 12:7, 11; I Chron. 17:4, 7.
36. II Sam. 24:12; I Chron. 21:10-11.
37. I Ki. 11:31; 14:7.
38. I Ki. 12:24; II Chron. 11:4; 12:5.
39. I Ki. 17:14; 21:19, II Ki. 1:4, 16.
40. II Ki. 2:21; 3:16-17; 4:43; 7:1; II Chron. 21:12.
41. II Chron. 24:20.
42. II Ki. 19:6, 20, 32-33; 20:1, 5, 17; 21:12; Is. 1:24; 29:22; 37:33; 38:1, 5; 43:16; 45:1, 14; 49:8, 25; 50:1; 52:3; 56:1, 4; 65:8; 66:1, 12.
43. II Ki. 22:15-16, 18-19; II Chron. 34:23, 24, 26.
44. II Chron. 20:14-15.
45. Jer. 2:2, 5; 4:3; 5:14; 6:9, 16, 21; 8:4; 9:7, 15, 17, 22, 23; 10:2, 18; 11:3, 11, 21, 22; 12:14; 13:1, 9, 12, 13; 14:10, 15; 15:2, 19; 16:3, 5, 9; 17:5, 21; 18:11, 13; 19:1, 3, 11, 15; 20:4; 21:4, 8, 12; 22:1, 3, 11, 18, 30; 23:2, 15, 16; 24:5, 8; 25:8, 15, 27, 28, 32; 26:2, 4; 27:2, 4, 16, 19, 21; 29:4, 8, 10, 17, 21, 31; 30:5, 12, 18; 31:2, 7, 15, 16, 23, 35, 37; 32:28, 36, 42; 33:2, 4, 10, 12, 17, 20, 25; 34:2, 4, 13, 17; 35:13, 18, 19; 36:29, 30; 37:7, 9; 38:2, 3, 17; 39:16; 42:9, 15, 18; 43:10; 44:2, 7, 11, 25, 30; 45:2; 47:2; 48:40; 49:1, 7, 12, 28, 35; 50:18, 33; 51:1, 33, 36, 58.
46. Ezek. 2:4; 3:11, 27; 5:5, 7, 8; 6:3, 11; 7:2, 5; 11:5, 7, 16, 17; 12:10, 19, 23, 28; 13:3, 8, 13, 18, 20; 14:4, 6, 21; 15:6; 16:3, 36, 59; 17:3, 9, 19, 22; 20:3, 5, 27, 30, 39, 47; 21:3, 9, 24, 26, 28; 22:3, 19; 23:22, 28, 32, 25, 46; 24:3, 6, 9, 21; 25:3, 6, 8, 12, 13, 15, 16; 26:3, 7, 15, 19; 27:3; 28:2, 6, 12, 22, 15; 29:3, 8, 13, 19; 30:2, 6, 13, 22; 31:10, 15; 32:3, 11; 33:25, 27; 34:2, 10, 11, 17, 20; 35:3, 14; 36:2, 3, 4, 5, 6, 7, 13, 22, 33, 37; 37:5, 9, 12, 19, 21; 38:3, 10, 14, 17; 39:1, 17, 25; 43:18; 44:6, 9; 45:9, 18; 46:1, 16; 47:13.
47. Amos 1:3, 6, 9, 11, 13; 2:1, 4, 6; 3:11, 12, 13; 5:3, 4; 7:17.
48. Obad. 1:1.
49. Jer. 27:18; Mi. 2:3; 3:5.

Nahum,[50] Haggai,[51] Zechariah,[52] Malachi,[53] Nephi,[54] Jacob,[55] King Benjamin,[56] Abinadi,[57] Alma,[58] Nephi, the son of Helaman,[59] Samuel the Lamanite,[60] and Joseph Smith.[61]

It is significant to note that in numerous instances in the scriptures, the identifying phrase, "Thus saith the Lord," was carefully recorded, even though the individual who delivered the inspired message was so obscure that the person's name was omitted. Obviously, the authors of the scriptural records felt that it was necessary to identify the messages recorded as being the revealed words of God, even though other significant details were lacking. This occurred with the accounts of an unnamed prophet in the days of Gideon;[62] a prophet in the days of Eli;[63] an unnamed man of God, from Judah, whom the Lord sent to prophesy to an altar;[64] and to a prophet sent to prophesy to that same man of God.[65] It was also the case with an unnamed prophet the Lord sent to Ahab,[66] with another man of God sent to that same king,[67] and to yet another man, one of the sons of the prophets, who was also sent to that wicked king of Israel.[68]

Must a prophet always use the exact words, "Thus saith the Lord" when indicating that the message he is revealing or delivering is the result of revelation? It appears that those exact words are not required. Among the Old Testament prophets, for instance, the scriptures do not record those exact words being used by the prophets Daniel, Hosea, Joel, Jonah,

---

50. Nah. 1:12.
51. Hag. 1:5, 7; 2:6, 11.
52. Zech. 1:3, 4, 14, 16, 17; 2:8; 3:7, 10; 8:2, 3, 4, 6, 7, 9, 14, 19, 20, 23; 11:4.
53. Mal. 1:4.
54. 2 Ne. 5:22; 26:17-18; 27:33; 28:30; 29:4.
55. 3 Ne. 10:7; Jac. 2:23, 25, 28; 5:3.
56. Mos. 3:23-24.
57. Mos. 11:20, 25; 12:2.
58. Mos. 23:7; Al. 8:29; 45:16.
59. Hel. 7:23; 10:11, 14.
60. Hel. 13:8, 11.
61. D&C 21:7, 12; 36:1; 38:1; 44:1; 49:5; 50:6; 52:1, 11; 54:1; 55:1; 56:14; 57:3; 60:1; 61:2; 64:1; 66:1, 13; 70:2; 71:1, 9; 72:2; 73:1; 75:13, 23; 76:5, 31; 78:8; 80:1; 83:1; 86:1, 8; 87:8; 95:10, 16; 97:28; 98:3, 14, 38, 48; 107:60; 112:24, 25, 26, 27; 117:4, 5, 7, 11, 12, 13, 14, 16; 118:5; 119:4; 120:1; 121:16; 124:15, 17, 21, 32, 35, 47, 48, 50, 51, 52, 53, 54, 59, 69, 71, 72, 75, 76, 88, 101, 119, 120, 122, 135, 136, 137, 140, 145; 125:4; 127:4, 6, 8, 9; 132:6, 8, 9, 11, 12, 13, 18, 26, 27, 29, 39, 46, 47, 48, 51, 52, 54, 60, 64; 133:1, 36, 64.
62. Jud. 6:8.
63. I Sam. 2:27-30.
64. I Ki. 13:2.
65. I Ki. 13:21.
66. I Ki. 20:14.
67. I Ki. 20:28.
68. I Ki. 20:42.

Habakkuk, or Zephaniah. Yet in each of these prophetic books, with their own terminology, the prophet identifies his message, or portions of it, as being the revealed word of God.[69]

Many other identifying phrases are used in the scriptures by Revelators to identify their message as being the word of God. The most common of these is "saith the Lord."[70] But there are dozens of other variations, including the following:

—"Thus saith God. . . ."[71]
—"Thus saith the Lord God. . . ."[72]
—"Thus saith the Lord God of hosts. . . ."[73]
—"Thus saith the Lord of hosts. . . ."[74]
—"Thus saith God the Lord. . . ."[75]
—"Thus saith the Lord that created thee. . . ."[76]
—"Thus saith the Lord, thy redeemer, and he that formed thee from the womb. . . ."[77]
—"Thus saith the Lord the King of Israel, and his redeemer the Lord of hosts. . . ."[78]
—"Thus saith the Lord, the Holy One of Israel, and his Maker. . . ."[79]
—"Thus saith the Lord that created the heavens. . . ."[80]
—"Thus saith the Lord the Redeemer of Israel, and his Holy One. . . ."[81]
—"Thus saith thy Lord the Lord, and thy God that pleadeth the cause of his people. . . ."[82]
—"Thus saith the high and lofty One that inhabiteth eternity, whose name is Holy. . . ."[83]
—"Thus saith the Father. . . ."[84]
—"Thus saith the Spirit. . . ."[85]

---

69. See, for instance, Dan. 1:17; 2:19-23, 28, 45; 3:25; 4:8; 5:5; 6:22; 7:1, 2, 13, 15, 16; 8:1-3, 15-19, 26; 9:21-22; 10:5-10; Hos. 1:1, 2, 4, 6, 9; 3:1; 4:1; 12:9-10; 13:4; Joel 1:1; 2:12; Hab. 1:1; 2:2-3; Zeph. 1:1; 2:9.

70. In Isaiah, for instance, this phrase occurs as follows: Is. 14:22; 30:1; 31:9; 33:10; 37:6, 34; 39:6; 41:21; 43:10, 12; 48:22; 49:18; 52:5; 54:1, 17; 55:8; 57:19; 59:20, 21; 65:7, 25; 66:2, 17, 20, 21, 22, 23. It occurs hundreds of other places in the scriptures, particularly in the Old Testament.

71. II Chron. 24:20; Is. 54:6.

72. Is. 7:7; 28:16; 49:22; 52:4; 65:13.

73. Is. 10:24.

74. Is. 14:22, 23; 17:3; 22:25; 45:13.

75. Is. 42:5.

76. Is. 53:1; 44:2.

77. Is. 44:24.

78. Is. 44:6.

79. Is. 45:11.

80. Is. 45:18.

81. Is. 49:7.

82. Is. 51:22.

83. Is. 57:15.

84. 2 Ne. 31:20; 3 Ne. 24:1.

85. Al. 5:50.

—"Wherefore saith the Lamb of God. . . ."[86]
—"And the angel of the Lord said unto me. . . ."[87]
—"I spoke . . . making known unto him the things which the Lord had manifested unto me by his Holy Spirit. . . ."[88]
—"I am called by his Holy Spirit to teach these things. . . ."[89]
—"The voice of the Lord came into my mind again, saying. . . ."[90]
—"The voice of the Lord, by the mouth of angels, doth declare it. . . ."[91]
—". . . Having been visited by angels and also the voice of the Lord, therefore having seen angels, and being eyewitness, and having power given unto him that he might know. . . ."[92]
—"The Lord hath said. . . ."[93]
—"The Lord hath shown unto me. . . ."[94]
—"Saith the Holy One. . . ."[95]
—"Saith your God. . . ."[96]
—"Saith thy God. . . ."[97]
—"Saith my God. . . ."[98]
—"Saith the Lord, the Lord of hosts. . . ."[99]
—"Saith the Lord God of hosts. . . ."[100]
—"Saith the Holy One of Israel. . . ."[101]
—"Saith the Lord God, the Holy One of Israel. . . ."[102]
—"Saith the Lord, and thy redeemer, the Holy One of Israel. . . ."[103]
—"Saith the King of Jacob. . . ."[104]
—"Saith the Lord that formed me from the womb to be his servant. . . ."[105]
—"Saith the Lord that hath mercy on thee. . . ."[106]
—"The Lord God which gathereth the outcasts of Israel saith. . . ."[107]
—"Hear ye the word of the Lord. . . ."[108]
—"The Lord saith thus. . . ."[109]
—"The Lord of hosts, the God of Israel, saith. . . ."[110]
—"The Lord, the God of hosts, the Lord, saith thus. . . ."[111]
—"I have spoken it, saith the Lord God. . . ."[112]
—"Hear ye now what the Lord saith. . . ."[113]
—"Then the word of the Lord came unto Jeremiah the prophet, . . . saying. . . ."[114]
—"Thus saith the Holy Ghost. . . ."[115]

86. 1 Ne. 13:33.
87. 1 Ne. 13:24.
88. 1 Ne. 2:17.
89. Al. 18:34.
90. Enos 1:10.
91. Al. 13:22.
92. 3 Ne. 7:15.
93. Mos. 7:29, 27:13; Al. 34:36.
94. Morm. 8:34.
95. Is. 40:25.
96. Is. 40:1.
97. Is. 66:9.
98. Is. 57:21.
99. Is. 19:4.
100. Is. 22:14, 15.
101. Is. 30:12.
102. Is. 30:15.
103. Is. 41:14; 43:14; 48:17; 54:8.
104. Is. 41:21.
105. Is. 49:5.
106. Is. 54:10.
107. Is. 56:8.
108. Jer. 21:11.
109. Jer. 28:12.
110. Jer. 46:25.
111. Amos 5:16.
112. Ezek. 23:34; 26:5; 39:5.
113. Mi. 6:1.
114. Jer. 28:12.
115. Acts 21:11.

—"He that hath an ear, let him hear what the Spirit saith unto the churches. . . ."[116]
—"These things saith the first and the last, which was dead, and is alive. . . ."[117]
—"These things saith he which hath the sharp sword with two edges. . . ."[118]
—"These things saith the Son of God. . . ."[119]
—"These things saith he that is holy, he that is true, he that hath the key of David, he that openeth and no man shutteth; and shutteth, and no man openeth. . . ."[120]
—"These things saith the Amen, the faithful and true witness, the beginning of the creation of God. . . ."[121]
—"Yea, saith the Spirit. . . ."[122]

There are other identifying phrases used by the prophets in the scriptures, but the above listing should certainly suffice as examples. Several observations should be made. One is that different prophets used different styles in identifying the revelations they had received as being the word of God. Ezekiel usually used the words "Thus saith the Lord God." Jeremiah alternated between "Thus saith the Lord" and "Saith the Lord." In contrast, Isaiah—the prophet with great literary skill—used dozens of different identifying phrases.

Another observation that should be made is that a phrase identifying words as being revealed from God does not necessarily indicate that the words are truly inspired. False prophets also use the term "Thus saith the Lord."[123]

The Lord has revealed His promise that

> *I will give unto you a pattern in all things, that ye may not be deceived;* for Satan is abroad in the land, and he goeth forth deceiving the nations—[124]

And then, in explanation of how this revealed pattern is to be applied, the Lord said:

> . . . He that trembleth under my power shall be made strong, and shall bring forth fruits of praise and wisdom, *according to the revelations and truths which I have given you.*
>
> And again, he that is overcome and bringeth not forth fruits, *even according to this pattern,* is not of me.
>
> Wherefore, *by this pattern ye shall know* the spirits in all cases under the whole heavens.[125]

116. Rev. 2:7, 11, 17, 29; 3:6, 13, 22.
117. Rev. 2:8.
118. Rev. 2:12.
119. Rev. 2:18.
120. Rev. 3:7.
121. Rev. 3:14.
122. Rev. 14:13.
123. See, for instance, II Chron. 18:10-12; Jer. 28:11; Ezek. 13:6; 22:28; etc.
124. D&C 52:14.
125. D&C 52:17-19.

In hundreds of passages in all dispensations, and in all of the Standard Works, the Lord has commanded[126] that His Prophets and Revelators are to identify revelations given to the Lord's people as being the word of God. This author, at least, knows of no other doctrinal principle so emphatically drawn, with so many hundreds of substantiating passages of scripture. The Lord has stated the principle repeatedly and plainly, "And he doeth nothing save it be plain unto the children of men."[127] The words of God "are made known unto us *in plain terms, that we may understand, that we cannot err.*" [128]

Yes, some revelations have been revealed which have not been clearly identified with "Thus saith the Lord" or other identifying phraseology, but they must surely be seen as the exception and not the established program. Problems, sometimes serious problems, arise when the revealed pattern is not obeyed. The Lord "is the same yesterday, to-day, and forever,"[129] and "in him there is no variableness neither shadow of changing."[130] Unless He reveals that this procedure is to be changed, and that revelation be accepted by the Church through the principle of common consent, the saints should not deviate from His previously-revealed word.

This becomes a safeguard to protect the saints in the days to come— for future prophets to refuse to identify their words as being the word of God when they are conveying a revelation from Him would be an extreme departure from the manner in which God has spoken to His people throughout the scriptures.

It is logical that a spokesman of God would choose to identify the word of God when it is revealed through him, for he is responsible for the fate of his people if he does not give them God's warning, and clearly identify it as such.[131] Conversely, it is illogical that a Revelator would refuse

---

126. Note that many, *many* of the passages cited in this section contain the Lord's words commanding the Prophet to identify the revealed message he is to deliver with "Thus saith the Lord."

127. 2 Ne. 26:33.

128. Al. 13:23.

129. 1 Ne. 10:18. See 2 Ne. 2:4; 27:23; 29:9; Al. 31:17; D&C 20:12; 35:1.

130. Morm. 9:9. See 10:19.

131. The Lord stressed this responsibility to Ezekiel when He commanded:

Son of man, speak to the children of thy people, and say unto them, When I bring the sword upon a land, if the people of the land take a man of their coasts, and *set him for their watchman;*

If when he seeth the sword come upon the land, he blow the trumpet, and warn the people;

Then whosoever heareth the sound of the trumpet, and taketh not warning; if the sword come, and take him away, his blood shall be upon his own head.

He heard the sound of the trumpet, and took not warning; his blood shall be upon him. But he that taketh warning shall deliver his soul.

to identify a commandment of God as being such when it is revealed, or hold it back from the people and incur God's displeasure, "For if the trumpet give an uncertain sound, who shall prepare himself to the battle?"[132] The Lord has revealed that

> If a man be called of my Father, as was Aaron, by mine own voice, and by the voice of him that sent me, and I have endowed him with the keys of the power of this priesthood, if he do anything *in my name, and according to my law and by my word,* he will not commit sin, and *I will justify him.* [133]

If he has the guarantee that the Lord will shield him from sin and justify him if he will identify the word of God with the Lord's name, it is most improbable that a Revelator would do otherwise when he receives a revelation for the Church.[134]

The Lord has said,

> He that receiveth of God, *let him account it of God;* and let him rejoice that he is accounted of God worthy to receive.[135]

And He has also pronounced the solemn warning that

> . . .In nothing doth man offend God, or against none is his wrath kindled, *save those who confess not his hand in all things,* . . .[136]

> But if the watchman see the sword come, and blow not the trumpet, and the people be not warned; if the sword come, and take any person from among them, he is taken away in his iniquity; but his blood will I require at the watchman's hand.
> So thou, O son of man, *I have set thee a watchman unto the house of Israel; therefore thou shalt hear the word at my mouth, and warn them from me.*
> When I say unto the wicked, O wicked man, thou shalt surely die; *if thou dost not speak to warn the wicked from his way, that wicked man shall die in his iniquity; but his blood will I require at thine hand.*
> Nevertheless, *if thou warn the wicked of his way to turn from it; if he do not turn from his way, he shall die in his iniquity; but thou hast delivered thy soul.* (Ez. 33:2-9)

132. I Cor. 14:8.
133. D&C 132:59.
134. The prophet is to magnify his calling unto the Lord and not to himself. He must teach the people the word of God with all diligence so that their blood will not be found upon his garments, as Jacob explained:

> And we did magnify our office unto the Lord, taking upon us the responsibility *answering the sins of the people upon our own heads if we did not teach them the word of God with all diligence;* wherefore, by laboring with our might their blood might not come upon our garments; otherwise their blood would come upon our garments, and we would not be found spotless at the last day. (Jac. 1:19)

135. D&C 50:34.
136. D&C 59:21.

The Prophets and Revelators of today and tomorrow will have to make an accounting of their stewardship in this regard, as in the days of Joseph Smith and his fellow Church leaders, of whom the Lord said,

> I, the Lord, have appointed them, and ordained them to be *stewards over the revelations* and commandments which I have given unto them, and *which I shall hereafter give unto them;*
> And an account of this stewardship will I require of them in the day of judgment.[137]

In scriptural times, the Prophet was not assumed to be speaking for the Lord unless he so identified his words. It would seem appropriate to assume the same relationship today. Some commentators have tended, in recent years, to reverse this pattern, making the assertion that the Prophet is speaking for the Lord except when he identifies a statement as being his own opinion. Such an assumption is definitely in opposition to the weight of scriptural evidence, and should so be regarded. As Joseph Smith clearly stated, ". . . A prophet was a prophet *only when he was acting as such.*"[138]

The Revelator Is to Abide in Christ So He May Retain His Gift— A "Worthiness" Limitation

The Lord revealed that His Revelator would be the only one appointed at that time to receive commandments for the Church, but with an important stipulation: *"if he abide in me."*[139] He then continued to warn that a Revelator can lose his revelatory gift, saying that *"if it be taken from him he shall not have power. . . ."*[140]

The Lord requires the Church to be bound by the Revelator's inspired words only when the Revelator is walking in righteousness and holiness before the Lord. Perhaps the same relationship exists between the Lord and His Revelator as between Alma and his missionary son, Corianton. Alma told Corianton, when the latter had fallen into wickedness, "When they saw your conduct they would not believe in my words."[141]

Throughout the scriptures, God has warned that His spokesmen might fall into wickedness and lose their prophetic calling. The Lord demands a high degree of righteousness from His prophets and leaders. At times He has rebuked them openly. To Joseph Smith He warned,

> Although a man may have many revelations, and have power to do many mighty works, yet if he boasts in his own strength, and sets at naught the

---

137. D&C 70:3-4.
138. HC 5:265.
139. D&C 43:3.
140. D&C 43:4.
141. Al. 39:11.

counsels of God, and follows after the dictates of his own will and carnal desires, he must fall and incur the vengeance of a just God upon him.

Behold, you have been entrusted with these things, but how strict were your commandments; and remember also the promises which were made to you, if you did not transgress them.

And behold, how oft you have transgressed the commandments and the laws of God, and have gone on in the persuasions of men.[142]

Indeed, a study of the revelations in the Doctrine and Covenants concerning the status of Joseph Smith as the Prophet of the Church yields the inescapable conclusion that the position of Prophet, Seer and Revelator is by no means "guaranteed," nor an indication that its holder is free from sin. As he established Joseph as His example of the prophetic calling, the Lord continually rebuked Joseph for his faults, and continually warned Joseph that he could fall and be removed from his position. Even before the Church was restored the Lord told Joseph:

Behold, thou art Joseph, and thou wast chosen to do the work of the Lord, but because of transgression, *if thou art not aware thou wilt fall.*

But remember, God is merciful; therefore, repent of that which thou hast done which is contrary to the commandment which I gave you, and thou art still chosen, and art again called to the work;

Except thou do this, *thou shalt be delivered up and become as other men, and have no more gift.*[143]

In a revelation given eight months later, in March, 1829, the Lord told Joseph:

And now I command you, my servant Joseph, to *repent and walk more uprightly before me,* and to yield to the persuasions of men no more; . . .[144]

The next month, the Lord told Oliver Cowdery to "stand by my servant Joseph, faithfully, . . ." and to *"admonish him in his faults."*[145]

---

142. D&C 3:4-6. Other such rebukes were found in D&C 3:7-11; 10:1-2; 24:1-2; 67:5; 93:47-49, etc. See also D&C 6:18-19.

143. D&C 3:9-11. Because of his errors in judgment at this time, Joseph lost his privileges "for a season—" (D&C 3:14). The Lord told him, *"you also lost your gift at the same time, and your mind became darkened."* (D&C 10:2.) It will be readily apparent that this revelation, and the fifteen passages which follow in this book, are not complimentary to the Prophet Joseph Smith. Yet they stand as a testimony to the world that Joseph truly was called of God, and set forth the messages he received from on high without "doctoring" them so they spoke well of him. Certainly a false prophet or an impostor would be reluctant to publish such stinging rebukes and intimate warnings. A much more complimentary view of the Prophet Joseph is found in the author's book, *The Prophecies of Joseph Smith* (Salt Lake City: Bookcraft, Inc., 1963).

144. D&C 5:21. And then the Lord told him that if he would be firm in keeping the commandments, "I grant unto you eternal life, even if you should be slain." (D&C 5:22.)

145. D&C 6:18-19. In another revelation that month, given through Joseph to Oliver, the Lord said that "neither of you have I condemned." (D&C 9:12.)

The Lord's promises to Joseph, throughout most of his ministry, were conditional, and dependent upon whether Joseph would be obedient. The Lord said concerning Joseph, "*If* he shall be diligent in keeping my commandments he shall be blessed unto eternal life."[146]

Prophets, like the rest of us, must continually deal with temptation. Joseph Smith, the Lord's first Prophet and example in this dispensation, was no exception. Revelations on several occasions spoke of the prophet Joseph being forgiven for sin but again being tempted. As the Church was restored, the Lord revealed that "After it was truly manifested unto this first elder that he had received a remission of his sins, *he was entangled again in the vanities of the world,* . . ."[147]

In July, 1830, the Lord told Joseph and Oliver Cowdery,

> . . .*Thou art not excusable in thy transgressions;* nevertheless, go thy way and *sin no more.*[148]

And six months later, in December, 1830, the Lord revealed that the possibility existed, even with His prophet Joseph, that His spokesman might have to be replaced. In a revelation to Joseph and Sidney Rigdon, Sidney was told,

> I have sent forth the fulness of my gospel by the hand of my servant Joseph; and *in weakness have I blessed him;*
> And I have given him the keys . . .*if he abide in me, and if not, another will I plant in his stead.*
> Wherefore, watch over him *that his faith fail not,* . . .[149]

Sidney was also commanded to test the Revelator's prophetic utterances by comparing his words to the scriptures:

> . . .It shall be given unto him to prophesy; and thou shalt preach my gospel and *call on the holy prophets to prove his words, as they shall be given him.*[150]

The conditional role of the prophet, and the possibility that the prophetic gift might be forfeited, was again asserted in a revelation given in February, 1831, even as the Lord instructed the saints that commandments for the Church were to be given through Joseph:

> And this ye shall know assuredly—that there is none other appointed unto you to receive commandments and revelations until he be taken, *if he abide in me.*

---

146. D&C 18:8. See verse 46 also.

147. D&C 20:5. But the Lord acknowledged that Joseph repented, humbled himself, and was therefore endowed with additional power from on high. (D&C 20:6-8.) See D&C 21:8; 23:5.

148. D&C 24:2.

149. D&C 35:17-19.

150. D&C 35:23. Thus the Lord clearly stated His intent that the saints should test and evaluate the validity of words spoken by the prophets. Note the time this testing is to take place: as the words of prophecy are given to the Prophet.

But verily, verily, I say unto you, that none else shall be appointed unto this gift except it be through him; *for if it be taken from him he shall not have power* except to appoint another in his stead.[151]

The conditional nature of the prophetic calling yet again was emphasized in a revelation given through Joseph Smith in September, 1831, with obedience to the ordinances specified as the action required of Joseph to retain the prophetic calling:

And the keys of the mysteries of the kingdom shall not be taken from my servant Joseph Smith, Jun., through the means I have appointed, while he liveth, *inasmuch as he obeyeth mine ordinances.*
There are those who have sought occasion against him without cause; *Nevertheless, he has sinned;* but verily I say unto you, I, the Lord, forgive sins unto those who confess their sins before me and ask forgiveness, who have not sinned unto death.[152]

A revelation given two months later again alluded to the prophet Joseph's weaknesses:

Your eyes have been upon my servant Joseph Smith, Jun., and his language you have known, and *his imperfections you have known;* . . .[153]

And then the Lord again granted forgiveness of his sins to Joseph in March, 1833:

Thus saith the Lord, verily, verily I say unto you my son, *thy sins are forgiven thee,* according to thy petition, for thy prayers and the prayers of thy brethren have come up into my ears.[154]

Yet, in the same revelation, the Lord still cautioned Joseph and his counselors in the First Presidency:

. . . *Be admonished in all your high-mindedness and pride, for it bringeth a snare upon your souls.*
Set in order your houses; keep slothfulness and uncleanness far from you.[155]

And promised blessings to the First Presidency remained conditional:

. . . All things shall work together for your good, *if* ye walk uprightly and remember the covenant wherewith ye have covenanted one with another.[156]

---

151. D&C 43:3-4.
152. D&C 64:5-7.
153. D&C 67:5.
154. D&C 90:1. In this same revelation Joseph was promised that "the keys of this kingdom shall never be taken from you, while thou art in the world, neither in the world to come." (D&C 90:3.) The sins of Sidney Rigdon and Frederick G. Williams, Joseph's counselors in the First Presidency, were also forgiven. (Verse 6.)
155. D&C 90:17-18.
156. D&C 90:24.

And two months later, in May, 1833, the Lord rebuked each of the members of the First Presidency. He again raised the possibility that the Prophet could be removed from his place, as he said to Joseph:

> . . . *You have not kept the commandments, and must needs stand rebuked before the Lord;*
> Your family must needs repent and forsake some things, and give more earnest heed unto your sayings, or *be removed* out of their place.
> What I say unto one I say unto all; pray always *lest that wicked one have power in you, and remove you out of your place.*[157]

In 1836, when Joseph, with several others journeyed to Massachusetts in a futile effort to obtain funds for the Church, a revelation said, "I, the Lord your God, am not displeased with your coming this journey, *notwithstanding your follies.*"[158]

But the Lord, though he repeatedly alluded to Joseph's imperfections and the possibility that his calling might be taken away in His revelations to Joseph, gave assurance to others that Joseph would not forfeit his keys. To Thomas B. Marsh, then president of the Twelve, the Lord commanded,

> Exalt not yourselves; rebel not against my servant Joseph; for verily I say unto you, *I am with him,* and my hand shall be over him; and *the keys which I have given unto him, and also to youward, shall not be taken from him* till I come.[159]

It is interesting to note that as Joseph endured the severe trials of the Missouri persecutions, the cautionary tone of the revelations given to him diminished, and the Lord began to speak in a more commendatory manner to the prophet.[160]

Yet the implications of this series of revelations remains clear. Prophets can sin, and they do have their weaknesses. And more important, the Lord stated repeatedly that prophets can and will be removed from their calling and position, and lose their prophetic gift, if they do not render strict obedience to the Lord's commandments.

Joseph understood full well the danger of falling into wickedness which confronts all priesthood leaders and warned, "The higher the authority, the greater the difficulty of the station."[161] Concerning the temptations which come to Church leadership, he recorded,

---

157. D&C 93:47-49.

158. D&C 111:1.

159. D&C 112:15. It is interesting that Thomas B. Marsh was commanded to admonish sharply the Twelve for their sins in this revelation. (D&C 112:11-13.)

160. See D&C 115:19; 122:4; and 124:1.

161. HC 2:478, April 6, 1837. He also said, *"The nearer a person approaches the Lord, a greater power will be manifested by the adversary to prevent the accomplishment of His purposes."* (Whitney, Orson F., *Life of Heber C. Kimball*, (Salt Lake City, Utah: Bookcraft, Inc., 3rd ed., 1967), p. 132.)

Behold, there are many called, but few are chosen. And why are they not chosen?

Because their hearts are set so much upon the things of this world, and aspire to the honors of men, that they do not learn this one lesson—

That *the rights of the priesthood are inseparably connected with the powers of heaven, and that the powers of heaven cannot be controlled nor handled only upon the principles of righteousness.*

That they may be conferred upon us, it is true; but *when we undertake to cover our sins, or to gratify our pride, our vain ambition, or to exercise control or dominion or compulsion upon the souls of the children of men, in any degree of unrighteousness, behold, the heavens withdraw themselves; the Spirit of the Lord is grieved; and when it is withdrawn, Amen to the priesthood, or the authority of that man.*

Behold, ere he is aware, he is left unto himself, to kick against the pricks, to persecute the saints, and to fight against God.

We have learned by sad experience that it *is the nature and disposition of almost all men, as soon as they get a little authority, as they suppose, they will immediately begin to exercise unrighteous dominion.*

Hence many are called, but few are chosen.[162]

In His infinite wisdom, God has seen fit to include, in His checks and balances, provision for the trial by the Church of even the President of the Church is he transgresses. Though this procedure has not been used within the Church, yet the fact that the Master included the provision in His plan for Church government indicates that the possibility that the Prophet may transgress is a real one:

And inasmuch as a President of the High Priesthood shall transgress, he shall be had in remembrance before the common council of the church, who shall be assisted by twelve counselors of the High Priesthood;

And their decision upon his head shall be an end of controversy concerning him.

Thus, none shall be exempted from the justice and the laws of God, that all things may be done in order and in solemnity before him, according to truth and righteousness.[163]

He also provides a way for the Church to judge the Quorum of the Twelve and the First Council of Seventy in the event they make unrighteous decisions:

The decisions of these quorums, or either of them, are to be made in all righteousness, in holiness, and lowliness of heart, meekness and long suffering, and in faith, and virtue, and knowledge, temperance, patience, godliness, brotherly kindness and charity;

Because the promise is, if these things abound in them they shall not be unfruitful in the knowledge of the Lord.

And in case that any decision of these quorums is made in unrighteousness, it may be brought before a general assembly of the several quorums,

---

162. D&C 121:34-40.
163. D&C 107:82-84.

which constitute the spiritual authorities of the church; otherwise there can be no appeal from their decision.[164]

In recent years, several discourses have been given on the theme that the Lord will not allow prophets to lead His people astray. Where did that concept originate, and is it scriptural?

It appears that this belief originated, not in the scriptures, but in an incident pertaining to Heber C. Kimball in 1842, as the doctrine of plural marriage was revealed to him by Joseph Smith. Heber C. Kimball was one of the original twelve apostles chosen in this dispensation in 1835. The prophet Joseph saw fit to test Heber in a manner similar to the way that Abraham of old was tested when he was commanded to offer up his son, Isaac, to the Lord.[165]

The test which was required of Heber stretched the apostle to the limits of his faith and endurance. "Three days he fasted and wept and prayed."[166] Then, after that trial was over, Heber was instructed by the Prophet Joseph to take another wife, which again brought crisis into Heber's life. As his daughter later recorded,

> In Nauvoo, shortly after his return from England, my father, among others of his brethren, was taught the plural wife doctrine, and *was told by Joseph, the Prophet, three times, to go and take a certain woman as his wife; but not till he commanded him in the name of the Lord did he obey. At the same time Joseph told him not to divulge this secret, not even to my mother, for fear that she would not receive it;* for his life was in constant jeopardy, not only from outside influences and enemies, who were seeking some plea to take him back to Missouri, but from false brethren who had crept like snakes into his bosom and then betrayed him.
>
> My father realized the situation fully, and *the love and reverence he bore for the Prophet were so great that he would sooner have laid down his life than have betrayed him. This was one of the greatest tests of his faith he had ever experienced.* The thought of deceiving the kind and faithful wife of his youth, whom he loved with all his heart, and who with him had borne so patiently their separations, and all the trials and sacrifices they had been called to endure, was more than he felt able to bear.
>
> He realized not only the addition of trouble and perplexity that such a step must bring upon him, but his sorrow and misery were increased by the thought of my mother hearing of it from some other source, which would no doubt separate them, and *he shrank from the thought of such a thing, or of causing her any unhappiness.*[167]

Heber's deep concern over the matter caused him to again consult with the Prophet Joseph, and that interview resulted in a revelation saying that,

164. D&C 107:30-32.
165. See Gen. 22:1-19.
166. Whitney, Orson F., *Life of Heber C. Kimball* (Salt Lake City, Utah: Bookcraft, Inc., 1957), p. 324.
167. *Ibid.*, p. 325. The account is related by his daughter, Helen.

if Heber was ever in danger of apostatizing, the Lord would end his mortal probation:

> Finally he was so tried that he went to Joseph and told him how he felt—that he was fearful if he took such a step he could not stand, but would be overcome. The Prophet, full of sympathy for him, went and inquired of the Lord. His answer was, *"Tell him to go and do as he has been commanded, and if I see that there is any danger of his apostatizing, I will take him to myself."* [168]

Others, who were intimate acquaintances of Heber C. Kimball, grasped the principle involved in this revelation to Heber and eventually made reference to it in their discourses, applying what the Lord said to Heber in a broader context. Their emphasis was on the aspect that the Lord would remove leaders if those leaders functioned unrighteously. President Brigham Young taught, for instance,

> The Lord will not permit me or any other man to lead His people astray. *If the leaders do wrong, the Lord will take them away.* If an apostle does not magnify his calling, *the Lord will remove him* and not permit him to lead away the people. [169]

Though the teaching was infrequently mentioned, it was Wilford Woodruff who preserved the concept. He referred to it in a discourse he delivered October 6, 1890, following the Church's acceptance of the Manifesto:

> I say to Israel, *the Lord will never permit me nor any other man who stands as the President of this Church, to lead you astray.* It is not in the programme. It is not in the mind of God. *If I were to attempt that, the Lord would remove me out of my place, and so He will any other man who attempts to lead the children of men astray from the oracles of God and from their duty.* [170]

Those who comment on this principle today generally quote the above statement by Wilford Woodruff as their source. But the change in emphasis—from "the Lord removing leaders who do wrong" to "leaders not leading the saints astray"—should be noted. Those who have quoted it in recent times have neglected to point out that shift in emphasis and have not made note of the individual, rather than general, application of what appears to be the original source. It was not a revelation foretelling the future course of the Church, but rather a specific promise made to one

---

168. *Ibid.,* pp. 325-26. Heber C. Kimball obeyed Joseph's commandment, married Sarah Noon, and found relief from his dilemma when the Lord revealed the matter and the doctrine which occasioned the situation to his wife, Vilate. See *Life of Heber C. Kimball,* pp. 326-328, for the touching account of the incident.

169. Discourse given July 21, 1861, as recorded by Wilford Woodruff in his personal journal. See Cowley, Mathias F., *Wilford Woodruff: History of His life and Labors* (Salt Lake City, Utah: Bookcraft, Inc., 1964), p. 418.

170. *Ibid.,* p. 572.

particular individual, Heber C. Kimball, in his time of personal trial. That is not a proper basis for the promulgation of new doctrine, and the teaching should be handled with caution today.

Have leaders who have done wrong altered the course of the Church in these latter days? Unfortunately the answer to that question has to be yes. For instance, their influence has caused the bypassing of two apostles in the line of succession for the presidency of the Church. The position of seniority held in the Council of the Twelve by Orson Hyde and Orson Pratt was altered later in their lives because those two brethren were led astray and hence were excommunicated for short periods in the early days of the Church. Though those two men stood senior to John Taylor in the Council of the Twelve for many years,[171] the rearranging of their seniority to the position they held at the time of their reentry into the Church following their excommunications caused John Taylor to be the President of the Quorum of the Twelve and, consequently, the third President of the Church, following the demise of President Brigham Young.[172]

And why were Orson Hyde and Orson Pratt excommunicated? Both men were led into improper actions by leaders who presided over them in the Church—leaders who fell into apostasy. Orson Hyde was led astray by Thomas B. Marsh, President of the council of apostles. Thomas Marsh swore out an affidavit which harmed the reputation of the Church in Richmond, Missouri, on October 24, 1838. At that time, Orson Hyde also swore to an affidavit saying that "The most of the statements in the foregoing disclosure I know to be true; the remainder I believe to be true."[173] This statement led to Orson's excommunication, and he remained outside the Church for several weeks until the priesthood was restored to him again on June 27, 1839.[174]

171. Orson Hyde was ordained an apostle Feb. 15, 1835; Orson Pratt was ordained an apostle April 26, 1835; John Taylor was ordained an apostle Dec. 19, 1838. Orson Hyde presided as President of the Quorum of the Twelve for 28 years, from April 6, 1848, until June, 1875, when this change took place.

172. For historical details on the matter, see Brigham H. Roberts, *A Comprehensive History of The Church of Jesus Christ of Latter-day Saints* (Salt Lake City, Utah: Deseret News Press, 1930), Vol. 5, pp. 518-524.

173. HC 3:167-68. These affidavits concerned the existance of an organization called the "Danites," which enemies of the Church asserted was retaliating to the attacks made by the Missourians. The affidavits were of great consequence to the Church because they were the immediate impetus which caused Governor Boggs to issue his infamous "extermination order," which caused thousands of Mormons to be driven from their homes.

Both men were excommunicated on January 16, 1839. Orson, because of a vision he received, repented and returned to the Church, being restored to the priesthood on June 30, 1839, and to the apostleship at the October conference of that year. Marsh returned to the Church in 1857. See Barron, Howard H., *Orson Hyde* (Bountiful, Utah: Horizon Publishers & Distributors, 1977), pp. 102-107.

174. HC 3:379.

Orson Pratt was led astray by statements of John C. Bennett,[175] a former Assistant President of the Church,[176] mayor of the city of Nauvoo,[177] and high officer in the Nauvoo Legion.[178] These false statements by Bennett portrayed Joseph Smith in an unfavorable light in regards to Orson's wife. Orson took hasty and unwise action, before ascertaining the facts of the matter and becoming aware of Bennett's duplicity. Because of his hasty action, he was cut off from the Quorum of the Twelve, and found himself outside the Church for a brief interim before Joseph Smith himself re-baptized him and ordained him to his former office in the Quorum of the Twelve.[179]

Other examples can be cited, but these should suffice to show that the course of the Church has, at least in these two situations, been significantly altered by leaders who led others astray. Certainly we should trust our leaders and have confidence in them, but that allegiance should never be so all-encompassing that we cease to make personal judgments in situations that affect our eternal standing before the Lord.

In his *Essentials of Church History,* which he published in 1950, Elder Joseph Fielding Smith gives a brief biographical outline which includes information pertaining to the excommunication of general authorities. Of the ninety-five men who have been apostles or members of the First Presidency to 1950, including assistant presidents, twenty-one have apostatized or been excommunicated or disfellowshipped from the Church or resigned from their position as a general authority in disharmony with their quorum.

---

175. See CHC 2:47-50 concerning his character and motivations. See also the "Affidavit of Hyrum Smith," HC 5:71, concerning the conduct of John C. Bennett while the latter was associated with the First Presidency. Earlier in this subtopic numerous conditional revelations from the Doctrine and Covenants were cited concerning Joseph Smith. Joseph rendered obedience to the Lord's commandments and gained the promised blessings. Similar conditional blessings were promised to John C. Bennett, who failed to remain obedient and fell into apostasy. His case is one that shows the truly conditional nature of these revelations. D&C 124:16-17 says concerning John C. Bennett:

> Again, let my servant John C. Bennett help you in your labor in sending my word to the kings and people of the earth, and stand by you, even you my servant Joseph Smith, in the hour of affliction; and his reward shall not fail *if he receive counsel.*
> And for his love he shall be great, for he shall be mine *if he do this,* saith the Lord. I have seen the work which he hath done, which I accept *if he continue,* and will crown him with blessings and great glory.

176. Called April 8, 1841. HC 4:341; CHC 2:69.
177. Elected Feb. 1, 1841. HC 4:287-292.
178. HC 4:295-296. He was second in command to Joseph Smith.
179. HC 5:256.

Fifteen[180] did so between 1830 and 1860, two[181] between 1861 and 1890, three[182] between 1891 and 1920, and one[183] from 1921 to the present. Several of these men who left the Church later returned and were rebaptized; two of them were reinstated in the Quorum of the Twelve.

Another teaching sometimes voiced in recent years is that if a prophet or Church leader tells the saints to do something, the saints should do it even if the action is wrong—they'll still be blessed for their obedience. Again, this is an unscriptural teaching that embraces dangerous principles.

Personal responsibility for one's sins is a fundamental doctrine of the Church: *"We believe that men will be punished for their own sins. . . ."* [184] Just as the saints are responsible for obtaining their own exaltation, and no one can gain that great reward for them, they also hold the ultimate responsibility for determining what is sin and what is detrimental to their eternal progress. Though the Church is charged with the responsibility of teaching correct principles and providing just and righteous leadership, yet the ultimate responsibility for discernment, obedience to correct principles, and rejection of false precepts and incorrect counsel remains with each individual member.

The concept that the saints are to follow Church leaders in wrong actions is repugnant and is not the position of the Church. This is clearly seen, for instance, in the problems encountered by Orson Hyde and Orson Pratt, mentioned previously. Action was quickly taken by the Church, for instance, against Thomas B. Marsh's "Danite" affidavit which asserted that some saints "have taken an oath to support the heads of the Church in all things that they say or do, *whether right or wrong.*"[185] That allegation was categorically rejected as being false, and was regarded as such a serious offense that it brought the excommunication of both Thomas B. Marsh and Orson Hyde.

The concept that the saints should follow Church leaders in *wrong* actions again was energetically rejected when John C. Bennett tried to introduce it to satisfy his own passions with illicit relationships, as was shown in the affidavit of Hyrum Smith:

> . . .Several females . . . testified that John C. Bennett endeavored to seduce them, and accomplished his designs by *saying it was right; that it was*

---

180. These were Sidney Rigdon, Frederick G. Williams, William Law, Oliver Cowdery, John C. Bennett, Thomas B. Marsh, Orson Hyde, William E. McLellin, Luke S. Johnson, William Smith, John F. Boynton, Lyman E. Johnson, John E. Page, Orson Pratt, and Lyman Wight.
181. These were Amasa M. Lyman and Albert Carrington.
182. These were Moses Thatcher, John W. Taylor, and Mathias F. Cowley.
183. Richard R. Lyman.
184. Article of Faith 2.
185. See again HC 3:167.

one of the mysteries of God, which was to be revealed when the people was strong enough in faith to bear such mysteries—that it was perfectly right to have illicit intercourse with females, providing no one knew it but themselves, . . . bringing witnesses of his own clan to *testify that there were such revelations and such commandments, and that they were of God;* also stating that *he would be responsible for their sins,* if there were any, and that he would give them medicine to produce abortions, providing they should become pregnant.[186]

John C. Bennett was removed from his positions of authority and excommunicated from the Church for promulgating this false teaching.

The scriptures also teach the principle that man is ultimately responsible for his own conduct. If he follows the false or improper instructions of even one who is an authorized prophet of God, he is not blessed for obeying that prophet, but instead is punished by God for disobeying the instructions he has previously been given from on high. Such was the case, for instance, with the man of God who prophesied to Jeroboam of the future birth of Josiah and foretold the destruction of the altar Jeroboam was using for his wicked purposes. The man was sent by God with the specific instruction that "Thou shalt eat no bread nor drink water there, nor turn again to go by the way that thou camest."[187] The man of God delivered his prophecy to Jeroboam and obediently refused that king's offer of food. He also started homeward by a different route, as the Lord commanded. But there "dwelt an old prophet in Bethel"[188] who was lonesome for company. The old prophet went out and found the man of God. To entice the man of God to come visit with him, the old prophet told the man of God a lie:

I am a prophet also as thou art; and an angel spoke unto me by the word of the Lord, saying, Bring him back with thee into thine house, that he may eat bread and drink water. *But he lied unto him.*[189]

The man of God who had prophesied to Jeroboam recognized the old man to be a prophet, so he did not test and verify through the Spirit the old prophet's message, even though it conflicted with what God had previously instructed him to do. He went with the old prophet and sat down to break bread with him. Then, *through the old prophet,* came this stinging rebuke to the man of God:

And it came to pass, as they sat at the table, that the word of the Lord came unto the prophet that brought him back:

And he cried unto the man of God that came from Judah, saying, *Thus saith the Lord, Forasmuch as thou hast disobeyed the mouth of the Lord, and hast not kept the commandment which the Lord thy God commanded thee,*

186. HC 5:71.
187. I Ki. 13:17.
188. I Ki. 13:11.
189. I Ki. 13:18.

But comest back, and hast eaten bread and drunk water in the place, of which the Lord did say to thee, Eat no bread, and drink no water; *thy carcase shall not come unto the sepulchre of thy fathers.*[190]

As he journeyed homeward, the man of God was slain by a lion, in fulfillment of the prophetic warning revealed through the old prophet who led him astray. His body never was taken to his home for burial, but was entombed in Bethel, in literal fulfillment of the prophecy.[191]

Diligent service and obedience does not of itself bring God's reward. It must be obedience to correct causes, true teachings, and authorized leaders for that obedience to bring God's approbation. Obeying false prophets, or false counsel, does not bring blessings, it brings the cursings and disapproval of God. This will be clearly shown in another chapter.[192]

One further passage should suffice in this context—the words of the prophet Isaiah:

Therefore the Lord will cut off from Israel head and tail, branch and rush, in one day.

The ancient and honourable, he is the head; and *the prophet that teacheth lies,* he is the tail.

For the leaders of this people cause them to err; and they that are led of them are destroyed.[193]

In this passage, the people had obeyed false prophets, and that obedience had made the people err. Were they blessed for their obedience to false revelation? No, they were cursed—and eventually were destroyed for obeying false prophets and corrupt religious leaders.

Thus, the Church must always be aware that the Lord has placed a "worthiness requirement" upon those who are the recipients of His revealed word, be the recipients His prophets or the saints. There is no reward promised for diligent obedience to false prophets or incorrect doctrines. Indeed, the Savior's warning in the Sermon on the Mount speaks directly to this issue:

Beware of false prophets, which come to you in sheep's clothing, but inwardly they are ravening wolves.

Ye shall know them by their fruits. Do men gather grapes of thorns, or figs of thistles?

Even so every good tree bringeth forth good fruit; but a corrupt tree bringeth forth evil fruit.

A good tree cannot bring forth evil fruit, neither can a corrupt tree bring forth good fruit.

---

190. I Ki. 13:20-22.
191. I Ki. 13:23-32.
192. See chapter 9.
193. Is. 9:14-16. See also Mi. 3:5-7, a passage with similar condemnation of the people for obeying false prophets.

Every tree that bringeth not forth good fruit is hewn down, and cast into the fire.
Wherefore by their fruits ye shall know them.
Not everyone that saith unto me, Lord, Lord, shall enter into the kingdom of heaven; but he that doeth the *will of my Father* which is in heaven.
Many will say to me in that day, Lord, Lord, *have we not prophesied in thy name?* and in thy name have case out devils? and in thy name done many wonderful works?
And then will I profess unto them, *I never knew you: depart from me, ye that work iniquity.*[194]

Revelation Must Appoint Nothing Contrary to the Church Covenants—A "Content" Requirement

Now to return to the basic passages which form the outline for this chapter. The Lord has revealed that *"neither shall anything be appointed unto any of this church contrary to the church covenants."*[195] Thus, a test has been established for verifying revelations received by the President or anyone else in the Church. The test is narrow in scope, for it refers only to Church covenants, not to the broad range of Church doctrines.

What are the Church covenants which will not be contradicted by new revelations from God? The Doctrine and Covenants lists a number of covenants including

1. the new and everlasting covenant, the fulness of the gospel based on the ordinances in which the Lord promises that He will give power to obtain eternal life to those who believe on His name;[196]

2. the Lord's covenant to give the saints a land of promise which will be their eternal inheritance;[197]

3. the Lord's covenant to recover His people, the house of Israel;[198]

4. the consecration of properties with a covenant to support the poor;[199]

5. the oath and covenant of the priesthood;[200]

6. the Lord's promise to answer prayers;[201]

7. the eternal marriage covenant;[202]

8. and the pledge of the saints to keep the commandments, statutes, and ordinances of the Lord.[203] Other covenants, such as baptism, the sacrament, and the temple endowment could be added to this list.

194. Mt. 7:15-23.
195. D&C 28:12.
196. D&C 45:8-9; 66:2; 101:39; 133:57; 22:1-4; 1:15, 22; Is. 24:5.
197. D&C 38:17-20.
198. D&C 39:11.
199. D&C 42:30; 78:3-12; 82:11-12, 15-21; 90:23-24; 104:1-5.
200. D&C 84:33-41, 48.
201. D&C 98:1-3.
202. D&C 131:2; 132:4, 6, 19, 26-27, 41, 51.
203. D&C 136:2, 4.

To verify revelation by the standard of Church covenants is far different than comparing it to Church doctrine today, for the latter term is often expanded to include the interpretive sermons and expressions of opinion of various Church leaders which are actually not part of doctrine. The Lord doesn't assert that His revelations will always square with the opinions of His servants, but rather with the covenants He has revealed and into which He has entered.

This test is not infallible and should not stand by itself, for the activities of the saints in regards to several of these covenant areas have been changed. Examples of such changes are the delay in the return to establish the New Jerusalem, the discontinuance of the United Order, and the abolition of plural marriage.

All Things Must Be Done in Order—A "Procedure" Requirement

While revealing His will concerning the inspired messages He would grant through His Revelator, the Lord commanded that *"all things must be done in order,* and by common consent in the church, by the prayer of faith."[204]

Indeed, an insistence on orderly procedure characterizes the revelations of God concerning His Church.

The Lord's revelations give evidence of the order He desires. First of all, order means truthful, righteous, and ethical procedure. No one, at any level of responsibility in the Church, is exempt from God's requirement that his actions and words be performed and spoken in righteousness. Concerning even the President of the High Priesthood himself, the Lord spoke specifically, saying that *"none shall be exempted from the justice and the laws of God, that all things may be done in order and in solemnity before him, according to truth and righteousness."*[205] "The Lord God worketh not in darkness."[206] His servants must not do so either. If an action or policy would be improper or unethical in a secular setting, it should have no place within the Church. There should be no room for discrimination, favoritism, suspect business practices, or improper use of the power and influence of the Church to advance personal status or to perpetuate personal prejudices. An impropriety is an impropriety in any situation—there may be no double standard.

Even in combatting evil and falsehood, those who administer the Lord's work on earth are bound by the Lord to function only by orderly, righteous procedure. For instance, though enemies may circulate falsehoods

---

204. D&C 28:13.
205. D&C 107:84.
206. 2 Ne. 26:23.

to thwart the Lord's work, the saints are not allowed to retaliate in kind by spreading falsehoods or rumors in return. Indeed, the Lord has warned that "wo be unto him that lieth to deceive because he supposeth that another lieth to deceive, *for such are not exempt from the justice of God.*"[207]

Secondly, the principle of order requires the keeping of careful and valid records, and that such records be open to the examination of those who would do so for a legitimate purpose. A record of current revelations should certainly be kept and should somehow be available to the Church, for the saints have been commanded that "ye shall bear record of me, even Jesus Christ. . . ;"[208] How can this be done unless the record is made available of the Lord's messages to the Church and of His dealings with the saints? If revelations are being constantly received by the Church today, they are not being released to the Church membership. Certainly the *Ensign,* the *New Era,* the *Conference Reports,* or the *Church News* do not report them with any degree of frequency. They tell of policy changes but not revelations. These is a widespread hunger among the saints for knowledge in this area.

On one occasion the Lord spoke concerning His future revelations to the Church, and stressed the importance of their availability so they can be "held in remembrance from generation to generation:"

> For *I am about to restore many things to the earth,* pertaining to the priesthood, saith the Lord of Hosts.
> And again, *let all the records be had in order, that they may be put in the archives of my holy temple, to be held in remembrance from generation to generation, saith the Lord of Hosts.*[209]

A letter from the Prophet Joseph Smith shows the importance of a careful record being kept of "actual revelation," and that such a record has been necessary in all dispensations:

> In all ages of the world, whenever the Lord has given a dispensation of the priesthood to any man *by actual revelation,* or any set of men, this power has always been given. Hence, *whatsoever those men did in authority, in the name of the Lord, and did it truly and faithfully, and kept a proper and faithful record of the same, it became a law on earth and in heaven.*[210]

Another type of order required by the Lord is that revelations be presented to the Church and accepted by the principle of common consent, as is discussed in the next section.

---

207. D&C 10:28.
208. D&C 68:6. See D&C 1:39; 76:113; 85:1; 124:96; 128:2-4; Moses 6:5, etc.
209. D&C 127:8-9.
210. D&C 128:9.

All Things Must Be Done by Common Consent— An "Acceptance" Requirement

While revealing His will concerning the nature of revelation, the Savior proclaimed that "all things must be done in order, and *by common consent* in the church."[211] Another revelation requires that *"all things shall be done by common consent in the church,* by much prayer and faith, for all things you shall receive by faith."[212]

It should be understood that acceptance of a leader or a policy becomes *binding* upon the general *Church membership* only through the principle of common consent. A doctrine does not become binding upon the general Church membership until it is *canonized* through acceptance by the assembled Church membership or its authorized representatives in compliance with the revealed "common consent" limitation. Just as a contract is not binding until one signs it, a revelation is not binding upon the Church until it is accepted as the Lord's word in the Church by the sustaining vote of the membership. A revelation may be true, but the saints do not have the obligation to live by its precepts until after it has been voted upon and accepted. They should not be subject to Church judicial proceedings concerning the revelation, for instance, unless it has been accepted by common consent.

The Church as a whole, or its representatives[213] *from the various congregations assembled together, is continually represented in the scriptures and in the History of the Church as the highest decision-making body of The Church of Jesus Christ of Latter-day Saints.* It is the sustaining vote of that body which ultimately directs the course of the Church. The first scriptural example showing the decision-making power of the assembled body of the Church is in the New Testament, and pertains to a doctrinal dispute concerning the Jewish law of circumcision. The matter was discussed and debated before the "multitude,"[214] with both the apostles and those who were not general authorities[215] voicing their views. The decision made had the approbation of "the apostles and elders, with the *whole church.*"[216] This account, in the fifteenth chapter of Acts, is of great

---

211. D&C 28:13.
212. D&C 26:2.
213. D&C 20:61-62, 81-83. The conferences of the Church are times when doctrinal and policy agreement are to be reached by the saints. See D&C 41:2-3; 72:7; 73:1-2, 5.
214. Acts 15:12.
215. For instance, the James who spoke and won his point (Acts 15:13-21) was not a general authority. He was not the apostle James, for that apostle had previously been slain (see Acts 12:1-2).
216. Acts 15:22.

scriptural and historical importance, for it establishes the assembled body of the Church as the place where doctrine is ultimately decided.

This pattern was followed in the early days of the restored church also, when doctrinal decisions were also made in general conference and conferences were frequently the occasion for new revelations to be given and presented to the Church. For instance, the Doctrine and Covenants was not *binding* upon the Church as doctrine until it became "a law and a rule of faith and practice to the Church"[217] by its acceptance at a general assembly of the Church held August 17, 1835.[218]

—The Pearl of Great Price, though first published in 1857, was not accepted as a standard work and as a *binding* statement of doctrine until it was presented to and accepted by the Church in general conference assembled on October 10, 1880.[219]

—The Word of Wisdom, given at first "not by commandment or constraint, but by revelation,"[220] was accepted as being a *binding* commandment and requiring the compliance of the saints when accepted by the saints at a meeting on September 9, 1851.[221]

—The Official Declaration, or "Manifesto," was issued September 24, 1890, but did not become *binding* on the Church until October 6, 1890, when the body of the Church, in general conference, voted unanimously to accept President Wilford Woodruff's "declaration concerning plural marriages as authoritative and binding."[222]

The meeting held following the martyrdom of Joseph Smith, on August 8, 1844, in which the Church voted to follow the Twelve rather than Sidney Rigdon, gives ample evidence that the decision-making power ultimately rests with the saints. Brigham Young presented the matter in these words:

---

217. HC 2:243. The acceptance as scripture of certain revelations given to the prophet Joseph Smith and certain of his writings has a definite implication which should not be overlooked. The act of canonizing some teachings at the same time relegates other teachings to a place of lesser prominence and acceptance. The other writings of the prophet Joseph, as well as the writings of later prophets, hold lesser weight than the standard works. They are not to be regarded as being on a par with scripture or they would have been canonized as such.

218. See HC 2:244-246.

219. See Hunter, Milton R., *Pearl of Great Price Commentary* (Salt Lake City, Utah: Stevens & Wallis, Inc., 1951), pp. 246-247. See also Clark, James R., *The Story of the Pearl of Great Price* (Salt Lake City, Utah: Bookcraft, Inc., 1955), pp. 204-212.

220. D&C 89:2.

221. Smith, Joseph Fielding, *Answers to Gospel Questions,* (Salt Lake City, Utah: Deseret Book Co., 1957), Vol. 1, p. 197.

222. *The Doctrine and Covenants of the Church of Jesus Christ of Latter-day Saints,* (Salt Lake City, Utah: by the Church), pp. 256-257.

> Here are the Apostles, the Bible, the Book of Mormon, the Doctrine and Covenants—they are written on the tablet of my heart. If the church want the Twelve to stand as the head, the First Presidency of the Church, and at the head of this kingdom in all the world, stand next to Joseph, walk up into their calling, and hold the keys of this kingdom, every man, every woman, every quorum is now put in order, and *you are now the sole controllers of it.*
>
> All that are in favor of this, in all the *congregation of the saints,* manifest it by holding up the right hand. *(There was a universal vote).* If there are any of the contrary mind, every man and every woman who does not want the Twelve to preside, lift up your hands in like manner. *(No hands up).* This supersedes the other question, and trying it by quorums.[223]

In the same meeting, President Young sought from the body of the Church, and received authority delegated from the saints, for the Twelve to make certain decisions and to exercise control in the financial matters of the Church, as follows:

> *Is it the will of this congregation* that they will be tithed until the Temple is finished, as they have hitherto been? If so, signify it by the uplifted hand. *(The vote was unanimous).*
>
> The men will act that have never acted before, and they will have the power and authority to do it. *Is it the mind of this congregation to loose the hands of the Twelve,* and enable us to go and preach to all the world? *We want to know the feelings of the people. Is it your will* to support the Twelve in all the world in their missions? *(The congregation sustained this question by a unanimous vote). Will you leave it to the Twelve to dictate about the finances of the church?* and *will it be the mind of this people* that the Twelve teach what will be the duties of the bishops in handling the affairs of the church? I want this, because twelve men can do it just as well as calling this immense congregation together at any other time. *(A unanimous vote).*
>
> We shall have a patriarch, and the right is in the family of Joseph Smith, his brothers, his sons, or some one of his relations. Here is Uncle John, he has been ordained a patriarch. Brother Samuel would have taken the office if he had been alive; it would have been his right; the right is in Uncle John, or one of his brothers (read sec. iii, par. 17, Doctrine and Covenants). I know that it would have belonged to Samuel. But as it is, if you leave it to the Twelve, they will wait until they know who is the man. *Will you leave it to the Twelve, and they dictate the matter. (A unanimous vote).* I know it will be let alone for the present.
>
> I feel to bring up Brother Rigdon; we are of one mind with him and he with us. *Will this congregation uphold him in the place he occupies* by the prayer of faith and let him be one with us and we with him. *(Unanimous).* The Twelve will dictate and see to other matters. There will be a committee for the Temple; and now let men stand to their posts and be faithful.[224]

The responsibility of the body of the Church in sustaining Church officials is an important portion of the Lord's set of checks and balances.

223. HC 7:240. See Brigham Young's statement that it was the voice of the people that made Joseph Smith the President of the Church (JD 1:133), cited on p. 35.
224. HC 7:241-242.

In the early days of the restored Church the saints were quick to perceive the importance of the procedure, and used it with concern and diligence. There is danger in the recent philosophy that calls for automatic acceptance of recommendations made as an act of obedience to Church leadership. The saints do not serve Church authorities—they serve the Lord, and they retain the responsibility for choosing correctly their personal and collective courses of action. The automatic acceptance teaching some individuals have promulgated in recent years is directly counter to the purposes of the common consent principle—it removes the power of checks and balances from the saints.

As the Lord clearly revealed in the Doctrine and Covenants, the process of sustaining the authorities in conferences is the opportunity for the saints to either "*approve* of those names which I have mentioned, or else *disapprove* of them *at my general conference.*"[225] In many of the early conferences, the process of sustaining officials was conducted in this light. In the April 1841 general conference, Joseph Smith announced to the saints that "the presidents of the different quorums would be presented before them *for their acceptance or rejection.*"[226]

In the general conference held April 6, 1843, Joseph Smith stated that the first object of the meeting was "to *ascertain the standing* of the First Presidency, which he should do by presenting himself before the conference."[227] "President Joseph then asked the conference if they were satisfied with the First Presidency, so far as he was concerned as an individual to preside over the whole Church, *or would they have another?*"[228]

---

225. D&C 124:144. Note that the officials of whom the saints were to approve or disapprove included the President of the Church, the First Presidency, the Quorum of the Twelve, the presidents of the First Quorum of the Seventy, and the Church Patriarch, as well as local officials. See verses 91-97, 123-144.

226. HC 4:340. April 8, 1841. In this process:

> The presidents and counselors belonging to the several quorums were then presented to each quorum separately, *for approval or rejection,* when *the following persons were objected to,* viz., John A. Hicks, *President of the Elders' quorum,* Alanson Ripley, *Bishop;* Elder John E. Page, *one of the Twelve Apostles;* and Noah Packard, *High Priest.* Bishop Newel K. Whitney moved their cases be laid over, to be tried before the several quorums. (HC 4:341.)

Earlier in this conference, Elder John C. Bennett of the First Presidency, had addressed the saints and stated that "he wished to know how many of the saints who were present *felt disposed to continue to act in concert and follow the instructions of the First Presidency;* and called upon all those who did so, to arise on their feet—when immediately the saints, *almost without exception,* arose. (HC 4:340.)

227. HC 5:327.

228. HC 5:328. The position in the presidency of Sidney Rigdon was challenged, but answered to the satisfaction of the Church, and he was accepted unanimously as were Joseph Smith and William Law. At that time, "President Hyrum Smith,

As he conducted the sustaining of Church leaders at the April conference in 1845, Brigham Young "said he would now present the authorities of the Church *for the approval or disapproval of the conference.*"[229]

In the October 1845 conference, "President Brigham Young then rose and said: the first business that will come before this conference, will be to present the authorities of the church *to ascertain whether they are in good standing.*"[230]

To be sure, the process of sustaining officials and giving common consent to doctrinal proposals must not be allowed to deteriorate to the level of an election,[231] for that is not its purpose. Inspired appointments made by inspired officials will be approved and sustained by the saints if they are also being led by the Holy Spirit.

It is when error creeps in that the saints must use the principle of common consent with special care. In the early church the body of the saints refused to sustain leaders in whom they had lost confidence on several occasions. For instance, the "Minutes of a Conference Assembled in *Committee of the Whole Church* at Kirtland on Sunday, the 3rd of September, 1837," contain the following items:

> President Smith then presented Sidney Rigdon and Frederick G. Williams as his counselors, and to constitute with himself the three first Presidents of the Church. Voted unanimously in the affirmative, except for Frederick G. Williams, *which was not carried unanimously.*
>
> President Smith then introduced Oliver Cowdery, Joseph Smith, Sen., Hyrum Smith, and John Smith for assistant counselors. These last four, together with the first three, are to be considered the heads of the Church. Carried unanimously.
>
> The Twelve Apostles were then presented one by one, when Thomas B. Marsh, David W. Patten, Brigham Young, Heber C. Kimball, Orson Hyde, Parley P. Pratt, Orson Pratt, William Smith, and William E. M'Lellin were received unanimously in their Apostleship, *Luke S. Johnson, Lyman E. Johnson, and John F. Boynton were rejected and disfellowshiped though privileged with confessing and making satisfaction.*

Patriarch, *said he wished to be tried,* when it was voted unanimously that he retain his office of Patriarch." (HC 5:329.)

229. HC 7:391. April 7, 1845. See also HC 7:293, 296 concerning the October 1844 conference.

230. HC 7:458. October 6, 1845. In this conference the membership refused to sustain William Smith as one of the Twelve, and Lyman Wight was challenged. See HC 7:458-460.

231. However, many Church officials have been elected, as a review of minutes of general conferences in the early days of the Church will show. Lyman Wight, for instance, was *nominated* in conference to fill a vacancy to the apostleship and was "accepted" or elected. See HC 4:341. There is no indication of revelation being received in the matter.

The President then arose and said he would call upon the Church to know if they were satisfied with their High Council, and should proceed to name them individually.

John Johnson, Joseph Coe, Joseph C. Kingsbury, and Martin Harris were objected to, also John P. Greene, but his case went over until he should be present.

Noah Packard, Jared Carter, Samuel H. Smith, were sustained.

Oliver Granger, Henry G. Sherwood, William Marks, Mayhew Hillman, Harlow Redfield, Asahel Smith, Phinehas Richards, and David Dort, *were chosen to fill the places of those objected to,* (and Thomas Grover having moved west) John Smith, chosen one of the presidents of the Church, all having belonged to the High Council.

The President then called upon the congregation to know if the recently appointed presidents of the Seventies should stand in their calling.

Voted that John Gaylord, James Forster, Salmon Gee, Daniel S. Miles, Joseph Young, Josiah Butterfield, and Levi W. Hancock, should retain their offices as presidents of Seventies; *John Gould was objected to.*[232]

The minutes of this conference were sent to the saints at Far West, Missouri, that they might "know how to proceed to set in order and regulate the affairs of the Church in Zion whenever they become disorganized."[233]

Two months later, on November 7, 1837, Joseph Smith conducted a conference of the "general assembly of the Church of Latter-day Saints assembled at Far West," in which the first presidency was reorganized because of the refusal of the saints to sustain one of the counselors:

President Smith then made a few remarks accepting the appointment, requesting the prayers of the Church in his behalf. He also *nominated* President Sidney Rigdon to be one of his counselors, and *he was unanimously chosen.*

He then *nominated* Frederick G. Williams to be his second counselor, *but he was objected to by Elder Lyman Wight* in a few remarks referring to a certain letter written to this place by the said Frederick G. Williams.

Also *Elder Marsh objected* to President Williams.

Elder *James Emmet also objected* to President Williams.

---

232. HC 2:509-510. See also p. 512. D&C 107:22, while speaking of the Melchizedek and Aaronic priesthoods, states that the quorum of the Presidency of the Church is to be *"chosen by the body,* appointed and ordained to that office, and upheld by the confidence, faith and prayer of the church."

On or about the same day, Joseph Smith made the following announcement concerning an assistant to the First Presidency:

DEAR BRETHREN—Oliver Cowdery, has been in transgression, but as he is now chosen as one of the presidents or counselors, I trust that he will yet humble himself and magnify his calling, but if he should not, *the Church will soon be under the necessity of raising their hands against him; therefore pray for him.* (HC 2:511.)

233. HC 2:509.

Bishop Edward Partridge said *he seconded President Williams' nomination* and should vote for him; and as to said letter, he had heard it and saw nothing so criminal in it.

President David Whitmer also made a few remarks in President Williams' favor.

Elder Marsh made further remarks.

Elder *Thomas Grover also objected* to President Williams.

President Sidney Rigdon then nominated President Hyrum Smith to take President Williams' place.

The moderator called for a vote in favor of President Williams, but he was rejected.

He then called for a vote in favor of President Hyrum Smith, which was carried unanimously.[234]

Again, in a conference held on March 17, 1839, at Quincy, Illinois, the president of the twelve and a former member of the First Presidency, along with other brethren who had previously been regarded as leaders, were removed from the Church by the vote of the general membership because of their disaffection during the Missouri persecutions.

After the conference had *fully expressed their feelings upon the subject* it was *unanimously voted that the following persons be excommunicated* from the Church of Jesus Christ of Latter-day Saints, viz.: George M. Hinkle, Sampson Avard, John Corrill, Reed Peck, *William W. Phelps, Frederick G. Williams, Thomas B. Marsh,* Burr Riggs, and several others. After which the conference closed by prayer.[235]

An incident in the October, 1843, conference indicates that the decision of the "Committee of the Whole Church" takes priority over a decision made by the President of the Church. In this conference Joseph Smith sought the removal of Sidney Rigdon as a counselor in the First Presidency. "He stated his dissatisfaction with Elder Sidney Rigdon as a Counselor, not having received any material benefit from his labors or counsels since their escape from Missouri."[236] Sidney Rigdon's defense, however, was such that "the sympathies of the congregation were highly excited." Several authorities spoke in Rigdon's defense, then

On motion by President William Marks, and seconded by Patriarch Hyrum Smith, conference voted that Elder Sidney Rigdon be permitted to retain his station as Counselor in the First Presidency.

President Joseph Smith arose and said, "I have thrown him off my shoulders, and you have again put him on me. You may carry him, but I will not."[237]

---

234. HC 2:522-523.
235. HC 3:284.
236. HC 6:47. October 6, 1843.
237. HC 6:49.

These incidents are sufficient to show that the "Committee of the Whole Church" retains the power to determine what doctrine is binding upon the Church, to reject leadership which has lost the confidence of the membership, or to retain authorities which others attempt to depose. Thus, the pattern set in previous general conferences of the Church indicates that the "Committee of the Whole Church" (meaning the representatives of the various wards and stakes convened in general conference) stands as the highest decision-making body in the Church and retains the power to override decisions made by even the President of the Church.

The sustaining of Church leaders, through the principle of common consent, may be a mere formality in good times, but in times of stress and crisis it becomes the Lord's balancing power, which checks the possibility of leaders guiding the people improperly.

All Things Must Be Done by the Prayer of Faith— A "Dependence Upon God" Requirement

More than any other member of the Church, the Revelator must be "as the clay is in the potter's hand"[238]—pliable, and receptive to the will of God. He must be a channel of communication through which men can approach Diety. His prayer of faith, which God requires,[239] is the means for keeping the channel clear. He must be so in tune with the Holy Ghost that he will be prompted in the requests he directs to God, for "He that asketh in the Spirit asketh according to the will of God; wherefore it is done even as he asketh."[240] He must also diligently seek, through the prayer of faith, for further knowledge which will lead the saints toward their goals. His prayerful seeking is what the Lord requires in preparation for the outpouring of heavenly blessings:

> *If thou shalt ask,* thou shalt receive revelation upon revelation, knowledge upon knowledge, that thou mayest know the mysteries and peaceable things— that which bringeth joy, that which bringeth life eternal.[241]

Blessings Are Promised to Revelators

The basic passages, which state the detailed requirements God has imposed on the process of transmitting revelation to the Church, also contain rich promises for the servants of God who faithfully fulfill their responsibility as revelators of God's word. Concerning the first to function as Revelator in this dispensation, the Lord revealed, "Him have I inspired

---

238. Jer. 18:6.
239. D&C 28:13.
240. D&C 46:30.
241. D&C 42:61. See also D&C 8:10-11.

to move the cause of Zion in mighty power for good."[242] Certainly the privilege of receiving inspiration for the furtherance of God's work is a choice blessing. How exquisite it is for a man to know he is actually a tool through which God is bringing to pass His divine plan here on the earth!

The Lord revealed other blessings which are enjoyed by His revelator:

> *His diligence I know, and his prayers I have heard.*
> *Yea, his weeping for Zion I have seen, and I will cause that he shall mourn for her no longer; for his days of rejoicing are come unto the remission of his sins, and the manifestations of my blessings upon his works.*
> For behold, I will bless all those who labor in my vineyard with a mighty blessing, and they shall believe on his words, which are given him through me by the Comforter.[243]

Other Revelators have written of the blessings they have received in their callings. One of them was Nephi, son of Lehi:

> I know in whom I have trusted.
> *My God hath been my support;* he hath led me through mine afflictions in the wilderness; and *he hath preserved me* upon the waters of the great deep.
> *He hath filled me with his love,* even unto the consuming of my flesh.
> *He hath confounded mine enemies,* unto the causing of them to quake before me.
> Behold, *he hath heard my cry by day, and he hath given me knowledge by visions in the nighttime.*
> And by day have I waxed bold in mighty prayer before him; yea, my voice have I sent up on high; and *angels came down and ministered unto me.*
> And *upon the wings of his Spirit hath my body been carried away upon exceeding high mountains.* And mine eyes have beheld great things, yea, even too great for man; therefore I was bidden that I should not write them.[244]

Great power and blessings were given to another Revelator, also named Nephi, who lived at the time of Christ's birth:

> *Blessed art thou, Nephi,* for those things which thou hast done; for I have beheld how thou hast with unwearyingness declared the word, which I have given unto thee, unto this people. And thou hast not feared them, and hast not sought thine own life, but hast sought my will, and to keep my commandments.
> And now, because thou hast done this with such unwearyingness, behold, *I will bless thee forever; and I will make thee mighty in word and in deed, in faith and in works; yea, even that all things shall be done unto thee according to thy word, for thou shalt not ask that which is contrary to my will.*
> Behold, thou art Nephi, and I am God. Behold, I declare it unto thee in the presence of mine angels, that *ye shall have power* over this people, and *shall smite the earth* with famine, and with pestilence, and destruction, according to the wickedness of this people.

---

242. D&C 21:7.
243. D&C 21:7-9.
244. 2 Ne. 4:19-25.

> Behold, *I give unto you power, that whatsoever ye shall seal on earth shall be sealed in heaven; and whatsoever ye shall loose on earth shall be loosed in heaven; and thus shall ye have power among this people.*
>
> And thus, if ye shall say unto this temple it shall be rent in twain, it shall be done.
>
> And *if ye shall say unto this mountain, Be thou cast down and become smooth, it shall be done.*[245]

Surely, the blessings of serving the Lord as His spokesman are great!

Summary

1. Dissention on the question of "when is a prophet a prophet?" caused the apostasy of almost half of the Quorum of the Twelve and almost a third of the total Church membership in 1837-1838. The question still remains unanswered to many of the saints today. It must not be allowed to cause a similar problem in the future.

2. Because God knows the frailties of men who wield power, He has established systems of checks and balances which control those who lead. The Constitution of the United States, which Latter-day Saints hold to be inspired of God, is an example of these checks and balances.

3. Within the Church God has also established a set of checks and balances. He has revealed guidelines and safeguards which direct and also limit both the prophets and also the membership of the Church. Each have responsibilities to fulfill in order to insure that the proper channels of communication are open.

4. There has been a tendency on the part of some Latter-day Saints to overstate and to draw meanings and interpretations on this subject not supported by scripture and the history of God's dealings with His Church. It is important to recognize what the scriptures do *not* say, as well as what they *do* say.

5. This chapter considers the guidelines the Lord has revealed concerning His revelations to the prophets. The next chapter will deal with His guidelines concerning the membership of the Church.

6. When the President of the Church receives commandments of God for the Church, he is usually functioning in the role of "Revelator" rather than in the role of "Prophet" or "Seer."

7. Three passages in particular in the Doctrine and Covenants describe the manner in which the President of the Church is to receive commandments for the Church. These passages form the basis for most discourses which attempt to define the nature of revelation to the Church. These passages are D&C 21:4-9, D&C 28:2-13, and D&C 43:1-7. They out-

---

245. Hel. 10:4-9.

line responsibilities of both the Revelator and the Church membership. The statements they contain form the outline for much of this chapter and also the next chapter.

8. A number of responsibilities of a Revelator are listed in these passages. These responsibilities have been established by the Lord through revelation and serve to indicate to the Church how the Master intends to reveal His commandments concerning the Church. They serve as requirements, or limitations, upon the Revelator, as follows:

A. A "time" requirement—a Revelator is to give the Lord's commandments unto the Church when he receives them, clearly establishing that a new revelation has been given.

B. An "inspiration" requirement—a Revelator is to communicate to the Church the words of Christ given through the Comforter, but he is not to represent uninspired items as being the revealed word of God.

C. An "identification" requirement—the Lord requires His Revelator to identify revelations from God as being revelations; he is to clearly differentiate between those revelations and his personal observations and preachments.

D. A "worthiness" requirement—a Revelator is to abide in Christ so he may retain his gift and calling.

E. A "content" requirement—a Revelator must appoint nothing contrary to the Church covenants.

F. A "procedure" requirement—all things must be done in order.

G. An "acceptance" requirement—all things must be done by common consent.

H. A "dependence upon God" requirement—all things must be done by the prayer of faith.

9. If a Revelator fails to deliver the word of God to its intended recipients, he brings condemnation upon himself. Examples of judgments and threatened judgments upon Revelators who failed for a time to deliver revealed messages are cited from the scriptures and from historical items pertaining to the restored Church.

10. The words of a Revelator which are to become binding upon the Church as doctrine are only those which he has received from God through revelation or inspiration. Other opinions, statements, and writings of a Revelator are frequently of great value and interest, but are not to be regarded as doctrine—their acceptance is not obligatory upon the saints.

11. Revelators who receive and deliver the word of God are to identify revelations as being such so that the Church can know when a new message from God has been received. In scriptural times a prophet was not assumed to be speaking for the Lord unless he so identified his words. There is no scriptural or doctrinal justification for altering that approach today.

12. The scriptures indicate that many different phrases have been used to identify items as having been revealed by God. "Thus saith the Lord" and "saith the Lord" are the most frequently used phrases. Different identifying phrases have been used by various prophets, and no specific phrase appears to be *the* phrase required. But that God requires that His revelations be identified as such is the best-substantiated doctrine in all scripture. Hundreds of examples were cited in support of this conclusion.

13. The revelatory gift can be lost if an individual does not abide in Christ. The scriptures contain numerous warnings that prophets and revelators can and do fall into wickedness and cease to be the mortal instrument for the revealing of God's will.

14. The danger that a prophet might "fall" is most clearly demonstrated by citing the many warnings and conditional promises revealed to Joseph Smith in the Doctrine and Covenants. As part of His system of checks and balances, the Lord also revealed, in the Doctrine and Covenants, provisions for examining the conduct of general authorities, including the President of the Church, should they fall into sin and error.

15. The idea that a prophet will never lead the Church astray is not a scriptural teaching. It appears to have originated with a revelation given through Joseph Smith to Heber C. Kimball in 1842 as Heber wrestled with a serious challenge to his personal testimony. The Lord said that "if I see that there is any danger of his apostatizing, I will take him to myself." The concept evolved, in the few instances where it was quoted by intimate acquaintances of Elder Kimball. In that evolution the emphasis shifted from "the Lord removing those who do wrong" to "leaders not leading the saints astray." It was not a revelation fortelling the future course of the Church, but rather a specific promise made to one particular individual.

16. Examples of leaders who led others astray as they fell into apostasy, thereby significantly altering the future course of the Church, were cited. Orson Hyde and Orson Pratt both lost their positions of seniority in the Quorum of the Twelve, which caused John Taylor to be next in line to become the President of the Church, instead of them. The change was made because both were excommunicated in the early days of the Church, and lost their positions in the Quorum of the Twelve during the few days or weeks they held no Church membership. Both were excommunicated because of the influence and actions of higher Church leaders who were apostatizing, which affected their thoughts and actions.

17. The concept that the saints should obey Church leaders, even in wrong acts—that they'll be blessed for their obedience—is an unscriptural teaching that has been repudiated by the Church on several occasions. The message of the scriptures is that man is responsible for his own sins, and will incur divine punishment, even if he is following the directions of his leaders, when he sins.

18. New revelations are not to conflict with Church covenants. The Lord has stated that Church covenants, rather than doctrinal beliefs of leaders and members, are the standard for measuring the authenticity of new revelations. But such a test does not encompass all situations and should not be used as the only criterion for judgment.

19. The Lord requires that His servants perform their duties "in order and in solemnity before him, according to truth and righteousness." Righteous conduct, based on correct motives and procedures, is the standard of conduct which must prevail within the Church. Proper records should be kept and made available for the inspection of Church members. Procedures or actions which would be suspect or improper in a secular setting have no place within the Church.

20. A doctrine or policy does not become binding upon the Church until the matter is accepted by the membership by means of a sustaining vote through the principle of common consent.

21. Instances from Church history show that the "Committee of the Whole Church," assembled in general conference, is the highest decision-making body of the Church. While Church authorities may receive revelation and personal priesthood power from God, they receive the authorization to preside and govern within the Church from the sustaining vote of the membership. They remain subject to that vote throughout their term of office. Several instances in Church history demonstrate that the "Committee of the whole Church" holds and sometimes exercises the power to remove even apostles and members of the First Presidency from office.

22. The principle of common consent is an important element of the system of checks and balances established by the Lord. There is danger in the recent philosophy that asserts that recommendations made by Church leaders should be automatically accepted as an act of obedience to that Church leadership. The saints do not serve Church authorities—they serve the Lord. The Church exists for the saints, not the saints for the Church. The responsibility for correctly choosing their personal and collective courses of action remains with the Church membership, whatever the consequences may be.

23. More than any other member of the Church, the Revelator must be receptive and "in tune" with God. The expectation that he can and does seek and obtain revelation showing the will of God, on any matter that arises concerning the Church, is essential to the faith of the general membership.

3

What Does God Require of the Saints as He Reveals His Will?

As was shown in the preceding chapter, God has established an extensive series of checks and balances to safeguard the workings of His Church. That chapter reviewed the responsibilities God has placed on His Revelators. This chapter will focus on the duties and obligations of the general membership. Both areas are part of the system of checks and balances God has established.

That which is desired, of course, is a combination of a strong, inspired Church leadership which frequently receives, and always acts in accordance with, the revealed will of God, plus a valiant and dedicated Church membership which is anxious to serve the Lord and which renders obedience to the counsels of their leaders because they receive the revealed witness that their leaders' instructions and actions are directed by God.

The Saints Are to Give Heed to the Words and Commandments of God Given Through the Revelator—An "Obedience" Requirement

The basic passages which define the relationship between the Revelator and the saints are D&C 21:4-9, D&C 28:2-13, and D&C 43:1-7. In this chapter, as in the preceding chapter, statements found in them will provide the outline.

These basic passages reveal God's checks upon His Prophets, Seers, and Revelators. He has commanded that His spokesman is to

—give commandments unto the Church at the time he receives them,
—communicate to the Church the words revealed to him,
—represent his words as being from the mouth of God,
—abide in Christ, so he may retain his gift to receive revelations and commandments,
—appoint nothing contrary to the Church covenants,

95

—do all things in order,
—do all things by common consent in the Church, and
—do all things by the prayer of faith.

When he has fulfilled these requrements, then the responsibility for obedience shifts from his shoulders to the membership of the Church, to whom the Lord has commanded:

> Wherefore, meaning the church, *thou shalt give heed* unto all his words and commandments which he shall give unto you as he receiveth them, walking in all holiness before me;
> For his word ye shall receive as if from mine own mouth in all patience and faith. [1]

Obedience to the commandments and revelations of God is the vital element to joyful gospel living. It is the duty of the saints. It is also the premise upon which Church membership is based. Great blessings are promised to those who obey the Lord's revelations and commandments, of which the following is typical:

> *And all saints who remember to keep and do these sayings, walking in obedience to the commandments,* shall receive health in their navel and marrow to their bones;
> And shall find wisdom and great treasures of knowledge, even hidden treasures.
> And shall run and not be weary, and shall walk and not faint.
> And I, the Lord, give unto them a promise, that *the destroying angel shall pass by them, as the children of Israel, and not slay them. Amen.* [2]

Unwillingness or inability of the saints to render obedience to God's revealed word can retard the progress of the Lord's work. It can prevent the Church from receiving the blessings God desires to bestow upon it and can cause the membership to receive chastening and correction from the Lord. This was the intent of a revelation given in 1834, for instance, which concerned the redemption of Zion:

> Verily I say unto you who have assembled yourselves together that you may learn my will concerning the redemption of mine afflicted people—
> Behold, I say unto you, *were it not for the transgressions of my people, speaking concerning the church and not individuals, they might have been redeemed even now.*
> *But behold, they have not learned to be obedient to the things which I required at their hands,* but are full of all manner of evil, and do not impart of their substance, as becometh saints, to the poor and afflicted among them;
> And *are not united* according to the union required by the law of the celestial kingdom;

---

1. D&C 21:4-5.
2. D&C 89:18-21.

> *And Zion cannot be built up unless it is by the principles of the law of the celestial kingdom; otherwise I cannot receive her unto myself.*
> *And my people must needs be chastened until they learn obedience, if it must needs be, by the things which they suffer.* [3]

There must be no confusion, however, over that which God expects man to obey. It is to the words of God, revealed through the Revelator, that the saints are commanded to render obedience, rather than to the Revelator himself. A number of passages stress the importance of this understanding. While speaking of the relationship of the Church to the Revelator, the Lord instructed the saints:

> I will bless all those who labor in my vineyard with a mighty blessing, and *they shall believe on his words, which are given him through me by the Comforter,* which manifesteth that Jesus was crucified by sinful men for the sins of the world, yea, for the remission of sins unto the contrite heart. [4]

The relationship was redefined to Oliver Cowdery, who was instructed to obey the revelations given through Joseph Smith rather than Joseph, the man: "Thou shalt be obedient *unto the things which I shall give unto him.*"[5] Jesus has revealed, "I am the Lord thy God, and ye shall obey *my voice,*"[6] and "I, the Lord, utter my voice, and *it* shall be obeyed."[7]

The Lord limits the responsibility of the Church for acceptance of the Revelator's words as being the word of God to situations where the Revelator is actually setting forth that which he has received by revelation or inspiration. The responsibility of acceptance and adherence to the Revelator's other commentaries, writings and remarks, etc., is not placed upon the saints. The test cannot be "who said it?" but rather must be, *"Is it the revealed word of God?"* Just as Joseph Smith distinguished between when a man spoke in the prophetic role and when he acted without inspiration,[8] the saints are instructed by God to make the same distinction.

Our present general authorities have set forth this principle without hesitation, observing that with all the inspiration they receive, prophets are still mortal men with all the opinions, prejudices and imperfections common to mankind in general. They have acknowledged that the opinions and views of the prophets, unless they are inspired, can contain error, and that in many instances the Lord leaves them to work out their problems

---

3. D&C 105:1-6.
4. D&C 21:9.
5. D&C 28:3.
6. D&C 132:53.
7. D&C 63:5.
8. Recall, in this context, Joseph's statement "that a prophet was a prophet *only when he was acting as such."* (HC 5:265.)

without inspiration, just as He does with the rest of us.[9] This is not a criticism of their fulfillment of their prophetic role, but rather an acknowledgment that the Lord does not guide and command in all things, and that He expects His servants to use their own free agency as much as possible.

The Saints Are to Receive the Revealed Words of God in Patience and Faith—An "Attitude" Requirement

With the commandment that the saints are to receive His revealed word through the Revelator "in all patience and faith,"[10] the Lord reasserted the attitude which should characterize the Church membership. Jesus taught His followers to "be not faithless, but believing,"[11] and this attitude must be manifested among the saints of the latter days.

Those who preside in the Church must have the confidence and support of the membership. This is especially true of the President. As was shown in the preceding chapter, it is proper that the saints expect great faith from their Revelator. By the same token, he should expect great faith from them—faith that the Lord will speak through him, confidence that he is serving the Lord and the Church to the best of his ability, and prayerful support for his labors.

The saints are to pray for their Revelator. The Lord commanded the saints, for instance, "If ye desire the mysteries of the kingdom, appoint ye my servant Joseph Smith, Jun., and *uphold him before me by the prayer of faith.*"[12]

On another occasion the Lord commanded the saints to combine their faith and prayers in behalf of their leader in these words:

> *Ask and ye shall receive; pray earnestly that peradventure my servant Baurak Ale [Joseph Smith, Jun.] may go with you, and preside in the midst of my people,* and organize my kingdom upon the consecrated land, and establish the children of Zion upon the laws and commandments which shall be given unto you.
> *All victory and glory is brought to pass unto you through your diligence, faithfulness, and prayers of faith.*[13]

---

9. See, for instance, McConkie, Bruce R., "Are the General Authorities Human?" (Salt Lake City, Utah: Institute of Religion, Forum Talk for Oct. 28, 1966), and *Mormon Doctrine* (Salt Lake City, Utah: Bookcraft, Inc., 1958, pp. 283-284, 544-547.

10. D&C 21:5.

11. Jn. 20:27.

12. D&C 43:12.

13. D&C 103:35-36. For explanation concerning the name Baurak Ale, see the heading of D&C 78.

Concerning the First Presidency, the Savior has commanded that they be "upheld by the confidence, faith, and prayer of the church."[14] To Oliver Cowdery, who was intimately associated with Joseph Smith, the Revelator, the Lord commanded:

> . . . *Be diligent; stand by my servant Joseph, faithfully, in whatsoever difficult circumstances he may be for the word's sake.*
>
> Admonish him in his faults, and also receive admonition of him. Be patient; be sober; be temperate; have patience, faith, hope and charity.[15]

Oliver was also told, concerning his responsibility to Joseph Smith:

> And I have sent forth the fulness of my gospel by the hand of my servant Joseph; and in weakness have I blessed him;
>
> And I have given unto him the keys of the mystery of those things which have been sealed, even things which were from the foundation of the world, and the things which shall come from this time until the time of my coming, if he abide in me, and if not, another will I plant in his stead.
>
> *Wherefore, watch over him that his faith fail not.*[16]

It is essential for the work of the Lord that the saints fully sustain their leaders. The Church is now so large that few of the members know the Revelator and other general authorities personally. Yet those who are closest to the President of the Church testify frequently of his inspired leadership, and there is wisdom in their words. A typical statement is that of Elder Thorpe B. Isaacson, a former counselor in the First Presidency, to students at the Brigham Young University:

> I congratulate you on your good judgment and your loyalty to support the decision of the Prophet of God. I have learned to follow his counsel completely and without reservation. *He is constantly inspired of the Lord in his deliberations and decisions. I have learned that it is our responsibility and obligation, and even our blessing to follow the counsel of the prophet, the President of the Church.*[17]

No Man Is Appointed to Receive Commandments For the Church Except the Revelator Appointed by God

An important aspect of God's checks and balances is His stipulation that He will *command* the Church through only one man—His Revelator,

---

14. D&C 107:22.
15. D&C 6:18-19.
16. D&C 35:17-19.
17. Isaacson, Thorpe B., "Always Follow the Prophet," an address given to the Brigham Young University Student Body, January 18, 1966, (Provo Utah: Extension Publications, Division of Continuing Education, Brigham Young University), p. 3. See also Packer, Boyd K., "Follow the Brethren," a BYU talk given March 23, 1965, and available from the same source. Many addresses given in general conferences have followed this theme and are readily available.

the President of the Church. Concerning the first leader of the restored Church, Joseph Smith, the Lord revealed:

> . . . I say unto thee, *no one shall be appointed to receive commandments and revelations in this church excepting my servant Joseph Smith, Jun., for he receiveth them even as Moses.*[18]

A revelation given half a year later restated the principle:

> Ye have received a commandment for a law unto my church, through him whom I have appointed unto you to receive commandments and revelations from my hand.
>
> And this ye shall know assuredly—that *there is none other appointed unto you to receive commandments and revelations until he be taken, if he abide in me.*
>
> But verily, verily, I say unto you, that none else shall be appointed unto this gift except it be through him; for if it be taken from him he shall not have power except to appoint another in his stead.[19]

Again, in 1843, a revelation was recorded which spoke of

> *Revelation and commandment through the medium of mine annointed,* whom I have appointed on the earth to hold this power (and I have appointed unto my servant, Joseph to hold this power in the last days, *and there is never but one on the earth at a time on whom this power and the keys of the priesthood are conferred).*[20]

The message of these passages is clear: only one man, whom God has appointed, is authorized to *command* the Church in the name of the Lord through revelation. No other individual, either outside or within the Church, has that authorization. The appointed Revelator is empowered to pass on this responsibility through the procedure of ordination and transmitting of keys. It is the faith of the saints that this power has been transmitted and rests in the current President of the Church. He holds the keys of the kingdom,[21] the keys of the mysteries,[22] the keys of this dispensation,[23] and the keys of the priesthood.[24]

In both D&C 28:2 and 43:3 the Lord uses the words "revelations" and "commandments" as synonyms. Both words are used in the sense of "instructions to Church leaders and/or to the saints to perform duties for God." As will be seen, these words do not imply that revelation within the Church is given only to the Revelator, for such an interpretation would conflict with dozens of passages of scripture and the practice of the Lord

18. D&C 28:2.
19. D&C 43:2-4.
20. D&C 132:7.
21. D&C 27:12-13; 42:69; 65:2; 90:2-4, 6; 97:14; 115:19.
22. D&C 28:7; 35:18; 64:5; 84:19; 124:95,97.
23. D&C 110:16; 112:32.
24. D&C 132:19,40-47.

long established and recorded in the history of the Church. The sense of these passages is that God will *command* the saints through only one man at a time. In this way He protects the saints and prevents confusion. Failure to discern this distinction apparently has caused some saints, on occasion, to quote the above passages and draw erroneous conclusions. To be properly understood, D&C 28:2 and 43:3 must be seen and interpreted in the light of the broad spectrum of passages dealing with personal revelation to the saints.

The Lord is speaking, in both D&C 28:2 and D&C 43:1-7, concerning possible attempts to supplant the President as the one who is to set forth commandments to the Church. These passages were revealed to prevent possible usurpation of authority by individuals not called of God to be His spokesman.

The first of the above messages draws a distinct parallel between Joseph Smith in the latter days and Moses in Old Testament times, saying they were to receive revelation in the same manner. This provides an informative clue as to what the Lord means when he speaks of the Revelator as the only man appointed to receive commandments for the Church. Just as Moses was chosen of God to be His spokesman,[25] Joseph Smith was appointed as the only man to receive "commandments and revelations" for the Church in his day.[26] Yet, while both Moses and Joseph Smith were the only men "appointed" by God to give His commandments to the people in their eras, it must be understood that others received important revelations from God in the days of both Moses and Joseph Smith. Other men received and spoke the will of the Lord under inspiration in Moses' day, even though they were not the one "appointed" to give commandments in the name of God. Though there were some who did not understand it and sought to prevent it, yet the reception of revelation by others was right and proper, and it was accepted by Moses. The following incident took place at the time God and Moses delegated his authority by calling a group of seventy elders to assist in governing the people. Moses showed his attitude about others receiving revelation by his refusal to chastise Eldad and Medad:

> Moses went out, and *told the people the words of the Lord,* and gathered the seventy men of the elders of the people, and set them round about the tabernacle.
> And the Lord came down in a cloud, and spake unto him, and *took of the spirit that was upon him, and gave it unto the seventy elders:* and it came to pass that, *when the spirit rested upon them, they prophesied, and did not cease.*

---

25. See Ex. 3:12; 4:12-17.

26. It is an assumption, without direct scriptural basis, that later prophets have held the same relationship with God as Joseph Smith did. Yet certainly it is an appropriate assumption which seems to have been born out by evidence concerning the Lord's dealings with other Presidents of the Church since the time of Joseph Smith.

But there remained two of the men in the camp, the name of the one was Eldad and the name of the other Medad; and the spirit rested upon them; and they were of them that were written, but went not out unto the tabernacle: and *they prophesied in the camp.*

And there ran a young man, and told Moses, and said Eldad and Medad do prophesy in the camp.

And Joshua the son of Nun, the servant of Moses, one of his young men answered and said, *My Lord Moses, forbid them.*

And Moses said unto him, *Enviest thou for my sake? would God that all the Lord's people were prophets, and that the Lord would put his spirit upon them!* [27]

Thus others besides the "appointed" one received revelations and prophesied unto the people.

Their revelations represented an outpouring of the Lord's spirit upon His people, not a challenge and threat to Moses' authority as the official spokesman. In the latter days, as in Moses' time, there have been those who have envied for the sake of the prophet, and have attempted to forbid others to prophesy and to receive revelations. Yet the Lord specifically reveals that the Prophet in the latter days will hold the same relationship as did Moses, and Moses was highly pleased when others prophesied!

Another event in the life of Moses gives important insight concerning the relationship between the "appointed" Revelator and others who receive revelation from God. While others may receive revelation from God, if they begin to exalt themselves and to proclaim themselves as being "appointed" as official intermediaries between God and man as is the designated Revelator, they may incur the wrath of God. This lesson was taught to Moses' sister, Miriam, and to his brother, Aaron, by the Lord:

And Miriam and Aaron spake against Moses because of the Ethiopian woman whom he had married: for he had married an Ethiopian woman.

And they said, Hath the Lord indeed spoken only by Moses? hath he not spoken also by us? And the Lord heard it.

(Now the man Moses was very meek, above all the men which were upon the face of the earth.)

And the Lord spake suddenly unto Moses, and unto Aaron, and unto Miriam, Come out ye three unto the tabernacle of the congregation. And they three came out.

And the Lord came down in the pillar of the cloud, and stood in the door of the tabernacle, and called Aaron and Miriam: and they both came forth.

And he said, Hear now my words: *If there be a prophet among you, I the Lord will make myself known unto him in a vision, and will speak unto him in a dream.*

---

27. Num. 11:24-29. See also verse 17.

My servant Moses is not so, who is faithful in all mine house. With him will I speak mouth to mouth, even apparently, and not in dark speeches; and the similitude of the Lord shall he behold: wherefore then were ye not afraid to speak against my servant Moses? [28]

The message is evident. In addition to the "appointed" Revelator, there may be other prophets, and the Lord promises that he will make himself known unto them in dreams and visions! Yet the experience of continual face-to-face communication with the Lord was to be reserved for the "appointed" spokesman.

While others might enjoy the privilege of receiving the Lord's revealed will, yet they may not exalt themselves and count themselves equal with the "appointed" Revelator without displeasing God. Such was the revealed word of God concerning Moses' day; so it has also been in the latter days.

Two statements by Joseph Smith are pertinent to the discussion of who can receive revelation, and they are frequently quoted in this context. The first is found in a letter written by Joseph to the brother of Jared Carter on April 13, 1833 and reads,

> Respecting the vision you speak of we do not consider ourselves bound to receive any revelation from any one man or woman without his being legally constituted and ordained to that authority, and giving sufficient proof of it.
>
> I will inform you that it is contrary to the economy of God for any *member of the Church, or any one, to receive instructions for those in authority, higher than themselves;* therefore you will see the impropriety of giving heed to them: but *if any person have a vision or a visitation from a heavenly messenger, it must be for his own benefit and instruction;* for the fundamental principles, government, and doctrine of the Church are vested in the keys of the kingdom. [29]

The second statement was spoken by Joseph at a priesthood assembly held in the Kirtland Temple on April 6, 1837. He said,

---

28. Num. 12:1-8. The Lord punished Miriam for attempting to make herself equal to the "annointed" one by temporarily smiting her with leprosy. See verses 9-16.

29. HC 1:338. A later portion of the letter contains comments about revelation to the Church and about personal revelation which are of interest:

> *We never inquire at the hand of God for special revelation only in case of there being no previous revelation to suit the case; and that in a council of High Priests.*
>
> It is a great thing to inquire at the hands of God, or to come into His presence; and we feel fearful to approach Him on subjects that are of little or no consequence, to satisfy the queries of individuals, *especially about things the knowledge of which men ought to obtain in all sincerity, before God, for themselves, in humility by the prayer of faith;* and more especially a Teacher or a High Priest in the Church. (HC 1:339)

The Presidents or Presidency are over the Church; and revelations of the mind and will of God to the Church, are to come through the Presidency. This is the order of heaven, and the power and privilege of this Priesthood. *It is also the privilege of any officer in this Church to obtain revelations, so far as relates to his particular calling and duty in the Church. All are bound by the principles of virtue and happiness, but one great privilege of the Priesthood is to obtain revelations of the mind and will of God.* It is also the privilege of the Melchizedek Priesthood, to reprove, rebuke, and admonish, *as well as to receive revelation. If the Church knew all the commandments, one half they would condemn through prejudice and ignorance.*[30]

The meanings of these statements may be summarized by saying

1. God's commandments to the general Church membership are to come through the Presidency of the Church,

2. It is the privilege of any Church officer to receive revelation pertaining to his own particular Church assignment, and

3. Church members will not receive revelation which consists of instructions for those in higher offices in the Church than they themselves hold.

Many Saints Have Received Revelation which Influenced the Course of the Church

These instructions are valuable in matters of Church organization and government, for which they were intended. They become less useful and quite confusing, however, when men attempt to use them as infallible guides for interpreting who may receive revelation and who may not. The Lord's ways are not man's ways,[31] and the interpretation men have placed on these statements have sometimes failed to conform to the pattern of revelation God has established.

For instance, while the revelations have not commanded or instructed those in authority, there are *many* examples which show that individuals in lesser positions of authority have received revealed insights which have been accepted, utilized, and taught by those in higher positions, and also that others have received doctrinal or organizational insights before the President of the Church has received them.

For instance, in the early days of the Church, the established practice was that individuals were to perform the vicarious temple ordinances only for their own kindred dead. This practice was altered in 1877 to allow others to perform the vicarious ordinances besides those of the family of the deceased. This, of course, was a major policy change which was to affect the entire Church. The policy was changed, not by revelation to the President

---

30. HC 2:477.
31. Is. 55:8.

of the Church, Brigham Young, but by revelation to one of the Twelve, Wilford Woodruff. As Elder Woodruff explained in a discourse delivered March 1, 1877, the day the change took place:

> A few days ago I went before the Lord in this holy Temple, where I often go to pray. There is no more acceptable spot of this earth to the Lord than this Temple. *While in humble prayer, with the subject of temple ordinances resting upon my mind, I prayed the Lord to open the way for the redemption of my dead.* The spirit of the Lord rested upon me and gave me the following testimony: *"Let my servant Wilford call upon the daughters and mothers in Zion, and let them enter into My holy Temple* on the lst day of March, the day that my servant Wilford shall see the time allotted to man, three score years and ten. *There let them receive their endowments for his dead kindred, and this shall be acceptable unto me,* saith the Lord. The dead relatives of My servant shall be redeemed in the spirit world and be prepared to meet My servant at the time of his coming, which shall be at the time appointed unto him, yet not revealed to men in the flesh. Now, go to and perform this work and all shall be accomplished according to the desires of thy heart."
>
> This was merely a key to me, a light burst upon my understanding, and I saw an effectual door opened to me for the redemption of my dead. When I beheld this I felt like shouting, "Glory hallelujah to God and the Lamb." [32]

In another example of revelation being given to someone other than the President of the Church, significant prophecies—of a future temple and a major earthquake—were voiced. This incident also involved both Wilford Woodruff and Brigham Young, and took place at a conference in Logan, Utah in 1863. President Young was present and seated on the stand during the conference. Since he was the one in highest authority and the President of the Church, it is logical to assume that the revelation would have been given through him, but the Lord apparently chooses the recipient He desires for such manifestations, rather than holding to the pattern He has established for *commanding* the Church. The prophecy was as follows:

> You are to become men and women, fathers and mothers; yea, the day will come, after your fathers, and these prophets and apostles are dead, *you will*

---

32. Cowley, Mathias F., *Wilford Woodruff, op cit.,* p. 496. Elder Woodruff did not disregard the organizational structure of the Church, however. He told President Young of the revelation which he had received, and received the President's approval to make the change:

> I did not pursue this course, however, without first making known my testimony to President Young. Upon consulting him, *he said that my course was proper; what I did was right; and what I received came from the Lord.* He offered to provide several persons himself. In the assembly on this occasion were three of his wives and five of his daughters. (Ibid., p. 496.)

Note, however, that while organizational lines were respected, this revelation which affected the entire Church did not come through the Prophet, except possibly in confirmation of revelation given to someone else.

have the privilege of going into the towers of a glorious temple built unto the
name of the Most High (pointing in the direction of the bench), east of us upon
the Logan bench; and while you stand in the towers of the Temple and your
eyes survey this glorious valley filled with cities and villages, occupied by tens
of thousands of Latter-day Saints, you will then call to mind this visitation of
President Young and his company. You will say: That was in the days when
Presidents Benson and Maughan presided over us; *that was before New York*
was destroyed by an earthquake. It was before Boston was swept into the sea,
by the sea heaving itself beyond its bounds; it was before Albany was destroyed
by fire; yea, at that time you will remember the scenes of this day. Treasure
them up and forget them not. President Young followed and said: *"What*
Brother Woodruff has said is revelation and will be fulfilled." [33]

Various programs and practices observed Church-wide have come into
being through the efforts and inspiration of Church members rather than
through revelation to the President of the Church. The Sunday School
organization, for instance, had its beginning on December 9, 1849, when
the first Sunday School was held by Elder Richard Ballantyne at his home
in the Old Fort at Salt Lake City. When asked what motivated him to do
so he replied:

I was early called to this work by the voice of the spirit, and I have felt many
times that I have been ordained to this work before I was born, for even before
I joined the Church, I was moved upon to work for the young. Surely no more
joyful and profitable labor can be performed by an Elder. [34]

Although he requested and received permission from his Bishop to establish
his small Sunday School, he carried the full load himself without Church
assistance at the beginning, even constructing an addition to his home to
accommodate the students. The inspiration granted to Richard Ballantyne
long preceded any revelation which may have come to the Church authorities to bring about the organization of the Sunday Schools of the Church.
It was not until seventeen years later, in 1866, that the Sunday School came
under direct control of the Church. Again, this was not the result of revelation to the President of the Church, but of the efforts of various other
Church members. Elder B. H. Roberts summarized the matter as follows:

In the 15th of April number of the *Juvenile, 1866, a letter written by*
Wm. H. Sherman, appeared, urging the organization of a Sunday School
Union, to give organic uniformity to this movement and greater efficiency
that could only come from such a central body. At the following October conference of the church some attention was given to Sunday School work and the

---

33. *Deseret News,* Vol. 33, p. 678. This prophecy was made August 22, 1863.
See also JD 21:299 and D&C 84:114-115.

34. Jenson, Andrew, *Latter-day Saint Biographical Encyclopedia,* (Salt Lake
City, Utah: Andrew Jenson History Company, 1901), vol. 1, p. 705.

necessity of a central organization to direct its course. On November the 4th, such an organization was effected, of which George Q. Cannon was chosen president, Edward L. Sloan was chosen secretary, and George Goddard and Robert L. Campbell, corresponding secretaries. A committee of three was chosen to decide upon suitable books for Sunday School libraries. This organization for several years bore the name of the "Parent Sunday School Union." In 1872 the central organization took the name by which it has ever since been known—"The Deseret Sunday School Union."[35]

A similar situation exists with the organization of the Primary Association. Sister Aurelia S. Rogers, a resident of Farmington, Utah, felt strongly about the need for weekday religious education for young boys and girls. It was she who initiated contacts with the President of the Church, John Taylor, and with Eliza R. Snow, Emmeline B. Wells, and others, which led to the organization of this important Church auxiliary. It was not her assigned calling or duty within the Church. According to the narrow definition of who may receive revelation set forth by some commentators, she had no right to act. Yet God used her, and she was able to demonstrate the need for a Primary Association to the President of the Church and to other influential Church leaders. On August 11, 1878, Sister Rogers was set apart to preside over a Primary Association in Farmington. The first meeting was held two weeks later, on August 25th. The movement began spreading within the Church. Finally, on June 19, 1880, Louise B. Felt was called to preside over the Primary Association on a Church-wide basis.

Missionary teaching plans are another example of programs which have come into being through the inspiration and efforts of particular Church members rather than through direct revelation to the President of the Church. Programs have been initiated in various missions which have met with improved success and then have been used on a widespread or Church-wide basis. The Anderson plan, Great Lakes Mission plan, and Northwestern States mission plan are examples.

An earlier situation, however, provides a more striking example. A revelation which greatly affected the missionary activities of the Church was given to President German E. Ellsworth, president of the Northern States Mission, in June of 1907. At this time President Ellsworth was visiting the Sacred Grove and the Hill Cumorah in the company of an apostle, Elder George Albert Smith, for the purpose of purchasing the Joseph Smith homestead for the Church. While waiting for the title to be cleared, President Ellsworth frequently walked the three miles from Palmyra to Cumorah to pray and meditate there. One morning, at sunrise, a voice from beyond

35. CHC 5:479. The term "Juvenile" had reference to the "Juvenile Instructor," a newspaper which was begun January 1, 1866, by George Q. Cannon, as a semi-monthly publication. Thus Wm. H. Sherman's letter appeared in the seventh issue.

the veil spoke to him and told him to *"Push the distribution of the record taken from this hill; it will help bring the world to Christ."* [36]

Again, this is an example of revelation which came, not to the President of the Church, but to an individual holding less jurisdictional authority. Yet the revelation affected the course of missionary work throughout much of the Church for many years.

An interesting example is recorded in early Church history concerning the moving of the remainder of the saints from Kirtland to Missouri in 1838. This group was later known as Kirtland Camp. The presidency of the Seventies had met to plan how the move could be done, but without success. The matter had been referred to the First Presidency, from whom the suggestion was made that the saints come by steamboat, but this plan was unsuccessful. The quorum leaders met with the quorum and said that

> It seemed to them almost an impossible thing for the quorum [as such] to move from this place under existing circumstances; that the measures entered into by the High Council and High Priests for removing the Saints had failed and

---

36. Ellsworth, German E. and Ellsworth, Mary Smith, *Our Ellsworth Ancestors,* (Salt Lake City: Utah Printing Company, 1956), p. 55. The genealogical account which records the incident details the result of this manifestation as follows:

> German followed the admonition by injecting enthusiasm and inspiration for the value of the God-given Book of Mormon as a witness for Christ. A postcard picture of the Hill Cumorah with this statement was sent to all Northern States missionaries and to all Mission Presidents. *German E. was invited to visit all U. S. Missions in order to spark the wider use of the Book of Mormon as a missionary medium.* At one mission, Apostle George Albert Smith said, 'President Ellsworth, you haven't said a thing I wanted you to say. Get up and give them your conviction that there is no missionary book equal to the Book of Mormon, the one given by the Lord for the convincing of both Jew and Gentile, that Jesus is the Christ.' (The Book of Mormon was the exclusive book used by early missionaries from 1830-1837.)
>
> *President Joseph F. Smith sent for President Ellsworth to spend a day with Elder Melvin J. Ballard before going as a new Mission President to the Northwestern States Mission in order to encourage the wider use of the Book of Mormon in that Mission.* From a few hundred copies shipped to the Missions of the Church (at 37½ cents per copy) from the Deseret News in Salt Lake City, a Chicago edition of ten thousand from new plates was printed at a cost of 27 cents, including new plates. This was followed by a fifteen thousand edition at 24 cents per copy, and then many editions of twenty-five thousand at 18 cents per copy over the years, and finally a hundred thousand-copy edition of the same quality was printed in in Chicago at 12½ cents per copy just prior to the establishing of Zion's Printing Company in Independence, Missouri to which place all Book of Mormon plates and all plates for various tracts and books that had been printed in Chicago were shipped, from which place millions of books and tracts were printed. (p. 56.)

they had given up making any further attempts after their scheme of going by water had fallen through, and that they had further advised every individual of the Church wishing to go up unto Zion to look out for himself individually and make the best of it he could.[37]

Then as the meeting progressed, the spirit of prophecy was poured out upon the members present, and another approach to the move was set forth:

> *The Spirit of the Lord came down in mighty power, and some of the Elders began to prophesy that if the quorum would go up in a body together, and go according to the commandments and revelations of God, pitching their tents by the way, that they should not want for anything on the journey that would be necessary for them to have; and further that there should be nothing wanting towards removing the whole quorum of Seventies that would go in a body, but that there should be a sufficiency of all things for carrying such an expedition into effect.*[38]

It was not until after these manifestations that one of the quorum leaders told of the vision he had seen:

> President James Foster arose in turn to make some remarks on the subject and in the course of his address *he declared that he saw a vision in which was shown unto him a company (he should think of about five hundred) starting from Kirtland and going up to Zion.* That he saw them moving in order, encamping in order by the way, and that he knew thereby that it was the will of God that the quorum should go up in that manner.
>
> *The Spirit bore record of the truth of his assertions for it rested down on the assembly in power,* insomuch that all present were satisfied that it was the will of God that the quorum should go up in a company together to the land of Zion, and that they should proceed immediately to make preparations for the journey.[39]

In a meeting a week later, Elder Hyrum Smith, of the First Presidency, made the following comments concerning the previous plan of going by steamboat:

> *President Hyrum Smith* came in and addressed the meeting at some length on the movements of the Saints in Kirtland in relation to their emigration to the land of Zion since the commandment had gone forth for the honest in heart to rise up and go up unto that land. *He stated that what he had said and done in reference to chartering a steamboat, for the purpose of removing the Church as a body, he had done according to his own judgment without reference to the testimony of the Spirit of God; that he had recommended that course and had advised the High Council and High Priests to adopt that measure, acting solely by his own wisdom,* for it had seemed to him that the whole body of the Church in Kirtland could be removed with less expense in the way he had proposed than in any other. *He said further that the Saints had to act oftentimes upon their own responsibility without any reference to the testimony of*

---

37. HC 3:88, March 6, 1838.
38. *Ibid.*
39. *Ibid.*, pp. 88-89.

the Spirit of God in relation to temporal affairs, that he has so acted in this
matter and has never had any testimony from God that the plan of going by
water was approved of by Him, and that the failure of the scheme was evidence
in his mind that God did not approve of it.

He then declared that he knew by the Spirit of God that the movements
they were making by the quorum of the Seventies for their removal and the
plan of their journeying was according to the will of the Lord.[40]

The point is obvious—God pours out His Spirit upon the Church as
well as upon His Prophet, the President of the Church. The members themselves are often the recipients of revelation which ultimately becomes the
basis for inspired Church-wide programs or activities which shape the lives
of many of the saints. The revelation they receive is in proper perspective.
They claim no authority to reveal the Lord's will to the Church, neither do
they command the Church membership. In no way do they challenge the
authority of Church leaders. Yet God grants to them revelation which
ultimately affects the status of His people. Often the revelation they receive
is beyond their assigned callings within the Church, yet God uses whom He
chooses to further His purposes. Those who fail to recognize the reality of
this principle are sometimes confused in their personal understanding of
how revelation is granted and upon whom it may be bestowed.

Prophecy Does Not Conform to the Usual Pattern of Revelation

It should be noted in particular that prophecy does not conform to the
usual patterns of revelation. It often cannot be tested and evaluated with the
same criteria as other revelations, and confusion results when one attempts
to do so.

The tendency has been to indicate that an individual will *only* prophesy
or receive revelation pertaining to a personal problem or to his own family,
or to his particular assignment in the Church. This, once again, is contrary
to the pattern established by *many* revelations recorded in the history of the
Church and the biographies of the saints. A host of examples can be cited
which demonstrate that individuals may be shown events involving things
far into the future, revelations concerning future Church activities, prophecies concerning other individuals, etc. Their revelation is by no means
limited to their own personal sphere.

Consider a few examples. When Heber C. Kimball and Willard Richards
were preaching the gospel in England, Heber baptized Jennetta Richards,
the daughter of an English reverend. Willard Richards had never yet met
Jennetta. Heber, however, was able to make this prophecy to his fellow
missionary: *"Willard, I baptized your wife today."*[41] Willard subsequently

---

40. HC 3:94.
41. Whitney, Orson F., *Life of Heber C. Kimball, op. cit.,* p. 143. Why didn't
the revelation come directly to Willard Richards?

met Jennetta Richards and married her in fulfillment of Heber's prophecy. Willard apparently regarded the prophecy as a promise that she would be given to him by the Lord, for he recorded in his journal these words:

> Sept. 24, 1839, I married Jennetta Richards, daughter of the Rev. John Richards, independent minister at Walkerfold, Chaigley, Lancashire. *Most truly do I praise my Heavenly Father for His great kindness in providing me a partner according to His promise. I receive her from the Lord, and hold her at His disposal.* I pray that He may bless us forever. Amen.[42]

John Young, Brigham Young, Joseph Young and Heber C. Kimball received this prophetic manifestation in 1831, prior to their baptism into the Church:

> While we were thus engaged we were pondering upon those things which had been told us by the Elders, and upon the saints gathering to Zion, when the glory of God shone upon us, and *we saw the gathering of the saints to Zion, and the glory that would rest upon them; and many more things connected with that great event, such as the sufferings and persecutions that would come upon the people of God, and the calamities and judgments that would come upon the world.*
>
> These things caused such great joy to spring up in our bosoms that we were hardly able to contain ourselves, and we did shout aloud 'Hosannah to God and the Lamb.'[43]

Again, while Heber C. Kimball was a missionary in England, he converted two sisters, Mary Ann and Margaret Heaton Topping. To one of them he made a prophecy which presumably, by the "one only receives revelation for his own affairs" concept, would have come only to her:

> He warned one of these sisters not to marry a young man she was engaged to, as *he would apostatize and leave the Church,* and told her that her future husband was not then in the Church, but would come in and remain faithful; and, said he, *'You shall see the man you are going to marry at the conference that I will notify you to attend.'* These remarkable promises were all fulfilled, and Sister Topping bore witness of their truth.[44]

Daniel Tyler was the eventual recipient of a prophecy concerning his future which seemingly, according to the "one only receives revelation for his own affairs" philosophy, should have come directly to him. It was made

---

42. *Ibid.,* p. 144.
43. *Ibid.,* p. 19. Why did they see this manifestation? It did not directly concern them, for they were not among those who settled in Jackson County, Missouri. Note its significance—here four men who were not even members of the Church were shown much of the Church's future course, and also foresaw many of the calamities of the last days.
44. *Ibid.,* pp. 433-34. See other examples on pp. 436-37 (concerning George Nebeker) p. 439 (recorded by Solomon F. Kimball), and p. 448 (concerning A. F. McDonald).

a year prior to his entry into the Swiss mission at a prayer meeting in Salt Lake City. At that time his leg had been broken for seven months and he had despaired of ever being able to use it again:

> After the meeting was opened, *Sister More arose and began to speak in tongues.* She addressed her remarks to me, and I understood her as well as though she had spoken the English language. She said: '*Your leg will be healed, and you will go on a foreign mission and preach the gospel in foreign lands. No harm shall befall you, and you shall return in safety, having great joy in your labors.*'
>
> This was the substance of the prophecy. It was so different from my own belief and the fears of many others that I was tempted not to give the interpretation, lest it should fail to come to pass. The Spirit, however, impressed me and I arose, leaning upon my crutches, and gave the interpretation.[45]

Such incidents of people prophesying concerning other than their own future are commonplace. The above, however, are sufficient to show that prophecy does not conform to the usual pattern by which individuals sometimes attempt to evaluate revelation in general.

Revelations or Manifestations Given to Others Are Not Commandments to the Church

The Lord has revealed that

> This shall be a law unto you, that ye receive not the teachings of any that shall come before you *as revelations or commandments;*
>
> And this I give unto you that you may not be deceived, that you may know they are not of me.[46]

It is important to discern both what this passage *does* say and what it *does not* say. Its message is that the Church is not to allow itself to be *commanded* by anyone else than the Lord speaking through the Revelator. Its message is also that teachings voiced by others beside the Revelator are not to be regarded as revelations or commandments which are *binding* upon the Church as doctrine. This message is part of the Lord's protection for the saints. The above meanings are quite explicit and little confusion exists concerning them. Confusion does exist, however, concerning what the passage does not say. It does *not* say:

1. only the President of the Church can receive revelation;
2. a revelation is false if it was not revealed through the President of the Church;

45. Tyler, Daniel, "Incidents of Experience," *Scraps of Biography* (Tenth Book of the Faith-Promoting Series, Juvenile Instructor. Reprinted in Salt Lake City, Utah by Bookcraft, Inc., 1969), 41-42.
46. D&C 43:5-6.

3. revelations which do not come from the President of the Church
   may not be received by Church members as revealed truth;
4. Church members who receive revelations are not to share them with
   other Church members.

Indeed, such assertions are in direct conflict with other passages of scripture
and with many instances where the will of the Lord has been revealed, as
recorded in the history of the Church.

The principle which should be recognized is that while only the President of the Church is to command the Church in the name of the Lord,
many other members have received, do receive, and will receive revelations
which provide them with information concerning eternal truths which very
likely will be of value and interest to others. Many people are shown visions
of future events. Some are shown what the Church will do, or what the fate
of the saints will be. Yet they do not command the Church. To be equipped
with foreknowledge is not to command. In no way do such manifestations
conflict with the guidelines which the Lord has revealed. To cast doubt
and aspersions upon such sacred things is to deny the power and Spirit of
God. Those who have done so have spread a spirit of doubt and skepticism
within the Church which is inappropriate to the workings of the Lord's
Spirit. When the Lord promised that He "will give unto the children of
men line upon line, precept upon precept, *here a little and there a little. . . ,"*[47]
He also warned of such skeptics within the Church, who are "at ease in
Zion," who say, "We have received, and we need no more!" with these
words:

> Wo be unto him that hearkeneth unto the precepts of men, and denieth
> the power of God, and the gift of the Holy Ghost!
> *Yea, wo be unto him that saith: We have received, and we need no more!*
> And in fine, wo unto all those who tremble, and are angry because of
> the truth of God! For behold, *he that is built upon the rock receiveth it with
> gladness; and he that is built upon a sandy foundation trembleth lest he shall
> fall.*[48]

The Saints Are to Have Revelations and Bear Witness

Others besides the Revelator may receive revelation concerning the
things of God, and the Lord has revealed that it is appropriate to share
their knowledge with other Church members. What the recipients of revelation may *not* do is (1) represent themselves as being the one "appointed"
to receive revelation for the Church, nor (2) put the revelation forth "by
way of commandment." What they write must be by way of "wisdom"
only. With Oliver Cowdery this relationship was revealed in detail. Oliver

47. 2 Ne. 28:30.
48. 2 Ne. 28:26-28. See verses 24-25.

was promised the privilege of receiving direct revelation from the Lord in several sections of the Doctrine and Covenants[49] and was even promised, *"Thou shalt exercise thy gift, that thou mayest find out mysteries, that thou mayest bring many* to the knowledge of the truth."[50] Yet, the Lord cautioned him, saying, *"Thou shalt have revelations, but write them not by way of commandment."*[51]

The Lord carefully explained the relationship Oliver was to have with the appointed Prophet of the Church:

> Behold, I say unto thee, Oliver, that it shall be given unto thee that *thou shalt be heard by the church in all things whatsoever thou shalt teach them by the Comforter,* concerning the revelations and commandments which I have given.
>
> But, behold, verily, verily, I say unto thee, no one shall be appointed to receive commandments and revelations in this church excepting my servant Joseph Smith, Jun., for he receiveth them even as Moses.
>
> *And thou shalt be obedient unto the things which I shall give unto him,* even as Aaron, to declare faithfully the commandments and revelations, with power and authority unto the church.
>
> *And if thou art led at any time by the Comforter to speak or teach, or at all times by the way of commandment unto the church, thou mayest do it.*
>
> And *thou shalt not write by way of commandment, but by wisdom;*
>
> *And thou shalt not command him who is at thy head, and at the head of the church;*
>
> For I have given him the keys of the mysteries, and the revelations which are sealed, until I shall appoint unto them another in his stead.[52]

David Whitmer is another example of one who was promised revelation and was commanded to share what he received with others. The Lord promised him:

> It shall come to pass, that if you shall ask the Father in my name, in faith believing, *you shall receive the Holy Ghost, which giveth utterance, that you may stand as a witness of the things of which you shall both hear and see,* and also that you may declare repentance unto this generation.
>
> Behold, I am Jesus Christ, the Son of the living God, who created the heavens and the earth, a light which cannot be hid in darkness;
>
> Wherefore, I must bring forth the fulness of my gospel from the Gentiles unto the house of Israel.
>
> And behold, thou art David, and thou art called to assist; which thing if ye do, and are faithful, ye shall be blessed both spiritually and temporally, and great shall be your reward.[53]

49. See D&C 6:10-11,14-15; 8:1-7,11.

50. D&C 6:11. Note the implication that his personal revelations were to be communicated to others. How would he be able to use the revelations he received to bring many others to a knowledge of the truth unless he shared the revelations with them?

51. D&C 28:8.

52. D&C 28:1-7.

53. D&C 14:8-11.

To Orson Pratt, then a nineteen-year-old member of six weeks, the Lord also spoke, telling him to prophesy and to preach the things revealed to him: "Wherefore, lift up your voice and *spare not,* for the Lord God hath spoken; *therefore prophesy, and it shall be given by the power of the Holy Ghost.* "[54]

To twelve unidentified elders the Lord gave commandment that they should prophesy and speak concerning their prophecies, and He promised them many revelations:

> As ye shall lift up your voices by the Comforter, ye shall speak and prophesy as seemeth me good; . . .
> If thou shalt ask, thou shalt receive revelation upon revelation, knowledge upon knowledge, that thou mayest know the mysteries and peaceable things— that which bringeth joy, that which bringeth life eternal.[55]

Concerning four departing missionaries (Lyman Wight, John Corrill, John Murdock, and Hyrum Smith), the Lord commanded that they should add the things revealed to them by the Comforter to the standard doctrines they were to preach:

> Let them journey from thence preaching the word by the way, saying none other things than that which the prophets and apostles have written, *and that which is taught them by the Comforter through the prayer of faith.*[56]

An oft-quoted passage on the subject of revelation is found in the sixty-eighth section of the Doctrine and Covenants. It is unfortunate that some who cite it fail to recognize that it is not speaking of the President of the Church, but rather of priesthood holders in general and of four young converts (Orson Hyde, Luke S. Johnson, Lyman E. Johnson, and William E. M'Lellin) in particular. They are being commanded to speak and to bear record of the manifestations they receive through the Holy Ghost:

> This is an *ensample unto all those who were ordained unto this priesthood,* whose mission is appointed unto them to go forth—
> And this is the ensample unto them, that *they shall speak as they are moved upon by the Holy Ghost.*
> And whatsoever they shall speak when moved upon by the Holy Ghost shall be scripture, shall be the will of the Lord, shall be the mind of the Lord, shall be the word of the Lord, shall be the voice of the Lord, and the power of God unto salvation.
> Behold, this is the promise of the Lord unto you, O ye *my servants.*
> Therefore, be of good cheer, and do not fear, for I the Lord am with you, and will stand by you; and ye shall bear record of me, even Jesus Christ, that I am the Son of the living God, that I was, that I am, and that I am to come.

---

54. D&C 34:10.
55. D&C 42:16,61.
56. D&C 52:9.

> This is the word of the Lord unto you, my servant Orson Hyde, and also unto my servant Luke Johnson, and unto my servant Lyman Johnson, and unto my servant William E. M'Lellin, and *unto all the faithful elders of my church.*[57]

The History of the Church also contains numerous examples of individuals who saw sacred things or who received revelation concerning doctrine or concerning future events within the Church. Their visions and manifestations were regarded as blessings and were considered as completely appropriate. For instance, the Prophet Joseph himself recorded the manifestation given to Newel Knight, a convert of two weeks:

> Much exhortation and instruction was given, and the Holy Ghost was poured out upon us in a miraculous manner—*many of our number prophesied, whilst others had the heavens opened to their view,* and were so overcome that we had to lay them on beds or other convenient places; among the rest was Brother Newel Knight, who had to be placed on a bed, being unable to help himself. By his own account of the transaction, he could not understand why we should lay him on the bed, as he felt no sense of weakness. He felt his heart filled with love, with glory, and pleasure unspeakable, and could discern all that was going on in the room; when all of a sudden *a vision of the future burst upon him. He saw there represented the great work which through my instrumentality was yet to be accomplished. He saw heaven opened, and beheld the Lord Jesus Christ, seated at the right hand of the majesty on high, and had it made plain to his understanding that the time would come when he would be admitted into His presence to enjoy His society for ever and ever.* When their bodily strength was restored to these brethren, they shouted hosannas to God and the Lamb, and *rehearsed the glorious things which they had seen and felt, whilst they were yet in the spirit.*[58]

---

57. D&C 68:2-7. This passage has been seriously abused by some who quote it as having reference to the general authorities of the Church—an unjustified interpretation. Though several of the men later became general authorities (and, incidentally, fell from their positions), yet at this time there was no quorum of the twelve in existence. When this revelation was given, the recipients were only young missionaries. None of the four men had been members of the Church for more than a few months; Orson Hyde was the newest, and had been a member only about a month. See HC 1:217, 220, 260, 322. None of them were holders of high Church offices when this revelation was given in November, 1831. Though all of them later became General Authorities of the Church, any assertion that this particular passage had reference to statements made by General Authorities rather than lay members of the Church is a forced interpretation made contrary to reason and sound methods of scriptural and historical interpretation.

It becomes clear that a revealed item may be "scripture" and the "will of the Lord," yet it is not binding upon the Church unless it has been canonized through the accepting and sustaining vote of the Church assembled in general conference. Like many things, it may be true, and yet not be a stated doctrine of the Church.

58. HC 1:84-85. June 9, 1830. Note that Newel Knight
  (1) received revelations concerning the Church, not just his own jurisdiction;

On January 21, 1836, Warren Parrish, a secretary to Joseph Smith, was one of several men who received revelations. Concerning the event, Joseph Smith wrote,

> My scribe also received his anointing with us, and saw, in a vision, *the armies of heaven protecting the Saints in their return to Zion, and many things which I saw.*[59]

In a meeting one week later, the following manifestations took place:

> Elder Roger Orton *saw a mighty angel* riding upon a horse of fire, with a flaming sword in his hand, followed by five others, encircle the house, and protect the Saints, even the Lord's annointed, from the power of Satan and *a host of evil spirits,* which were striving to disturb the Saints.
>
> President William Smith, one of the Twelve, saw the heavens opened, and *the Lord's host* protecting the Lord's annointed.
>
> President Zebedee Coltrin, one of the seven presidents of the Seventy, *saw the Savior,* extended before him, as upon the cross, and a little after crowned with glory upon his head above the brightness of the sun.[60]

In a meeting on February 6, 1836,

> President William Smith, one of the Twelve, saw a vision of the Twelve, and Seven in counsel together, in old England, and *prophesied that a great*

---

    (2) saw both Christ and the Father, though he held no position of authority within the Church;

    (3) did not keep his manifestation secret, but openly shared it with others within the Church;

    (4) allowed it to be published and circulated among the saints.

59. HC 2:381. Note that Warren Parish

    (1) received revelation concerning the Church, not just his own jurisdiction;

    (2) saw many things which the Lord had revealed to the President of the Church;

    (3) did not keep his manifestation secret, but openly shared it with others within the Church;

    (4) allowed it to be published and circulated among the saints.

60. HC 2:386-387. January 28, 1836. Note that

    (1) revelations given to ordinary members of the Church were regarded by the Prophet Joseph as being as important as revelations given by general authorities and were recorded with equal treatment. In this instance, Roger Orton was a seventy, while William Smith was an apostle and Zebedee Coltrin was in the presidency of the first quorum of Seventy;

    (2) direct revelation was given to others even though the President of the Church was present;

    (3) in each case the individuals received revelation which had no relation to his jurisdiction within the Church;

    (4) they did not keep their manifestations secret, but bore witness of them to others within the Church;

    (5) they allowed word of their manifestation to be published and circulated among the saints.

work would be done by them in the old countries, and God was already beginning to work in the hearts of the people. [61]

There are numerous examples of other revelations given throughout the history of the Church which show that doctrine, the will of the Lord, and foreknowledge of future activities of the Church are constantly revealed to other individuals besides the President of the Church. They were shared with others; recorded and commented upon by others; and were accepted as valid manifestations by others, including the prophet Joseph Smith and other Church leaders.

One other well-known example will suffice. Consider the prophetic statement made by Heber C. Kimball to Parley P. Pratt in 1836:

> It was now April. I had retired to rest one evening at an early hour, and was pondering my future course, when there came a knock at the door. I arose and opened it, when Elder Heber C. Kimball and others entered my house, and being filled with the spirit of prophecy, they blessed me and my wife, and prophesied as follows:
>
> 'Brother Parley, *thy wife shall be healed from this hour, and shall bear a son, and his name shall be Parley; and he shall be a chosen instrument in the hands of the Lord* to inherit the Priesthood and to walk in the steps of his father. He shall do a great work in the earth in ministering the Word and teaching the children of men. Arise, therefore, go forth in the ministry, nothing doubting. Take no thoughts for your debts, nor the necessaries of life, for the Lord will supply you with abundant means for all things.
>
> *Thou shalt go to Upper Canada, even to the city of Toronto, the capital, and there thou shalt find a people prepared for the fulness of the gospel, and they shall receive thee, and thou shalt organize the Church among them, and it shall spread thence into the regions round about, and many shall be brought to the knowledge of the truth and shall be filled with joy; and from the things growing out of this mission, shall the fulness of the gospel spread into England, and cause a great work to be done in that land.'* [62]

---

61. HC 2:392. Note that
    (1) though he did not command the Church, William Smith received revelation which shaped the Church's future. Before this time there had been no plan set forth to send missionaries to England in the near future, yet within sixteen months Joseph sent missionaries there. (See Whitney, *Life of Heber C. Kimball,* p. 103).
    (2) revelation was given to another even though the President of the Church was present.
    (3) although others were present who actually went on the mission, the Lord did not reveal the vision to them. Visions do not always come to the person one might consider to be the most logical recipient.
    (4) he did not keep his manifestation secret, but bore witness of it to others within the Church.
    (5) he allowed word of his manifestation to be published and circulated among the saints.
62. Pratt, Parley P., *Autobiography of Parley P. Pratt* (Salt Lake City, Utah: Deseret Book Company, 1966), pp. 130-131. Note that

It is therefore clear that examples of individuals receiving revelation through the spirit and being prompted or commanded to share it are legion, both in the scriptures and in the history of the Church. That Spirit which reveals to man the truths of eternity is the same Spirit *"which giveth utterance, that you may stand as a witness of the things you shall both hear and see."*[63] Those who are enlightened by the word of God cannot, and should not be compelled to bury their knowledge. As the Savior taught, "Neither do men light a candle, and put it under a bushel, but on a candlestick; and *it giveth light unto all* that are in the house."[64]

While the Savior cautioned the saints to "Give not that which is holy unto the dogs, neither cast ye your pearls before swine, lest they trample them under their feet, and turn again and rend you,"[65] yet this was never meant to mean that the choice manifestations of the Spirit must never be shared. Rather, let the matter be handled as the Lord revealed in the latter days: *"Make not thy gift known unto any save it be those who are of thy faith."*[66] And above all, let not the members of the Church be the skeptics and disbelievers who "trample them under their feet, and turn again and rend," through lack of knowledge concerning the nature of revelation.

---

(1) revelation concerning intimate family matters (the healing of his wife, the birth and naming of his son) were not given to Parley P. Pratt, the head of the family, but to another individual;

(2) extensive prophecy which was to affect the course of the Church in both Canada and England was given through someone besides the President of the Church;

(3) though a prophecy, the revelation took the form of a commandment to the individual who was to execute it;

(4) he did not keep the manifestation secret, but bore witness of it to others within the Church;

(5) Parley P. Pratt, himself an apostle, wrote the manifestation to be published and circulated among the saints.

63. D&C 14:8.

64. Mt. 5:15. The next verse adds *"Let your light so shine before men, that they may see your good works. . ."* (Mt. 5:16). The Book of Mormon rendition makes a significant change which is pertinent to the subject at hand, saying, "Therefore let your light so shine *before this people,* that they may see your good works. . ." (3 Ne. 12:16). Thus the Book of Mormon account limits the recipients of these good tidings to members of the Church.

65. Mt. 7:6.

66. D&C 6:12. There have been occasions when God has commanded that particular aspects of a revelation not be shared. (See 3 Ne. 17:15; 28:25; Eth. 3:27, 4:5; II Cor. 12:4, etc.) but these are an infinitesimal fraction compared to the host of manifestations God has brought forth. There is no scriptural basis whatsoever for any assertion that other experiences and truths granted to individual members must be kept secret. If God desires that a revelation is to be kept secret, He will reveal the need for that secrecy to its recipient; otherwise the scriptural injunction above would seem to have precedence.

Personal Revelation Is Essential to an Unwavering Testimony

The receiving of personal revelation is an absolute necessity for every Latter-day Saint if he is to gain his salvation.[67] He may gain an intellectual testimony without it, but a "revealed" testimony can only be possessed by those who have received a personal, revealed witness by direct revelation. Without the guidance of the Holy Spirit, no man can bear valid testimony to the truthfulness of the gospel or to the divinity of Jesus Christ.[68]

Every member of the Church has the right and responsibility to receive revelation. As President Brigham Young explained, personal revelation "is the very life of the church of the living God:"

> *This church has been led by revelation, and unless we forsake the Lord entirely, so that the priesthood is taken from us, it will be led by revelation all the time.* The question arises with some who has the right to revelation? I will not ascend any higher than a priest, and ask the priest what is your right? You have the right to receive the administration of angels. If an angel was to come to you and tell you what the Lord was going to do in this day, you would say you had a revelation. *The president of the priests has a right to the Urim and Thummim, which gives revelation.* He has the right of receiving visits from angels. Every priest then in the church has the right of receiving revelations. *Every member has the right of receiving revelations for themselves, both male and female. It is the very life of the church of the living God, in all ages of the world.* The Spirit of Truth is sent forth into all the world to reprove the world of sin and unrighteousness, and of a judgment to come. If we were here today and had never heard this gospel, and a man was to come bounding into our midst, saying he had come to preach the gospel, to tell us that God was about to restore the priesthood, and save the people, etc., *it would be your privilege and my privilege to ask God in the name of Jesus Christ, as individuals, concerning this thing, whether it was of God, and get a testimony from God that it was true, and this would be revelation.* Let us take some of these old fathers for an example, they have heard the gospel, they have been baptized, etc., had the hands laid on them for the gift of the Holy Ghost—he has got a family of children, he has been led all his days by his own spirit, but now begins to come to understand *he has the right to bow before the Lord and receive instruction from God, from day to day, how to manage his family, his farm, his merchandise, and to govern all the affairs of his hours. . . . It is the*

---

67. On this theme Joseph Smith taught

> *Salvation cannot come without revelation; it is in vain for anyone to minister without it.* No man is a minister of Jesus Christ except he has the testimony of Jesus; and this is the spirit of prophecy. (HC 3:389, July 2, 1839).

68. Joseph Smith explained,

> According to John, the testimony of Jesus is the spirit of prophecy; therefore, *if I profess to be a witness or teacher, and have not the spirit of prophecy, which is the testimony of Jesus, I must be a false witness;* but if I be a true teacher and witness, I must possess the spirit of prophecy, and that constitutes a prophet. (HC 5:215, January 1, 1843.)

right of an individual to get revelations to guide himself. It is the right of the head of a family to get revelations to guide and govern his family. It is the right of an elder when he has built up a church to get revelations to guide and lead that people until he leads them and delivers them up to his superiors.[69]

"By the power of the Holy Ghost ye may know the truth of all things."[70] A revealed testimony tells one those things upon which he may rely as truth. Oliver Cowdery, for instance, received a revealed witness concerning the truthfulness of the Book of Mormon manuscript which he had recorded as it was dictated by Joseph Smith. Concerning this witness the Lord revealed,

> Behold, I have manifested unto you, by my Spirit in many instances, that the things which you have written are true; wherefore you know that they are true.
> *And if you know that they are true, behold, I give unto you a commandment, that you rely upon the things which are written;*
> *For in them are all things written concerning the foundation of my church, my gospel, and my rock.*[71]

---

69. HC 7:285-6. October 6, 1844. Note that he is saying that the right to receive revealed confirmation of the truthfulness of the gospel is possessed by every person, even non-members of the Church. Wilford Woodruff recorded in his journal a discourse by Brigham Young which contained these instructions:

> *It is our duty to make every sacrifice (if it may be called a sacrifice) required of us by our Father in Heaven, that He and His holy angels may know our integrity. I see a thousand weaknesses in myself that I now regret, and it is with all those who have the spirit of God, and they will try to overcome them.* People may be guilty of various sins, and do you think they can be forgiven in a moment. No, every Latter-day Saint knows better. This would be sectarianism. The religion of the world is that a man may commit murder, and when on the gallows, he can repent and be forgiven and go straightway to Abraham's bosom. It is a false doctrine. It is not true. Some may say that they cannot overcome their passions when they are tempted and tried, they cannot help scolding, swearing, etc., but *I tell you they can help it, and must overcome it sooner or later or they cannot be saved. We should improve day by day, be a better man or woman tomorrow than we are today.* Mothers, when you are cross and attempt to correct your children, *conquer yourselves first.* Fathers, when you feel angry passions rise, then you need the grace of God to bring yourselves into subjection to Him that you may gain victory over your feelings. *Live so that you may have the revelations of God concerning you in all things—that you cannot be deceived.* When Sidney Rigdon claimed to be the leader of the people, the people knew not his voice. *Parents are under the greatest obligation to live their religion,* so also the young men and women, that when they marry and have a posterity their children may be born in holiness and righteousness, and it will then be hard to make anything out of them but Latter-day Saints. (Cowley, Mathias F., *Wilford Woodruff, op. cit.,* pp. 365-366.)

70. Moro. 10:5.

71. D&C 18:2-4.

The Danger of Blind Acceptance of Leaders and Doctrines

It is proper, and an absolute necessity, that Church members receive a revealed witness of gospel doctrines and of the inspired leadership of those who preside over them. This can only be done by study and questioning. Blind faith and acceptance without questioning is self-defeating, for it often prevents the occurrence of situations which cause a revealed witness to be given. Elder John A. Widtsoe explained this principle when he wrote,

> It seems to be the opinion of some that Latter-day Saints do not think, but accept the doctrines and follow the practices of the Church without an intelligent consideration of what they believe and do. There could not be a more unfounded and erroneous view.
>
> *The doctrine of the Church cannot be fully understood unless it is tested by mind and feelings, by intellect and emotions, by every power of the investigator. Every Church member is expected to understand the doctrine of the Church intelligently. There is no place in the Church for blind adherence.*
>
> *This is indispensable in a Church which rests upon the individual testimonies of its members, and in which there is no professional ministry.* Church government lies in the hands of the membership, every man of which may hold the priesthood. That requires *more than a blind following.*
>
> A Church member who does not study the gospel and try it out in his life is not really in good Church standing. Such a man cannot intelligently perform the work of the Church. With insufficient knowledge he sees things obliquely and obscurely. Indeed, he is a danger to the progress of the latter-day work.
>
> There is nothing new in this. *From the beginning of its history the Church has opposed unsupported beliefs.*[72]

---

72. Widtsoe, *Evidences and Reconciliations, Ibid.,* p. 226. In his discussion Elder Widtsoe pointed out that the Church has been given certain eternal laws which are unchangeable. He wrote,

> It is this open-eyed understanding of the gospel that makes the Latter-day Saints so certain of their faith. *A blind acceptance is an incomplete acceptance, and usually leaves a person in doubt. . . .*
>
> It must be understood that some Church practices rest upon unchangeable gospel principles. We may not always understand these, but no amount of argument can change them. The strength of the gospel lies in these eternal, undeviating laws. . . .
>
> All such queries, designed to question the propriety of the basic laws of the gospel, are a waste of time. Every future revelation of the Church will be in the nature of an extension of these spiritual foundation stones of the latter-day kingdom of the Lord. This is accepted open-eyes not blindly by Latter-day Saints. (*Ibid.* p. 227-228).

These eternal laws he contrasted with less fundamental practices in the Church which are subject to evaluation and change:

> However, there are practices within the Church of less fundamental nature.
>
> The Saints must gather in meetings. That is a divine commandment. But the time of the meetings is set by the people of the Church upon the

On another occasion Brigham Young cautioned the saints that they must not rely so heavily on the leadership of the Church that they cease to receive personal revelation:

> What a pity it would be if we were *led by one man to utter destruction!* Are you afraid of this? *I am more afraid that this people have so much confidence in their leaders that they will not inquire for themselves of God whether they are led by Him.* I am fearful they settle down in a state of blind self-security, trusting their eternal destiny in the hands of their leaders with a reckless confidence that in itself would thwart the purposes of God in their salvation, and weaken that influence they could give to their leaders, did they know for themselves, by the revelations of Jesus, that they are led in the right way. *Let every man and woman know, by the whispering of the Spirit of God to themselves, whether their leaders are walking in the path the Lord dictates, or not. This has been my exhortation continually.*[73]

Heber C. Kimball warned that "unless a man *knew* that Jesus was the Christ, he could not stand in this Church.["][74] The pattern of prophecy makes it abundantly clear that the "many close places" through which the Church must pass of which Heber C. Kimball warned, are not yet over. The saints still need a strong personal testimony:

> President Kimball opened by stating that there were many within hearing who had often wished that they had been associated with the Prophet Joseph. 'You imagine,' said he, 'that you would have stood by him when persecution raged and he was assailed by foes within and without. You would have defended him and been true to him in the midst of every trial. You think you would have been delighted to have shown your integrity in the days of mobs and traitors.

---

recommendation of the sustained leaders. There may in many cases be a justifiable difference of opinion as to the best time.

The Saints must study and learn. That is in the revelations to Joseph Smith. But the value of the various study courses provided by the different Church organizations may with propriety be discussed by all.

Whether tithing shall preferably be paid in kind or in cash, is a question dependent on existing circumstances. It is subject to lawful discussion.

Every open-eyed Latter-day Saint, who refuses to accept things blindly, will distinguish clearly between the fundamental and the derivative, the essential and the nonessential, in the program and practices of the Church.

Those who confuse the two are either immature, perhaps honest seekers after truth, or faultfinders, perhaps enemies of the Church.

But Latter-day Saints who sustain their leaders, are always willing to try out debatable regulations, before passing judgment on them, and then report their objections, if any, to the proper Church officers.

Latter-day Saints should not and do not accept Church doctrine blindly. (Ibid., p. 228).

73. JD 9:150. January 12, 1862.

74. Whitney, Orson F., *Life of Heber C. Kimball, op. cit.,* p. 441. This statement was made in 1856.

'Let me say to you, that many of you will see the time when you will have all the trouble, trial and persecution that you can stand, and plenty of opportunity to show that you are true to God and His work. *This Church has before it many close places through which it will have to pass before the work of God is crowned with victory. To meet the difficulties that are coming, it will be necessary for you to have a knowledge of the truth of this work for yourselves. The difficulties will be of such a character that the man or woman who does not possess this personal knowledge or witness will fall.* If you have not got the testimony, live right and call upon the Lord and cease not til you obtain it. If you do not you will not stand.

'Remember these sayings, for many of you will live to see them fulfilled. *The time will come when no man nor woman will be able to endure on borrowed light. Each will have to be guided by the light within himself. If you do not have it, how can you stand?* Do you believe it?

'How is it now? *You have the First Presidency, from whom you can get counsel to guide you, and you rely on them. The time will come when they will not be with you. Why? Because they will have to flee and hide up to keep out of the hands of their enemies. You have the Twelve now. You will not always have them, for they too will be hunted and will have to keep out of the way of their enemies.* You have other men to whom you look for counsel and advice. Many of them will not be amongst you, for the same reason. *You will be left to the light within yourselves. If you don't have it you will not stand; therefore seek for the testimony of Jesus and cleave to it, that when the trying time comes you may not stumble and fall.*'

The main object of the discourse was to impress the people with the importance of having light and knowledge from God within themselves. The prophetic part was given as the leading reason why they should be in possession of an individual testimony, as it defined to some extent the character of the trials to which the Saints would be subjected. That Brother Kimball's predictions have been, in part, at least, already fulfilled must be clear to all who are familiar with the events of the last few years. In the course of his remarks on the occasion in point he several times said: *'You will have all the persecution you want and more too, and all the opportunity to show your integrity to God and truth that you could desire.'*[75]

The Saints May Teach and Write by Inspiration and Wisdom, but May Not Command the Church

A series of commandments to Oliver Cowdery defines the role members of the Church are to play in teaching and writing on doctrinal matters. Concerning teaching, it says:

Thou shalt be heard by the church in all things whatsoever thou shalt teach them by the Comforter, concerning the revelations and commandments which I have given.[76]

---

75. *Ibid.,* pp. 449-451. This passage is an account of an 1867 discourse reported by Elder John Nicholson. Concerning the "you will be here when" statement, see p. 211.
76. D&C 28:1.

And also

> . . . Thou shalt be obedient unto the things which I shall give unto him, even as Aaron, to declare faithfully the commandments and the revelations, with power and authority unto the church.
> *And if thou art led at any time by the Comforter to speak or teach, or at all times by the way of commandment unto the church, thou mayest do it. . . .*
> And thou must open thy mouth at all times, declaring my gospel with the sound of rejoicing. Amen.[77]

Concerning that which was to be written, and the manner of writing, the revelation said,

> *Thou shalt not write by way of commandment, but by wisdom;*
> And *thou shalt not command him who is at thy head,* and at the head of the church;[78]

And also,

> Thou shalt cause my church to be established among them; and *thou shalt have revelations, but write them not by way of commandment.*[79]

Thus a pattern of what individual members of the Church can and cannot do is established by the Lord:

1. They *can* teach concerning the revelations and commandments already given, adding new insights they have received through personal revelation.
2. They *can* speak or teach by way of commandment unto the Church when led by the Comforter.
3. They *can* write by way of wisdom, but not by way of commandment.
4. They *can* have revelations.
5. They *cannot* write by way of commandment, even pertaining to the revelations they have received.
6. They *cannot* command the head of the Church.

In this era of "every member a missionary," every member of the Church holds the responsibilities of being personally prepared and of teaching those about .him. Concerning the teaching of His doctrine, the Lord has instructed the saints:

> I give unto you a commandment that *you shall teach one another the doctrine of the kingdom.*

---

77. D&C 28:3-4,16.
78. D&C 28:5-6.
79. D&C 28:8.

Teach ye diligently and my grace shall attend you, that you may be instructed more perfectly in theory, in principle, in doctrine, in the law of the gospel, in all things that pertain unto the kingdom of God, that are expedient for you to understand;[80]

He has also commanded:

As all have not faith, *seek ye diligently and teach one another words of wisdom;* yea, seek ye out of the best books words of wisdom; seek learning, even by study and also by faith.[81]

The commandments to teach one another relate particularly to warnings of the judgments of the last days:

---

80. D&C 88:77-78. Note that this passage, like D&C 97:14, divides the scope of gospel learning into categories:

(1) theory
(2) principle
(3) doctrine
(4) the law of the gospel
(5) all things that pertain unto the kingdom of God, that are expedient for you to understand.

By definition, the fifth of these categories is the *miscellaneous* area; the fourth refers to the *judicial system* of the Church and the commandments upon which it is based. *Doctrine,* the third area, deals with finite, specific teachings which can be documented in a pattern of instruction from the scriptures. A *principle* is formed from a combination of several doctrines. It is broader than a doctrine and represents a logical conclusion based on available evidence. It is regarded as a statement of truth, though it usually can't be documented from the scriptures except by documenting the doctrines upon which it is based. A *theory* is a hypothesis or tentative statement of how something is expected to be. It reaches beyond available evidence but is of great importance because it opens the way to new understandings. The line between a principle and a theory is often quite indefinite. *Note that the Lord commands the saints to teach theories as well as doctrines and principles.* This division of religious knowledge has often been diagrammed by the author as follows:

81. D&C 88:118.

Behold, I send you out to reprove the world of all their unrighteous deeds, and to *teach them of a judgment which is to come.*[82]

And,

> *. . . I say unto you, the rest of my servants, go ye forth as your circumstances shall permit, in your several callings, unto the great and notable cities and villages, reproving the world in righteousness of all their unrighteous and ungodly deeds, setting forth clearly and understandingly the desolation of abomination in the last days.*[83]

And also,

> *Behold, I sent you out to testify and warn the people, and it becometh every man who hath been warned to warn his neighbor. . . . and to prepare the saints for the hour of judgment which is to come;*
> That their soul may escape the wrath of God, the desolation of abomination which awaits the wicked, both in this world and in the world to come. Verily, I say unto you, let those who are not the first elders continue in the vineyard until the mouth of the Lord shall call them, for their time is not yet come; their garments are not clean from the blood of this generation.[84]

Before fulfilling these commandments to preach, the men of the Church are to "come in at the gate and be ordained."[85]

Just as they are to teach one another, the saints are also invited to strengthen the Church through writing. As was commanded to Oliver Cowdery, they should "not write by way of commandment, but by wisdom."[86] Their writings can be the source of good both to the saints and to themselves. Emma Smith, for instance, was commanded, *"Thy time shall be given to writing, and to learning much."*[87] John Whitmer was instructed to

> . . . Travel many times from place to place, and from church to church, that he may the more easily obtain knowledge—
> *Preaching and expounding, writing, copying, selecting, and obtaining all things which shall be for the good of the church,* and for the rising generations that shall grow up on the land of Zion. . . .[88]

Oliver Cowdery was told,

> Thou shalt continue in calling upon God in my name, and *writing the things which shall be given thee by the Comforter, and expounding all scriptures unto the church.*
> And it shall be given thee in the very moment what thou shalt speak and write, and they shall hear it.[89]

And what does it mean to write by wisdom? What can Latter-day Saint writers do that will further the Lord's work and strengthen their

---

82. D&C 84:87.
83. D&C 84:117.
84. D&C 88:81,84-85.
85. D&C 43:7.

86. D&C 28:8.
87. D&C 25:8.
88. D&C 69:7-8.
89. D&C 24:5-6.

brethren? Elder B. H. Roberts, on one occasion, expressed his observation that the "crying need" of the Church was for *"thoughtful disciples who will not be content with merely repeating some of its truths, but will develop its truths, and enlarge it by that development:"*

Disciples and partisans, in the world of religious and of philosophical opinion, are of two sorts. There are, first, the disciples pure and simple,—people who fall under the spell of a person or of a doctrine, and whose whole intellectual life thenceforth consists in their partisanship. *They expound, and defend, and ward off foes, and live and die faithful to the one formula.* Such disciples may be indispensable at first in helping a new teaching to get popular hearing, but *in the long run they rather hinder than help the wholesome growth of the very ideas that they defend: for great ideas live by growing, and a doctrine that has merely to be preached, over and over, in the same terms, cannot possibly be the whole truth.* No man ought to be merely a faithful disciple of any other man. Yes, no man ought to be a mere disciple even of himself. *We live spiritually by outliving our formulas,* and by thus enriching our sense of their deeper meaning. Now the disciples of the first sort do not live in this larger and more spiritual sense. They repeat. And true life is never mere repetition.

On the other hand, *there are disciples of a second sort.* They are men who have been attracted to a new doctrine by the fact that it gave expression, in a novel way, to some large and deep interest which had already grown up in themselves, and which had already come, more or less independently, to their own consciousness. They thus bring to the new teaching, from the first, their own personal contribution. The truth that they gain is changed as it enters their souls. The seed that the sower strews upon their fields springs up in their soil, and bears fruit, thirty, sixty, an hundred fold. They return to their master his own with usury. Such men are the disciples that it is worth while for a master to have. Disciples of the first sort often become, as Schopenhauer said, more magnifying mirrors wherein one sees enlarged, all the defects of a doctrine. *Disciples of the second sort co-operate in the works of the Spirit; and even if they always remain rather disciples than originators, they help to lead the thought that they accept to a truer expression. They force it beyond its earlier and cruder stages of development.*

I believe 'Mormonism' affords opportunity for disciples of the second sort; nay, that its crying need is for such disciples. It calls for thoughtful disciples who will not be content with merely repeating some of its truths, but will develop its truths; and enlarge it by that development. Not half—not one-hundredth part—not a thousandth part of that which Joseph Smith revealed to the Church has yet been unfolded, either to the Church, or to the world. The work of the expounder has scarcely begun. The Prophet planted by teaching the germ-truths of the great dispensation of the fulness of times. The watering and the weeding is going on, and God is giving the increase, and will give it more abundantly in the future as more intelligent discipleship shall obtain. The disciples of 'Mormonism,' growing discontented with the necessarily primitive methods which have hitherto prevailed in sustaining the doctrine, *will yet take profounder and broader views of the great doctrines committed to the Church; and, departing from mere repetition, will cast them in new formulas; co-operating in the works of the Spirit, until they help to give to the truths received a more forceful expression, and carry it beyond the earlier and cruder stages of its development.*[90]

President Hugh B. Brown expressed this same need for thoughtful discipleship in a talk to the studentbody of the Brigham Young University:

> We have been blessed with much knowledge by revelation from God which, in some part, the world lacks. *But there is an incomprehensibly greater part of truth which we must yet discover.* Our revealed truth should leave us stricken with the knowledge of how little we really know. It should never lead to an emotional arrogance based upon a false assumption that we somehow have all the answers—that we in fact have a corner on truth. For we do not.
>
> Whether you are in the field of economics or political science, history or the behavioral sciences—*continue your search for truth. And maintain humility sufficient to be able to revise your hypotheses as new truth comes to you by means of the spirit or the mind.* Salvation, like education, is an on-going process.
>
> *One may not attain salvation by merely acknowledging allegiance,* nor is it available in ready-to-wear stores or in supermarkets where it may be bought and paid for. *That it is an eternal quest must be obvious to all. Education is involved in salvation and may be had only by evolution or the unfolding or developing into our potential. It is in large measure a problem of awareness, of reaching out and looking up, of aspiring and becoming, pushing back our horizons, seeking for answers, and searching for God.*
>
> In other words, it is not merely a matter of conformity to rituals, climbing sacred stairs, bathing in sacred pools, or making pilgrimages to sacred shrines. *The depth and height and quality of life depends upon awareness, and awareness is a process of being saved from ignorance. Man cannot be saved in ignorance.*[91]

In the same discourse, he emphasized that Latter-day Saints are to "be unafraid to express your thoughts and to insist upon your right to examine every proposition:"

> One of the most important things in the world is freedom of the mind; from this all other freedoms spring. Such freedom is necessarily dangerous, for one cannot think right without running the risk of thinking wrong, but generally *more thinking is the antidote for the evils that spring from wrong thinking.* More thinking is required, and *we call upon you students to exercise your God-given right to think through on every proposition that is submitted*

---

90. Roberts, B. H., "Book of Mormon Translation—Interesting Correspondence on the Subject of the Manual Theory," *Improvement Era* (Salt Lake City, Utah: Young Men's Mutual Improvement Association, Church of Jesus Christ of Latter-day Saints), Vol, 9, pp. 712-713, 1905-1906. The first two paragraphs are a quotation drawn by Elder Roberts from the introduction to *Fiske's Work,* by Josiah Boyce.

91. "President Brown Addresses BYU," text of an address given by President Hugh B. Brown, first counselor in the First Presidency, May 13, 1969, on the BYU campus. (Salt Lake City, Utah: *Church News,* week ending May 24, 1969, p. 13.)

to you and be unafraid to express your opinions, with proper respect for those to whom you talk and proper acknowledgment of your own shortcomings.

You young people live in an age when freedom of the mind is suppressed over much of the world. *We must preserve it in the Church and in America and resist all efforts of earnest men to suppress it, for when it is suppressed, we might lose the liberties vouchsafed in the Constitution of the United States.*

Preserve, then, the freedom of your mind in education and in religion, and be unafraid to express your thoughts and to insist upon your right to examine every proposition. We are not so much concerned with whether your thoughts are orthodox or heterodox as we are that you shall have thoughts.[92]

The privilege of writing and teaching on gospel subjects is one of the most effective ways in which the saints can fulfill the Lord's admonition:

Verily I say, *men should be anxiously engaged in a good cause, and do many things of their own free will, and bring to pass much righteousness;*

For the power is in them, wherein they are agents unto themselves. And inasmuch as men do good they shall in nowise lose their reward.[93]

The Saints Are to Walk in Holiness Before the Lord— A "Worthiness" Requirement

As He admonished the saints to give heed to the words He would reveal through His Revelator, the Lord stipulated that they were to be *"walking in all holiness before me."* [94] The need for the membership to live worthy lives is often stated in the scriptures. For instance, the Savior has commanded that

The members shall manifest before the church, and also, before the elders by a godly walk and conversation, that they are worthy of it, that there may be works and faith agreeable to the holy scriptures—walking in holiness before the Lord.[95]

He has also commanded, "Let every man esteem his brother as himself, and practice virtue and holiness before me.[96]

That the saints must walk in holiness is part of the Lord's plan for their protection against being led astray by falsehood:

Ye are commanded in all things to ask of God, who giveth liberally; and *that which the Spirit testifies unto you even so I would that ye should do in all holiness of heart, walking uprightly before me, considering the end of your salvation,* doing all things with prayer and thanksgiving, that ye may not be seduced by evil spirits or doctrines of devils, or the commandments of men; for some are of men, and others of devils.

Wherefore, *beware lest ye are deceived.* [97]

Failure to walk in holiness and to keep the commandments of God leads to the spirit of criticism, which results in condemnation:

Who am I that made man, saith the Lord, that will hold him guiltless that obeys not my commandments?

92. *Ibid.*
93. D&C 58:27-28.
94. D&C 21:4.
95. D&C 20:69.
96. D&C 38:24.
97. D&C 46:7-8.

Who am I, saith the Lord, that have promised and have not fulfilled? I command and men obey not; I revoke and they receive not the blessing. Then they say in their hearts: This is not the work of the Lord, for his promises are not fulfilled. But wo unto such for their reward lurketh beneath, and not from above.[98]

The temptation to criticize the Church is one of Satan's most valued tools. He uses it at all levels of the Church, and it is a temptation against which the saints should be on guard. In an address to the Twelve, on July 2, 1839, Joseph Smith warned,

O ye Twelve! and *all Saints!* profit by this important Key—that in all your trials, troubles, temptations, afflictions, bonds, imprisonments and death, *see to it, that you do not betray heaven; that you do not betray the revelations of God, whether in the Bible, Book of Mormon, or Doctrine and Covenants, or any other that ever was or ever will be given and revealed unto man in this world or that which is to come.* Yea, in all your kicking and flounderings, see to it that you do not this thing, lest innocent blood be found upon your skirts, and you go down to hell. All other sins are not to be compared to sinning against the Holy Ghost, and proving a traitor to the brethren.

I will give you one of the Keys of the mysteries of the Kingdom. It is an eternal principle, that has existed with God from all eternity: *That man who rises up to condemn others, finding fault with the Church, saying that they are out of the way, while he himself is righteous, then know assuredly, that that man is in the high road to apostasy; and if he does not repent, will apostatize, as God lives.*[99]

---

98. D&C 58:30-33.

99. HC 3:385. Note that this address was actually instruction to the apostles, rather than to the Church at large, and that Joseph's intent was to warn of the danger of apostasy of Church leaders rather than the members at large. To be seen in proper perspective, this statement should be presented as a statement of that viewpoint. This speech was made shortly after the tragic apostasy of 1837-1838, which took a terrible toll of the membership and leadership of the Church. It is best understood in the light of the context which precedes it:

Ever keep in exercise the principle of mercy, and be ready to forgive our brother on the first intimations of repentance, and asking forgiveness; and should we even forgive our brother, or even our enemy, before he repent or ask forgiveness, our Heavenly Father would be equally as merciful unto us.

Again, let the Twelve and all Saints be willing to confess all their sins, and not keep back a part; and let the Twelve be humble, and not be exalted, and beware of pride, and not seek to excel one above another, but act for each other's good, and pray for one another, and honor our brother or make honorable mention of his name, *and not backbite and devour our brother.* Why will not man learn wisdom by precept at this late age of the world, when we have such a cloud of witnesses and examples before us, and not be obliged to learn by sad experience everything we know? *Must the new ones that are chosen to fill the places of those that are fallen, of the quorum of the Twelve, begin to exalt themselves, until they exalt themselves so high that they will soon tumble over and have a*

Four months earlier, on March 20, 1839, the following revelation was given through the prophet Joseph Smith, which shows the danger of the spirit of criticism:

> *Cursed are all those that shall lift up the heel against mine annointed saith the Lord, and cry they have sinned when they have not sinned before me,* saith the Lord, but have done that which was meet in mine eyes, and which I commanded them.
>
> *But those who cry transgression do it because they are the servants of sin, and are the children of disobedience themselves.*
>
> And those who swear falsely against my servants, that they might bring them into bondage and death—
>
> Wo unto them; because they have offended my little ones they shall be severed from the ordinances of mine house.
>
> *Their basket shall not be full, their houses and their barns shall perish, and they themselves shall be despised by those that flattered them.*
>
> *They shall not have right to the priesthood, nor their posterity after them from generation to generation.*
>
> *It had been better for them that a millstone had been hanged about their necks, and they drowned in the depth of the sea.*[100]

> *great fall, and go wallowing through the mud and mire and darkness, Judas like, to the buffetings of Satan, as several of the quorum have done, or will they learn wisdom and be wise? O God! give them wisdom, and keep them humble, I pray.*
>
> When the Twelve or any other witnesses stand before the congregations of the earth, and they preach in the power and demonstration of the Spirit of God, and the people are astonished and confounded at the doctrine, and say, 'That man has preached a powerful discourse, a great sermon,' then let that man or those men *take care that they do not ascribe the glory unto themselves, but be careful that they are humble, and ascribe the praise and glory to God and the Lamb; for it is by the power of the Holy Priesthood and the Holy Ghost that they have power thus to speak.* What art thou, O man, but dust? And from whom receivest thou thy power and blessings, but from God?
>
> Then O ye Twelve! notice this Key, and be wise for Christ's sake, and your own soul's sake. Ye are not sent out to be taught, but to teach. *Let every word be seasoned with grace. Be vigilant; be sober. It is a day of warning, and not of many words. Act honestly before God and man. Beware of Gentile sophistry; such as bowing and scraping unto men in whom you have no confidence. Be honest, open, and frank in all your intercourse with mankind.* (HC 3:383-4.)

100. D&C 121:16-22. The following description of the stages of apostasy was written by Susa Young Gates and published in the *Improvement Era:*

> There's the apostate now. He's a queer creature. Very queer! He has some remarkable notions. And *no matter who he is, or when he apostatized, he is all alike in some things. For instance, he always feels very much abused. No matter what has been done, or what left undone; your apostate, if he is the genuine article, feels that any number of people have been in league against him.* Of course, there are those who simply drift out of the Church through indifference or general neglect. And indifferent and neglectful they generally remain. Again, there are those who leave other

100. (Continued)

churches. But someway, such people never manifest the real apostate spirit. For they fail to manifest the infallible signs. Diagnose these cases, and the true symptoms will be found absent. *One apostatizes only from truth, not error.* But to return to our simon-pure apostate; for he generally turns on us. He not only feels he is abused, but in the abandonment of his self-piety he pictures whole co-horts of persons who have been conspiring for his overthrow. Symptom number one.

The next stage of his malady is exhibited when he begins to think he is twenty years ahead of the Church. The Church, according to him, is a good, old, doddering idiot, who has been a pretty fair specimen at one time, but now has lagged miles, leagues, eons behind your anxious apostate. If this—and but that—and perhaps in the days to come, if the Church can only be persuaded to get a hurry on itself—well, you know, it might be possible, in some dim and distant future for the poor old Church to catch the apostate and its own breath at the same time, and proudly linking arms with the soulful and condescending whilom apostate, together they might travel the comfortable broad way that leads to, you know where! Oh yes, and how graciously will your kingly apostate then forgive his long-time delinquent brethren, and how munificent will be his gifts, and self-applied donations; and how magniloquently will he pour out his healing eloquence to soothe all the wicked leaders who will then have repented and come bending and crawling to him. The picture of all this makes him weep in the night. And he weeps! Symptom number two!

Then this self-righteous individual, we are discussing, has another profound conviction: this usually is in the last stages of the complaint, and occurs about the time the officers have had to quarantine him; he resents being told of his affliction. It hurts his sensitive feelings to be told that he is an apostate. He is nothing of the kind! Don't you dare—. The story of the Indian here comes to mind, "Me no lost," grunts the wandering Lo, "me no lost, wickiup lost!" And that's the case with our impatient patient; he hasn't apostatized, not he! It's the Church that's apostatized! He has fought and bled all his life for the same things for which he is fighting and bleeding now, so to speak! He, the great, the good, the only, he apostatized? Perish the thought, and with it the four hundred and fifty thousand people who think the thought! And most of all, perish the local, stake or general authorities who are in the direct line of our apostate's vision. Down with the priesthood! Up with unbridled license! And thus ends sympton number three.

If the patient then gets the rabies, and goes out clothed with indignation and with flames bursting from his mouth, he is in the last stages of decomposition, and everybody should get out of the way. Keep out of the chamber of death and despair, unless duty calls you within. Then hang up all the disinfectants you can procure; be exceedingly careful of contagion, for the disease is said to be very catching for relatives and friends; cover up the malodorous remains of what was once a friend and brother, and depart as quickly as may be. Let us consign the rest to oblivion. *Dost like the picture? Then avoid the disease! (Improvement Era* (Salt Lake City, Utah: Young Men's Mutual Improvement Association, Church of Jesus Christ of Latter-day Saints), Vol. 8, pp. 463-465, 1904-1905.)

In this context, the counsel of Elder B. H. Roberts is appropriate:

> *I want to warn members of the Church against speaking lightly or slightingly of sacred things, or of the servants of God. In nothing, perhaps, can you more offend God or grieve his Spirit.* Have nothing to do, I pray you, with "smart" quips against the truth, however respectable their origins, or however popular or catchy their phraseology. I pray you give them no lodgment in your hearts. *Remember, we live under the law of God—Speak no evil of mine annointed; do my prophets no harm. And always that whatever the weakness they may have manifested before the Church in the past, or may manifest before it in the future (for the end is not yet) their weaknesses and imperfections affect not the truth that God has revealed.* The Lord will vindicate his truth, and at the last it will be found that,
>
> > 'Tis no avail to bargain, sneer, and nod
> > And shrug the shoulder for reply to God.
>
> *Remember also that ridicule is not argument; that a sneer, though it may not be susceptible of an answer, is no refutation of the truth; that though profane ribaldry may provoke a passing merriment, the profaner's 'laugh is a poor exchange for Deity offended.'* I therefore admonish you, as a friend and brother, to stand aloof from all these things. *Hold as sacred the truths of God; and hold in highest esteem, as indeed you may, those whom God has appointed to be his prophets, apostles and servants.*[101]

These statements deal with the fruits of unjust and unwarranted criticism of Church leaders. Certainly such criticism can have only an adverse effect upon those who participate in it.

On the other hand, these statements must never be allowed to become a shield for improper acts or unwise decisions by those in high positions. Just as the Lord instructed Oliver Cowdery to admonish Joseph Smith in his faults,[102] such admonition may be needed for others. It is the responsibility of their bishops or their brethren who preside over them to give Church leaders such admonition when needed. If an individual has a personal difference with one in authority, the procedure for resolving the problem is the same as a dispute with any other member, which is outlined by the Lord through revelation.[103] As was seen in the preceding chapter,[104] Church tribunals and action by the Committee of the Whole Church are the protection available to the saints if more serious problems arise. Backbiting, however, or anonymous criticism, or evil-speaking against the Lord's annointed are never proper means for solving problems which may arise within the Church.

---

101. Roberts, B. H., "Relation of Inspiration and Revelation to Church Government," *Improvement Era, op cit.,* Vol. 8, p. 370.
102. D&C 6:19.
103. See D&C 42:88-93.
104. See D&C 107:32, 35-37, 71-74, 77-84; also pp. 82-89.

There is also a place for constructive suggestions from the membership of the Church concerning Church policies, programs, curricula, and other matters. In government bureaucracies, the tendency is for officials to make more and more policies and rules, which tend to have a cumulatively adverse effect upon the citizenry. As the Church undergoes its rapid world-wide expansion, its staff is also growing at a rapid pace, with the attendant evils of red tape and bureaucracy an ever-present danger. The assumption should never be made that, because individuals are employed by the Church, their decisions are automatically inspired, correct, and infallible. More than ever, as the Church expands, it should be open and responsive to constructive suggestions and criticism from the general membership.

The Lord has given repeated warnings to the saints and the Church as to what will be their fate in the last days if they do not keep His commandments and walk in holiness before Him. He has revealed His warning that

> All they who receive the oracles of God, *let them beware how they hold them lest they are accounted as a light thing, and are brought under condemnation thereby, and stumble and fall when the storms descend,* and the winds blow, and the rains descend, and beat upon their house.[105]

Future Judgments Upon Unrighteous Saints Are Foretold.

In the "day of visitation and of wrath upon the nations," [106] when God's judgments are poured out, those judgments are to begin among the saints who have professed the name of God but have not known him, according to the Lord's revealed word:

> Behold, vengeance cometh speedily upon the inhabitants of the earth, a day of wrath, a day of burning, a day of desolation, of weeping, of mourning, and of lamentation; and as a whirlwind it shall come upon all the face of the earth, saith the Lord.

---

105. D&C 90:5.
106. D&C 56:1. The entire passage is a warning to the rebellious saints:

> Hearken, *O ye people who profess my name,* saith the Lord your God; for behold, *mine anger is kindled against the rebellious, and they shall know mine arm and mine indignation,* in the day of visitation and of wrath upon the nations.
> And he that will not take up his cross and follow me, and keep my commandments, the same shall not be saved.
> *Behold, I, the Lord, command; and he that will not obey shall be cut off in mine own due time, after I have commanded and the commandment is broken.*
> *Wherefore I, the Lord, command and revoke, as it seemeth me good; and all this to be answered upon the heads of the rebellious, saith the Lord.*
> (D&C 56:1-4.)

And upon my house shall it begin, and from my house shall it go forth, saith the Lord;

First among those among you, saith the Lord, who have professed to know my name and have not known me, and have blasphemed against me in the midst of my house, saith the Lord. [107]

Indeed, the Lord has warned His people,

Hearken, O ye people of my church, saith the Lord your God, and hear the word of the Lord concerning you—

The Lord who shall suddenly come to his temple; the Lord who shall come down upon the world with a curse to judgment; yea, upon all the nations that forget God, *and upon all the ungodly among you.* [108]

The gospel serves to bring either blessings or cursings upon the saints who will hear the Lord, and He has proclaimed this principle:

Hearken and hear, O ye my people, saith the Lord and your God, ye whom I delight to bless with the greatest of all blessings, ye that hear me; and *ye that hear me not will I curse, that have professed my name, with the heaviest of all cursings.* [109]

As early as 1832, the weaknesses of the saints caused the Lord to place a warning of possible future condemnation before the Church:

And your minds in times past have been darkened because of unbelief, and because you have treated lightly the things you have received—

Which vanity and unbelief have brought the whole church under condemnation.

---

107. D&C 112:24-26. In a discourse delivered August 25, 1844, Wilford Woodruff alluded to this prophecy as follows:

I have now one important declaration to make to you and that is that inasmuch as you have been anointed in heart, mind and action in supporting your counselors, the priesthood of God, the present authorities of the Church, as you have supported the Prophet while he was alive, you will be safe and you will be blessed. *You will also be protected, but if you are divided and reject the counsels of God, you will fall. Union and faithfulness are necessary for your salvation.* It is true that you have been led by one of the best men that ever graced humanity or tabernacled in the flesh, but he is gone, he sealed his testimony with his blood, he loved this people unto death.

I now call upon the people to be united in building upon the foundation which the Prophet laid during his lifetime. *You have been called to suffer much for the cause in which you are engaged, but if judgement begins at the House of God, Babylon will not escape.* If there is fire in the green tree, what shall happen to the dry tree. No people are better prepared for the shock that is coming to this world than are the Latter-day Saints. *The real object we have is to secure the blessings which lie beyond the veil and which will be found in the first resurrection. For these blessings we are preparing ourselves.* (*Wilford Woodruff, op cit.,* p. 229.)

108. D&C 133:1-2.
109. D&C 41:1. See also D&C 133:63-73.

And this condemnation resteth upon the children of Zion, even all.

And they shall remain under this condemnation until they repent and remember the new covenant, even the Book of Mormon and the former commandments which I have given them, not only to say, but to do according to that which I have written—

That they may bring forth fruit meet for their Father's kingdom; *otherwise there remaineth a scourge and judgment to be poured out upon the children of Zion.*

For shall the children of the kingdom pollute my holy land? Verily, I say unto you, Nay.[110]

The following year, the Lord again revealed his conditional warning:

Thus saith the Lord, let Zion rejoice, for this is Zion—THE PURE IN HEART; therefore, *let Zion rejoice, while all the wicked shall mourn.*

For behold, and lo, vengeance cometh speedily upon the ungodly as the whirlwind; and who shall escape it?

The Lord's scourge shall pass over by night and by day, and the report thereof shall vex all people; yea, it shall not be stayed until the Lord come;

For the indignation of the Lord is kindled against their abominations and all their wicked works.

Nevertheless, *Zion shall escape if she observe to do all things whatsoever I have commanded her.*

But if she observe not to do whatsoever I have commanded her, I will visit her according to all her works, with sore affliction, with pestilence, with plague, with sword, with vengeance, with devouring fire.

Nevertheless, let it be read this once to her ears, that I, the Lord, have accepted of her offering; and if she sin no more none of these things shall come upon her;

And I will bless her with blessings, and multiply a multiplicity of blessings upon her, and upon her generations forever and ever, saith the Lord your God. Amen.[111]

These judgments, if and when they come, will be associated with the fulfilling of the times of the Gentiles:[112]

And in that generation shall the times of the Gentiles be fulfilled.

And there shall be men standing in that generation that shall not pass until they shall see an *overflowing scourge; for a desolating sickness shall cover the land.*

But my disciples shall stand in holy places, and shall not be moved; but among the wicked, men shall lift up their voices and curse God and die.

And there shall be earthquakes also in divers places, and many desolations; yet men will harden their hearts against me, and they will take up the sword, one against another, and they will kill one another.[113]

110. D&C 84:54-59.
111. D&C 97:21-28.
112. See *Prophecy—Key to the Future*, pp. 18-20 for an explanation of this term.
113. D&C 45:30-33.

What can be done to avert these judgments? President Wilford Wood-ruff attempted to answer that question in a general epistle to the Church and to all the world which he wrote in 1879. After warning of the judgments to come upon the earth he wrote,

> You Latter-day Saints, do you know these things are true? You do, and so do I, for the spirit of God bears record, and the record is truth, and truth abideth forever. Under the circumstances, what manner of men and women ought we to be? *Are we prepared as a people for the great events which await us; which await both Zion and Babylon? Judge ye!* What is our duty as Saints of the living God? *It is our duty to humble ourselves before the Lord and call upon His name, until we are filled with the Holy Ghost and the spirit of inspiration, which is the light of Christ. Pay our tithes and offerings, keep the commandments of God and have faith in His word, remember and honor the ordinances we have observed,* and the covenants and obligations we have entered into in the holy places and temples of our God. *We should unite ourselves together in a temporal as well as in a spiritual point of view, as directed by the wise men of Israel. We should seek to build up the Kingdom and Zion of our God,* and not ourselves alone. When we do these things we are prepared as a people to let our prayers ascend into the ears of the Lord of Sabbaoth, and they will be heard and answered upon our heads. Again, this testament which Joseph Smith left contains a revelation and commandment from God, out of heaven, concerning the patriarchal order of marriage. *The Lord has commanded us to have our wives and children sealed to us, for time and eternity, that we may have them with us in our family organizations in the resurrection to dwell with us forever in the eternal worlds,* that we may have an increase of posterity forever in connection with Abraham, Isaac, Jacob, and all the ancient patriarchs. *I would say to all Israel, treat your wives and children kindly, and keep the commandments of God and trust in Him, and He will fight your battles.* And I will say, in the name of Jesus Christ, the Son of the living God, that "Mormonism" will live and prosper, Zion will flourish, and the *Kingdom of God will stand in power and glory and dominion as Daniel saw it, when this nation is broken to pieces as a potter's vessel and laid in the dust, and brought to judgment, or God never spoke by my mouth.* Therefore I say to all the Saints throughout the world, *be faithful and true to your God and to your religion, to your families and to yourselves.*[114]

Blessings Are Promised to the Faithful

While judgments and scourging are foretold upon the wicked and rebellious among the saints, blessings are promised to those who remain stalwart and faithful. In the first of the basic passages being considered in this chapter, the Lord revealed.

> Wherefore, meaning the church, thou shalt give heed unto all his words and commandments which he shall give unto you as he receiveth them, walking in all holiness before me;
> For his word ye shall receive, as if from mine own mouth, in all patience and faith.

114. Cowley, Matthias F., *Wilford Woodruff, op cit.*, pp. 508-9.

*For by doing these things the gates of hell shall not prevail against you;
yea, and the Lord God will disperse the powers of darkness from before you,
and cause the heavens to shake for your good, and his name's glory. . . .*
*For, behold, I will bless all those who labor in my vineyard with a mighty
blessing, and they shall believe on his words, which are given him through
me by the Comforter, which manifesteth that Jesus was crucified by sinful
men for the sins of the world, yea, for the remission of sins unto the contrite
heart.*[115]

Though the Church may yet pass through difficult times, the faithfulness of the saints during that period will ultimately be a source of rich blessings for them. So it has been before, and the principle remains unchanged.
The Lord has revealed,

Hearken, O ye elders of my church, and give ear to my word, and learn
of me what I will concerning this land unto which I have sent you.

For verily I say unto you, *blessed is he that keepeth my commandments,
whether in life or in death; and he that is faithful in tribulation, the reward
of the same is greater in the kingdom of heaven.*

Ye cannot behold with your natural eyes, for the present time, the design
of your God concerning those things which shall come hereafter, and the
glory which shall follow after much tribulation.

*For after much tribulation come the blessings. Wherefore the day cometh
that ye shall be crowned with much glory; the hour is not yet, but is nigh at
hand.*

*Remember this, which I tell you before, that you may lay it to heart,
and receive that which is to follow.*

Behold, verily I say unto you, for this cause I have sent you that you
might be obedient and that your hearts might be prepared to bear testimony of
the things which are to come.[116]

And also,

After much tribulation, as I have said unto you in a former commandment, cometh the blessings.

Behold, *this is the blessing which I have promised after your tribulations, and the tribulations of your brethren—your redemption, and the redemption of your brethren, even their restoration to the land of Zion,* to be
established, no more to be thrown down.[117]

In the last days, as throughout the history of God's dealings with His
children, the principle of receiving blessings through obedience to eternal
law remains:

115. D&C 21:4-6,9.
116. D&C 58:1-6.
117. D&C 103:12-13. Yet the Lord qualifies this promise in the next verse,
warning that, "Nevertheless, if they pollute their inheritances they shall be thrown
down; for I will not spare them if they pollute their inheritances. (D&C 103:14).

All who will have a blessing at my hands shall abide the law which was appointed for that blessing, and the conditions thereof, as were instituted from before the foundation of the world.

And as pertaining to the new and everlasting covenant, it was instituted for the fulness of my glory; and *he that receiveth a fulness thereof must and shall abide the law, or he shall be damned, saith the Lord God.*[118]

Summary

1. This chapter, like the preceding chapter, considers the system of checks and balances God has established to safeguard His Church. The preceding chapter discussed responsibilities placed on the Revelator. This chapter considers the duties and obligations of the general membership, as pertaining to revelations given to the Church through the Revelator.

2. The basic passages which define the relationship between the Revelator and the Saints, D&C 21:4-9, D&C 28:2-13, and D&C 43:1-7, provide much of the outline for this, as well as the preceding chapter.

3. When the Revelator brings forth revelation in conformance with the limitations God has revealed, an obligation for obedience is placed upon the saints. Blessings are promised in the scriptures to those who are obedient.

4. Disobedience to revealed commandments can retard the progress of the Lord's work and can cause the members of the Church to receive chastening and correction from the Lord.

5. It is to God's words revealed through the Revelator, rather than the Revelator himself, that the saints are commanded to give obedience. The responsibility of acceptance and adherance to the Revelator's other commentaries, writings, remarks, etc., is not placed upon the saints. Yet Church leaders are recognized as men of wisdom, experience, and good judgment, whose counsel deserves careful consideration.

6. General authorities are authorities in the sense of holding power to administer Church affairs. Their calling, however, does not necessarily make them authorities in the sense of superior doctrinal knowledge, outstanding knowledge of Church procedures, or increased reception of the promptings of the Spirit. The nature of their labors, however, affords them opportunity for greater growth in these areas than is commonly experienced by other Latter-day Saints.

7. The saints are to receive the revealed word of God in patience and faith. They are to "be not faithless, but believing." They are to place their confidence in the Revelator and to uphold him by the power of their faith and prayers.

---

118. D&C 132:5-6.

8. Today, with the rapid growth which the Church has experienced, few of the saints know the President of the Church personally. They must, and do, rely heavily on the expressions of testimony as to the quality and inspired nature of his leadership made by those who are intimately associated with him.

9. The Lord has revealed that He will *command* the Church through only one man at a time—His Revelator. The appointed Revelator is empowered to pass on this responsibility through the procedure of ordination and transmittal of keys. It is the faith of the saints that this power has been transmitted and rests in the current President of the Church.

10. In several passages, such as D&C 28:2 and 43:3, the Lord uses the words "revelations" and "commandments" as synonyms. Both words are used in the sense of "instructions to Church leaders and/or to the saints to perform duties for God."

11. To interpret the above passages to mean that revelation within the Church is given *only* to the Revelator is erroneous. Such an interpretation conflicts with many passages of scripture, and also with the revelatory practices of the Lord which are long established and recorded in the history of the Church. The sense of these passages is that God will *command* the saints through only one man at a time.

12. In D&C 28:2 it is indicated that modern Revelators are to receive the word of God "even as Moses." In Moses' day, others received revelation and prophesied as well as he did. However, when others attempted to establish themselves as the ones "appointed" to receive God's revelations for the people, they were punished by God. The parallel seems to be appropriate for today.

13. Two often quoted statements by Joseph Smith (HC 1:338 and HC 2:477) may be summarized as follows:

A. God's commandments to the Church are to come through the Presidency of the Church,

B. It is the privilege of any Church officer to receive revelation pertaining to his particular Church assignment, and

C. Church members will not receive revelation which consists of instructions for those in higher offices in the Church than they themselves hold.

While these instructions are valuable in matters of Church organization and government, they are not infallible rules by which men may discern who may receive revelation and who may not. When used in that manner, confusion is sometimes created, because revelations received by Church leaders and members have not always conformed to that outline.

14. There are many examples recorded in Church history which demonstrate that individuals in lesser positions of authority have received revealed

insights which have been accepted by those in higher positions, and also that others have received doctrinal or organizational insights before the President of the Church has received them. It is apparent that some commonly-held beliefs concerning who may receive revelations conflict with the actual evidence of how and to whom God reveals His will.

15. Prophecy does not conform to the usual patterns of revelation and often cannot be evaluated by the same criteria.

16. Confusion exists because some have failed to recognize what the basic scriptural passages concerning revelation to the Church do *not* say and have therefore drawn conclusions which contradict the evidence at hand. The basic passages do *not* say:

   A. only the President of the Church can receive revelation,
   B. a revelation is false if it is not revealed through the President of the Church,
   C. revelations which do not come from the President of the Church may not be regarded by Church members as revealed truth, and
   D. Church members who receive revelations are not to share them with other Church members.

17. The scriptures clearly assert that others besides the President of the Church are to receive revelation and that they are to bear witness of it.

18. Recipients of revelation within the Church are forbidden by the scriptures

   A. to represent themselves as the one "appointed" to receive revelation for the Church, and
   B. to put the revelation forth "by way of commandment."

19. Church members, through the Holy Ghost, may receive revelation which the Savior calls "scripture, . . .the will of the Lord, . . .the mind of the Lord, . . .the word of the Lord, . . .the voice of the Lord, and the power of God unto salvation." (D&C 68:4) Though such revelation represents truth, it is not binding upon the saints unless canonized by the vote of the Church assembled in conference. This is true both for revelations given to Church members and revelations given to the President of the Church.

20. The scriptural counsel concerning the sharing of revelations, manifestations, and faith-promoting experiences is to share them within, but not without, the Church. "Sacred" and "secret" are not synonyms. Many things are shared and yet retain their sacred character.

21. In the early decades of the restored Church, it was customary to share revelations and manifestations within the Church, and this practice was frequently encouraged by the example of Church leaders. Since the early decades of the twentieth century, however, a spirit of skepticism has been manifested within the Church, and many have become reluctant to share their faith-promoting experiences with others. This attitude of skep-

ticism and secrecy has perhaps served to quench the Spirit and to retard the outpouring of the spiritual gifts among the saints.

4

What Do the Scriptures Teach About Who Can Prophesy?

> *Salvation cannot come without revelation;* it is in vain for anyone to minister without it. *No man is a minister of Jesus Christ without being a prophet.* No man can be a minister of Jesus Christ except he has the testimony of Jesus; and *this is the spirit of prophecy.*[1]

This was the teaching of the prophet Joseph Smith as he described the vital role revelation must play in the life of every individual who seeks to serve the Lord Jesus Christ. The gift of prophecy is one of the choice spiritual gifts[2] promised by the Master for the benefit of those who love Him and seek to serve Him.[3] Indeed, the apostle Paul, who taught the saints to "covet earnestly the best gifts,"[4] gave preeminence to the gift of prophecy when he advised his flock to particularly seek the gift of prophecy[5] and emphasized that *"he that prophesieth edifieth the church."*[6] His message was that *"prophesying serveth not for them that believeth not, but for them which believe."*[7] As will be seen in this chapter, Paul clearly understood that prophecy was to be enjoyed and experienced by even the least of the saints, and that prophetic utterances were to be shared for the edification of the entire congregation.

It is unfortunate that confusion exists today in some areas concerning *who* can enjoy the gift of prophecy, and *how* that gift is to be regarded by its recipients. The tendency is sometimes manifested to prohibit or reject spiritual experiences which are not understood, accepting the lowest common denominator—of Church "activity" without the outpouring of the Spirit—as the proper level of Latter-day Saint life.

---

1. HC 3:389.
2. D&C 46:22.
3. D&C 46:9. See verses 7-30.
4. I Cor. 12:31.
5. I Cor. 14:1.
6. I Cor. 14:4.
7. I Cor. 14:22.

Misconceptions concerning who *can* and who *may* prophesy appear to
have increased in recent years, as various individuals have stressed different
points of Church procedure in their discourses and writings without showing all aspects of the doctrines involved. Frequently-heard comments in
Sunday School, Priesthood, and other Church classes seem to indicate the
pendulum of understanding has swung increasingly far away from essential
principles found in the scriptures.[8]

This chapter is written to clarify, from the scriptures, a series of doctrinal principles concerning who can prophesy. It is hoped that the passages
compiled will add balance and new insights to the understanding of the
saints on the subject.

Prophets Are Not Always Church Leaders

One important theme which is repeatedly set forth in the scriptures is
that the gift of prophecy is not related to Church position, but is rather a
blessing received by many lay members of the Church. By the same token,
whether or not a person holds a high calling in the Church is in no way
a valid test of the veracity of his prophecy.

Scriptural examples to demonstrate these points are many and varied.
Typical is the account of prophecies made by other individuals to Eli, the
priest, who lived in the final days of the judges of Israel. Eli was, presumably, the head of the Church for he was the priest and keeper of the tabernacle and "had judged Israel forty years."[9] His sons, Hophni and Phinehas,

---

8. One of the inevitable results of being an author of several books on LDS
themes is that telephone calls are frequently received in which questions are asked on
various doctrinal subjects. Those who call are often seeking insights to resolve
questions that have arisen in various Church classes, or are attempting to resolve
difficulties on doctrine which have arisen in their area. This author has used the
utmost care to avoid any involvement in those doctrinal disagreements, all of which
are beyond his area of jurisdiction and personal responsibility. Yet the frequency
of calls on questions related to matters of revelation clearly indicates that many
Church members have questions and misunderstandings in this area, and that
counsel given by various individuals is sometimes in direct conflict with the scriptures.

9. I Sam. 5:18. The actual existence of the Church among the Old Testament
Israelites must be acknowledged. They had a definite, clearly-defined form of
worship which they had received by revelation through a prophet, religious law to
which they rendered obedience and by which they were governed and judged, and a
covenant relationship with their God, Jehovah. The Abrahamic covenant, under
which the Church still functions today, promised that *"they shall bear this ministry
and priesthood"* (Abra. 2:9), that those who received the Gospel would be adopted
into their race and be accounted the seed of Abraham (Abra. 2:10), and that through
the Israelite lineage all the families of the earth would receive "the blessings of the
Gospel, which are the blessings of salvation, even of life eternal." (Abra. 2:11.)

were also priests, though they were wicked.[10] Eli held power and authority from God, and was able to grant blessings in the name of diety.[11] Yet others prophesied *to* Eli, the Church leader.

An unidentified "man of God" came and rebuked Eli for failing to chastize his errant sons. He prophesied judgments upon the house of Eli, the death of both his sons, and that the Lord would raise up priests from another lineage to lead his people.[12] The man of God's identity is unknown, but he did not stand as the leader of the Church, for that presumably was Eli's calling. A short time later, the Lord spoke to another individual, the young child Samuel, who repeated the prophecy he received to Eli:

> Behold, *I will do a thing in Israel, at which both the ears of every one that heareth it shall tingle.*
> *In that day I will perform against Eli all things which I have spoken concerning his house;* when I begin, I will also make an end.
> For I have told him that *I will judge his house for ever for the iniquity which he knoweth; because his sons made themselves vile, and he restrained them not.*
> And therefore I have sworn unto the house of Eli, that the iniquity of Eli's house shall not be purged with sacrifice nor offering for ever.[13]

In this instance, God used both an unidentified man and a small child as the spokesmen for prophecies which ultimately affected both a leader of the Church and the people at large. It should be noted that the Lord used the law of witnesses in this instance. Two separate individuals prophesied the same message to Eli.[14]

Later, while Samuel ruled as the head of the Church and as judge of Israel, a young man, Saul, was chosen to be a future king of Israel. As Saul journeyed with his servant,

> *A company of prophets met him, and the Spirit of God came upon him, and he prophesied among them.*
> And it came to pass, when all that knew him before time saw that, behold, *he prophesied among the prophets,* then the people said one to another, What is this that is come unto the son of Kish? Is Saul also among the prophets?[15]

---

10. They were "sons of Belial," or "worthless, lawless fellows." (I Sam. 2:12.) Among their sins was the committing of whoredoms with the harlots of Israel (I Sam. 2:22).

11. See I Sam. 1:17-20, in which Eli promised the barren mother of Samuel a son by the power of God.

12. I Sam. 2:27-36. Eli was a descendant of Ithamar, Aaron's youngest son. Years later, in fulfillment of this prophecy, the right to be high priest was taken from his line and restored to the line of Eleazar, the elder son of Aaron, through Zadok's appointment by King Solomon (I Ki. 2:35).

13. I Sam. 3:11-14. See verses 1-20.

14. See Jn. 8:17; Deut. 19:15; Mt. 18:16; II Cor. 13:1; D&C 6:28; D&C 128:3; Deut. 17:6; Num. 35:30; Heb. 10:28; I Tim. 5:19; D&C 42:80.

15. I Sam. 10:10-11.

In this instance Saul was able to prophesy, though he wasn't the leader of the Church.

Another prophetic incident of significance occurred during David's reign as king of Israel. After David's sin with Bathsheba and Uriah the Hittite, the Lord rebuked him through the prophet Nathan. Among other prophecies, Nathan warned David of the Lord's promise, "I will raise up evil against thee out of thine own house. . . ."[16] A second witness also prophesied against David. The man was Shimei, a descendant of Saul. Shimei challenged David on the road, and prophesied that "the Lord hath delivered the kingdom into the hand of Absalom thy son; and, behold thou art taken in thy mischief, because thou art a bloody man."[17] Again the Lord supported his word according to the law of witnesses; again men who were not the leaders of the Church[18] made prophecies of events which ultimately affected the entire nation.

An assumption frequently made is that the authors of the prophetic books of the Old Testament were the constituted authorities of the Church in their eras. This, however, was not always the case. Some of them were even considered rebels by the religious leaders of Israel in their days. Jeremiah was one such prophet who stood outside of the Church. The established Church, through its priests, even attempted to put Jeremiah to death.[19] Micah, Amos, Hosea and Zephaniah were also prophets who were critical of corruption within the Church.

These Old Testament prophets did not speak as representing the church, but as representing the Lord. Though the prophets may have held the higher priesthood authority,[20] there is no Biblical indication that the general church membership of that time was aware of it.

---

16. II Sam. 12:11. See verses 1-14.
17. II Sam. 16:8. See verses 5-12.
18. Nathan was not the high priest; Zadok was the high priest. See II Sam. 8:15-17. Abiathar also served as high priest in the early days of David's reign, but he allied himself with rebels during the rebellion of Adonijah while Zadok remained faithful (I Ki. 1:7-8, 24-26).

In fulfillment of their prophecies, Absalom captured Jerusalem and David was an outcast for a short time until Absalom fell in battle (II Sam. 17, 18).
19. Jer. 26:8-11.
20. Joseph Smith, on one occasion, is reported to have given this answer to the question, "Was the Priesthood of Melchizedek taken away when Moses died?":

All Priesthood is Melchizedek, but there are different portions or degrees of it. That portion which brought Moses to speak with God face to face was taken away; but that which brought the ministry of angels remained. *All the prophets had the Melchizedek priesthood and were ordained by God himself.* (Smith, Joseph Fielding, comp., *Teachings of the Prophet Joseph Smith* (Salt Lake City, Utah: The Deseret News Press, 1938), pp. 180-181. No original source is given.)

Many times the Lord spoke through the prophets to rebuke the established church which was still conveying the Priesthood authority.[21] They were regarded as spokesmen of God by the righteous, but as enemies and nuisances by the wicked priestly officials. Hireling prophets were engaged to counter their words. Many times the people of Israel were unable to discern which prophets were foretelling the truth.[22]

Jeremiah spoke in strong words against the corrupt church and its hireling prophets, giving this warning to the people:

> Thus saith the Lord of hosts, *Hearken not unto the words of the prophets that prophesy unto you:* they make you vain: *they speak a vision of their own heart, and not out of the mouth of the Lord.*[23]

Hosea also spoke out against the false prophets entrenched within the Church, saying,

> The days of visitation are come, the days of recompence are come; Israel shall know it: *the prophet is a fool, the spiritual man is mad, for the multitude of thine iniquity, and the great hatred.*
> The watchman of Ephraim was with my God: but *the prophet is a snare of a fowler in all his ways, and hatred in the house of his God.*
> *They have deeply corrupted themselves, . . .*[24]

Micah commented on the low caliber of the church officials in his day, and how they, though being evil, still insisted that God was with them:

> The heads thereof judge for reward, and the priests thereof teach for hire, and the prophets thereof divine for money: *yet will they lean upon the Lord, and say, Is not the Lord among us? none evil can come upon us.*[25]

And Zephaniah observed, concerning the church in Jerusalem, that

> *Her prophets are light and treacherous persons:* her priests have polluted the sanctuary, they have done violence to the law.[26]

These passages are cited in this context only to show that in some periods of Old Testament history, the prophets we recognize and study today were not the church leaders, but instead were outspoken critics of corrupt practices and officials within the church.[27]

---

21. Joseph Smith taught, for instance, that "the Levitical Priesthood is forever hereditary—fixed on the head of Aaron and his sons forever, and *was in active operation down to Zachariah the father of John.*" Smith, Teachings (*Ibid.,* p. 319. Original source listed only as "MSS. Historian's Office.")

22. See, for instance, Jer. 28.

23. Jer. 23:16.

24. Hos. 9:7-9.

25. Mi. 3:11.

26. Zeph. 3:4.

27. Their messages concerning the danger of prophets leading people astray will be considered in detail later in this book. See chapter 9.

These prophets represented the avenue of communication with God, while the priests within the church represented the ritualistic elements of daily living to the people and continued the line of priesthood authority. The prophets were regarded with varying degrees of respect as the righteousness of the church membership fluctuated.

The Book of Mormon also depicts some of the prophets as being individuals who were not church leaders. For instance, the following is recorded concerning Gidgiddoni, a Nephite general who utilized the gift of prophecy during the era when Nephi was the head of the Church:

> Now it was the custom among all the Nephites to appoint for their chief captains, (save it were in their times of wickedness) some one that had the spirit of revelation and also prophecy; therefore, this Gidgiddoni was a great prophet among them, as also was the chief judge.
>
> Now the people said unto Gidgiddoni: Pray unto the Lord, and let us go up upon the mountains and into the wilderness, that we may fall upon the robbers and destroy them in their own lands.
>
> But Gidgiddoni saith unto them: The Lord forbid; for if we should go up against them the Lord would deliver us into their hands; therefore we will prepare ourselves in the center of our lands, and we will gather all our armies together, and we will not go against them, but we will wait till they shall come against us; therefore as the Lord liveth, if we do this he will deliver them into our hands. [28]

Many more examples could be cited from the scriptures to show that prophets, in ancient times, were not always Church leaders. These, presumably, are sufficient to make the point. Church position is not the test by which the validity of prophecy is measured.

Prophets Were Not Always Apostles in New Testament Times

The same pattern of prophets sometimes being separate from the heads of the church, found in the Old Testament, also appears in the New Testament. In the early Christian Church, the prophets were consistently listed as separate officials, subordinate to the apostles but still with a high calling.

Paul, while writing to the Corinthian saints, clearly emphasized this differentiation:

> Now ye are the body of Christ, and members in particular.
>
> And God hath set some in the church, first apostles, secondarily prophets, thirdly teachers, after that miracles, then gifts of healings, helps, governments, diversities of tongues.
>
> Are all apostles? are all prophets? are all teachers? are all workers of miracles?
>
> Have all the gifts of healing? do all speak with tongues? do all interpret?
>
> But covet earnestly the best gifts: and yet shew I unto you a more excellent way. [29]

28. 3 Ne. 3:19-21.
29. I Cor. 12:27-31.

In his epistle to the Ephesians he again separated the functions of apostle and prophet, saying that Christ *"gave some, apostles; and some, prophets; and some, evangelists; and some pastors and teachers. . . ."*[30] He also wrote that the Ephesian saints were "built upon the foundation of the apostles *and* prophets. . . ."[31]

The prophetic and apostolic functions are also considered as separate in the Revelation of St. John. While speaking of the future fall of a great and evil city in the last days the scripture says:

> Rejoice over her, thou heaven, and ye holy apostles *and* prophets; for God hath avenged you on her.[32]

Instances in the Book of Acts show that the prophets were not necessarily apostles in New Testament times, yet their prophecies were held in high regard by the Church. While Paul was at Antioch, prior to his first missionary journey, the following occurred:

> And in these days came *prophets* from Jerusalem unto Antioch.
> And there *stood up one of them named Agabus, and signified by the spirit that there should be great dearth throughout all the world: which came to pass* in the days of Claudius Caesar.
> Then came the disciples, every man according to his ability, determined to send relief unto the brethren which dwelt in Judaea:
> Which also they did, and sent it to the elders by the hands of Barnabas and Saul.[33]

The identity of the apostles of that era is known, and Agabus was not one of them. Yet he prophesied an event of world-wide importance. And though he was not a Church leader, the saints in Antioch acted upon his prophecy and immediately began to collect articles to aid those at Jerusalem whom they knew would suffer hardships because of the famine.

Years later the same prophet foretold Paul's imprisonment at Jerusalem. This was an instructive situation, for in this instance a prophecy was made by a man who was not a general authority, rather than by the apostle himself, telling the fate of the general authority:

> And as we tarried there many days, there came down from Judaea *a certain prophet, named Agabus.*
> And when he was come unto us, he took Paul's girdle, and bound his own hands and feet, and said, *Thus saith the Holy Ghost, So shall the Jews at Jerusalem bind the man that owneth this girdle, and shall deliver him into the hands of the Gentiles.*

---

30. Eph. 4:11.
31. Eph. 2:20. See also 3:5.
32. Rev. 18:20. This same pattern of separation appears in the Doctrine and Covenants. See D&C 52:9, 36; 64:39; 98:32.
33. Acts 11:27-30.

And when we heard these things, both we, and they of that place, besought him not to go up to Jerusalem.

Then Paul answered, What mean ye to weep and to break mine heart? for I am ready not to be bound only, but also to die at Jerusalem for the name of the Lord Jesus.

And when he would not be persuaded, we ceased, saying, *The will of the Lord be done.*[34]

Others who were not among the authorities of the Church were recognized as prophets by the New Testament saints. Judas and Silas were prophets,[35] though not among the twelve. Barnabas, Simeon Niger, Lucius of Cyrene, and Manaen (the foster brother of Herod the tetrarch) were prophets and teachers in Antioch. The Lord spoke through them to call the apostles Barnabas and Saul on their first missionary journey.[36] The four young daughters of Philip the evangelist also were blessed with the ability to prophesy.[37]

Thus the pattern is repeated. People who were not church leaders were accepted as being prophets of the Lord. They foretold future events of worldwide consequence and the saints acted on their prophecies; they prophesied events in the life of a church leader rather than that authority receiving the revelation himself. These scriptural events are far broader than the narrow doctrinal confines some today assert concerning who can and may prophesy in the name of the Lord.

Many Prophets May Function at One Time

Another principle taught in the scriptures is that God may use a number of prophets at the same time. The scriptures in many instances refer to groups of prophets or tell of various prophets whose messages are heard during the same era. For example, in Moses' day, seventy of the elders of Israel prophesied.[38] Samuel prophesied to Saul that he should meet "a *company* of prophets."[39] During Ahab's wicked reign as king of Israel, "When Jezebel cut off the prophets of the Lord, . . . Obadiah took *an hundred prophets* and hid them by fifty in a cave."[40]

The plural nature of the prophetic calling is frequently stressed in the scriptures. Thus, prophet*s* accompanied King Josiah as he read from the

---

34. Acts 21:10-14. Paul, however, had some intimation of a future time of imprisonment. See Acts 20:22-23.
35. Acts 15:32.
36. Acts 13:1-3.
37. Acts 21:8-9.
38. Num. 11:25-29.
39. I Sam. 10:5, 10-11.
40. I Ki. 18:4, 13.

book of the covenant;[41] the Lord sent prophets to turn Judah from idolatry following the death of Jehoiada;[42] and in the days of King Zedekiah of Judah the people "mocked the messengers of God, and despised his words, and misused his prophets until the wrath of the Lord arose against his people."[43] Amos spoke the word of the Lord when he said, "I raised up of your sons for prophets, and of your young men for Nazarites. Is it not even thus, O ye children of Israel? saith the Lord."[44] As Zerubbabel and his followers labored to rebuild the wall of Jerusalem, "the prophets of God [were] helping them."[45] Paul gave instruction to *"Let the prophets speak two or three"*[46] in the meetings of the Corinthian saints. James spoke of "my brethren, the prophets."[47]

Scriptural prophecies of the last days indicate that there will be various prophets laboring simultaneously in a period yet future, also. John the Revelator foresaw a time when two prophets would be slain and lie in the streets of Jerusalem.[48] He also spoke of a time of destruction of a great city, and saw that it will be a time of rejoicing for prophets.[49] Through the prophet Joel the Lord spoke of a future period following a great battle, presumably the Battle of Armageddon, and promised:

> It shall come to pass afterward, that I will pour out my spirit upon all flesh; and *your sons and your daughters shall prophesy,* your old men shall dream dreams, your young men shall see visions:
> And also upon the servants and upon the handmaids in those days will I pour out my spirit.
> And I will shew wonders in the heavens and in the earth . . .[50]

The message of the scriptures, then, is that God in His wisdom has chosen to inspire many men as prophets at the same time. These prophets often prophesy the same thing, for the Lord uses many witnesses to establish and proclaim His truths. Just as all the prophets have spoken of Christ,[51] their testimonies have combined and do combine to proclaim events of the future.

---

41. II Ki. 23:2.
42. II Chron. 24:19.
43. II Chron. 36:16.
44. Amos 2:11.
45. Ezra 5:2.
46. I Cor. 14:29. See also Acts 11:27-28; 15:32; 13:1.
47. Jas. 5:10.
48. Rev. 11:3-12.
49. Rev. 18:20.
50. Joel 2:28-30.
51. See Jac. 7:11; Hel. 8:19-20; 3 Ne. 7:10; 1:10, etc.

Individual Church Members May Prophesy

The ability to prophesy is one of the most important of the spiritual gifts. As such it stands among the list of manifestations of the Spirit "given to *every man* to profit withal."[52] Paul placed a high premium on the gift of prophecy, for he wrote to the Corinthian saints to "follow after charity, and desire spiritual gifts, *but rather that ye may prophesy.*"[53] He also wrote, "I would that ye all spake with tongues, but *rather that ye prophesied. . . ,*"[54] and also, "Brethren, *covet to prophesy.*"[55] It should be noted that all these admonitions were written by Paul to recent converts in the new young branch established in Corinth, not to saints long established in the Church. To the saints at Rome Paul also gave counsel concerning the gift of prophecy, telling them that "having then gifts differing according to the grace that is given to us, whether prophecy, *let us prophesy according to the proportion of faith. . . .*"[56]

Thus the ability to prophesy is one of the most choice of the spiritual gifts, and presumably one to which Paul had reference when he instructed the saints to "covet earnestly the best gifts."[57] That person who enjoys the companionship and guidance of the Holy Ghost will prophesy, upon occasion, for the Lord Himself promised that the Spirit "will shew you things to come."[58]

Moses, when he found Joshua wanting to forbid Eldad and Medab from prophesying among the Israelites, rebuked Joshua, and clearly asserted his understanding that the gift of prophecy should be available to all God's children:

> And Moses said unto him, Enviest thou for my sake? *would God that all the Lord's people were prophets, and that the Lord would put his spirit upon them!*[59]

---

52. I Cor. 12:7. Paul also wrote that "every man hath his proper gift of God, one after this manner, and another after that." (I Cor. 7:7.) While revealing the nature of spiritual gifts in the latter days, the Lord said,

> For all have not every gift given unto them; for there are many gifts, and to every man is given a gift by the Spirit of God.
> To some is given one, and to some is given another, that all may be profited thereby. (D&C 46:11-12.)

In his treatment of spiritual gifts, Moroni wrote that "all these gifts come by the Spirit of Christ; and *they come unto every man severally*, according as *he* will." (Moro. 10:17.)

53. I Cor. 14:1.
54. I Cor. 14:5.
55. I Cor. 14:39.
56. Ro. 12:6.
57. I Cor. 12:31.
58. Jn. 16:13.
59. Num. 11:29. See verses 24-30.

Note that the same problem existed in Moses' day as sometimes occurs today—over-zealous followers attempt to limit to the leader of the Church a gift and ability to which all the saints are entitled.

Concerning the privilege of every man to prophesy, Joseph Smith's statement, cited earlier in this chapter, should be recalled:

> *Salvation cannot come without revelation; it is in vain for anyone to minister without it. No man is a minister of Jesus Christ without being a Prophet.* No man can be a minister of Jesus Christ except he has the testimony of Jesus; and this is the spirit of prophecy.[60]

On another occasion, while answering a series of questions, Joseph commented on the query "Do you believe Joseph Smith, Jun., to be a Prophet?" with the answer:

> Yes, *and every other man who has the testimony of Jesus.* For the testimony of Jesus is the spirit of prophecy.—Revelation, xix:10th verse.[61]

Wilford Woodruff also emphasized the same principle, saying

> *Anybody is a prophet who has the testimony of Jesus Christ, for that is the spirit of prophecy. The Elders of Israel are prophets.* A prophet is not so great as an Apostle. Christ has set in his Church, first, Apostles; they hold the keys of the kingdom of God.[62]

Sharing Prophecies and Revelations

The instructions Paul wrote to the branch of the Church at Corinth give explicit directions concerning how prophecies, revelations and spiritual experiences received by individual members should be regarded. It should be recalled that his epistle was written to a new branch, only about four years old, and located many hundreds of miles from the center of the Church. Paul wrote that

> *He that prophesieth edifieth the church.* . . . . greater is he that prophesieth than he that speaketh with tongues, except he interpret, *that the church may receive edifying.*[63]

Again, the apostle asked,

> What shall I profit you, except I shall speak to you either *by revelation,* or by knowledge, *or by prophesying*, or by doctrine?[64]

---

60. HC 3:389. July 2, 1839. His statement is based on I Cor. 12:3.

61. HC, 3:38. May 8, 1838. He made repeated comments to this effect. See HC, 5:215-16; 5:427; 5:516.

62. JD, 13:165. Dec. 12, 1869.

63. I Cor. 14:4-5. How can the Church be edified by prophecy or revelation unless the prophecy or revelation be shared?

64. I Cor. 14:6.

And also,

> But *if all prophesy, and there come in one that believeth not, or, one unlearned, he is convinced of all,* he is judged of all:
> And thus are the secrets of his heart made manifest; and so falling down on his face he will worship God, and report that God is in you of a truth.[65]

His instruction concerning the meetings of the saints was the following:

> How is it then, brethren? when ye come together, *every one of you hath a psalm, hath a doctrine, hath a tongue, hath a revelation, hath an interpretation.* Let all things be done unto edifying.[66]

In the above passages, Paul is apparently saying that prophecies and revelations which Church members have received are to be shared with one another by the saints, and that they are fit subjects for Church gatherings and discourses. Paul clearly expected that a sizeable number of the members of the congregation would receive such manifestations. His counsel was

> Let the prophets speak two or three, and let the other judge.
> *If any thing be revealed to another* that sitteth by, let the first hold his peace.
> *For ye may all prophesy one by one, that all may learn and all may be comforted.*
> *And the spirits of the prophets are subject to the prophets.*[67]

As was previously seen,[68] the instruction to share manifestations received is frequently repeated in the Doctrine and Covenants and is the counsel of the Lord, revealed in the scriptures in the latter days as it was in New Testament times.

Words of caution have been expressed in the scriptures concerning the sharing of prophecies and manifestations, however. *First,* prophecies revealed within the Church should be kept among the saints. As Paul wrote, "Prophesying serveth not for them that believe not, but for them which believe."[69] The Lord in the last days, has commanded, "Make not thy gift known unto any *save it be those who are of thy faith.*"[70]

---

65. I Cor. 14:24-25.
66. I Cor. 14:26.
67. I Cor. 14:29-32.
68. See pp. 113-119.
69. I Cor. 14:22.
70. D&C 6:12. Joseph Smith commented on this theme in these words:
> Some people say I am a fallen Prophet, because I do not bring forth more of the word of the Lord. Why do I not do it? Are we able to receive it? No! Not one in this room. He then chastened the congregation for their wickedness and unbelief, "for whom the Lord loveth he chasteneth, and scourgeth every son and daughter whom he receiveth," and if we do not receive chastisements then we are bastards and not sons.

Second, many people are given a revealed glimpse of future events but they fail to seek and fully understand the meaning and interpretation of what they have seen.[71] Joseph Smith gave counsel on this matter. He said, "When you see a vision, pray for the interpretation; *if you get not this, shut it up; there must be certainty in this matter.* An open vision will manifest that which is more important."[72] The saints should be careful not to share items for which they do not have a revealed understanding, and should be even more careful not to link an uninspired interpretation to a manifestation that has been received.

Third, in rare instances[73] the Lord, as part of a manifestation, will reveal the instruction that portions of it are not to be shared with others. Certainly such instructions should be faithfully heeded. However, careful study of the scriptures and of numerous manifestations recorded throughout the history of the Church clearly shows that revealed instructions to keep personal revelations secret are quite infrequent. They are the exception, the rare exception, not the rule. Generally, there is no reason for secrecy. It is interesting to read the discourses, biographies, and histories of early Church leaders and members and to see how readily they shared their personal faith-promoting experiences and the manifestations granted unto them. Various collections of such items were also made and circulated throughout the Church, both privately and under the direction of Church authorities. Church leaders frequently told of their personal experiences and manifestations as they spoke in local and general conferences, and in their various writings.

But somehow, in recent years, two words have been accepted as synonyms by some Latter-day Saints which are very different in meaning.

On the subject of revelation, he said, a man would command his son to dig potatoes and saddle his horse, but before he had done either he would tell him to do something else. This is all considered right; but as soon as the Lord gives a commandment and revokes that decree and commands something else, then the Prophet is considered fallen. *Because we will not receive chastisement at the hands of the Prophets and Apostles, the Lord chastiseth us with sickness and death.* Let not any man publish his own righteousness, for others can see that for him; sooner let him confess his sins, and then he will be forgiven, and he will bring forth more fruit. When a corrupt man is chastised he gets angry and will not endure it. *The reason we do not have the secrets of the Lord revealed unto us, is because we do not keep them but reveal them; we do not keep our own secrets, but reveal our difficulties to the world, even to our enemies, then how would we keep the secrets of the Lord?* I can keep a secret till Doomsday. (HC, 4:478-79. Dec. 19, 1841.)

71. See, for example, the dreams granted to Nebuchadnezzar, Pharoah, the baker and the butler, mentioned on pp. 159-160.

72. HC, 3:391. July 2, 1839.

73. See 3 Ne. 17:15; 28:25; Eth. 3:27-4:5; II Cor. 12:4.

The two words, "sacred" and "secret," are far apart in their implications. To hold and regard something as "sacred" in no way requires that it be kept a "secret." Something "sacred" is something which is dedicated to God, worthy or reverence, and holy. Our chapels are sacred edifices, but that does not mean that our attendance there requires secrecy. The scriptures are sacred, but that does not mean that we must read them and discuss them in secret. The name of God is sacred, but that does not mean we cannot address Him. Revelations from God are also sacred because of their source, but that does not mean that they cannot be shared for the edification of others. "Sacred" does not mean "secret," and those who have represented the two words as being synonyms, thus quenching the flow of enlightening and faith-promoting experiences, have done a grave disservice to the Saints.

Fourth, it has been seen[74] that while many individuals receive prophecies and other manifestations which may indicate future developments in the Church, yet they are not to (1) "command" the Church nor (2) assert in any way that they are "appointed" to receive revelations *for* the Church.

It is possible that there are prophetic, and even doctrinal items, with which individual Church members, through personal revelation and study, may be acquainted to a greater degree than those who preside as Church authorities.[75] Yet if the Lord sees fit to "command" the Church to perform a specific act, He will reveal it through the "appointed" prophet, seer and revelator: the President of the Church.

Finally, Church members would do well to recognize that the Church has relatively little doctrine. Doctrine[76] within the Church is a limited core of knowledge drawn primarily from specific scriptural statements. But much additional truth has come to light since the scriptures were published. Most of this newly-discovered truth has not been made doctrine, yet it is truth,[77] and "if there is anything virtuous, lovely, or of good report, or praiseworthy, we seek after these things."[78] The policy followed by Church authorities for many years was one of not enlarging the body of scripture through canonizing[79] new revelations and statements of principle. Their wisdom in this matter is accepted in faith by the Saints.

---

74. See pp. 112-119.

75. See pp. 104-110.

76. See chapter 8 for comments on the nature of doctrine.

77. The scriptures define truth as "knowledge of things as they are, and as they were, and as they are to come." (D&C 93:24.)

78. Article of Faith 13.

79. Canonization is the act of stating a principle to be the official belief of the Church and hence requiring it to be accepted and obeyed by the Church membership. This is done by the vote of the Church in general conference; in obedience to the law of common consent. For example, see the heading to D&C 134, (D&C p. 250), the Manifesto (D&C pp. 256-57), etc.

But it must also be realized that new discoveries, new prophecies and other manifestations, new insights, etc., continue to be received. They may not be doctrine, nor required to be believed by the membership of the Church, and yet they are revealed truth. The test of "what is or is not doctrine" is not the same as the test of "what is or is not truth." The vast majority of truth known today has not been made doctrine and binding upon the saints. It remains "independent in that sphere in which God has placed it. . . ."[80]

Man's agency compels him to acquire and evaluate new truth and to respond to it in an appropriate manner:

> Behold, here is the agency of man, and here is the condemnation of man; because that which was from the beginning *is plainly manifest unto them, and they receive not the light.*[81]

And as man examines new insights, and finds them to be true, it is folly for others to reject those insights or assert them to be falsehoods because the Church does not yet accord them the status of doctrine. Again, doctrine is limited and far from all-encompassing—there are multitudes of truths which have not been canonized, and the body of truth, both revealed and discovered, grows continually larger.

Prophecy Is Not Limited to Church Members

Yet another important message of the scriptures often misunderstood by Latter-day Saints is that not only the members of the Lord's Church, but also non-members of the Church may receive prophecies inspired of God.

Perhaps the Old Testament prophecy most often quoted in Mormondom is a manifestation given to Nebuchadnezzar, the pagan king of Babylonia. It was he who saw the great image with a head of gold, breast and arms of silver, belly and thighs of brass, legs of iron, and feet of iron and clay. The king also saw a stone which was cut out without hands which smote the feet of the image and broke it in pieces and then filled the whole earth. As Nebuchadnezzar later learned, the dream was a panorama of world events for centuries to come. Little of it concerned him personally. The vision was repeated to the prophet Daniel, but only because Daniel and his companions pleaded to see it so that their lives could be spared.[82]

King Nebuchadnezzar also prophesied a period of exile and insanity which was to come upon himself for seven years.[83] On another occasion

---

80. D&C 93:30.

81. D&C 93:31.

82. The account of the dream is found in Dan. 2. For interpretive comment see the author's book, *Prophets and Prophecies of the Old Testament*, pp. 499-502.

83. See Dan. 4.

he heard a voice speak to him from heaven, saying, "O king Nebuchadnezzar, to thee it is spoken; the kingdom is departed from thee."[84]

Prophetic dreams were given to a butler and a baker who were in prison with Joseph in Egypt. One of them foresaw his release from prison while the other foresaw his own death.[85]

Prophetic dreams were given to Pharoah of Egypt in the days of Joseph, which led the king to store food to protect his prople from a seven-year famine.[86] The revelation which he received was of international importance, for Egypt became the storage area upon which surrounding nations drew during the famine.

A prophetic dream saved Abimelech, the king of Gerar, from sin and the penalty of death in the days of Abraham.[87]

In yet another instance, during the reign of the judges, the Lord called Gideon to fight against the Midianites. Through a series of revealed instructions, the Lord caused Gideon to reduce his army from 32,000 to 300 men. Yet Gideon was reluctant to attack the Midianites until he overheard a God-inspired prophetic dream and its interpretation related by enemy soldiers:

> It came to pass the same night, that the Lord said unto him, Arise, get thee down unto the host; for I have delivered it into thine hand.
> *But if thou fear to go down, go thou with Phurah thy servant down to the host:*
> *And thou shalt hear what they say;* and afterward shall thine hands be strengthened to go down unto the host. Then went he down with Phurah his servant unto the outside of the armed men that were in the host.
> And the Midianites and the Amalekites and all the children of the east lay along in the valley like grasshoppers for multitude; and their camels were without number, as the sand by the sea side for multitude.
> And when Gideon was come, behold, there was a man that told a dream unto his fellow, and said, Behold, *I dreamed a dream, and, lo, a cake of barley bread tumbled into the host of Midian, and came unto a tent, and smote it that it fell, and overturned it, that the tent lay along.*
> *And his fellow answered and said, This is nothing else save the sword of Gideon the son of Joash, a man of Israel: for into his hand hath God delivered Midian, and all the host.*
> And it was so, when Gideon heard the telling of the dream, and the interpretation thereof, that he worshipped, and returned into the host of Israel, and said, *Arise; for the Lord hath delivered into your hand the host of Midian.*[88]

In the latter days, non-members have also prophesied under the influence of God, speaking inspired words which foretold, and perhaps

84. Dan. 4:31.
85. Gen. 40.
86. Gen. 41.
87. Gen. 20.
88. Judg. 7:9-15.

influenced, the course of the restored Church. Two well-known examples were recorded by Wilford Woodruff in his journal. One concerns Robert Mason, an old man who befriended Wilford in his youth. The following is President Woodruff's account:

Father Mason did not claim that he had any authority to officiate in the ordinances of the gospel, nor did he believe that such authority existed on the earth. He did believe, however, that it was the privilege of any man who had faith in God to fast and pray for the healing of the sick by the laying on of hands. *He believed it his right and the right of every honest-hearted man or woman to receive light and knowledge, visions, and revelations* by the prayer of faith. He told me that *the day was near when the Lord would establish His Church and Kingdom upon the earth with all its ancient gifts and blessings. He said that such a work would commence upon the earth before he died, but that he would not live to partake of its blessings. He said that I should live to do so, and that I should become a conspicuous actor in that kingdom.*

The last time I ever saw him he related to me the following vision which he had in his field in open day: 'I was carried away in a vision and found myself in the midst of a vast orchard of fruit trees. I became hungry and wandered through this vast orchard searching for fruit to eat, but I found none. While I stood in amazement finding no fruit in the midst of so many trees, they began to fall to the ground as if torn up by a whirlwind. They continued to fall until there was not a tree standing in the whole orchard. I immediately saw thereafter shoots springing up from the roots and forming themselves into young and beautiful trees. These budded, blossomed, and brought forth fruit which ripened and was the most beautiful to look upon of anything my eyes had ever beheld. I stretched forth my hand and plucked some of the fruit. I gazed upon it with delight; but when I was about to eat of it, the vision closed and I did not taste the fruit.'

At the close of the vision I bowed down in humble prayer and asked the Lord to show me the meaning of the vision. Then *the voice of the Lord* came to me saying: *"Son of man, thou hast sought me diligently to know the truth concerning my Church and Kingdom among men.* This is to show you that my Church is not organized among men in the generation to which you belong; but *in the days of your children the Church and Kingdom of God shall be made manifest with all the gifts and the blessings enjoyed by the Saints in past ages.* You shall live to be made acquainted with it, but shall not partake of its blessings before you depart this life. *You will be blest of the Lord after death because you have followed the dictation of my Spirit in this life."* '

When Father Mason had finished relating the vision and its interpretation, he said, calling me by my Christian name: "Wilford, I shall never partake of this fruit in the flesh, but *you will and you will become a conspicuous actor in the new kingdom."* He then turned and left me. These were the last words he ever spoke to me upon the earth. To me this was a very striking circumstance. I had passed many days during a period of twenty years with this old Father Mason. He had never mentioned this vision to me before. On this occasion *he said he felt impelled by the Spirit of the Lord to relate it to me.*[89]

89. Cowley, Matthias F., *Wilford Woodruff—History of His Life and Labors* (Salt Lake City, Utah: Bookcraft, 1964), pp. 16-17. Elder Woodruff also made this statement about Robert Mason:

Wilford Woodruff also recorded the prophetic manifestation recorded by his brother, Philo, in which Philo was visited by an angel and told the date of his own death. Again, this manifestation was granted to a non-member, for the Church was not yet restored at this time:

> A few months prior to his death, *Philo dreamed that an angel from heaven was going through the streets of the town* with a roll containing a list of those who should die during the year in that town. *The angel approached Philo and unfolded to him the roll, at the same time he informed his that on November 27th there would be a funeral at his father's house.* Philo recorded the dream in his journal. On the very day named by the angel his own funeral occurred at his father's home. The fulfillment of this strange dream made a lasting impression on Wilford's mind.[90]

Like Wilford Woodruff, the prophet Joseph Smith also recorded a prophecy given to a non-member of the Church which related to the rise of the restored gospel. He wrote that

> My grandfather, Asael Smith, *long ago predicted that there would be a prophet raised up in his family,* and my grandmother was fully satisfied that it was fulfilled in me. My grandfather Asael died in East Stockholm, St. Lawrence county, New York, after having received the Book of Mormon, and read it nearly through; and *he declared that I was the very Prophet that he had long known would come in his family.*[91]

These incidents, cited both from the scriptures and from LDS historical sources, give clear indication that prophecy is not limited to Church members, but that others outside the Church also receive God-inspired manifestations. Church membership is not a valid criterion for ascertaining the validity of prophecy.

Women Can Prophesy

Another message clearly established in the scriptures is that the prophetic gift can also be enjoyed by women. It is not limited to men, and therefore is not necessarily a priesthood function. Like any of the spiritual gifts, it can be manifested in any person upon whom God, through His Holy Spirit, chooses to bestow it.

The first opportunity I had after the truth of baptism for the dead was revealed, I went forth and was baptized for him in the temple font at Nauvoo. He was a good man, *a true prophet; for his prophecies have been fulfilled.* There was so much reason in the teachings of this man, and such harmony between them and the prophecies and teachings of Christ and of the apostles and prophets of old, that I believed in them with all my heart. (*Ibid.,* p. 18.)

90. *Ibid.,* p. 25.
91. HC, 2:443. May 17, 1836.

The Old Testament records in detail the visit of Hilkiah the high priest, Shapan the scribe, and others, to Huldah the prophetess. They, being the Church leaders of the day, were sent by Josiah the king to "inquire of the Lord" for him, so he could better understand God's will concerning the book of the law which had been discovered in the temple after being lost for many years. When they met with the prophetess she told them,

> *Thus saith the Lord God of Israel,* tell the man that sent you to me,
> *Thus saith the Lord,* Behold, *I will bring evil upon this place,* and upon the inhabitants thereof, even all the words of the book which the king of Judah hath read:
> Because they have forsaken me, and have burned incense unto other gods, that they might provoke me to anger with all the works of their hands; therefore my wrath shall be kindled against this place, and shall not be quenched.
> But to the king of Judah which sent you to inquire of the Lord, thus shall ye say to him, *Thus saith the Lord God of Israel,* As touching the words which thou hast heard;
> *Because thine heart was tender, and thou hast humbled thyself before the Lord, when thou heardest what I spake against this place, and against the inhabitants thereof, that they should become a desolation and a curse, and hast rent thy clothes, and wept before me; I also have heard thee, saith the Lord.*
> Behold therefore, I will gather thee unto thy fathers, and *thou shalt be gathered into thy grave in peace;* and thine eyes shall not see all the evil which I will bring upon this place.[92]

Other women in the scriptures possessed the ability to prophesy. We read of *"Miriam the prophetess,* the sister of Aaron,"[93] and of *"Deborah, a prophetess,* the wife of Lapidoth."[94] They tell of "the prophetess Noadiah,"[95] who was allied with the enemies of Judah. Isaiah's wife was a prophetess, and he wrote that "I went unto the prophetess; and she conceived, and bore a son."[96]

In the meredian of time, when Jesus was first presented in the temple, his parents encountered *"Anna, a prophetess,* the daughter of Phanuel."[97] Philip, the evangelist, *"Had four daughters, virgins, which did prophesy."*[98]

And John the Revelator also spoke of a woman who had the ability to prophesy, though she worked against the Lord's servants. As he wrote to the saints at Thyatira he commented,

---

92. II Ki. 22:15-20. See also II Chron. 34:22-28.
93. Ex. 15:20.
94. Judg. 4:4.
95. Neh. 6:14. She, it would appear, worked against Nehemiah in his rebuilding of the Jerusalem wall.
96. Is. 8:3. See also 2 Ne. 18:3.
97. Lk. 2:36.
98. Acts 21:8-9.

Notwithstanding I have a few things against thee, because thou sufferest that woman *Jezebel, which calleth herself a prophetess,* to teach and seduce my servants to commit fornication, and to eat things sacrificed unto idols."

Thus women, married and unmarried, young and old, are shown in the scriptures to be the possessors of prophetic ability. They have served God, and also opposed His work, by means of their prophetic gift. The pattern is clear, though, that women as well as men can and may prophesy with God's authorization and inspiration.

Summary

1. Joseph Smith taught that "salvation cannot come without revelation," that "no man is a minister of Jesus Christ without being a prophet," and that a testimony of Jesus "is the spirit of prophecy."

2. The apostle Paul counseled the Church to seek, particularly, the gift of prophecy, and emphasized that "he that prophesieth edifieth the church."

3. This chapter is written to clarify, from the scriptures, the doctrinal patterns pertaining to who can prophesy.

4. Scriptural accounts show that the Lord has sometimes revealed prophecies and messages to leaders of the Church through individuals who were not members of the Church hierarchy. The Lord used the boy Samuel and an unknown man of God, for instance, to rebuke the high priest Eli for the corruption he had allowed within the Church and within his own family.

5. Church position is not the test by which validity of prophecy is measured. Many of the Old Testament prophets, including Jeremiah, Micah, Amos, Hosea and Zephaniah, were not Church leaders. They stood outside the organized Church and were highly critical of the corruption that existed within it. The corrupt priesthood regarded these prophets as rebels and apostates. Men who were not Church leaders were also regarded as prophets among the Book of Mormon saints. Gidgiddoni, head of the Nephite army, for instance, was "a great prophet among them."

6. In the New Testament, prophets, such as Agabus, who were not Church leaders foretold events of world-wide significance and even warned apostles of events which would shape their personal lives. Other New Testament prophets who were not part of the Church hierarchy included Judas, Silas, Barnabas, Simeon Niger, Lucius of Cyrene, and Manaen. The daughters of Philip the evangelist also prophesied.

7. The scriptures show that many prophets may function at one time, with as many as one hundred prophets of Jehovah on record as functioning

---

99. Rev. 2:20.

at one time (I Ki. 18:13). Prophecies of events yet future indicate that numerous prophets will be functioning at the same time. The Lord uses many witnesses to establish and proclaim his truths.

8. Individual members are entitled to prophetic abilities, and are admonished in the scriptures to "prophesy according to the proportion of faith" which is theirs. Moses desired that "all the Lord's people were prophets, and that the Lord would put his spirit upon them."

9. According to the scriptures, prophecies are given to edify the Church. The apostle, Paul, for instance, commanded that members of the Church are to share prophecies they've received with others. Numerous examples in scripture show that inspired prophecies were shared for the uplifting of others.

10. Some cautions concerning the sharing of prophecies and revelations were noted, as follows:

A. Prophecies revealed within the Church should be kept among the saints.

B. Prophecies should be properly understood and interpreted before being shared. Caution should be exercised with items for which the saints do not have a revealed understanding, and particular care should be used so that an uninspired interpretation is not linked to a manifestation that has been received.

C. In rare instances, the Lord has given instructions that portions of manifestations are not to be shared with others. It was observed that such situations are the rare exceptions rather than the usual occurrence.

D. While many individuals receive prophecies and other manifestations which may indicate future developments in the Church, they are not to (1) "command" the Church nor (2) assert that they are "appointed" to receive revelations *for* the Church.

E. The Church has relatively little doctrine. Most newly-revealed insights, though they may be truth, have not been canonized and therefore are not items requiring the mandatory belief of the saints.

11. There are multitudes of truths which have not been canonized, and the body of truth, both revealed and discovered, grows continually larger. Man's agency compels him to acquire and evaluate new truth and to respond to it.

12. Prophecy is not limited to Church members. Some of the most notable prophecies recorded in scripture, such as Nebuchadnezzar's vision of the great image and Pharaoh's foreknowledge of impending famines, were revealed to non-members.

13. In these last days, various non-members have foreseen events which were to transpire within the Church, and their prophetic statements have been accepted by contemporary Church leaders as being inspired.

14. Women, as well as men, can prophesy, thus indicating that prophecy is among the spiritual gifts available to all, rather than being a function of the priesthood.

5

What Are the Characteristics
of True Prophecy?

In previous chapters we have considered definitions of the terms "Prophet," "Seer," and "Revelator," and also examined the messages of the scriptures concerning who may receive prophecies inspired by the Lord. This chapter treats some of the characteristics associated with true prophecy, as defined in the scriptures.

God Has Promised to Fulfill His Words

Throughout the history of His dealings with man, God has forcefully proclaimed that His revealed prophecies and promises will all be fulfilled. The scriptures repeatedly assert His determination to bring to pass all that He has revealed unto man. For instance, to Isaiah the Lord declared that

> . . . I am God, and there is none else; I am God, and there is none like me,
> *Declaring the end from the beginning, and from ancient times the things that are not yet done,* saying, My counsel shall stand, and I will do all my pleasure:
> Calling a ravenous bird from the east, the man that executeth my counsel from a far country: yea, *I have spoken it, I will also bring it to pass; I have purposed it, I will also do it.*[1]

God's revelations of what will come to pass, long before the prophesied events take place, serve to establish His power and the reality of His divinity in the minds of men. As He revealed to ancient Israel,

> *I have declared the former things from the beginning; and they went forth out of my mouth, and I shewed them; I did them suddenly, and they came to pass.*
> Because I knew that thou art obstinate, and thy neck is an iron sinew, and thy brow brass;

---

1. Is. 46:9-11.

> *I have even from the beginning declared it to thee; before it came to pass I shewed it thee:* lest thou shouldest say, Mine idol hath done them, and my graven image, and my molten image, hath commanded them.[2]

In His infinite power and wisdom, God is able to make His revealed word bear fruit and accomplish His purposes. Yet He does so in ways incomprehensible to man:

> *My thoughts are not your thoughts, neither are your ways my ways, saith the Lord.*
>
> For as the heavens are higher than the earth, so are my ways higher than your ways, and my thoughts than your thoughts.
>
> For as the rain cometh down, and the snow from heaven, and returneth not thither, but watereth the earth, and maketh it bring forth and bud, that it may give seed to the sower, and bread to the eater:
>
> *So shall my word be that goeth forth out of my mouth: it shall not return unto me void, but it shall accomplish that which I please, and it shall prosper in the thing whereto I sent it.*[3]

To Habakkuk, God also affirmed that the visions He reveals unto man come to pass. Though fulfillment may be reserved for a later time, man is to preserve revelation and then wait patiently until it comes to pass:

> *Write the vision,* and make it plain upon tables, that he may run that readeth it.
>
> *For the vision is yet for an appointed time, but at the end it shall speak, and not lie: though it tarry, wait for it; because it will surely come,* it will not tarry.[4]

The Lord proclaimed to Jeremiah, *"I will hasten my word to perform it,"*[5] and to the wicked Chaldeans the Lord promised,

> I will bring upon that land all my words which I have pronounced against it, even all that is written in this book, which Jeremiah hath prophesied against all the nations.[6]

Book of Mormon prophets also bore witness that God will fulfill His revealed words. It was Alma who warned that even if man opposed the word of God, that word would yet come to pass. To the people of Zarahemla he announced, "I say unto you, if ye speak against it, it matters not, for *the word of God must be fulfilled.*"[7] Years later, Helaman, another Book of Mormon prophet, observed that "We see how merciful and just

---

2. Is. 48:3-5. This was also Alma's teaching as he explained to his son, Helaman, "God is powerful to the fulfilling of all his words." Al. 37:16.)
3. Is. 55:8-11.
4. Hab. 2:2-3.
5. Jer. 1:12.
6. Jer. 25:13.
7. Al. 5:58.

are all the dealings of the Lord, *to the fulfilling of all his words unto the children of men; yea, we can behold that his words are verified.*"[8]

In the meridian of time, because of their knowledge that God's word must surely be fulfilled, the Nephites repented and lived in righteousness in order to be prepared for an expected visit from the Savior:

> *Behold, there was not a living soul among all the people of the Nephites who did doubt in the least the words of all the holy prophets who had spoken;* for they knew that it just needs be that they must be fulfilled.
> And they knew that it must be expedient that Christ had come, *because of the many signs which had been given according to the words of the prophets; and because of the things which had come to pass already they knew that it must needs be that all things should come to pass according to that which had been spoken.*
> Therefore they did forsake all their sins, and their abominations and their whoredoms, and did serve God with all diligence day and night.[9]

When the Savior came among them, He taught them of His Father and told them *"He fulfilleth the words which he hath given, and he lieth not, but fulfilleth all his words."*[10] Four centuries later the prophet Moroni wrote his conviction that "the eternal purposes of the Lord shall roll on, until *all his promises shall be fulfilled.*"[11]

In the last days the Lord has asserted repeatedly that His revealed prophecies and promises will all be fulfilled. In His revealed preface to the Doctrine and Covenants, He commanded the inhabitants of the earth to

> *Search these commandments, for they are true and faithful, and the prophecies and promises which are in them shall all be fulfilled.*
> What I the Lord have spoken, I have spoken, and I excuse not myself; and though the heavens and the earth pass away, *my word shall not pass away, but shall all be fulfilled, whether by mine own voice, or by the voice of my servants, it is the same.*[12]

Of these commandments and revelations He warned mankind, saying,

> Fear and tremble, O ye people, for *what I the Lord have decreed in them shall be fulfilled.*[13]

While speaking of the "desolating scourge"[14] which is to go forth in the last days "until the earth is empty" the Lord again asserted that His words would see fulfillment as He warned,

> Behold, I tell you these things, even as I also told the people of the destruction of Jerusalem; and *my word shall be verified at this time as it hath hitherto been verified.*[15]

---

8. Al. 50:19.
9. 3 Ne. 5:1-3.
10. 3 Ne. 27:18.
11. Mor. 8:22.

12. D&C 1:37-38.
13. D&C 1:7.
14. See the warnings in chapter 9.
15. D&C 5:20.

In later revelations Jesus repeatedly emphasized the fulfillment of His
revealed word by saying that "as the words have gone forth out of my
mouth even so shall they be fulfilled;"[16] "My word must needs be fulfilled;"[17] and "I, the Lord, promise the faithful and cannot lie."[18]

That God will fulfill all the events He has revealed concerning the
last days is therefore a true and abiding principle. The Lord will come in
His glory, but the many events He has revealed which are to take place
prior to His coming will surely precede His advent. Indeed, He proclaimed,

> Ye say that ye know that the end of the world cometh; ye say also that
> ye know that the heavens and the earth shall pass away;
>   And in this ye say truly, for so it is; but *these things which I have told
> you shall not pass away until all shall be fulfilled.*[19]

Though His advent in glory will be sudden, "as a thief in the night,"[20]
Christ's coming will not be a surprise to "those servants, whom the Lord
when He cometh shall find watching,"[21] for they will know the prophecies
and will recognize their fulfillment. They will be firm in the Savior's pledge
that "although the days will come, that heaven and earth shall pass away;
yet my words shall not pass away, but all shall be fulfilled."[22]

Prophecy Usually is Specific, Accurate, and Receives Literal Fulfillment

True prophecies have features which serve as identifying characteristics
of their validity. The scriptures abound with examples which show that
inspired prophecy is almost always specific, accurate, and receives literal
fulfillment. Such examples are equally commonplace in the early history
of the Church restored in the latter days. In most instances, prophecies
are revealed in plainness,[23] "for the Lord God *giveth light unto the under-*

---

16. D&C 29:30.
17. D&C 101:64.
18. D&C 62:6.
19. D&C 45:22-23.
20. I Thess. 5:2.
21. Lk. 12:37. See alsp Eph. 6:18.
22. JS 1:35. See also D&C 56:11.
23. However, frequently what is plain to one individual is extremely compli-
cated to another person. Many people fail to search the scriptures with the aid of
the Holy Spirit, and thus find their understanding limited to a great degree. As
Nephi explained,

> The words of Isaiah are not plain unto you, nevertheless.*they are plain unto
> all those that are filled with the spirit of prophecy.* But I give unto you a
> prophecy, according to the spirit which is in me: wherefore *I shall prophesy
> according to the plainness* which hath been with me from the time that I

standing; for he speaketh unto men according to their language, unto their understanding.''[24]

Old Testament prophecies clearly depict the literal fulfillment which prophecy receives. A good example is the detailed prophecy of Ahijah the Shilonite to Jeroboam:

> It came to pass at that time when Jeroboam went out of Jerusalem, that the prophet Ahijah the Shilonite found him in the way: and he had clad himself with a new garment; and they two were alone in the field:
>
> And Ahijah caught the new garment that was on him, and rent it in twelve pieces:
>
> And he said to Jeroboam, Take thee ten pieces: for *thus saith the Lord,* the God of Israel, Behold, *I will rend the kingdom out of the hand of Solomon, and will give ten tribes to thee:*
>
> *(But he shall have one tribe* for my servant David's sake, and for Jerusalem's sake, the city which I have chosen out of all the tribes of Israel:)
>
> Because that they have forsaken me, and have worshipped Ashtoreth the goddess of the Zidonians, Chemosh the god of the Moabites, and Milcom the god of the children of Ammon, and have not walked in my ways, to do that which is right in mine eyes, and to keep my statutes and my judgments, as did David his father.
>
> Howbeit I will not take the whole kingdom out of his hand: but I will make him prince all the days of his life for David my servant's sake, whom I chose, because he kept my commandments and my statutes:
>
> But *I will take the kingdom out of his son's hand,* and will give it unto thee, even ten tribes.
>
> And *unto his son will I give one tribe,* that David my servant may have a light alway before me in Jerusalem, the city which I have chosen me to put my name there.
>
> And I will take thee, and thou shalt reign according to all that thy soul desireth, and *shalt be king over Israel.*

> came out from Jerusalem with my father; for behold, my soul delighteth in plainness unto my people, that they may learn. (2 Ne. 25:4.)

Some individuals pray for guidance but fail to pay the price of adequate preparation through prayerful study. Certainly the area of scriptural and prophetic interpretation is a prime example of the need for the approach set forth by the Lord in the early days of the restoration:

> Behold, you have not understood; you have supposed that I would give it unto you, when you took no thought save it was to ask me.
>
> But behold, I say unto you, that you must study it out in your mind; then you must ask me if it be right, and if it is right I will cause that your bosom shall burn within you; therefore, you shall feel that it is right. (D&C 9:7-8.)

However, some prophetic utterances have lost portions which are "plain and most precious," (see 1 Ne. 13:26) and they are far from plain to even the most qualified students of scripture.

24. 2 Ne. 31:3.

> And it shall be, if thou wilt hearken unto all that I command thee, and
> wilt walk in my ways, and do that is right to my sight, to keep my statutes and
> my commandments, as David my servant did; that I will be with thee, and
> build thee a sure house, as I built for David, and will give Israel unto thee.
> And I will for this afflict the seed of David, but not forever.[25]

Shortly after the prophecy was made, the kingdom was divided. Jeroboam
became the king over ten of the tribes of Israel while Solomon's son
Rehoboam retained authority over the tribe of Judah. The account of the
exact, literal fulfillment of the prophecy may be read in 1st Kings 11:40-43;
12:1-24. Note the literal fulfillment of prophecy in that
1. ten tribes followed Jeroboam (compare I Ki. 11:31,35 with 12:20)
2. one tribe remained with the house of Solomon (compare I Ki. 11:32,
   11:36 with 12:17, 20-21)
3. the kingdom was taken from Solomon in the days of his son,
   Rehoboam (compare I Ki. 11:34-35; 11:11-13 with 11:41-43, 12:1-16).
For the greatest degree of understanding similar lists should be prepared by
interested readers pertaining to the examples that follow.

Another instance of literal fulfillment is the prophecy made by the man
of God to King Jeroboam:

> Behold, there came a man of God out of Judah by the word of the Lord unto
> Bethel: and Jeroboam stood by the altar to burn incense.
> And he cried against the altar in the word of the Lord, and said, O altar,
> altar, *thus saith the Lord;* Behold, *a child shall be born unto the house of
> David, Josiah by name; and upon thee shall he offer the priests of the high
> places that burn incense upon thee, and men's bones shall be burnt upon
> thee.*[26]

The exact fulfillment of this remarkable prophecy came three hundred and
thirty years later, when a young king of Judah named Josiah began a
program of reform which extended into Israel. The altars were destroyed
and defiled by burning the bones of the dead upon them. This fulfillment
can be read in II Ki. 23:1-18 and II Chron. 34:3-7.

On some occasions, prophecy took the form of a promise of victory
in battle, as demonstrated by the words of the prophet to Ahab, an Israelite
king who was being attacked by the armies of Syria:

> Behold, there came a prophet unto Ahab king of Israel, saying, *Thus saith the
> Lord,* Hast thou seen all this great multitude? behold, *I will deliver it into thine
> hand this day;* and thou shalt know that I am the Lord.
> And Ahab said, By whom? And he said, *Thus saith the Lord, Even by
> the young men of the princes of the provinces.* Then he said, Who shall order
> the battle? And he answered, Thou.[27]

25. I Ki. 11:29-39.
26. I Ki. 13:1-2. See also verses 3 through 10.
27. I Ki. 20:13-14.

In true fulfillment of the prophecy, the Israelites conquered their foe that same day (I Ki. 20:16-21).

But at the end of the battle another prophecy was made:

> The prophet came to the king of Israel, and said unto him, Go, strengthen thyself, and mark, and see what thou doest: for *at the return of the year the king of Syria will come up against thee.*[28]

I Kings 20:23-30 records the fulfillment of the later prophecy.

A similar prophecy was made by Jahaziel unto the people of Judah, in which he prophesied they would gain a military victory without even having to fight their enemies:

> Hearken ye, all Judah, and ye inhabitants of Jerusalem, and thou king Jehoshaphat, *Thus saith the Lord* unto you, Be not afraid nor dismayed by reason of this great multitude; for the battle is not yours, but God's.
>
> Tomorrow go ye down against them: behold, they come up by the cliff of Ziz; and *ye shall find them at the end of the brook, before the wilderness of Jeruel.*
>
> *Ye shall not need to fight in this battle:* set yourselves, stand ye still, and see the salvation of the Lord with you, O Judah and Jerusalem: fear not, nor be dismayed; tomorrow go out against them: for the Lord will be with you.[29]

The prophecy saw literal fulfillment the next day when the Ammonites, Moabites, and Edomites fought among themselves, and completely destroyed each other's armies. (II Chronicles 20:20-24.)

During a Syrian seige of Samaria in which the beseiged Israelites were so near starvation that they were slaying and eating their own children, the prophet Elisha spoke this prophecy:

> Hear ye the word of the Lord; *Thus saith the Lord, Tomorrow about this time shall a measure of fine flour be sold for a shekel, and two measures of barley for a shekel, in the gate of Samaria.*
>
> Then a lord on whose hand the king leaned answered the man of God, and said, Behold, if the Lord would make windows in heaven, might this thing be? And he said, Behold *thou shalt see it with thine eyes, but shalt not eat thereof.*[30]

The miraculous way in which food was supplied by the Syrians deserting their camp, and also the death of Elisha's skeptical critic without eating of it, are reported in II Kings 7:3-20.

In II Kings chapters 24 and 25 is recorded the destruction which came upon Jerusalem in fulfillment of these prophetic words;

> Shaphan the scribe shewed the king, saying, Hilkiah the priest hath delivered me a book. And Shaphan read it before the king.

---

28. I Ki. 20:22.
29. II Chron. 20:15-17.
30. II Ki. 7:1-2.

And it came to pass, when the king had heard the words of the book of the law, that he rent his clothes.

And the king commanded Hilkiah the priest, and Ahikam the son of Shaphan and Achbor the son of Michaiah, and Shaphan the scribe, and Asahiah a servant of the king's saying,

Go ye, inquire of the Lord for me, and for the people, and for all Judah, concerning the words of this book that is found: for great is the wrath of the Lord that is kindled against us, because our fathers have not hearkened unto the words of this book, to do according unto all that which is written concerning us.

So Hilkiah the priest, and Ahikam, and Achbor, and Shaphan, and Asahiah, went unto *Huldah the prophetess,* the wife of Shallum the son of Tikvah, the son of Harhas, keeper of the wardrobe; (now she dwelt in Jerusalem in the college;) and they communed with her.

And she said unto them, *Thus saith the Lord* God of Israel, Tell the man that sent you to me,

Thus saith the Lord, Behold, *I will bring evil upon this place, and upon the inhabitants thereof, even all the words of the book* which the king of Judah hath read:

Because they have forsaken me, and have burned incense unto other gods, that they might provoke me to anger with all the works of their hands; therefore *my wrath shall be kindled against this place,* and shall not be quenched.[31]

These are but a few of the hundreds of examples found in the scriptures which have received literal fulfillment. To review them all would be to undertake a complete review of the scriptures—a task too broad for this context.[32]

These examples are typical of the scriptural pattern that prophecies receive literal fulfillment and that events do come to pass as foretold by God's inspired prophets. Exceptions to this pattern are rare.

Occasionally, interpreters force interpretations upon prophecies which are incorrect. In such instances, the interpreter is unable to recognize the true fulfillment when the prophecy does come to pass. His interpretation is erroneous, but the revealed word of God has not failed.

Prophecy Is Not Predestination: Prophetic Outcomes May Be Changed

Several misunderstandings have been observed which should be commented upon in this setting. One such misunderstanding is the erroneous belief that prophecy is a type of predestination, which inalterably fixes the course of future events.

31. II Ki. 22:10-17. For its fulfillment, see II Ki. 24 and 25.

32. For those who might desire further examples, a detailed analysis of the prophecies recorded in the Old Testament beginning with the era of the divided kingdoms is found in the author's book, *Prophets and Prophecies of the Old Testament* (Bountiful, Utah: Horizon Publishers & Distributors). Chapter VI, "The Early Prophets and Their Messages," examines the messages of numerous prophets

Prophecy is not predestination. It does not *govern* what will come to pass. The scriptures teach that when conditions pertinent to the prophesied situation change, the outcome of prophecy may also change. Revealed prophecy pre-states the manner God will later manifest His will. If God chooses to alter His intentions, He may reveal new prophecy to His spokesmen indicating different outcomes to earth events. An understanding of this principle is basic to man's understanding of many of the manifestations of God.

---

over a 200-year span. In it is repeatedly documented a series of insights concerning the nature of prophecy which is later summarized as follows:

A. God reveals the future to His prophets.

B. Prophecy is specific and accurate.

C. Prophecy is literally fulfilled.

D. God warns His prophets of approaching challenges and dangers.

E. God directs people, through His prophets, as to how they should conduct their lives.

F. God rules the destiny of nations.

G. God will not allow men to disturb His plans.

H. When situations change, the outcome of prophecy may change.

I. When God changes a prophetic outcome, He reveals the change to His prophet.

J. Man can avert or soften a prophecy of the Lord's punishment against him by truly repenting and manifesting humility.

K. A prophet can forsee events hundreds of years into the future, and in differing national situations.

L. God often shows the truthfulness of a prophecy by giving a sign which receives immediate fulfillment.

M. A prophet can call upon the powers of God to smite and curse his enemies.

N. A prophet can call upon the powers of God to heal and remove curses.

O. God demands that His prophets be treated with reverence and respect.

P. God can use a man as a prophet even though the man is not free from sin.

Q. God demands strict obedience from His prophets.

R. Man should test the prophets and their prophecies by the spirit of discernment.

S. Revelation serves for commendation as well as reproof.

T. Man's life is not predestined. Man himself determines his fate by establishing in the present a cause-and-effect relationship with the future. Prophecy merely pre-states what the ultimate effect of present actions will be.

U. God often uses many prophets at the same time.

V. A calling as a prophet did not necessarily require that the person with this calling stand at the head of the Church.

W. God gives His prophets control over nature to further His work.

X. God protects his prophets and supplies their needs.

Y. Prophets have the power to perform miracles.

Z. Some miracles are performed by the powers already vested in the prophet. For other miracles he must call upon God.

AA. Miracles are often used to establish the divinity of Jehovah and the authority of His prophets.

Many examples of this principle from the scriptures can be cited. One instance is the extension of life granted to Hezekiah, a righteous king of Judah. At one time during his reign, the king became ill. The word of the Lord concerning his fate was revealed through the prophet Isaiah:

> In those days was Hezekiah sick unto death. And Isaiah the prophet the son of Amoz came unto him, and said unto him, *Thus saith the Lord,* Set thine house in order: *for thou shalt die, and not live.* [33]

But Hezekiah was a righteous man who knew how to prevail with God. He pleaded with the Lord for the privilege of a longer sojourn upon the earth:

> Hezekiah turned his face toward the wall, and prayed unto the Lord,
> And said, Remember now O Lord, I beseech thee, how I have walked before thee in truth and with a perfect heart, and have done that which is good in thy sight. And Hezekiah wept sore. [34]

God heard Hezekiah's prayer and had compassion upon him. He changed His decision that Hezekiah was to die at that time, but He didn't just extend the king's life without revealing His new decision through His prophet:

> Then came the word of the Lord to Isaiah, saying,
> Go, and say to Hezekiah, *Thus saith the Lord,* the God of David thy father, *I have heard thy prayer, I have seen thy tears:* behold, *I will add unto thy days fifteen years.*
> And I will deliver thee and this city out of the hand of the king of Assyria: and I will defend this city.
> *And this shall be a sign unto thee from the Lord, that the Lord will do this that he hath spoken;*
> Behold, I will bring again the shadow of the degrees, which is gone down in the sun dial of Ahaz, ten degrees backward. So *the sun returned ten degrees,* by which degrees it was gone down. [35]

BB. On special occasions God gives His servants strength beyond the normal limits of endurance.
CC. Many miracles are designed for the convenience of God's servants.
DD. Some servants of God are transferred from this earth to another. They become translated beings.
EE. Prophets have the power to discern the thoughts and deeds of others.
FF. At times people perform specific actions to intentionally fulfill prophecies.
GG. The Bible does not record the fulfillment of some prophecies. This does not, however, make them untrue.
HH. At times prophets must suffer martyrdom for their testimony.
II. Women can also speak the Lord's will, as prophetesses.
33. Is. 38:1. The full account is also given in II Ki. 20:1-11.
34. Is. 38:2-3.
35. Is. 38:4-8. Note that a sign was given with the prophecy. This is a common occurrence. While men are expressly cautioned not to seek after signs (see, for example, D&C 46:9; 63:7-12; Mt. 12:38-39, etc.), signs are often given by the Lord in connection with prophecies. (See Is. 38:7-8; Jud. 6:17-21, 36-40; I Sam. 2:34; 14:10; I Ki. 13:3-5; Is. 37:30; 7:11-16; 19:19-20; 55:13; Jer. 44:29; Lk. 2:12, etc.)

Another example of new, altered prophecy being revealed is the account of Ahab, a wicked king of Israel. Ahab caused Naboth to be slain in order to obtain a vineyard which Naboth owned. Because of the king's wickedness, the Lord sent Elijah to make this prophecy to Ahab:

> *Thus saith the Lord,* Has thou killed, and also taken possession? And thou shalt speak unto him, saying, *Thus saith the Lord, In the place where dogs licked the blood of Naboth shall dogs lick thy blood,* even thine.
>
> And Ahab said to Elijah, Hast thou found me, O mine enemy? And he answered, I have found thee: because thou hast sold thyself to work evil in the sight of the Lord.
>
> Behold, *I will bring evil upon thee, and will take away thy posterity,* . . .
>
> . . . for the provocation wherewith thou hast provoked me to anger, and made Israel to sin.[36]

Yet the scripture records the repentance of Ahab, which altered the condition upon which the prophecy was based. Because of Ahab's penitence, the will of the Lord changed. A new prophecy was revealed through Elijah, in which God's retribution was postponed:

> And it came to pass, when Ahab heard those words, that he rent his clothes, and put sackcloth upon his flesh, and fasted, and lay in sackcloth, and went softly.
>
> And the word of the Lord came to Elijah the Tishbite, saying,
>
> *Seest thou how Ahab humbleth himself before me? Because he humbleth himself before me, I will not bring the evil in his days:* but in his son's days will I bring the evil upon his house.[37]

Another example of new prophecy being revealed because of changing conditions is found early in the history of the nation of Judah, when Rehoboam and his people were under attack by Shishak, king of Egypt. A prophetic warning was spoken against the princes of Judah by the prophet Shemaiah, who warned, *"Thus saith the Lord,* Ye have forsaken me, and therefore have *I also left you in the hand of Shishak."*[38] But then the condition changed. "The princes of Israel and the king humbled themselves; and they said, The Lord is righteous."[39] With their repentance, the Lord chose to lighten His judgment upon them. A new prophecy was revealed through His prophet:

> When the Lord saw that they humbled themselves, the word of the Lord came to Shemaiah, ·saying, *They have humbled themselves; therefore I will not destroy them, but I will grant them some deliverance; and my wrath shall not be poured out upon Jerusalem by the hand of Shishak.*

36. I Ki. 21:9-22.
37. I Ki. 21:27-29. For the fulfillment of the prophecy on Ahab's wicked son, Joram, see II Ki. 9:22-10:11.
38. II Chron. 12:5.
39. II Chron. 12:6.

> Nevertheless they shall be his servants; that they may know my service, and the service of the kingdoms of the countries.[40]

In yet another situation which exemplifies this principle of altered prophecy, a conditional warning was spoken by a man of God to King Amaziah during his rule in Jerusalem. The king was told that he would die in a contemplated battle against the Edomites if he used the 100,000 mercenaries he had hired from Israel:

> There came a man of God to him, saying, O king, let not the army of Israel go with thee; for the Lord is not with Israel, to wit, with all the children of Ephraim.
> But if thou wilt go, do it, be strong for the battle: *God shall make thee fall before the enemy:* for God hath power to help, and to cast down.[41]

Amaziah took heed to the prophecy and sent the mercenaries away. Consequently, in the battle his life was spared and he was able to conquer the Edomites (the children of Seir).[42]

Another example of a prophetic outcome being altered is found in the account of the prophet Jonah, who cried a warning of impending destruction against the people of the Assyrian city of Nineveh:

> The word of the Lord came unto Jonah the second time, saying, Arise, go unto Nineveh, that great city, and preach unto it the preaching that I bid thee.
> So Jonah arose, and went unto Nineveh, according to the word of the Lord. Now Nineveh was an exceeding great city of three days' journey.
> And Jonah began to enter into the city a day's journey, and he cried and said, *Yet forty days, and Nineveh shall be overthrown.*[43]

But the people of Nineveh repented in sackcloth and ashes,[44] "and God saw their works, that they turned from their evil way;" and *God repented of the evil that he had said that he would do unto them; and he did it not.*"[45] Because of all the tribulation Jonah had suffered before delivering his warning message, "it displeased Jonah exceedingly" that God changed His will, yet the prophet had no choice but to accept the new revelation that came to him.[46]

Twice God revealed to the prophet Amos judgments He had determined to bring against Israel, yet the pleadings of that prophet were sufficient to

---

40. II Chron. 12:7-8. Verses 9-12 tell the fulfillment of the latter prophecy.
41. II Chron. 25:7-8.
42. See II Chron. 25:9-12.
43. Jon. 3:1-4.
44. Jon. 3:5-9.
45. Jon. 3:10. In the Inspired Version, this verse reads, "And God saw their works that they turned from their evil way and repented; and God turned away the evil that he had said he would bring upon them."
46. See Jon. 4:11.

alter the conditions and prevent the curse from coming upon his people. Instead of the judgment, God revealed His promise not to send it:

> *Thus hath the Lord God shewed unto me;* and, behold, he formed grasshoppers in the beginning of the shooting up of the latter growth; and, lo, it was the latter growth after the king's mowings.
>
> And it came to pass, that when they had made an end of eating the grass of the land, then I said, O Lord God, forgive, I beseech thee: by whom shall Jacob arise? for he is small.
>
> *The Lord repented for this: It shall not be, saith the Lord.*
>
> *Thus hath the Lord God shewed unto me:* and, behold, the Lord God called to contend by fire, and it devoured the great deep, and did eat up a part.
>
> Then said I, O Lord God, cease, I beseech thee: by whom shall Jacob arise? for he is small.
>
> *The Lord repented for this: This also shall not be, saith the Lord God.*[47]

Similar examples are found in latter-day scripture. For instance, the Lord revealed His will that the saints should gather to Zion, the New Jerusalem, in numerous revelations through His prophets.[48] Yet the saints were not willing to support the gathering process fully. Less than half the number specified by the Lord, for example, were willing to participate in Zion's Camp.[49] Some members of the Church, within Zion's Camp and elsewhere, fell into transgression; others refused to contribute their funds for the upbuilding of Zion. The conditions changed. The Lord, altering His will because of the attitudes of the Church members, revealed a new policy through the prophet Joseph Smith:

> Verily I say unto you who have assembled yourselves together that you may learn my will concerning the redemption of mine afflicted people—
>
> Behold, I say unto you, *were it not for the transgressions of my people, speaking concerning the church and not individuals, they might have been redeemed even now.*
>
> *But behold, they have not learned to be obedient to the things which I required at their hands, but are full of all manner of evil, and do not impart of their substance, as becometh saints, to the poor and afflicted among them;*
>
> *And are not united according to the union required by the law of the celestial kingdom;*
>
> And Zion cannot be built up unless it is by the principles of the law of the celestial kingdom; otherwise I cannot receive her unto myself.
>
> *And my people must needs be chastened until they learn obedience, if it must needs be, by the things which they suffer.*
>
> I speak not concerning those who are appointed to lead my people, who are the first elders of my church, for they are not all under this condemnation;
>
> But I speak concerning my churches abroad—there are many who will say: Where is their God? Behold, he will deliver them in time of trouble, otherwise we will not go up unto Zion, and will keep our moneys.

---

47. Amos 7:1-6. See also Ex. 32:9-14; Gen. 18:20-33.

48. See, for example, D&C 45:64-66; 57:1-9; 66:11; etc.

49. The call was for 500 men; they eventually marched with 205. See D&C 103:30-36; HC 2:87-88; also D&C 105:16-17.

> Therefore, *in consequence of the transgressions of my people, it is expedient in me that mine elders should wait for a little season for the redemption of Zion—*[50]

And still the saints wait, for the Lord desires that the Church as a people "may be prepared, and that my people may be taught more perfectly, and have experience, and know more perfectly concerning their duty, and the things which I require at their hands."[51]

When the Lord reveals through His prophets that which will come to pass, it is not absolute, it is not unalterable, it does not *govern* the future. If conditions change, God, in His justice and mercy, will alter the events He brings to pass. Man, in his wickedness, may forfeit promised blessings, but it is man upon whom the responsibility must rest. As the Master revealed,

> Who am I, saith the Lord, that have promised and have not fulfilled? I command and men obey not; I revoke and they receive not the blessing. *Then they say in their hearts: This is not the work of the Lord, for his promises are not fulfilled. But wo unto such, for their reward lurketh beneath, and not from above.*[52]

His is the pledge that *"I, the Lord, am bound when ye do what I say: but when ye do not what I say, ye have no promise."*[53]

Thus a pattern is established. A prophecy may be given which foretells future events. It may reach far into the future and deal with events completely foreign to the era in which it was spoken, yet it will describe or imply a condition and foresee the results of that condition. However, if when the time of fulfillment draws near, those involved alter the condition through wickedness, repentance, or other pertinent action, God may exercise His power and change the outcome. If the outcome is to be different from that foretold by His prophets, He will reveal new prophecy to his servants which will set forth the altered course of events.

Two further comments should be made in connection with this principle. First, there may be some instances where God has revealed to his prophets a change in His previously-prophesied program, yet the change has not been recorded or a knowledge of it made available to mankind. Such a situation, obviously, can be a cause for confusion and doubt. In instances of this kind, the saints are left with incomplete evidence, and it becomes impossible to fully understand the situation at hand unless further revelation is made known to them. However, it is fortunate that there have been few times in either scriptural history or the history of the Church where such a problem has occurred.

---

50. D&C 105:1-9.
51. D&C 105:10.
52. D&C 58:31-33.
53. D&C 82:10. See also D&C 132:5; 130:20-21; 82:3.

Second, it should also be noted that scriptural evidence of prophecies being altered is very limited. The evidence indicates that prophetic alteration has taken place occasionally, but the weight of evidence clearly shows that such happenings are comparatively rare. There are but few times when the future course previously outlined by prophecy has been changed. Such instances are not indications of indecision on the part of God. Instead, they usually are examples of God's mercy and love, in situations where wicked men have repented or righteous men have sought special favors from Him.

Prophecy Does Not Limit Free Agency

Relatively little is said in the scriptures concerning the agency of man. That which has been revealed, however, indicates that man's agency is "moral agency"[54]—the privilege of choosing between good and evil and thus determining his eternal fate—"that every man may be accountable for his own sins in the day of judgment."[55] The privilege of agency is guaranteed only in the domain of moral choice, "that sphere in which God has placed it:"

> *All truth is independent in that sphere in which God has placed it, to act for itself,* as all intelligence also; otherwise there is no existence.
> *Behold, here is the agency of man,* and here is the *condemnation* of man; because that which was from the beginning is plainly *manifest unto them, and they receive not the light.*[56]

The scriptural passages related to the theme of free agency consistently deal with man's freedom of choice in matters of good or evil only.[57] Though man on numerous occasions may make other decisions, yet those decisions are often subject to the overruling influence of divine will if they conflict with God's eternal purposes. Man, in his *mortal* state, usually has little or no control over his time and place of birth,[58] the length of his life,[59] the time of his death,[60] bodily afflictions,[61] and the major world events which shape his life.

---

54. D&C 101:78.
55. *Ibid.*
56. D&C 93:30-31.
57. The major doctrinal passages in this area include Gen. 2:16-17; Deut. 11:26-28; Josh. 24:14-15; 2 Ne. 2:11-29; Al. 12:30-35; 29:4-5; 41:3-8; Hel. 13:10-11; 14:29-31; Moses 4:3; 7:32; D&C 29:35-40; 101:78; 58:28-29; 104:17-19.
58. Acts 17:26-27. Note that the times determined by God are "before appointed." Who appointed them before God did? Is this an allusion to a greater degree of agency man possessed in his pre-mortal state? Interesting references on this theme are contained in the author's book, *Life Everlasting* (Salt Lake City, Utah: Bookcraft, Inc., 1967), pp. 36-42. See also Deut. 32:7-8.
59. See D&C 29:43-44; Job 14:5; Al. 40:10.
60. See Eccles. 3:1-2; D&C 42:28; D&C 122:9.
61. See Jn. 9:103; 11:1-4.

There is a common tendency to assume that man possesses a far greater degree of agency and ability to choose between good and evil than is taught by the scriptures. The assumption that man has complete control over all his life circumstances is neither scriptural, logical, nor realistic. Because the concept of free agency has been frequently misunderstood and overstated, the relationship of free agency to prophecy has appeared to be one of opposition and contradiction.

God rules in the affairs of men, and often alters the course of man's affairs. He is a "discerner of the thoughts and intents of the heart."[62] He "knoweth all things" and He has taught man that "all things are present before mine eyes."[63] With His understanding of the intent and purposes of men, God is constantly shaping the lives of both men and nations. The scriptures bear repeated witness to this truth.[64] It is folly to disregard the effect of God's control in the affairs of man, for the Lord has warned that "in nothing doth man offend God, or against none is his wrath kindled, save *those who confess not his hand in all things,* and obey not his commandments."[65]

Though God rules in the affairs of men, man's life is not predestined. Man can greatly alter his life's course through the exercising of moral agency. Man may not be able to prevent the wars, pestilences, and judgments which God has decreed must come upon the earth, but through his personal righteousness man can remain firmly fixed on a course towards his personal exaltation in the time of trial. Man may not be able to alter the intent and actions of wicked men in positions of power, yet he often can shield himself and his loved ones from the effects of their evil policies

---

62. D&C 33:1.

63. D&C 38:2. See also verses 7-8.

64. Consider such passages as the following, which give clear indication that God controls the actions and fate of nations: I Ki. 12:24; 14:14; 20:13, 23; II Ki. 3:18; 8:19; 10:32; 13:5; 15:37; 17:20; 19:34; 21:14; 24:2-3; II Chron. 13:15-17; 20:6-7, 27; 24:24; 29:8; 30:12; 32:21; 36:17; Mic. 1:6; Is. 3:1-3; 7:20; Obad. 2, 4, 8; Jer. 5:15-17; 6:8; 7:3-7; 12:12, 17; 14:12; 15:4; 19:7; 20:5; 21:4-6,7; 22:7; 25:9, 12; 27:8; 32:3; 46:26; Ezek. 20:18-26; 29:19; 30:23-24; 38:16; 39:1-2; Dan. 1:1-2; 2:21.

That God controls the actions and fate of individuals is also shown in numerous passages, of which the following are typical: I Ki. 11:14, 21, 34, 36; 12:15; 20:42; 22:20-3; II Ki. 3:10; 9:7; 10:30; 15:5, 12; 19:7; 24:20; II Chron. 10:15; 11:4; 13:2-20; 15:6-7; 16:7, 8; 18:31; 21:18; 25:16, 10; 26:16-20; 28:10; 33:11; 36:22; Mic. 7:8-9; Is. 29:10; 63:17; Ezek. 24:16-18; Ezra 7:6; Dan. 1:9, 17; 2:37; 4:17; 4:25, 32; Zech. 8:10.

God also controls nature and the elements, which in turn affect the affairs of man. This is demonstrated in passages such as: II Ki. 8:1; Jon. 1:4, 17; 2:6, 8; Amos 4:7-10, 13; 5:8; 8:9; 9:5, 6; Is. 23:11; 29:6; 42:15; 43:16; 44:3; 50:2; 51:10, 15; Nahum 1:3, 4; Hab. 3:6-11; Jer. 3:3; 5:22, 24; 10:10, 13; 14:22; Dan. 2:22; Neh. 9:11; Joel 2:23.

65. D&C 59:21.

through the exercise of righteous faith and priesthood power. Trials and sufferings may fall on the just as well as the wicked, and the righteous may be unable to turn them from their course. Yet the righteous may still, through the exercise of their moral agency, remain firm in the faith and reap eventual good from the experience. As the Lord revealed to His servant, Joseph Smith:

> If thou art called to pass through tribulation; if thou art in perils among false brethren; if thou art in perils among robbers; if thou art in perils by land or by sea;
>
> If thou art accused with all manner of false accusations; if thine enemies fall upon thee; if they tear thee from the society of thy father and mother and brethren and sisters; and if with a drawn sword thine enemies tear thee from the bosom of thy wife, and of thine offspring, and thine elder son, although but six years of age, shall cling to thy garments, and shall say, My father, my father, why can't you stay with us? O, my father, what are the men going to do with you? and if then he shall be thrust from thee by the sword, and thou be dragged to prison, and thine enemies prowl around thee like wolves for the blood of the lamb;
>
> And if thou shouldst be cast into the pit, or into the hands of murderers, and the sentence of death passed upon thee; if thou be cast into the deep; if the billowing surge conspire against thee; if fierce winds become thine enemy; if the heavens gather blackness, and all the elements combine to hedge up the way; and above all, if the very jaws of hell shall gape open the mouth wide after thee, *know thou, my son, that all these things shall give thee experience, and shall be for thy good.*[66]

Man, through the exercise of his agency to choose between good and evil, often determines his fate by establishing in the present a cause-and-effect relationship with the future. When a prophecy has been made pertaining to a man's future actions, it is often a pre-statement of what the ultimate effect of the man's present actions will be. The prophecy is not an indication of predestination. Yet it is an indication of the future results of previous decisions, both mortal and pre-mortal.

This cause-and-effect relationship with the future is depicted in numerous scriptural passages. For instance, note the prophecy of future wars which was made to the Jewish king Asa because of his failure to exercise faith in God:

> At that time Hanani the seer came to Asa king of Judah, and said unto him, *Because thou hast relied on the king of Syria, and not relied on the Lord thy God, therefore is the host of the king of Syria escaped out of thine hand.*
>
> Were not the Ethiopians and the Lubims a huge host, with very many chariots and horsemen? Yet, because thou didst rely on the Lord, he delivered them into thine hand.
>
> *For the eyes of the Lord run to and fro throughout the whole earth, to shew himself strong in the behalf of them whose heart is perfect toward him. Herein thou hast done foolishly: therefore from henceforth thou shalt have wars.*[67]

---

66. D&C 122:5-7.   67. II Chron. 16:7-9.

Because he inquired of an idol rather than of the Lord concerning his health, the Israelite king, Ahaziah, received a prophecy of his impending death:

> Ahaziah fell down through a lattice in his upper chamber that was in Samaria, and was sick: and he sent messengers, and said unto them, Go, inquire of Baal-zebub the god of Ekron whether I shall recover of this disease.
>
> But the angel of the Lord said to Elijah the Tishbite, Arise, go up to meet the messengers of the king of Samaria, and say unto them, *Is it not because there is not a God in Israel, that ye go to inquire of Baal-zebub the god of Ekron?*
>
> *Now therefore thus saith the Lord, Thou shalt not come down from that bed on which thou art gone up, but shalt surely die.*[68]

The deathbed prophecy of Elisha concerning future conflicts between Syria and Israel was formulated on the basis of the lack of determination of king Joash:

> Now Elisha was fallen sick of his sickness whereof he died. And Joash the king of Israel came down unto him, and wept over his face, and said, O my father, my father, the chariot of Israel, and the horsemen thereof.
>
> And Elisha said unto him, Take bow and arrows. And he took unto him bow and arrows.
>
> And he said to the king of Israel, Put thine hand upon the bow. And he put his hand upon it: and Elisha put his hands upon the king's hands.
>
> And he said, Open the window eastward. And he opened it. Then Elisha said, Shoot. And he shot. And he said, The arrow of deliverance from Syria: for thou shalt smite the Syrians in Aphek, till thou have consumed them.
>
> And he said, Take the arrows. And he took them. And he said unto the king of Israel, Smite upon the ground. And he smote thrice, and stayed.
>
> *And the man of God was wroth with him, and said, Thou shouldest have smitten five or six times; then hadst thou smitten Syria till thou hadst consumed it: whereas now thou shalt smite Syria but thrice.*[69]

When Ahab of Israel failed to kill the wicked Benhadad whom the Lord had delivered into his hand, his action occasioned this prophecy:

> So the prophet departed, and waited for the king by the way, and disguised himself with ashes upon his face.
>
> And as the king passed by, he cried unto the king: and he said, Thy servant went out into the midst of the battles; and, behold, a man turned aside, and brought a man unto me, and said, Keep this man: if by any means he be for his life, or else thou shalt pay a talent of silver.
>
> And as thy servant was busy here and there, he was gone. And the king of Israel said unto him, So shall thy judgment be; thyself hast decided it.
>
> And he hasted, and took the ashes away from his face; and the king of Israel discerned him that he was of the prophets.

---

68. II Ki. 1:2-4.
69. II Ki. 13:14-19.

> *And he said unto him, Thus saith the Lord, Because thou hast let go out of thy hand a man whom I appointed to utter destruction, therefore thy life shall go for his life, and thy people for his people.*[70]

In another example, at the time of Moses' last counsel to the Israelites, he prophesied in great detail what would happen to them after they entered the Land of Promise. He predicted that they would later demand a king.[71] Centuries later, near the end of the life of the prophet Samuel, Moses' prophecy was fulfilled as the elders of Israel came to Samuel with the request for a king.[72] Samuel then prophesied to the Israelites the bondage and trials to which they would submit themselves and their descendants if they insisted upon a monarch:

> This will be the manner of the king that shall reign over you: He will take your sons, and appoint them for himself, for his chariots, and to be his horsemen; and some shall run before his chariots.
>
> And he will appoint him captains over thousands, and captains over fifties; and will set them to ear his ground, and to reap his harvest, and to make his instruments of war, and instruments of his chariots.
>
> And he will take your daughters to be confectionaries, and to be cooks, and to be bakers.
>
> And he will take your fields, and your vineyards, and your oliveyards, even the best of them, and give them to his servants.
>
> And he will take the tenth of your seed, and of your vineyards, and give to his officers, and to his servants.
>
> And he will take your manservants, and your maidservants, and your goodliest young men, and your asses, and put them to his work.
>
> He will take the tenth of your sheep: and ye shall be his servants.
>
> *And ye shall cry out in that day because of your king which ye shall have chose you; and the Lord will not hear you in that day.*[73]

Yet the people of Israel continued to clamor for a king. By the time the throne had passed from Saul to David to Solomon, Samuel's prophecy had received literal fulfillment.[74]

These examples combine to depict the relation of moral agency and prophecy. Prophecy merely pre-states what the ultimate effect of present or future actions will be. Man determines his eternal status by establishing, through exercise of his moral agency in the present, a cause-and-effect relationship with the future.

---

70. I Ki. 20:38-42.
71. Deut. 17:14.
72. I Sam. 8:5-9, 19-20.
73. I Sam. 8:11-18.
74. I Ki. 10:25-29; 11:1-10. Both Israel and Judah suffered to a far greater extent under other kings in the era of the divided kingdoms.

Summary

1. God has repeatedly promised in the scriptures that the prophecies and promises which He reveals to His people through His inspired servants will come to pass and be fulfilled.

2. Although the coming in glory of the Savior is believed to be near, those events which are prophesied to take place prior to His coming must actually happen preceeding His advent. They will not be excluded from the events of the last days, for God has promised that all His words will be fulfilled.

3. Analysis of scriptural prophecies and their fulfillment indicates that most inspired prophecies are specific, accurate, and are literally fulfilled.

4. The revelations of God are designed to be plain and easily understood by man. However, revelations regarded as easily understood by some individuals may be difficult for others to comprehend because of their lack of studious preparation and/or failure to have and heed the clarifying promptings of the Holy Spirit.

5. Students and interpreters of prophecy may make erroneous interpretations which prevent them from recognizing the true fulfillment of the prophecies. A distinction should always be made between the literal words of a prophecy and interpretations made concerning the prophecies by others.

6. Prophecy is not predestination. Prophetic outcomes may be changed.

7. Prophecy revealed by God is a pre-statement of the way in which the will of God will later be manifested.

8. If conditions change sufficiently to cause God to alter His will, God may reveal new prophecy to His spokesmen indicating that the outcome of earth events will be changed. A number of scriptural instances indicate that God uses this procedure.

9. When God reveals new prophecy to reflect altered conditions, the new prophecy should be regarded as superceding and replacing previous prophecy. The error of regarding the former and latter prophecies as being in conflict with each other should not be made. Hopefully, such new prophecy will stipulate clearly that a change is being made in the Lord's program.

10. It is possible that God may reveal prophetic changes to His spokesmen the prophets, but the prophets may then fail to adequately communicate such changes to the Church at large. In such instances the saints are left with incomplete evidence and are unable to fully understand the situation under consideration unless further revelation is given.

11. Instances in which prophetic outcomes are changed and God reveals substitute prophecies are rare. They are not indications of divine indecision, but usually reflect God's mercy and love in situations where men have repented or have sought special blessings from Him.

12. People sometimes assume they have the right to more free agency than God actually promises to man. The agency promised in the scriptures is moral agency—the privilege of choice between good and evil which determine man's eternal fate. Control over the various external events which shape one's life's course is not necessarily a part of man's moral agency. Prophecy does not restrict man's moral agency.

13. God rules in the affairs of man and shapes the affairs of both men and nations. Though man enjoys the privilege of moral agency, God directs the events of man's life (perhaps in accordance with pre-mortal choices made by man). Man's life is not predestined, but is shaped by God in order to give man experience and opportunity to merit eternal life.

14. Through the exercise of his moral agency, man often establishes a cause-and-effect relationship with the future. Prophecy is sometimes a pre-statement of what the ultimate effect of man's present actions will be.

6

How Should Prophecy Be
Verified and Interpreted?

Prophecies are given to help man shape his life in preparation for the future. One must decide whether to accept, reject, or ignore the prophecies which pertain to his life and situation, and he will make that decision on the basis of his estimate of whether or not the prophecies will come to pass. Indeed, the study of prophecy continually poses the question of validity. One needs to determine whether prophecies of forthcoming happenings are actually going to come to pass in a literal manner before he can allow them to shape his life.

The study of prophecy within the Church functions on at least two levels. One level is concerned with demonstrating that particular individuals and Church leaders have actually been prophets. A second, and higher, level of study draws meaning and pattern from the things the prophets have foretold. This chapter is intended to be an aid to the reader in evaluating the validity of prophecy on both of these levels.

Revealed Tests for Determining the
Validity of Revelation and Prophecy

A Latter-day Saint has both the right and the obligation to verify what appears to be revelation and prophecy. He must discern that it is valid and that it comes from the proper source. This was Paul's admonition to the Thessalonians, whom he told to *"Quench not the Spirit. Despise not prophesyings. Prove all things; hold fast that which is good."* [1] An individual should test his own inspiration and should also evaluate that which is revealed to others. This was the example set by the prophet, Alma, who testified,

---

1. I Thess. 5:19-21.

> Do ye not suppose that I know of these things myself? Behold, I testify
> unto you that I do know that these things whereof I have spoken are true. And
> how do ye suppose that I know of their surety?
>
> Behold, I say unto you *they are made known unto me by the Holy Spirit
> of God.* Behold, I have fasted and prayed many days *that I might know* these
> things of myself. *And now I do know of myself that they are true; for the
> Lord God hath made them manifest unto me by his Holy Spirit;* and this is the
> spirit of revelation which is in me.
>
> And moreover, I say unto you that *it has thus been revealed unto me, that
> the words which have been spoken by our fathers are true, even so according
> to the spirit of prophecy,* which is in me, which is also by the manifestation of
> the Spirit of God.[2]

Without the operation of this testing function in the Church, Satan
would be free to infiltrate his followers into the ranks of the members. The
obligation of all members to confirm by the Spirit the things of the Spirit is
a vital force in the maintaining of righteousness, truth, and harmony in the
Church. It is also the method whereby members can maintain a strong
testimony of the divine calling of their leaders.

Various standards for evaluating prophecies are set forth in the scriptures. They provide norms which man can apply to discern that which is
true. These revealed tests for establishing the validity of prophecy are:

1. *Fulfillment*—the coming to pass of a prophecy is the most valid
proof of its authenticity. As Jeremiah taught in his day, *"When the word of
the prophet shall come to pass, then shall the prophet be known,* that the
Lord hath truly sent him."[3] Conversely, "When a prophet speaketh in the
name of the Lord, *if the thing follow not, nor come to pass, that is the thing
which the Lord hath not spoken, but the prophet hath spoken it presump-
tuously:* thou shalt not be afraid of him."[4]

Knowledge of the fulfillment of other prophetic statements made by
prophets inspires confidence that subsequent prophecies they make will
also be fulfilled. In like manner, knowledge that some portions of a specific
prophecy have come to pass inspires confidence that the remainder of the
prophecy will also be fulfilled.

2. *Lack of conflict with other revelations*—The Lord revealed to
Sidney Rigdon that he was to test the prophecies of Joseph Smith, saying,
"It shall be given unto him to prophesy; and thou shalt preach my gospel
and *call on the holy prophets to prove his words, as they shall be given
him."* [5] The evaluation of a prophecy by comparing it with the words of
other prophecies and revelations, both scriptural and from latter-day

2. Al. 5:45-47. See also D&C 18:2-3; 6:14-17, 22-24.
3. Jer. 28:9.
4. Deut. 18:22.
5. D&C 35:23.

prophets, is a second approach in determining validity. This was Paul's method when he counseled the Corinthian saints that *"the spirits of the prophets are subject to the prophets."* [6] The comparison of prophecies, of course, is for two purposes: (1) to determine if they are free from conflict with each other, and (2) to note their parallels and combined insights.

Care must be taken that prophecies are compared with other prophecies or revelations, not merely with the opinions or private interpretations of prominent men. Since "no prophecy of the scripture is of any private interpretation," [7] the comparison must be made with other instances where "holy men of God spake as they were moved by the Holy Ghost." [8]

3. *The law of witnesses applied through parallel prophecies*—The Savior, on various occasions, has revealed that "in the mouth of two or three witnesses shall every word be established." [9] He has followed this policy Himself in restoring His work in the last days. [10] He has seen fit to reveal many prophetic insights of the same events to various prophets, both in ancient and in modern times. The prophet Amos was commenting on the principle of parallel revelation when he cried, "Surely the Lord God will do nothing, but he revealeth his *secret* unto his *servants* the *prophets*." [11] The Lord revealed to Hosea that "I have also spoken by the prophets, and *I have multiplied visions, and used similitudes,* by the ministry of the prophets." [12] Thus, prophecies are substantiated by each other when they are found to reveal the same events.

However, when a prophecy stands alone it isn't necessarily false. Other prophecies may parallel it which have not yet come to the attention of the student, or the prophecy may be the first of a series of revelations, and the later ones have not yet been given. A prophecy without parallel evidence should not be judged false on that basis alone; rather, judgment should be withheld until new evidence is forthcoming.

4. *Confirmation of validity through personal revelation*—The Lord has promised that "whosoever shall believe in my name, doubting nothing, *unto him will I confirm all my words, even unto the ends of the earth."* [13] Moroni promised that *"by the power of the Holy Ghost ye may know the truth of all things."* [14] In some instances, individuals receive confirming

---

6. I Cor. 14:32.

7. II Pet. 1:20.

8. II Pet. 1:21.

9. II Cor. 13:1. See also Deut. 17:6; 19:15; D&C 6:28; 42:80-81; 128:3.

10. See, for instance, D&C 5:10-15; 128:20; 2 Ne. 27:12-14; etc.

11. Amos 3:7. Note that the passage is saying that several prophets will be the recipients of a single message.

12. Hos. 12:10.

13. Morm. 9:25.

14. Moro. 10:5. See also verse 4.

testimony through the Holy Ghost that a prophecy is either true or false. This is a privilege exercised primarily by the faithful who are well conversant with the operations of the Spirit. This is a personal blessing—one must rely on his own communication through the Spirit and receive his own confirmation or warning.

Experience, including hundreds of frank discussions with bishops and members of stake presidencies, indicates that the receipt of such confirmation concerning prophecies of the latter-days and concerning sacred matters in general is relatively rare within the Church today. Many seemingly give lip-service to the principle but fail to apply it. Perhaps they fail to approach the matter without doubt,[15] or fail to pay the price of days of fasting and prayer,[16] or neglect the revealed instruction that "you must study it out in your mind; then you must ask me if it be right."[17] Perhaps they are not prepared to accept the responsibility that confirming revelation will place upon them, for the Lord has cautioned that He will give "unto the faithful line upon line, precept upon precept; and *I will try you and prove you herewith.*"[18] Man does not have control over such confirming revelations through the Spirit—they are gifts of God, given when He choses to do so. Yet those who gain such confirmations are blessed with an absolute assuredness which cannot be gained through academic means alone.

5. *Must not command the Church nor claim recipient is appointed to receive revelations for the Church*—As was seen in preceding chapters, the Lord has commanded that revelation granted to anyone else than the President of the Church is not to be regarded as valid if it either (1) commands the Church or (2) asserts that the recipient has been appointed by God to receive revelations for the Church.

However, this by no means implies that others besides the President of the Church cannot properly receive revelations, nor that revelations received by others may not foretell what the Church or its members will encounter in a future situation, and also foretell what the future actions of the Church and/or its members will be in those situations. A careful reading of early Church history and the journals of early Church members will make this abundantly apparent.

One other important test of the validity of revelation and prophecy should be included in this context. It is not scriptural, and hence will not be listed as are those above. It is, however, both basic and simple. The application of the test would save a great deal of difficulty in many situations. When a new teaching or prophetic statement is put forth, the question

---

15. Morm. 9:25, 27.
16. Al. 5:46.
17. D&C 9:8.
18. D&C 98:12.

should be tactfully asked, *"Is this a new revelation from God?"* A simple yes or no answer to that question would be extremely useful to all concerned.

Many statements of years gone by are today regarded as revelation although the persons who made them did not regard them as such when they were made. Similarly, many commentators tend to embellish previously-made prophecies with their own interpretive statements as they relate the prophecies in gospel discourses. The Church needs to be able to determine whether embellishing statements are intended as prophecies or as private interpretations. The tactful asking of this question could prove very helpful in instances of this kind.

Guidelines for Evaluating Historical Records and Testimonies

Emphasis should be placed on the importance of careful gathering of historical detail when attempting to determine the validity of prophecies. However, experience has shown that the study of prophecy and revelation cannot be limited solely to an historical approach. When a prophecy makes significant comment concerning the future, it can't be brushed aside as false simply because insufficient historical data is available to completely verify the manner in which it was given. The very nature of revelation tends to conflict with the techniques of historical research. Prophecies and revelations tend to be given to individuals when they are alone; hence, no witnesses are available to testify concerning the manner in which they were received. Also, when a revelation is received while the recipient is in the company of others, the group is often unaware of that which is taking place. They can only bear witness to that which the recipient tells them, and he may choose to tell nothing. Thus the historical approach is not completely applicable to the study of prophecy and revelation.

The study and analysis of prophecy is closer to genealogical research methodology than to the techniques of pure historical research. The very nature of the sources of evidence makes it so. As one studies the various items, he must be concerned with whether they are primary or secondary sources; original records or items which have been transcribed, compiled, and copied; and whether the evidence is direct or circumstantial. These terms fall more often from the lips of the genealogist than from the mouth of the historian. Sometimes things have to be demonstrated by the "lack of conflicting evidence" method, a technique more common to genealogical than to historical research.

When a student is seeking to determine the validity of a prophecy, he would do well to examine its

1. record source
2. record transmission
3. validifying historical evidence.

An examination of the source of a prophecy is an attempt to evaluate the accuracy with which the prophecy was first recorded. Sources may be divided into two general classifications: *primary sources* and *secondary sources*. These terms have been defined by one author as follows:

> A *Primary Source* is a record or statement of an event or a circumstance made by an eye-witness or someone closely connected with that event or circumstance, recorded or stated verbally at or near the time of the event or circumstance.
> A *Secondary Source* is a record or statement of an event or circumstance made by a non-eyewitness or by someone not closely connected with the event or circumstance, recorded or stated verbally either at or some time after the event, or by an eye-witness at a time *after* the event, *when the fallibility of memory is an important factor.*[19]

Within these two general classifications there are varying degrees of validity. For instance, among primary sources,

—a prophecy recorded by the recipient of the revelation would be considered more valid than the same prophecy recorded by an eye-witness who only heard the prophecy delivered;

—the recording of a prophecy made by one who claimed inspiration in recording it would be considered more valid than a prophecy recorded by one who admittedly wrote it down "as best he could";

—a prophetic recording written down and then submitted for the approval of the individual who received the revealed prophecy would be considered more valid than a recording which was never submitted for such approval;

—a prophetic recording which was properly witnessed and/or notarized would be considered more valid than one which was not;

—a prophetic recording which carefully detailed the historical circumstances and listed the participants would be considered more valid than one which related only the prophecy itself;

—a prophetic recording which is carefully written down would be considered more valid than a verbal retelling of the prophecy in a sermon or conversation, etc.

While primary sources are always considered more valid than secondary sources, they still need to be evaluated as to their relative strength.

Secondary source material is more likely to contain items of inaccuracy than is primary source material. Certainly there will be greater variance of reliability among secondary sources than among primary sources. However, "The passage of time between an event and its recording does not prove that the resulting records *must be incorrect* because it has been classified as

---

19. Harland, *Derek, Genealogical Research Standards* (Salt Lake City, Utah: Bookcraft, Inc., 1963), p. 39.

Secondary source material. In fact in many cases such Secondary source material may later be proved to be the more exact."[20] Often, however, secondary sources are the only sources available.

In summary, a study of the record's source is an effort to determine if the prophecy was recorded accurately when it was written down.

The manner in which a prophecy has been transmitted and circulated also deserves analysis. When any item is copied repeatedly, there is a very real danger of copy errors creeping in. In this area, an *original* copy of a prophecy is to be considered of greater validity than a *transcribed, compiled,* or *copied* record. Items repeatedly copied by hand and circulated "over the back fence" tend to have phrases omitted, punctuation altered, and interpretive statements added which later are absorbed into the text in continued copying. Errors which originate in a copy are embodied in later copies until "families of errors" exist which spring from parent copies. A careful study of Biblical translations and manuscripts, for instance, indicates that such difficulties can become quite extensive, even in scripture.

The possibility of copying errors and interpolations altering the sense of a prophecy, however, tends to be exagerated by some Latter-day Saints, in the opinion of the author. He has had repeated opportunities to compare various circulated accounts of well-known prophecies and other spiritual experiences in the Church, and has observed relatively few changes, and none of major consequence. While the danger of copying errors and interpolations does exist, it tends to be over-rated.

Another area of historical verification that should be pursued as prophecies are studied is the evaluation of validifying historical evidence. Details pertaining to the time, place, and circumstances in which the prophecy was given should be verified when possible. Allusions concerning the political, social, religious, and other conditions of the time when a prophecy was given should be checked when possible. An effort should be made to determine whether the participants mentioned in prophetic accounts were where the accounts claimed they were at the time specified in the account. In seeking such historical verifications, evidence of two types may be located, *direct* and *circumstantial.*

"Direct evidence is any information that points directly to the problem under discussion and which spontaneously brings about a conclusion upon a disputed issue."[21]

"Circumstantial evidence, on the other hand, does not give a direct answer to the issue, but requires inference or calculation to arrive at the required conclusion. It must be pointed out that there are two classes of

---

20. *Ibid.,* p. 40.
21. *Ibid.,* p. 52.

circumstantial evidence —Relevant and Irrelevant."[22] Circumstantial evidence has value in that it "provides clues and leads to future searches for better evidence."[23]

Direct evidence, of course, is preferable to circumstantial evidence. However, there are many instances when only circumstantial evidence is available, and that evidence is insufficient to establish the validity of the prophecy under consideration. In such instances, the strength of circumstantial evidence can be improved by trying to disprove it through seeking for contradictory evidence. A demonstrated *lack of conflicting evidence* gives support in cases of circumstantial or insufficient evidence.

The acceptability of witnesses and their testimony should be considered. Differentiations should be made between opinions and hearsay evidence as contrasted with definite knowledge and eye-witness accounts. The danger of accepting opinion as fact on religious matters is especially great when dealing with people of high standing in the community or in the Church. Neither social prestige, good character, nor religious authority is an acceptable substitute for actual knowledge when the question of the validity of witnesses is under consideration.

All of these items must be taken into consideration when considering the validity of prophecies from an historical approach. The search should be made for primary sources, original records, direct evidence, and qualified witnesses. Unfortunately, these elements are frequently missing to a large degree. It is well that the study of prophecy does not have to hinge on historical approaches alone.

The Characteristics of Prophecy Influence Study Approaches

There are five basic characteristics of prophecy which influence the manner in which prophecies should be studied. These are:

1. *A prophecy requires fulfillment.* Some historians have noted that people sometimes attempt to link themselves to a famous person by quoting things the person said or by relating stories of their experiences together. The tendency for such quotations and stories to be exaggerated sometimes causes increasingly invalid reportings of historical incidents as the years go by. As the stories and quotations receive wider and wider circulation, a halo effect of half-truths and myths begin to surround the image or memory of the famous person. Certainly this tendency must be noted and evaluated in each incident considered.

The tendency of historians to discount the validity of even comparatively reliable evidence by reference to this circumstance when the matter

---

22. *Ibid.,* p. 53.
23. *Ibid.,* p. 54.

pertains to prophecies, revelations, or other miraculous events which they disbelieve should receive equal note. This is an area where bias may be evidenced in both directions.

Within The Church of Jesus Christ of Latter-day Saints, however, prophecy tends to remain aloof from this type of give-and-take controversy because of its most basic characteristic: prophecy requires fulfillment. A belief in the validity of prophecy is a tenet of the Church,[24] and the saints generally regard prophecy as important and as something which should not be taken lightly. It would be obvious folly for a Church member to fabricate a prophecy of future events and attribute it to Joseph Smith or any other prophet if there were no anticipation that it would come to pass. The need for fulfillment places an effective curb on embellishment and imagination. The author has yet to find a journal or other original record by a Latter-day Saint, which reports a prophecy of Joseph Smith or other early leader, where there was reason to suspect inaccurate information has been deliberately inserted in the prophecy. Prophecies demand fulfillment; hence people listen to them carefully, record them with special care, and make special efforts to keep them free from error or embellishment. Historians should take this tendency into account.

2. *Parallel revelation is given.* God frequently sees fit to reveal the same thing to a number of different persons. The historian, who is accustomed to linking ideas and influences from one person to another, is ill-equipped to handle the phenomenon of a series of separate revelations being given to unrelated individuals. Historical methods, which generally exclude the possibility of revelation being a valid source for the transmittal of ideas, cannot provide an effective approach or understanding in such a situation.

The comparison of parallel revelations is the most important tool for verification of prophecy which the student has available. Indeed, to compare prophecies is to employ the law of witnesses,[25] for the Lord uses the message of one prophet to lend validity to the words of another of His spokesmen. Parallel prophecies give strong evidence to support each other, yet the explanation of parallel revelations is beyond the scope of usual historical methods and techniques. Verification through the comparison of parallel prophecies is especially useful in instances where the origin and/or accuracy of recording of a prophecy is uncertain.

3. *Preliminary fulfillment anticipates later fulfillment.* When early items of a prophecy which covers an extended period of time are fulfilled, it is but natural to accept the inspiration of the prophecy and anticipate the ultimate fulfillment of the other items prophesied. Thus the validity of the

---

24. Article of Faith 7.
25. See pp. 152-159, 190-191.

latter portion of a prophecy—that which is still future—may be at least partially established by the careful documentation of the fulfillment of the earlier portion. Prophecies frequently extend over a long period of time, and this is a useful approach which tends to establish their validity. In instances where there is historical uncertainty as to the origin or accuracy of recording of a prophecy, this technique is especially useful.

4. *Prophecy links future events.* The historical approach tends to try to explain prophecies as being the results of current events in a prophet's time, from which he has deduced the events of the future. Such a critical approach might be valid if the prophecy spoke on only one future happening. Most prophecies, however, link a series of future events together in a chronological order or other relationship. If most of the events prophesied have no link to current events in the prophet's day, then there is little justification for the assertion that one or two of the prophesied events are merely deductions made by the prophet based on current events. Unless the entire prophecy fits into the circumstances of the prophet's day, none of it belongs there. The only exception would be, possibly, the opening events of long, down-through-time utterances.

The manner in which a prophecy links various events is of great importance, for it is from this linking relationship that prophetic chronologies are drawn.

5. *Things of God are often recorded with the aid of the Spirit.* Historians are, and should be, concerned about whether statements are recorded accurately by those who hear them made. Can a person record from memory a statement several pages long which he or someone else has made without varying the wording, order, etc? In most cases, the answer to that question must be no. However, things revealed by God are sometimes different from the general rule and deserve special consideration. The Holy Spirit, who serves as the means of communication for many revelations, often remains with the recipient of a prophecy of revelation until the communication is written down. For instance, when the visions of the degrees of glory were granted to Joseph Smith and Sidney Rigdon, Joseph wrote, "This is the end of the vision which we saw, *which we were commanded to write while we were yet in the Spirit.*" [26] Indeed, the writing and preservation of sacred things is under the direction of Diety, for the Lord revealed to Oliver Cowdery,

---

26. D&C 76:113. See also verses 28, 49, 80, 115. Elder Parley P. Pratt left this description of the manner in which Joseph Smith recorded some of the revelations which he received:

> After we had joined in prayer in his translating room, he dictated in our presence the following revelation:—(each sentence was uttered slowly and very distinctly, and with a pause between each, sufficiently long for it to be recorded, by an ordinary writer, in long hand.)

If it be not right you shall have no such feelings, but you shall have *a stupor of thought that shall cause you to forget the thing which is wrong; therefore, you cannot write that which is sacred save it be given you from me.*[27]

A basic function of the Holy Ghost is to "bring all things to your remembrance."[28] Through the power of the Spirit, the exact words of sacred things long forgotten can be recalled and written down. For example, to his son Don Carlos in his final blessing, the first patriarch of the Church, Joseph Smith, Sr., made this promise:

> Carlos, my darling son, when I blessed thee thy blessing was never written, and I could not get it done, but now I want you to get my book, which contains the blessings of my family. *Take your pen and fill out all those parts of your blessing which were not written. You shall have the Spirit of the Lord and be able to fill up all the vacancies which were left by Oliver* when he wrote it. You shall be great in the sight of the Lord, for he sees and knows the integrity of your heart, and you shall be blessed; all that know you shall bless you. Your wife and your children shall also be blessed, and you shall live to fulfill all that the Lord has sent you to do. Even so. Amen.[29]

The Holy Ghost, then, serves to aid man in preserving sacred and important things, by calling them to man's remembrance.

Prophecies also tend to be better preserved than other items through the ordinary functions of memory. Because they are unusual, interesting, important, and inseparately connected with various aspects of one's faith and testimony, Latter-day Saints especially have tended to listen to them attentively and to record and preserve them with care.

These five characteristics of prophecy, then, are noteworthy:

1. a prophecy requires fulfillment;
2. parallel revelation is given;
3. preliminary fulfillment anticipates later fulfillment;
4. prophecy links future events; and
5. the things of God are often recorded by the aid of the Spirit.

Each has an influence on the manner prophecies should be studied, and each calls for understandings not found through the use of standard historical methods only.

This was the manner in which all his written revelations were dictated and written. There was never any hesitation, reviewing, or reading back, in order to keep the run of the subject; neither did any of these communications undergo revisions, interlinings, or corrections. As he dictated them so they stood, so far as I have witnessed; and I was present to witness the dictation of several communications of several pages each. (Pratt, Parley Parker, *Autobiography of Parley Parker Pratt* (Salt Lake City, Utah: Deseret Book Company, 6th ed., 1966), p. 62.)

27. D&C 9:9. See also 24:5-6.
28. Jn. 14:26.
29. Smith, Lucy Mack, *History of Joseph Smith by His Mother* (Salt Lake City, Utah: Bookcraft, 1958), p. 311.

A Checklist for Evaluating the Validity of Prophecy

It must be recognized that in almost every prophetic statement available for study, the supporting evidence is limited. Many of the questions asked will, unfortunately, go unanswered for lack of evidence, pro or con. This is particularly true in connection with the ancient scriptural prophecies found in the Bible and in the Book of Mormon. For the most part, they are accepted as valid because external and internal evidence shows that the books are true, not because the prophecies themselves can be validated. Indeed, there is much more substantiating evidence for almost all of the latter-day prophecies than for the prophecies of the ancient scriptures. The student should maintain this perspective concerning the quality of evidence available on the items as he studies them.

As one seeks to determine whether prophecies of future events are or are not valid, it soon becomes obvious that some type of organized study approach is necessary. Every serious student may wish to develop his own evaluating plan. The following list of questions, however, will aid the general reader to more effectively approach a prophetic statement and evaluate its validity.

I. The Prophet

A. Is there evidence that the recipient of the prophetic revelation has received other prophecies? Have they been fulfilled?

B. Does the prophetic statement claim to have an inspired basis, or is it merely an expression of opinion?

C. Is there evidence of any improper or ulterior motive in the setting forth of the prophecy?

D. Is there evidence that the individual setting forth the prophecy or anyone else may profit from it in any way?

E. What is the motive for the circulation and/or publication of the prophecy?

II. Circumstances Under Which the Prophecy Was Received

A. Is the historical setting for the reception of the prophecy known?

B. Do the statements embodied in the prophecy accurately correspond with known historical facts concerning the time and circumstances of its revelation? Is the evidence direct or circumstantial?

C. What witnesses testify to the veracity of the prophecy? What connects them to it? How reliable are they? What is their motive in testifying about the prophecy? Are they primary or secondary sources?

III. Recording of the Prophecy

A. Was the prophecy completely and accurately recorded?

B. Was the recording at or near the time of the prophecy?

C. What are the circumstances under which it was recorded?

D. Was the recording of the prophecy made by a primary or a secondary source?

E. Is there any claim or evidence that the prophecy was recorded under inspiration?

F. Is there any indication that private interpretations, either those of the recipient of the prophecy or of others, may have been inserted into the prophecy as it was recorded?

IV. Transmission of the Prophecy

A. Is there evidence that the prophecy has been altered in transmission? To what degree?

B. Are the discrepancies copying deviations or interpretive insertions?

C. Has the prophecy been "stabilized" by appropriate publication?

V. Lack of Conflicting Evidence

A. Does the prophecy conflict in any way with the scriptures or other revelations?

B. Is there evidence which would cast legitimate doubt on the validity of the prophecy?

C. Has the prophecy been the target of criticism? Is the criticism legitimate, or based on invalid assumptions? What evidence is cited by the critics to support their views? Is there evidence of bias or of improper or ulterior motives in their criticism?

D. Does the prophecy "command the Church" or assert that the recipient has been "appointed" to receive revelations for the Church?

E. Are there circumstances pertaining to the prophecy which are unexplainable if the validity of the prophecy is rejected?

VI. Comparison with Other Revelations

A. Does the prophecy correspond with other prophecies? Is the law of witnesses in effect?

B. Does the prophecy fit appropriately into a "pattern of prophecy," with a variety of links to a series of other prophetic statements?

VII. Fulfillment

A. What signs of the times presently visible seem to point towards future fulfillment of portions of the prophecy?

B. Does the prophecy call for specific, documentable fulfillment, or only for general, long-range fulfillment?

C. Can logical theories be advanced which would effectively explain the method in which the prophecy may find fulfillment?

VIII. Revealed Confirmation

A. Has confirmation or rejection of the prophecy been revealed to me?

B. Has confirmation or rejection of the prophecy been revealed to others? Should I accept their inspiration as valid without further examination of them or of the prophecy?

The above questions, while not an exhaustive treatment of the subject, will give the student a workable approach to the study of prophecy.

Some Suggestions on the Interpretation of Prophecy

The interpretation of prophecy is accomplished in the same manner as the interpretation of all scripture. The whole process of interpretation is a challenging task which needs to be performed with wisdom and understanding. The remainder of this chapter suggests a series of general approaches to the interpretation of prophecy[30] while giving a series of examples of interpretive pitfalls in connection with well-known passages.

---

30. The following suggestions on the interpretation of scripture are condensed from the author's text, *Prophets and Prophecies of the Old Testament,* pp. 29-34:

A. One should gain his own interpretation of scriptural passages first, before accepting the interpretations made by others.

B. One should seek personal inspiration in interpreting scripture.

C. One should seek an interpretive pattern, drawn from other passages, which clarifies the meaning of the passage under consideration.

D. One should determine the relative strength of a doctrinal interpretation. The validity of doctrinal statements and interpretations can be measured according to a descending scale of value, as follows:

1. Doctrinal statements from numerous scriptural witnesses, which need no external interpretation. They are clearly stated.

2. Doctrinal statements from only one scriptural witness, which needs no external interpretations.

3. Doctrinal statements from numerous scriptural witnesses, which still are subject to various interpretations.

4. Doctrinal statements from only one scriptural witness, which still are subject to various interpretations.

Observe Subject Statements in the Text and Context

A basic rule of interpretation is that subject statements in the text and context of a passage must be observed. If a passage clearly states that it is speaking of a specific event or place, it is improper to disregard the statement and force another meaning.

An example of failure to observe the subject statement is the citing of Isaiah 2:2-3 without including the subject explanation of verse one. This passage has occasionally been cited as a reference pertaining to the Salt Lake Temple. Such an interpretation entirely disregards the subject statement in verse one which clearly shows that it speaks of the temple to be built near Jerusalem:

> *The word that Isaiah the son of Amoz saw concerning Judah and Jerusalem.*
> And it shall come to pass in the last days, that the mountain of the Lord's house shall be established in the top of the mountains, and shall be exalted above the hills; and all nations shall flow unto it.

---

5. Doctrinal teachings from numerous authorized Church leaders, which need no external interpretation, based on their interpretation of the scriptures.

6. Doctrinal teachings from only one authorized Church leader, which need no external interpretation, based on his interpretation of the scriptures.

7. The interpretive opinions of sectarian Bible students and scholars.

E. One should determine the chronological relationship of a passage to aid in fixing its interpretation. Questions such as the following should be asked:

1. Who was prophesying?
2. To whom was he prophesying?
3. Who is to fulfill the prophecy?
4. Where is it to be fulfilled?
5. Has this prophecy already been fulfilled or does the fulfillment still lie in the future? What evidence supports this interpretation?
6. What clues are given to indicate the order of events into which its fulfillment will fall? What must precede its fulfillment? What must follow its fulfillment?
7. Is the determined chronological fulfillment of the prophecy supported by other prophecies and scriptural clues? What?

F. One should glean the interpretive clues from the context.

G. One should have a hypothesis.

H. One should contrast varying interpretations and attempt to find evidence which will substantiate or eliminate one of them. An effort should be made to determine which interpretation the speaker intended when he gave the passage.

I. One should continually propose alternative interpretations.

J. One should be consistent.

K. One should look for key words.

L. One should check his interpretations with other scriptures.

M. One should check his interpretations with the position of the Church.

N. One should compare his interpretations with the findings of sectarian scholars.

> And many people shall go and say, Come ye, and let us go up to the mountain of the Lord, to the house of the God of Jacob; and he will teach us of his ways, and we will walk in his paths: for out of Zion shall go forth the law, and the word of the Lord from Jerusalem.[31]

Apply Time Clues in the Text and Context

Numerous prophecies contain phrases showing a time relationship to other events. To understand and interpret the prophecies correctly, these time relationships must be properly observed. A typical example is Joel 2:28-29:

> And it shall come to pass *afterward,* that I will pour out my spirit upon all flesh; and your sons and your daughters shall prophesy, your old men shall dream dreams, your young men shall see visions:
> And also upon the servants and upon the handmaids in those days will I pour out my spirit.

The word *afterward* gives indication of a time relationship which is vital to the understanding of the passage. Almost the entire book of Joel is a description of a terrible last-days[32] conflict to rage in and around Jerusalem.[33] A careful reading of the entire book can leave little doubt that the time of which the prophecy speaks is yet future. Note also that it is a prophecy to a specific people, the inhabitants of the Land of Israel, who will have the Savior in their midst at that time.[34] Certainly there have been (and are now) dreams, visions, prophecies, and an outpouring of the Lord's Spirit in the Church. But this particular passage is a reference to experiences which are yet future. It is improper to interpret the passage as a reference to past or present events in disregard of the time clue contained therein.

Apply Place Clues in the Text and Context

Many scriptural and prophetic passages contain clues which will aid in determining the place of their fulfillment. The following verse is occasionally cited as one in which reference is made to growth in the western United States:

> The wilderness and the solitary place shall be glad for them; and the desert shall rejoice, and blossom as the rose.

---

31. Note that the quotation of the passage in the Book of Mormon also includes the same subject statement. See 2 Ne. 12:1-3.

32. Note that it is to be "in those days, and in that time," when the Lord shall end (bring again) the captivity of Judah and Jerusalem (Joel 3:1-2) and when the Lord will soon be dwelling in Zion, His holy mountain, and Jerusalem shall be holy (Joel 3:17). There can be little doubt that the book of Joel is a prophecy of the Battle of Armageddon.

33. See especially Joel 2:1, 15, 23; 3:2, 12, 16-17, 20-21.

34. See Joel 2:27.

Yet is it the deserts of Utah to which Isaiah had reference? The succeeding verses make it obvious that he had reference to his own area, Palestine. Note the next verse, for instance:

> It shall blossom abundantly, and rejoice even with joy and singing: *the glory of Lebanon shall be given unto it, and excellency of Carmel and Sharon, they shall see the glory of the Lord,* and the excellency of our God.[35]

Here he identifies places which are to blossom and rejoice: Carmel and Sharon. Carmel seemingly refers to the area around Mt. Carmel, overlooking the Mediterranean Sea, seventy miles northwest of Jerusalem.[36] Today the city of Haifa stands there, in fulfillment of Isaiah's prophecy. Sharon is the Plain of Sharon, which stretches along the Mediterranean Coast between the ancient cities of Joppa and Ceasarea. Today the area includes Israel's largest city, Tel Aviv-Jaffa. To the north along the seacoast lie Israel's choice resort areas, such as Natanya and Caesarea. Literal fulfillment can be found in the places which Isaiah identifies specifically in his prophecy. Though the Utah valleys have also grown, it is difficult to find in them the fulfillment of Isaiah's prophecy, for they do not contain the places to which the prophet made specific reference.

Be Aware of the Effect of Style and Writing Techniques

There are instances of interpretations of Biblical passages being made which show a complete disregard for the basic elements of Hebrew poetic form. A large portion of the Old Testament, especially the prophetic books, is written in Hebrew poetry.

A common technique of Hebrew poetic form is the employment of parallelism. Almost all Hebrew poetry makes use of this technique. Four types of parallelism have been identified: (1) synonymous parallelism, (2) antithetic[37] (contrasting) parallelism, (3) synthetic[38] (constructive) parallelism, and climactic[39] parallelism.

---

35. Is. 35:2.

36. This was the site of Elijah's encounter with the 450 priests of Baal. See I Ki. 18.

37. In Antithetic (or contrasting) parallelism, the second line of the couplet states a thought which is in contrast to the thought of the first line.

38. In synthetic parallelism (also known as constructive and continuing parallelism), the second line neither repeats or contrasts the thought of the first line, but supplements and completes it. The parallelism is often one of form rather than thought. In this type of parallelism one of the lines frequently expresses a motive, a reason, or a consequence.

39. Climactic parallelism is comparatively rare. In this type, the first line of the couplet is incomplete, the second line uses some of the same words from it and completes the thought. This type of parallelism is sometimes described as "ascending rhythm."

Synonymous parallelism is the type of parallelism most frequently used in Old Testament poetry and prophecy. In this poetic form the second line of a couplet echoes the first line by repeating a thought which is parallel or synonymous. For example:

> But Israel does not know,
> my people does not understand. (Is. 1:3)

> He will raise a signal for a nation afar off,
> and whistle for it from the ends of the earth; (Is. 5:26)

> Listen to me, O coastlands,
> and hearken, you peoples from afar. (Is. 49:1)

> Seek the Lord while he may be found,
> call upon him while he is near; (Is. 55:6)

It is in the interpretation of synonymous parallelism that difficulties occasionally arise. If the interpreter fails to note the existence of the poetic form he may mistakenly assume that the two lines of the couplet are speaking of different subjects. As an example of a passage where this difficulty has arisen, consider Micah 4:2:

> the law shall go forth of Zion,
> and the word of the Lord from Jerusalem.

This passage, and its counterpart, Isaiah 2:3, are occasionally cited and interpreted as indicating that two centers of divine power are to exist in the last days; one in the New Jerusalem in Jackson County, Missouri, and the other in the Jerusalem of the land of Israel. Certainly there are to be two centers of importance, but there is little justification for interpreting this particular passage as saying so. The context (Micah 4:1-2) gives no indication that more than one place is being discussed, and the context of its passage counterpart (Isaiah 2:1) emphatically states that the verses are speaking of Judah and Jerusalem. It seems to be a clear example of synonymous parallelism, with the terms Jerusalem and Zion (the name of the fortress of the pre-Israelite city of Jerusalem[40] being used as synonyms.

Avoid Being Influenced by Chapter and Verse Placement

The division of the Bible into chapters and verses is not a part of the scripture itself, but rather an aid added in the middle ages. No claim for inspiration is made in the placement of chapter and verse divisions. The division of the Bible into chapters is usually attributed to Stephen Langton

---

40. See 2 Sam. 5:7. After its fall, Zion came to be known also as the "City of David." The former home of the Jebusites had earlier become known as Jerusalem also. "Mt. Zion" was the name of the hill located within the second wall, west of the area of the temple of Solomon and north of the upper city of Josephus' day.

(1150-1228), a doctor of the University of Paris and later an archbishop of Cantebury. Verse divisions are believed to have first been made by the great printer-editor, Robert Ettienne, in his 1557 edition of the New Testament in Greek.

On occasion students of the scriptures are misled by the placement of chapter headings. Many tend to limit inspection of context to the chapter at hand, assuming the chapter heading marks the beginning of the pertinent material. Such may not be the case. Consider the verse which played such an important part in discussions of the validity of plural marriage prior to the issuing of the Manifesto in 1890. It is Isaiah 4:1:

> And *in that day* seven women shall take hold of one man, saying, We will eat our own bread, and wear our own apparel: only let us be called by thy name, to take away our reproach.

When is the "that day" when the prophecy was to be fulfilled? The context which follows seemingly indicates a last-days setting—fulfillment in a time yet future:

> In that day shall the branch of the Lord be beautiful and glorious, and the fruit of the earth shall be excellent and comely for them that are escaped of Israel.
> And it shall come to pass, that he that is left in Zion, and he that remaineth in Jerusalem, shall be called holy, even every one that is written among the living in Jerusalem:
> When the Lord shall have washed away the filth of the daughters of Zion, and shall have purged the blood of Jerusalem from the midst thereof by the spirit of judgment, and by the spirit of burning.
> And the Lord will create upon every dwelling place of Mount Zion, and upon her assemblies, a cloud and smoke by day, and the shining of a flaming fire by night: for upon all the glory shall be a defence.[41]

But what of the context of the preceding chapter? It prophecies of an event fulfilled over 2500 years ago: the fall of Jerusalem to Babylonia.[42] It describes the punishment which was to come to the haughty daughters of Jerusalem:

> Moreover the Lord saith, Because the daughters of Zion are haughty, and walk with stretched forth necks and wanton eyes, walking and mincing as they go, and making a tinkling with their feet:
> Therefore the Lord will smite with a scab the crown of the head of the daughters of Zion, and the Lord will discover their secret parts.
> In that day the Lord will take away the bravery of their tinkling ornaments about their feet, and their cauls, and their round tires like the moon,
> The chains, and the bracelets, and the mufflers,

---

41. Is. 4:2-5.
42. Compare Isaiah chapter 3 with chapters 1, 5, and 39. See II Ki. 24:14-16; 25:8-12; and Jer. 52 for the account of the fall of Jerusalem.

The bonnets, and the ornaments of the legs, and the headbands, and the tablets, and the earrings,

The rings, and nose jewels,

The changeable suits of apparel, and the mantles, and the wimples, and the crisping pins,

The glasses, and the fine linen, and the hoods, and the vails.

And it shall come to pass, that instead of sweet smell there shall be stink; and instead of a girdle a rent; and instead of well set hair baldness; and instead of a stomacher a girding of sackcloth; and burning instead of beauty.

Thy men shall fall by the sword, and thy mighty in the war.

And her gates shall lament and mourn; and she being desolate shall sit upon the ground.[43]

Thus the preceding chapter ends with a prophecy of the loss of the men of Jerusalem, which explains why such a shortage of men would exist. It would seem that the prophecy of the seven women seeking one man belongs with the warfare and desolation of chapter three, back at the time of the fall of Jerusalem, rather than in the context of the next chapter. This is an instance where the chapter divider is improperly placed, causing the "seven women" aspect to appear connected with the last days prophecy of chapter four rather than the fall of Jerusalem prophecy of chapter three.

Avoid Basing Interpretations on
Uncertain Chronological or Historical Conclusions

Occasionally interpretations are made which are based on extremely weak historical or chronological conclusions. Perhaps the most widely circulated of these interpretations is that which holds that Christ's final coming in glory will take place about the year 2,000 A.D. Note the shaky chain of logic by which such an interpretation is reached. It finds its "basis" in a single passage, Doctrine and Covenants 77:6; a passage which stands in question and answer form:

Q. What are we to understand by the book which John saw, which was sealed on the back with seven seals?

A. We are to understand that it contains the revealed will, mysteries, and works of God; the hidden things of his economy concerning *this earth during the seven thousand years of its continuance, or its temporal existence.*

The reasoning of this interpretation seems to take this form:

1. The earth is to have seven thousand years of temporal existence.

2. Christ's coming will begin the millennium, which will occupy the final thousand of the seven thousand years.

3. Earth-life began with Adam about 4,000 B.C.

4. Therefore, six thousand years will end about 2,000 A.D. and that will be the time of Christ's coming.

This interpretation has a number of assumptions concerning historical and chronological conclusions which deserve to be questioned.

---

43. Is. 3:16-26.

Assumption one—earth life began with Adam[44] in 4,004 B.C. To accept this date is to rely on the chronological study of one individual, while disregarding the chronological calculations of many others. In 1650-1654 an Irish theologian, archbishop James Ussher (1581-1656), published his *Annales Veteris et Novi Testamenti.* In this work he outlined Biblical chronology, according to which the Creation occurred in 4,004 B.C. Many other chronologies have been prepared, however, and a comparison of even a few of them make it clear that the time of Adam is extremely uncertain. Elder Orson Pratt was aware of this problem, and clearly warned of the dangers of calculations based on Old Testament chronologies:

> We are living, Latter-day Saints, near the close of the sixth thousand years from the fall of man; how near I do not know, and there is a great change about to take place. Inquires one—'Is there not some way by which we can fix the time, and arrive at a certainty in regard to the age of our globe since the fall of man?' *I do not know of any way except by new revelation, for chronology is so imperfect that many hundreds who have spent their lives and fortunes in studying it, differ from each other in their conclusions.* One has one date for the age of the world, and another has another. Let me give to you a few specimens. We will take one of the oldest eras—the Alexandrian—computed by Julius *Africanus.* In this Alexandrian era, the time from the creation to the birth of Christ is set down at 5,500 years; in the Antioch era, computed by *Pannorus,* it is set down at 5,493 years; in the Constantinople, or Greek era, it is set down at 5,509 years; you take *Scaliger,* another great chronoligist, and he, by a comparison of the text of various ancient manuscripts, makes the age of the world, from the creation to the coming of Christ, 3,950 years. Then you take another celebrated man, Father *Pezron,* and he makes it 5,873 years from the creation to Christ. Then you take the one who has given the chronology to the Bible, Archbishop *Ussher,* and he makes it 4,004 years from the creation to Christ. How are you going to judge? You may take over two hundred other chronologists, whose names are given, and they all have their special dates; consequently, you see, *we are utterly at a loss, and without new revelation, we are no more sure that Archbishop Ussher's chronology, contained in King James Bible, is correct, than we have to suppose that that many of those others are correct.*[45]

Assumption two—the millennium begins with Christ's coming in glory. Unfortunately, the scriptures are silent on the matter of what event begins the millennial era. While Christ's final coming in glory is a good possibility of being the event which begins it, as good a case can be made for His appearance at the Council at Adam-ondi-Ahman. At that time the Lord is to receive "dominion, and glory, and a kingdom, that all people, nations, and languages, should serve him."[46]

---

44. A discussion of conflicting theories of evolution is beyond the scope of this volume, as is also the consideration of where Adam came from, his condition, etc.
45. JD, 16:324. Nov. 22, 1873.
46. Dan. 7:13-14. For treatment in depth concerning this council, see *Prophecy—Key to the Future,* pp. 167-176.

Assumption three—the millennium begins at the beginning of the seventh thousand years. It should be recalled that Doctrine and Covenants 77:6, the passage which gave rise to this interpretation, is a portion of an interpretive statement concerning the Book of Revelation. A careful reading of the Book of Revelation itself will show that a number of events of tragic consequence are still to take place after the seventh thousand-year period begins. Doctrine and Covenants 77:12 indicates that the trumps of at least chapters eight to eleven of Revelation are to take place in the beginning of the seventh thousand years. These chapters tell of numerous plagues, a war in which the third part of men are slain, the Battle of Armageddon, etc. Much time will apparently elapse after the seventh thousand-year period begins but before Christ's final coming in glory.

The interpretation that Christ's coming will take place about the year 2,000 A.D. is thus seen to be extremely weak. The time itself is set from the calculations of a single individual: Archbishop Ussher, when those calculations are in direct variance with numerous other scholars. If the time of beginning the calculation is uncertain, the time of ending must also be uncertain.

Avoid Making Time Determinations Based on the Word "Generation"

Various individuals have based extensive time calculations on their interpretation of the word "generation." Some have assumed a generation to be thirty years, according to modern reckoning. Others have asserted that a generation is one hundred years, and base their calculation on Alma 45:10-12. With this time length assumed, some have interpreted Doctrine and Covenants 84:4-5, 31 to mean that the New Jerusalem temple would have been built before 1932. Others have interpreted a generation to be 120 years, basing their calculations on Genesis 6:3.[47] Yet all these calculations are so weak in their basic assumption as to lack validity. Prophetic dating can be an extremely valuable tool when it is properly used. The word "generation," however, carries so varied a meaning that to assign any definite number of years to it for purposes of interpretation is folly.

---

47. Much is being assumed here. The passage makes no reference to the word generation, but says merely, "The Lord said, My spirit shall not always strive with man, for that he also is flesh: *yet his days shall be an hundred and twenty years.*" (Gen. 6:3) The following passage, Mt. 24:34-39, is often cited in connection with the above:

> Verily I say unto you, This generation shall not pass, till all these things be fulfilled.
> Heaven and earth shall pass away, but my words shall not pass away.
> But of that day and hour knoweth no man, no, not the angels of heaven, but my Father only.

Avoid Accepting Statements of Opinion as Inspired Prophecy

Prominent people, such as presidents of the United States, famous inventors, LDS General Authorities, etc., often express their personal viewpoints on the events of the day. Many times those opinions appear pertinent to situations which arise in later years. There is little justification for later quotation of these opinions, however, with the assumption that they are inspired statements which reflect the will and intent of God. They remain merely opinions, whether correct or incorrect, and the passage of time does not make them inspired prophecy.

Some statements of opinion can be extremely misleading and harmful to the correct understanding of prophesied events if they are not understood in proper perspective. For instance, Abraham Lincoln once said,

> At what point, then, is the approach of danger to be expected? If it ever reaches us, it must spring up among us. It cannot come from abroad. If destruction be our lot, we must ourselves be its author and finisher; as a nation of freemen, we must live through all time or die by suicide.[48]

His opinion is interesting. Citing it as an inspired prophecy that the American nation will not be subject to foreign attack or defeat at the hands of foreign oppressors, however, has no validity. A personal opinion is an entirely different phenomenon from a prophecy made under inspiration. Compared to the latter, it is of little value.

Be Cautious of "You'll Be Here When" Statements in Prophecies

Numerous prophecies carefully describe future events, but contain the speaker's opinion that some who are then present will still be alive to see the fulfillment.[49] Some have rationalized these statements by holding that the individuals may carry out the predictions as resurrected beings, that translated beings such as the three Nephites were present, etc. Perhaps the matter can be better explained as was suggested by President Joseph Young, one of the seven presidents of Seventies. He cautioned that the Holy Spirit tends to make things appear vividly and close by, and inferred that because of the vividness in which visions and revelations are received, people tend

---

But as the days of Noe were, so shall also the coming of the Son of man be.

For as in the days that were before the flood they were eating and drinking, marrying and giving in marriage, until the day that Noe entered into the ark,

And knew not until the flood came, and took them all away, so shall also the coming of the Son of man be.

48. January 27, 1837; Springfield, Illinois.

49. See, for instance, HC, 1:176, 315-316, 386-387; 5:336. JD, 4:231-232; 8:350; 9:27; 12:344; 14:64; 18:25; 37; 23:122-123, etc.

to assume that the time of fulfillment is close by and express that assumption in recounting the manifestation. While speaking of the saints' dealings with the Indians, for instance, he said,

> . . . *the Holy Spirit brought many things close to their minds—they appeared right by, and hence many were deceived, and run into a mistake respecting them.* They (the Saints) undertook to make calculations for to establish the kingdom and restore Israel, and many were so excited, that they wanted to take the Gospel from the Gentiles immediately. They were for taking the Gospel clear away at once, and of course for sealing them all up to destruction. Many good men made great blunders upon the subject of 'redeeming Israel;' it was a great mystery, and perhaps I made as great mistakes as others in forming my opinions, but I had the caution not to utter my views to any one. I knew that *faith and the Holy Ghost brought the designs of Providence close by, and by that means we were enabled to scan them, and find out what they would produce when carried into effect, but we had not knowledge enough to digest and fully comprehend those things. . . .*[50]

Expressions like "You will see it come to pass," "You will know when it happens," "You will be here when it comes to pass," etc., appear to be a characteristic speech mannerism of the early saints, rather than a portion of the prophecies they recounted to their audiences. In general, such phrases lack validity as means of dating the fulfillment of the items prophesied.

Avoid Interpretations Involving the Misapplication of Scripture

There are frequent instances in which passages dealing with one subject are interpreted as being related to an entirely different event or subject. This misapplication of scripture can cause ideas to be formed which do not stand up under the light of close inspection. Indeed, the misapplication of scriptures is a major source of the doctrinal confusion which exists among the various denominations of Christianity today. The problem also exists among Latter-day Saints.

For instance, allusions are frequently made to the belief that the great Council at Adam-ondi-Ahman, which is prophesied to take place in a time yet future,[51] will be a secret meeting, unknown to the world at large and even to the general membership of the Church. When he prophesied of the event, the prophet Daniel said that a "thousand thousands" and "ten thousand times ten thousand"[52] would be in attendance, or a hundred million people! It is difficult to envision a meeting of that size and scope being held in secret, especially when Church conferences are, by nature, a gathering of representatives from each ward and stake of the Church. How did the "secret" belief arise? It began, apparently, with the misapplication

---

50. JD, 9:230. July 13, 1855.
51. See *Prophecy—Key to the Future*, pp. 167-176.
52. Dan. 7:10.

of I Thessalonians 5:2. In a written discussion concerning the Council at Adam-ondi-Ahman by a prominent General Authority, it was asserted that that council "shall precede the coming of Jesus Christ as a thief in the night, unbeknown to all the world." Yet the "thief in the night" passage, as seen by its context, has no reference to the Council at Adam-ondi-Ahman, but rather to the *time* (but not the manner) of the Savior's final coming in glory, an entirely different event:

> But I would not have you to be ignorant, brethren, concerning them which are asleep, that ye sorrow not, even as others which have no hope.
>
> For if we believe that Jesus died and rose again, even so *them also which sleep in Jesus will God bring with him.*
>
> For this we say unto you by the word of the Lord, that we which are alive and remain unto the coming of the Lord shall not prevent them which are asleep.
>
> *For the Lord himself shall descend from heaven with a shout, with the voice of the archangel, and with the trump of God: and the dead in Christ shall rise first:*
>
> *Then we which are alive and remain shall be caught up together with them in the clouds, to meet the Lord in the air: and so shall we ever be with the Lord.*
>
> Wherefore comfort one another with these words.
>
> But of the times and the seasons, brethren, ye have no need that I write unto you.
>
> For yourselves know perfectly that *the day of the Lord so cometh as a thief in the night.*[53]

It is appropriate to give careful scrutiny to the evidence upon which interpretations are made, for if the evidence is misapplied to the subject, how can the interpretation be correct?

Avoid Fallacious Assumptions Which Are Not the Actual Message of the Evidence Cited

At times certain assumptions are made which are not the actual message of the scriptural passages upon which they claim to be based. These assumptions can be misleading and detrimental to a clear understanding of the scriptures. For instance, one such assumption has its origin in a prophecy found in the Book of Mormon concerning the land of promise:

> Wherefore, I, Lehi, prophesy according to the workings of the Spirit which is in me, that there shall none come into this land save they shall be brought by the hand of the Lord.[54]

The fallacious assumption sometimes drawn from this passage is that the United States will never be subjected to attack by foreign powers on its

---

53. I Thess. 4:13-5:2. See also D&C 88:95-99.
54. 2 Ne. 1:6.

home territory. As can be seen, that isn't the message of the passage at all, as is evidenced by the following verse:

> Wherefore, this land is consecrated unto him whom he shall bring. And if it so be that they shall serve him according to the commandments which he hath given, it shall be a land of liberty unto them; wherefore, they shall never be brought down into captivity; *if so, it shall be because of iniquity; for if iniquity shall abound cursed shall be the land for their sakes,* but unto the righteous it shall be blessed forever.[55]

What the passage is saying is that others won't come to attack "this land" unless they are brought by the hand of the Lord. The scriptures indicate that the Lord has frequently caused or allowed enemies to come against His chosen people at times when His people have fallen into iniquity.[56] Therefore, there is no validity in the assumption based on this passage that America will always be free from external attack on her home soil. God can bring retribution upon the people of America and there are numerous prophecies that He may do so if the people turn to wickedness.

Summary

1. Man has both the right and the obligation to verify what appears to be revelation and inspiration. He is to "despise not prophesyings," and to "prove all things; hold fast that which is good."

2. The obligation of all members to confirm by the Spirit the things of the Spirit is a vital force in the maintaining of righteousness, truth, and harmony in the Church. It is also the method whereby members can maintain a strong testimony of the divine calling of their leaders.

3. Various standards for evaluating the validity of prophecies are set forth in the scriptures. They are:

A. fulfillment,

B. lack of conflict with other revelations,

C. the law of witnesses applied through parallel prophecies,

D. confirmation of validity through personal revelation, and

E. revelations received by one other than the President of the Church must not command the Church nor claim the recipient is "appointed" to receive revelations for the Church.

4. Care must be taken that prophecies are compared with other prophecies or revelations, not merely with the opinions or private interpretations of prominent men.

5. God has frequently revealed prophetic insights concerning the same event to many different individuals, thereby using multiple witnesses to

---

55. 2 Ne. 1:7.

56. See, for instance, I Ki. 11:14, 31-35; 14:14; II Ki. 10:32; 15:37; 17:20; 21:14; 24:2-3; II Chron. 13:15-16; 24:23-24; 36:16-17; Is. 3:1-3; Jer. 3:15-17; 14:11-12; 19:7; 20:5; 21:4-7; 22:7; 25:9; Ezek. 38:16; Dan. 1:1-2; etc.

establish the validity of His revelations. Prophecies are substantiated by each other when they are found to reveal the same events.

6. When a prophecy stands alone it should not be rejected as false solely on that basis. The student may have failed to locate parallels, or other verifying revelations may yet be forthcoming. Judgment should be withheld until other verifying or disqualifying evidence is found.

7. Revelations confirming the validity of prophecies and other revelations can be received. Relatively few people, however, seem to receive such manifestations. Possible reasons why others do not receive these confirming revelations are that they do not seek them, they have not prepared for them adequately or properly, or because God, in His wisdom, chooses not to place the burden of confirmed knowledge upon the individual.

8. It is appropriate and necessary to tactfully ask, "Is this a new revelation from God?" when a new teaching or prophetic statement is put forth. Many teachings and interpretations are assumed by others to be from God when they are actually only the personal belief of the individual expounding them.

9. When examining the validity of a prophecy, the student should examine its record source, record transmission, and its validifying historical evidence. In general, primary sources are stronger than secondary sources; an original copy is more accurate than a transcribed, compiled, or copied record; direct evidence is stronger than circumstantial evidence in historical verification, etc.

10. An important verifying technique borrowed from genealogical research methodology is to prove there is a definite lack of evidence which would conflict with the message of a prophecy or the circumstances under which it was given.

11. Neither social prestige nor religious authority is an acceptable substitute for actual knowledge when the question of the validity of witnesses is under consideration. Opinions should never be substituted for facts nor hearsay evidence substituted for valid testimony.

12. The validity of prophecy cannot be established by a solely historical approach. The traditional methodology of the historian is not able to deal effectively with the verification of revelation.

13. Five basic characteristics of prophecy influence the manner in which prophecies should be studied. These are

    A. a prophecy requires fulfillment—this restricts the circulation of false prophecies attributed to respected Church leaders;

    B. parallel revelation is given—one prophecy supports the message of another prophecy;

    C. preliminary fulfillment anticipates later fulfillment—it is proper, when a prophecy begins to be fulfilled, to expect the rest of it to be fulfilled also;

    D. prophecy links future events—prophecies tend to form patterns of chronological relationships which facilitate their interpretation, and

    E. things of God are often recorded with the aid of the Spirit—through the promptings of the Holy Ghost, things can be written down accurately long after they are received or heard.

14. Because they are interesting, important, and inseparately connected with aspects of one's faith and testimony, prophecies tend to be better preserved than other items through the normal functions of memory.

15. When one evaluates the validity of prophecy, one should seek information concerning

    A. the prophet,

    B. the circumstances under which the prophecy was received,

    C. the recording of the prophecy,

    D. the transmission of the prophecy,

    E. the existence of conflicting evidence,

    F. the parallels of the prophecy with other revelations,

    G. evidence of the prophecy's prior or approaching fulfillment, and

    H. revealed information confirming or rejecting the validity of the prophecy.

16. While considering common interpretation errors, the following suggestions were made, accompanied by examples:

    A. observe subject statements in the text and context,

    B. apply time clues in the text and context,

    C. apply place clues in the text and context,

    D. be aware of the effect of stylistic and writing techniques,

    E. avoid being influenced by chapter and verse placement,

    F. avoid basing interpretations on uncertain chronological or historical conclusions,

    G. avoid making time determinations based on the word "generation,"

    H. avoid accepting statements of opinion as inspired prophecy,

    I. be cautious of "you'll be here when" statements in prophecies,

    J. avoid interpretations involving the misapplication of scripture, and

    K. avoid fallacious assumptions which are not the actual message of the evidence cited.

7

What Is an Appropriate Response to Critics of Prophecy?

Over the years, prominent people and men of much worldly learning have sometimes attempted to challenge the validity and accuracy of important scriptural prophecies. Occasionally their criticism has been extended to non-scriptural prophecies made by Latter-day Saints in the era of the restored Church. As the Church moves into the perilous events of the last days, the scriptures warn that it is to encounter severe persecution and frequent challenges to the validity of its doctrines and to the authority of those who lead its members. From both without and within, critics and antagonists will challenge the words and precepts of the prophets, as the influence of Satan spreads across the earth.

There is a need for the saints to know how to respond to these antagonists, and to refute the challenges they raise, with precision and accuracy. Ignoring their accusations will only increase their vehemence, and tempt them to increase their agitation against the saints. This chapter is written to suggest ways in which adequate responses to their criticisms can be prepared.

The Motives of Critics and "Debunkers" Should Be Evaluated

Jesus said, *"Judge not, that ye be not judged, for with what judgment ye judge, ye shall be judged: and with what measure ye mete, it shall be measured to you again."* [1] Certainly those who challenge the validity of the scriptures and other prophecies must be prepared to defend their challenge. If an individual chooses to disbelieve something, that is his prerogative. He may disbelieve in silence without the need to justify his belief, but if he labels something as false or erroneous, and then publishes or voices his opinion to others, then his judgment must in turn be judged by others. He should be prepared to document and defend his criticism. Often it is the criticism, rather than that which is criticized, which is invalid.

It is appropriate to evaluate the motives of those who assume the role of critic as well as those they criticize. Such motives are many and varied. Elder Adam S. Bennion suggested three reasons why some people engage in criticism:

1. Mt. 7:1-2.

217

    1. To hurt a person or persons against whom they hold a grievance—real or imagined.

    2. To appear heroic. Some people like to appear to be "in the know." You no doubt have witnessed this form of self-elevation.

    3. To qualify as a detective. Life presents all sorts of dramatic situations. There seems to be a little of the detective in all of us.[2]

Other reasons also may be added to explain why individuals engage in religious criticism. Some may criticize because their stated personal views are endangered; they may, perhaps, be publicly committed to a certain doctrinal position and feel that outspoken criticism against new evidence is the way to "save face." Some may criticize because of a personal animosity for, or distrust of, the teachings of others. Others may challenge religious teachings because they regard them as contrary to the precepts of their particular faith and they are seeking to "shelter their flocks." Others may raise their voice in criticism of the scriptures or of prophecies in the belief that they are supporting or defending their particular religious leaders. Still others may criticize religious precepts or documents as an expression of their zeal in the role of a missionary for their faith.

When an individual judges or criticizes the scriptures, or prophecies, or any other religious precept or item of sacred history, the observer would do well to analyze that individual's motive for so doing. "Does the critic have a legitimate and unbiased reason for criticism?" should be the test his criticism should pass. Criticism of others and their teachings should never be allowed to serve as a smokescreen to cover improper motives of the critic. A basic rule of approach should be to *examine the critic's motives first, before examining either the validity of that which he challenges or the criticism he sets forth.*

Common sense should alert the observer to signs of improper motive. The real seeker of truth will be open to new evidence and will invite it; beware of the critic who would hinder the gathering of evidence.

The real seeker of truth will encourage careful examination of difficult issues by all interested and qualified observers; beware of the critic who seeks to prevent others from studying in sensitive areas.

The real seeker of truth will present and consider evidence he encounters on both sides of a controversial issue; beware of the critic who will pursue and publicize only his own narrow viewpoint.

The real seeker of truth will seek to let the evidence establish the validity of the item under consideration without involving personal strife; beware

---

    2. Bennion, Adam S., *The Ten Commandments Today* (Salt Lake City, Utah: Deseret Book Company, 1955), p. 137, as cited in *A Light Unto the World—A Course of Study for the Melchizedek Priesthood Quorums of The Church of Jesus Christ of Latter-day Saints* (Published by the First Presidency of The Church of Jesus Christ of Latter-day Saints, 1967), p. 98.

of the critic who attempts to bring social, economic, academic, political, or ecclesiastical pressure against those who disagree with his views.

The real seeker of truth will let the evidence determine his viewpoint; beware of the critic who lets his viewpoint determine the evidence he will accept.

The real seeker of truth will alter his viewpoint and acknowledge his error if new evidence proves him wrong; beware of the critic who clings to error when new evidence shows it is error.

The real seeker of truth will recognize and analyze the assumptions he makes in his investigation; beware of the critic who judges on the basis of assumptions with no regard to their validity.

The real seeker of truth regards all truth as appropriate for careful and discerning study; beware of the critic who would label things as "mysteries" and prohibit their study.

The real seeker of truth will discern where evidence ends and opinion begins; beware of the critic who does not discern between the two.

The Assumptions of Many Bible Critics Concerning Prophecy

After first examining the motives of those who would criticize scriptures and latter-day prophecy, their assumptions should next come under scrutiny. Almost all theological criticism is based on assumptions. If these underlying assumptions are invalid, the criticism itself has little validity. This is shown to be true, for instance, in the scholarly writings of many Bible scholars of the past two centuries.[3] Some Bible critics have made important contributions in helping man to better understand the revealed word of God, and are worthy of praise for their efforts. However, it is unfortunate that many who have engaged in Biblical criticism have lacked the faith in and guidance from God which they needed to balance their academic brilliance. The disbelief and irreverence of some Bible scholars has often bordered on atheism.

A basic technique of their work has been to raise needless doubts concerning the validity of numerous portions of the scriptures, and then to quote one another in book-long debates concerning these minute points. Some authors in the religious field dedicate their efforts to displaying their knowledge of the opinions of their predecessors and contemporaries. Others have shown themselves to be name-droppers and scholarly show-offs, with little depth, understanding, or personal application of the gospel principles.

---

3. For a recent commentary by a non-Mormon which stresses his concern in this matter, see Lewis, C. S., *Christian Reflections* (Grand Rapids, Michigan: William B. Eerdmans Publisher, 1967). His essay "Modern Theology and Biblical Criticism," one of fourteen in the book, is reprinted in *BYU Studies* (Provo, Utah: Brigham Young University), Autumn 1968, Vol. IX, No. 1, pp. 33-48.

The exegesis of many Bible critics concerning scriptural prophecy is frequently based on three assumptions, all of which are in direct opposition to principles of the restored gospel:

1. *A prophet speaks only to the people of his own generation, and only about his own time.*

2. *A prophet foretells the future only by discerning the signs of the times already evident and drawing correct conclusions about them.*

3. *A prophet anticipates future events only as the current events of his day indicate the future events are to come about.*

The first assumption tends to limit the time when a prophecy can be fulfilled to the lifetime of the prophet or shortly thereafter. The approach used by some Bible critics was that, since it was assumed that a prophet could not foretell events of the distant future, fulfillment had to take place in a limited period. Of course, since the prophecies often spoke of a time far into the future, no fulfillment could be found in the historical era they searched. Their conclusions and implications: the prophecy was false, the prophet was uninspired of God, the Bible is inaccurate and unreliable, God does not reveal His will through prophets, God does not control the events of the earth, God has no foreknowledge or knowledge of human affairs, etc. Yet without the misleading influence of the assumption, little problem exists.

The second assumption stems from the belief that a prophet's role is only to look around him, discern the signs of the time, and then draw significant conclusions based on his discernment. The prophet is reduced by the critics to his own wisdom and discernment as a source—the possibility of revelation from God is excluded. Of necessity, the first indications of future events must be already visible, they say; the prophet is just keen enough to recognize these indications earlier than others. He need not be a spokesman for God. His prophecies arise from natural sources. God functions only through the natural laws and processes known to man, say these critics. There is no need for the "miracle" of revelation.

The third assumption is that the prophet can only foretell the future when the current events of his day begin to show what the future will be. When the prophet does not know the events of his day, he cannot prophesy. He cannot prophesy far into the future because there are not yet any signs upon which he can base forecasts concerning the future situations. Biblical situations where prophets foretold events far ahead of their time, when no contemporary events could possibly have given clues to the prophets, are sometimes explained away by the critics as interpolations by later copiests of Biblical manuscripts or as forgeries.

The corollary which soon developed to these three false assumptions became a constant theme in Bible criticism: *since prophetic passages which speak of an era later than the prophet lived could not have been prophesied by him, they are interpolations by later authors.* Thus we have elaborate theories concerning a second Isaiah and even a third and a fourth Isaiah, as well as a host of other beliefs which have played havoc with Old and New Testament exegesis. These theories are usually the basis for criticism in doctrinal matters when voiced against The Church of Jesus Christ of Latter-day Saints by Bible critics.[4]

A prime technique of Bible critics is to drive a wedge, based on some theory related to the above assumptions, into a prophecy, until it has created sufficient doubt that the prophecy or scriptural passage becomes a matter of debate and controversy. Rarely is the full prophecy attacked at first, just a small portion of it. In the conflict that ensues, they rise to glory as the originator of the theory. They win; their opponents who oppose them with equal brilliance also win; only the faith of their readers in the scriptures suffers irreparable damage.

Most churches have a variety of assumptions, based on their particular dogmas, which affect their criticism of the Bible and of Latter-day prophecies. These assumptions, which stand as doctrine to those of the various sects, must be recognized by those who encounter their publications. The common tendency in modern Christianity is for the exponents of a particular theology to push it to an extreme—to expand a particular precept until its implications extend far beyond the bounds of supportable evidence. For example, by the middle ages Catholicism had extended the assumption that Peter was the first bishop of Rome to include the concepts of the papacy, the church as the intermediary between God and man, the church as the only valid interpreter of doctrine, the sacraments of the church were necessary for salvation, etc. In the reformation, to counteract the Catholic hold on the people, the Protestants took the concept of salvation only by the grace of God and expanded it into the concepts of individual rather than church interpretation of the Bible; the Bible being man's sole basis of authority without need for authority descending from Peter; man can be saved by faith alone without the need for the ordinances of the church; no further revelation other than the Bible is to be expected; etc. The assumption is that if one basic principle is true, then all related theology is also true. As

---

4. Some critics of Mormonism, having accepted the theories of Bible scholars as fact, have attempted to use them as a means of disproving the Book of Mormon. For instance, that book quotes twenty-one complete chapters of Isaiah plus parts of others. Since the critics assume that portions of the book of Isaiah were written after the time Lehi left Jerusalem, they say that the Book of Mormon quotations of Isaiah are not of ancient origin but were fabricated by Joseph Smith. This matter is explained in the author's book, *Prophets and Prophecies of the Old Testament,* pp. 377-380. Dr. Sidney B. Sperry treats it in greater depth in *The Voice of Israel's Prophets* (Salt Lake City, Utah: Deseret Book Company, 1952), pp. 75-94.

can readily be seen, in theological study an all-or-nothing approach holds little validity.

Inappropriate Criteria for the Criticism of Prophecy Used by Some Church Members

Over the years a number of assumptions have also come into existance among Latter-day Saints concerning the nature of prophecy. These assumptions have been expressed, from time to time, yet they have no scriptural nor doctrinal basis. Indeed, some of them are in direct conflict with the scriptures and with the manner in which the Lord has continually revealed His will to the Church. Unfortunately, these assumptions are occasionally used as criteria by which the validity of certain prophetic statements are "judged." The assumptions, themselves, deserve to be examined before they are accepted as valid criteria. Some of them are:

1. *Prophecies by Church leaders, if valid, are incorporated into printed histories of the Church.* Prophecies, by their very nature, tend to be excluded from historical works because they often do not speak of events which come to pass in the historical period covered in the printed history and hence are not germane to the subject of the book. The writer of an early history does not include them because the fulfillment comes later than the period he is covering; the writer of a later history doesn't record a prophecy because he researches too late a period to discover it. Church history books have shown a marked tendency to eliminate prophetic items, as well as miraculous experiences and accounts of supernatural manifestations, and to regard them as irrelevant to the mainstream of history. One can locate hundreds of such choice items about Joseph Smith, for instance, in the biographies and journals of other early saints, which have been omitted from the histories of the Church. It is quite probable that the Latter-day Saint historians never even knew of their existence. The matter does not rest in the validity of the prophecies at all, but rather in the knowledge, choice, and tastes of the compilers of history.

It should also be recognized that our two major histories were printed with an acute awareness of the non-Mormon viewpoint, during the period when "getting along with the Gentiles" was a guiding desire. Thus they omitted many items of prophetic and historical record which the editor and compilers recognized might tend to embarrass the Church if they did not come to pass as expected. The *Documentary History of the Church*[5] especially, has undergone heavy editing and suffered the deletion of many

---

5. Now published under the title *History of the Church of Jesus Christ of Latter-day Saints* in seven volumes, which extend from the earliest beginnings of the Church through most of 1848.

important items which the Prophet Joseph Smith himself preserved or ordered recorded.[6]

This assumption is sometimes stated in reverse form: *Prophecies by Church leaders which are not incorporated into printed histories of the Church are invalid.* In this form, the assumption has no more validity than in its previous guise. The truthfulness of a prophetic item is not determined by whether or not a historian chooses to include it in the book he is writing.

2. *Prophecies by Church leaders are false unless they personally recorded and preserved them.* It has become apparent that many events regarded as important today were considered inconsequential or so commonplace that they were not recorded in the early days of the Church. In the records kept by Joseph Smith, for instance, his main concern was to preserve the history of the Church, not to aggrandize himself in the eyes of future generations by recording his remarks of a prophetic nature. In the manuscript which became the *Documentary History of the Church,* Joseph Smith was keeping a history, not a personal diary. Comparison of Joseph's history with the records and journals kept by others closely indicate that many of the important prophetic statements which he made were not recorded in his record, nor were the majority of his discourses, many healings, and other miraculous deeds he performed, the private counsel he gave, etc. Significant manifestations such as visitations from angels, etc., which he received are also omitted in his record.[7] Are the visitations false because he didn't record them? or the counsel? or the healings? or the discourses? By the same token, the prophecies are not false simply because he did not record them.

The same is true for other Church leaders. Heber C. Kimball is frequently regarded as standing next to Joseph Smith in reputation as a prophet, yet many of his most famous prophecies were recorded by others rather than by himself.[8] The same is true of Orson Hyde.

It is probable that whether or not Church leaders recorded the inspired words which flowed from their own lips often depended upon the availability of time and opportunity in their busy schedules to do so. It appears that frequently they had to be content with the knowledge that someone else had recorded their statements. Examination of the records they left indicates

---

6. For example, Orson F. Whitney quotes from "The Prophet's History," a sketch of the organization of the "Young Gentleman and Ladies' Relief Society" (*Life of Heber C. Kimball, op. cit.,* pp. 332-334). The organization didn't stand the test of time, and thus also didn't manage to gain mention in later editions of the *Documentary History of the Church.*

7. For quotations to this effect, see the author's book, *The Prophecies of Joseph Smith* (Salt Lake City, Utah: Bookcraft, Inc., 1963), pp. 61-63, 32-33.

8. See, for instance, Whitney, *The Life of Heber C. Kimball, op. cit.,* pp. 431-471. Note also that he discontinued his personal record after being named to the First Presidency.

that their writings were often reduced in quantity during times of stress, travel, sickness, etc. They were busy men, and did not have the time-saving machines available which are in common usage today. It is little wonder that their statements were frequently preserved by others rather than themselves.

3. *Prophecies of Church leaders are always communicated to the membership of the Church through established channels: a letter from presiding authorities to bishops and/or stake presidents, publication by the Church in a Church-controlled periodical, or presentation in general conference.* It has been seen that prophecy does not always conform to the established pattern of revelation to guide the Church. While it is highly desirable that prophetic statements come forth to the saints by one of the above methods, such an occurrence is not common. Many bishops, and stake presidents with whom the author has conversed, for instance, have commented that they know of *no* prophetic statement released by the Church in this manner for decades; policy changes and new programs—yes, but prophecy, no. If significant prophetic statements have been released in the above ways, the general Church membership is unaware of them. Perhaps the reason prophecy rarely comes forth to the saints through the above channels is that prophecy, though significant, does not necessarily fall into the category of "revelation to guide or command the Church."

The validity or lack of validity of this assumption may be examined by ascertaining whether the prophecies of early Church leaders were made available through this practice. With the exception of those incorporated into the Doctrine and Covenants, the majority of other prophetic statements they made were not disseminated in the above manner.

Many prophecies were recorded in biographical studies published years after the statements were made. Surely it would be folly to take the stand that they were originally false because they were not circulated according to the above assumption, but became true upon publication.

The truthfulness of a prophetic item is not determined by the time or manner or particular periodical in which it is disseminated.

4. *A prophecy, if true, will be recorded by the Church Historian's Office.* The Church Historian's office is a library with an important collection of materials pertaining to the Church. However, it is by no means complete in its holdings, as its staff has emphasized.[9] In matters of old records, diaries, journals, etc., it is dependent upon the contributions of the saints for the enlarging of its holdings. However, many who have such materials have chosen to retain possession of them or to donate them to

---

9. See "The Era Asks About The Church Historian's Office," *The Improvement Era* (Salt Lake City, Utah: published by the Mutual Improvement Associations of The Church of Jesus Christ of Latter-day Saints), Vol. 71, No. 8, October 1968, pp. 34-39.

other libraries where interested parties will have easier access to them. A prophetic statement is found in the Church Historian's library only if an individual who has it in his possession has chosen to donate a copy of it or has given the librarians access to it.

It is unfortunate that some basic library record-keeping techniques were not employed in the early days of the Church Historian's office. A careful recording of acquisition dates and sources, for instance, would have been most useful in dating and identifying many prophetic items under recent scrutiny. Such information is now lost.

Because it is a library, it is no more appropriate for the Church Historian's office than for any other library or libraries to comment on the validity or lack of validity of a prophetic item. Such commentary is not the proper role for a library.

In summary, the validity of a prophetic item is not determined on the basis of in what library it is or is not found.

5. *A prophecy is false if quoted by anti-Mormon sources.* Although there is a reluctance to acknowledge it, a number of prophecies by, or attributed to, early Church leaders foretell a time of future strife and dissention within the Church and also within the United States. Unfortunately, anti-Mormon and apostate organizations have become aware of them and have circulated the portions pertaining to difficulties within the Church. The tendency among some of the saints has been to adopt a "guilt by association" attitude, by reasoning that if anti-Mormon sources quote them, the prophecies must be false and one should have nothing to do with them. The same non-Mormon groups quote extensively from the *Doctrine and Covenants* and other Church standard works, yet the validity of those inspired writings is not rejected because of their actions. Why should such reasoning prevail in regard to prophetic statements? The answer lies, perhaps, in the unpleasant nature of the content of the prophecies. The customary Mormon "look on the bright side" attitude takes precedence, and the use of the prophetic items by non-Mormon groups affords a convenient excuse for avoiding the issues they raise.

The validity of a prophetic item is not determined by who does or does not quote it.

6. *A prophecy is false if a respected person expresses his opinion that it is false.* If a respected scholar, or one in high position where he holds the confidence and respect of the people, states something is false, his statement must fall into one of three categories. It is either based on (1) revelation which has been received which states that the questioned item is false, (2) the conclusion he has reached after a careful study of all pertinent evidence has been made, or (3) an unsupported opinion. In matters of prophetic criticism, it is essential that the student evaluate the criticism and correctly classify it into the above category which best describes it.

If the statement that a prophetic item is false claims a revealed basis, then let that revelation be verified as any other revelation should be.[10] If God has revealed that the item in question is false, it can safely be assumed that factual evidence, when it is considered, will also verify the item's falsity.

If the critic makes no claim that his conclusion is based on revelation, then he is under obligation to support his criticism with evidence if the criticism is to be regarded as valid. That evidence, in turn, must be able to withstand careful scrutiny. Without the factual basis of sound evidence, his criticism must stand as an unsupported opinion.

There is difficulty in this area when the critic is one who holds a position of authority within the Church. Authority is not a substitute for proper evidence[11]—there is no doctrine of infallibility in Mormondom to shield his opinions from investigation. When one in authority labels something as "simply false," but fails to support his statement with appropriate evidence, he can be sure that his view will become a center of controversy, especially if evidence begins to come to light on the matter under consideration[12] which does not support his comment.

It is by concrete evidence, rather than the unsupported opinions of respected people, that prophetic validity must and will be determined.

7. *All revelation comes only from either God or Satan.* This assumption also finds its way into many discussions on revelation. There is a tendency to say, "God only does such and such, therefore any other manifestations must be from Satan," in typical missionary-style logic. There are, however, many dozens of accounts on record which show that individuals receive revelation from inhabitants in the spirit world rather than from God or Satan. There is clear evidence that a mortal often cannot tell whether he is receiving revelation from the Holy Ghost or from spirit-world inhabitants when he hears a voice, receives an impression, etc.[13] A host of examples exist which show that departed kindred, guardian angels,[14] and others in the

---

10. See chapter 6.

11. Other assumptions related to this area have sometimes been voiced: the ideas that "a proper test of the validity of a prophecy is the examination of a person's authority to receive it," "a proper test of the validity of the preserving and transmittal of a prophecy is the examination of the authority of the person who wrote it," etc. Again, authority is not a substitute for facts and proper evidence.

12. By the same token, if controversy exists, it is the careful presentation of all pertinent evidence which will bring it to an end. Withholding or suppressing evidence never will accomplish that end, nor will emotional appeals for unity nor admonitions to follow the lead of authorities. There will always remain those who desire the privilege of receiving and considering the evidence and making their own judgment on the basis of facts.

13. Numerous examples which illustrate this statement are found in the author's book, *Life Everlasting.*

14. Joseph Smith, for instance, saw his guardian angel just two weeks before his death. See HC 6:461-462, June 13, 1844.

spirit world have communicated important messages to Church members[15] —sometimes of a prophetic nature. Thus some people learn of future events even though they aren't the logical ones to receive the knowledge. Man's understanding of the processes and sources of revelation are so very limited that the logic he might advance concerning what God does or does not is of little value.

A Checklist for Evaluating the Validity of Prophetic Criticism

Just as an organized study approach is useful in the study of prophecy,[16] a step-by-step approach also has utility when considering criticisms leveled against prophetic items. The following outline will cover most situations which may arise:

I. The Critic

A. Who is the critic? Does he speak only for himself or is his view representative of some institution or organization?

B. What is his professed motive in making the criticism? Is it valid?

C. Is there evidence of any improper or ulterior motive in the setting forth of the criticism?

D. What qualifies him to make the criticism? Does he have a background of expertise in the area?

E. Does he claim that his rejection of the prophetic item is based on personal revelation which he has received?

II. The Critic's Approach

A. Is the critic allowing the evidence to shape his views, or is he speaking on the basis of prior bias? Will he change his stand if the evidence shows he is wrong?

B. Is he open to new evidence? Does he invite it?

C. Does he encourage the careful examination of the issue by other interested and qualified observers? Is he willing to share his findings with them to further the cause of truth?

D. Does he consider evidence on both sides of the issue?

E. Does he consider the issue objectively?

F. Does he recognize and justify the assumptions upon which he bases his investigation?

G. Does he discern where evidence ends and opinion begins?

H. Does he disqualify himself by:

    1. hindering the gathering of evidence by others?

---

15. And to non-members also.
16. See again chapter 6.

2. seeking to prevent others from studying in sensitive areas?

3. pursuing and publishing his own narrow viewpoint without at least acknowledging the existence of conflicting views?

4. attempting to bring social, economic, academic, political, or ecclesiastical pressure against those who disagree with his views?

5. letting his viewpoint limit and determine the evidence he will accept?

6. clinging to error when conclusive evidence shows that it is error?

7. judging on the basis of assumptions with no regard as to their validity?

8. labeling things "mysteries" and prohibiting their study?

9. failing to discern between fact and opinion?

III. His Assumptions

A. What standards and assumptions does he employ for his criticism? Are they valid? How does he show their validity?

B. Are there other standards, assumptions, and facts which should be applied to the issue at hand which would lend proper perspective?

IV. His Examination of Evidence

A. What evidence has he actually examined? Are there important items he has omitted?

B. Does he discern between primary and secondary sources, original and copied records, and direct and circumstantial evidence? Does he do so concerning both the prophecy itself and the evidence with which he has attempted to refute its veracity?

C. Has he carefully documented the circumstances concerning the receiving and recording and transmittal of the prophecy?

D. Has he investigated the prophecy in terms of

1. fulfillment? How does he explain the portions which have come to pass if he asserts that the prophecy is false?

2. lack of conflict with other revelations?

3. the existence of parallel prophecies which foretell the same events, thereby applying the law of witnesses?

4. confirmation or rejection of the verification which others may claim to have received through personal revelation?

5. whether it actually professes to be a revelation which commands the Church?

6. whether the prophecy's recipient claims to have been "appointed" by God to receive revelation for the Church?

E. Has he dealt with the main issue of controversy, or based his criticism on periferal issues?

V. His Evaluation of Evidence and Conclusions

A. Does his evidence actually support the conclusions he draws?

B. Does his evidence actually refute the validity of the prophecy or only raise questions concerning it?

C. Has he made a valid judgment concerning the motives of the person who claimed to have received or recorded the prophecy, if he criticizes it as false?

D. Does he make his evidence available for counter-examination by interested parties?

E. Does he satisfactorily answer the questions his conclusions raise? Does he refute the evidence which would cast legitimate doubt on the criticism he has voiced?

F. Are there circumstances pertaining to the prophecy which remain unexplainable if the validity of the prophecy is rejected?

Summary

1. Scholarly criticism of the scriptures and of prophecy is often valuable. Important contributions can be made by the critics and the questions they raise. Careful criticism lends perspective.

2. Just as it is important to verify and evaluate the prophecies themselves, it is equally important to identify and evaluate the methods, assumptions, and conclusions of the critics who challenge them.

3. Those who challenge the validity of the scriptures and other prophecies must be prepared to defend their challenge. When one publishes or voices his opinion to others, his judgment must in turn be judged by others.

4. Often it is the criticism, rather than that which is criticized, which is invalid.

5. Those who criticize in religious matters may do so

A. to hurt a person or persons against whom they hold a grievance,

B. to appear heroic and appear "in the know,"

C. to qualify as a detective,

D. to protect their endangered personal views,

E. to vent their animosity towards or distrust of the teachings of others,

F. to "shelter their flocks" from contrary views,

G. to defend and support their religious leaders, and

H. to demonstrate their zeal in the role of a missionary for their faith.

6. A basic rule is to examine the critic's motive first, before examining either the validity of that which he challenges or the criticism he sets forth. "Does the critic have a legitimate and unbiased reason for criticism?" should be the test his criticism should pass. One should be wary of those who criticize with improper motives.

7. Bible critics have made three incorrect assumptions about Biblical prophecy which directly oppose principles of Latter-day Saint theology:

   A. A prophet speaks only to the people of his own generation, and only about his own time.
   B. A prophet foretells the future only by discerning the signs of the times already evident and drawing correct conclusions about them.
   C. A prophet anticipates future events only as the current events of his day indicate the future events are to come about.

The corollary which developed to these assumptions has become a constant theme in Bible criticism: since prophetic passages which speak of an era later than the prophet lived could not have been prophesied by him, they are interpolations by later authors.

8. Some critics of Mormonism have based their challenges on the theories developed by Bible critics.

9. Most churches have a variety of assumptions, based upon their particular dogmas, which affect their criticism of the Bible and of latter-day prophecies. These precepts are sometimes expanded until their implications extend far beyond the bounds of supportable evidence.

10. Some Latter-day Saints also have assumptions concerning the nature of prophecy which lack validity. These assumptions include beliefs that

   A. Prophecies by Church leaders, if valid, are incorporated into printed histories of the Church. Prophecies which are not incorporated into printed histories of the Church are invalid.
   B. Prophecies by Church leaders are false unless they personally recorded and preserved them.
   C. Prophecies by Church leaders are always communicated to the membership of the Church through established channels: a letter from presiding authorities to bishops and/or stake presidents, publication by the Church in a Church-controlled periodical, or presentation in general conference.
   D. A prophecy, if true, will be recorded by the Church Historian's office.
   E. A prophecy is false if quoted by anti-Mormon sources.
   F. A prophecy is false if a respected person expresses his opinion that it is false.
   G. All revelation comes from either God or Satan.

11. The validity of prophecy is not determined by

   A. the decision of historians to include or exclude the prophecy in or from their works,
   B. who recorded and transmitted the prophecy,
   C. the time or manner or particular periodical in which the prophecy is disseminated,

D. in what library the prophecy is or is not found,

E. who does or does not quote the prophecy,

F. who does or does not regard the prophecy as being true, and

G. man's attempts, by logic, to decide what God will or will not do or reveal.

12. Prophecies are often excluded from histories. The writer of an early history does not include them because the fulfillment comes later than the period he is covering or has not yet taken place; the writer of a later history doesn't record a prophecy because he researches too late a period to discover it. They are also excluded because of author or editorial fears that they may be a source of embarrassment if they fail to come to pass as expected.

13. Many revelations, prophecies and other spiritual experiences were not personally recorded by early Church leaders. Many events regarded as important today were considered inconsequential or so commonplace that they were not recorded in the early days of the Church. The personal records of early leaders were often reduced in quantity during times of stress, travel, sickness, etc.

14. Prophecy does not conform to the established pattern of revelation to guide the Church. Prophecy has rarely come forth to the Church, at the time of its origin, through the accepted Church communication channels, except for the prophecies found in the Doctrine and Covenants. The general Church membership appears to be unaware of any authentic prophetic utterance released by Church authorities through these channels in recent decades. Since the practice of frequently adding to the body of scripture canonized by the Church was discontinued, the tendency to withhold the circulation of prophetic items and accounts of other manifestations has grown more pronounced.

15. The Church Historian's Office is a library, with many of the same responsibilities, limitations, and problems of any other library. The availability at the Church Historian's Office of records pertinent to important prophetic items often depends on whether those families which have them in their possession choose to donate them there or to other libraries where interested parties will have easier access to them. As a library, it is not the responsibility or proper role of the Church Historian's Office to issue commentaries on the interpretation and/or validity of materials housed therein.

16. Anti-Mormon sources cite prophetic statements by early Latter-day Saint leaders to support their views. This does not affect the validity of the prophecies they quote.

17. When an individual challenges a prophetic item, his statement is either (1) based on revelation which has been received which states that the questioned item is false, (2) the conclusion he has reached after a careful

study of all pertinent evidence has been made, or (3) an unsupported opinion. It is essential that the student determine which of the above is the proper category.

18. There is difficulty when a critic of prophecy holds a position of authority within the Church. Authority is not a substitute for proper evidence—there is no doctrine of infallibility in Mormonism to shield his criticism from the same investigation and judgment other criticism would receive.

19. When one in authority fails to support such a criticism with proper evidence, he can be sure his view will become a center of controversy, especially if evidence begins to come to light on the matter under consideration. If controversy of this type exists, probably the only effective means of ending it is the careful presentation and evaluation of all pertinent evidence. It is concrete evidence, rather than unsupported opinions, by which prophetic validity must and will be determined.

20. The assumption that all revelation comes only from either God or Satan does not conform to evidence concerning manifestations from the spirit world.

21. It appears that mortal beings usually cannot discern whether they are receiving revelation from the Holy Ghost or from other spirit-world inhabitants when they hear a voice, receive an impression, etc.

22. An organized approach is useful in examining the criticisms leveled against prophetic items. Such an approach should include the evaluation of
   A. the critic and his motives,
   B. the critic's approach and attitude towards gathering and examining evidence,
   C. the critic's standards of judgment and assumptions,
   D. the evidence the critic has examined,
   E. the critic's evaluation of evidence and conclusions, and
   F. questions and circumstances which he has left unanswered.

8

What Is 'Doctrine'?

The "Straw-Man" Technique Used in Anti-Mormon Literature

An approach frequently used by enemies of the Church in their efforts to counteract the rapid spread of the restored gospel has been to quote statements of various early LDS leaders and then to attempt to refute them. Often the statements they cite are utterances that have never been regarded by the Church as the doctrine of the Church, but which are the personal opinions of the individual who made the comments. The critics represent these opinions as being Church doctrine, making the unjustified assertion that if the opinions are voiced by a Church authority, they are of necessity a statement of the Church's doctrinal position.

The usual sources cited are the *Journal of Discourses* or the *Deseret News,* both of which recorded many discourses of the early brethren. A typical anti-Mormon treatment of such statements is that given by Jerald and Sandra Tanner in their book, *The Changing World of Mormonism.*[1] The approach is to present a photo of pages from the *Journal of Discourses* or *Deseret News,* with particular passages underscored. Statements by Brigham Young are favorites, and their book quotes and elaborates on quotations such as the following:

The Adam-God Theory

When our father Adam came into the garden of Eden, he came into it with a celestial body, and brought Eve, one of his wives, with him. He helped to make and organize this world. He is MICHAEL, the Archangel, the ANCIENT OF DAYS! about whom holy men have written and spoken—HE is our FATHER and our GOD, and the only God with whom WE have to do. . . . When the Virgin

---

1. Jerald and Sandra Tanner, *The Changing World of Mormonism—A Behind-the-Scenes Look at Changes in Mormon Doctrine and Practice* (Chicago, Ill.: Moody Press, 1980, 592 pp.)

Mary conceived the child Jesus, the Father had begotten him in his own likeness. He was *not* begotten by the Holy Ghost. And who is the Father? He is the first of the human family; [2]

How much unbelief exists in the minds of the Latter-day Saints in regard to one particular doctrine which I revealed to them, and which God revealed to me—namely that Adam is our father and God—[3]

Plural Marriage

Now, where a man in this church says, "I don't want but one wife, I will live my religion with one," he will perhaps be saved in the celestial kingdom; but when he gets there he will not find himself in possession of any wife at all. He has had a talent that he has hid up. He will come forward and say, "Here is that which thou gavest me, I have not wasted it, and here is the one talent," and he will not enjoy it, but it will be taken and given to those who have improved the talents they received, and he will find himself without any wife, and he will remain single for ever and ever. [4]

The only men who become Gods, even the Sons of God, are those who enter into polygamy. [5]

The Negro and the Priesthood

Shall I tell you the law of God in regard to the African race? If the white man who belongs to the chosen seed mixes blood with the seed of Cain, the penalty, under the law of God, is death on the spot. This will always be so. [6]

Cain slew his brother . . . and the Lord put a mark upon him, which is the flat nose and black skin. . . . How long is that race to endure the dreadful curse that is upon them? That curse will remain upon them, and they never can hold the Priesthood or share in it until all the other descendants of Adam have received the promises and enjoyed the blessings of the Priesthood and the keys thereof. Until the last ones of the residue of Adam's children are brought up to that favourable position, the children of Cain cannot receive the first ordinances of the Priesthood. They were the first that were cursed, and they will be the last from whom the curse will be removed. When the residue of the family of Adam come up and receive their blessings, then the curse will be removed from the seed of Cain, and they will receive blessings in like proportion. [7]

---

2. Brigham Young, *JD* 1:50, as cited in *The Changing World* . . . , p. 194. This quotation, and those that follow, have been typeset as they appeared in the original Journal of Discourses publication.

3. Brigham Young, *Deseret News,* June 18, 1873, as cited in *The Changing World.* . . , p. 197.

4. Brigham Young, *Deseret News,* September 17, 1873, as cited in *The Changing World* . . . , p. 288.

5. Brigham Young, *JD* 11:269, as cited in *The Changing World* . . . , p. 30.

6. Brigham Young, *JD* 7:290-291, as cited in *The Changing World* . . . , p. 314.

7. Brigham Young, *JD* 10:110, as cited in *The Changing World* . . . , p. 297.

Blood Atonement

> There is not a man or woman, who violates the covenants made with their God, that will not be required to pay the debt. The blood of Christ will never wipe that out, your own blood must atone for it; [8]

These statements, typical fare of apostates and critics of Mormonism, raise a question that should be resolved by Latter-day Saints: are they, or have they ever been, the official "doctrine" of the Church?

This author's response to that question is a resounding "No! They are not the doctrine of the Church today, nor have they ever been the doctrine of the Church!"

Anti-Mormon critics raise "straw men" which they then challenge and attempt to refute, without coming to grips with the actual doctrines and authority of the Church.[9] They tend to avoid any in-depth discussion of the central doctrines of Mormonism, such as the Biblical prophecies of the apostasy and restoration, authority, the nature of God, the first principles of the gospel, the fall and atonement of Christ, the relationship of faith and works, and similar themes, all of which have strong scriptural evidence which, when properly presented, provides clear refutation to their views. Their technique is to avoid the basics and to "nit-pik" on small items of peripheral significance. The statements, cited above as examples, represent private views expressed by the individual who spoke them. While they were, perhaps, shared by some of his associates, they were never accepted by the Church as being the Church's official "doctrine," and never became binding upon the membership of the Church. As will be shown later in this chapter, there is only one process the Lord has designated by which precepts become the official "doctrine" of The Church of Jesus Christ of Latter-day Saints, and that is the process of *canonization*, in which items are presented to the representatives of the Church assembled in General Conference, and

---

8. Brigham Young, *JD* 3:247, as cited in *The Changing World* . . . , p. 495.

9. Neither are their own precepts, nor personal and denominational histories, above reproach. Perhaps the only web that is more tangled and confused than protestant history since the days of the reformation is the maze of apostate cults who have separated from Mormonism. It's time Mormon authors gave their critics a dose of the same medicine, by examining not only their methods of criticism, but exposing the vagaries of their history, pointing out the unchristian conduct of some of their leaders and members, and comparing their doctrinal idiosyncrasies to the standards of Biblical doctrine. These outspoken critics of Mormonism need to be reminded of the implications of the Savior's admonition,

> Judge not, that ye be not judged.
> For with what judgment ye judge, ye shall be judged: and with what measure ye mete, it shall be measured to you again.
> And why beholdest thou the mote that is in thy brother's eye, but considerest not the beam that is in thine own eye? (Mt. 7:1-3)

by that body accepted through the application of the principle of common consent.

Certainly these statements by Brigham Young, cited above, are not the position of the Church today. Indeed, if a Latter-day Saint advocated any of these beliefs today, he would be regarded as apostate and his Church membership would be in jeopardy.

But the statements exist, and they were spoken by the President of the Church—he who was accepted as the "Prophet, Seer, and Revelator." They are cited here only to make the point that the existence of such items places the Church in an embarrassing position *if we fail to define "doctrine" and determine the position of the Church on various issues in the manner set forth in the scriptures.* And how statements of former leaders are regarded by Church authorities today ultimately provides the answer to the question, "How should the saints regard the statements, discourses, and writings of all Church leaders—as statements of infallible truths revealed by God, or as expressions of their own personal insights, counsel, and attitudes, which may or may not be inspired?"

Unfortunately, we can't "have our cake and eat it too"—we can't logically assert that pronouncements made by prophets today are to be automatically accepted, without question and testing by the Spirit and other standards, as the "mind and will of the Lord," yet discount the unacceptable teachings of former prophets in this dispensation as being only personal views. The same standard must apply—how we regard the statements of prophets on doctrinal matters[10] today is how we must regard the doctrinal statements of prophets who lived a century ago, and vice versa.

Yet the unwary among the saints will remain vulnerable to the tactics of anti-Mormon critics until we, as a Church, come to a clear reply and appropriate definition of the basic question, "What is Mormon doctrine?"

The problems caused by anti-Mormon "snipers" today is still in the "irritant" category rather than a major concern. But a significant theme in the scriptural prophecies of last-days events[11] is that the Church will be subjected to intense persecution. This book, and this chapter and the remaining

---

10. Note that this does not apply to matters pertaining to matters of "policy," as contrasted with "doctrine." As will be seen, "doctrine" pertains to religious precepts regarded as statements of eternal, unchanging truths. "Policy" refers to instructions as to how particular current situations are to be met or regarded, or how particular tasks are to be accomplished at the present time. Policy changes frequently; doctrine remains fixed. Certainly we look to current prophets in matters of policy, and their instructions supersede previous instructions. In matters of doctrine, however, previous doctrine is on a par with newly-revealed doctrine. Truth is eternal and absolute. Something is not more true if revealed today, or less true if revealed yesterday.

11. See chapter 9 of this book, and also chapter 9 of the author's book, *Prophetic Warnings To Modern America,* for extensive documentation on this subject.

chapters in particular, are written to fortify the saints against the difficulties which lie ahead. In the author's view, a careful definition of what is and is not the actual doctrine of the Church will play a significant role in stabilizing the faith of the saints in preparation for that which is to come.

There are many questions to be answered as we attempt to define the word "doctrine" in Latter-day Saint terms—questions such as

—Is our definition broad or restrictive?

—Do we use the term as it is understood by others outside of our faith?

—How is the term doctrine used in the scriptures?

—Exactly how does something become doctrine?

—Is it doctrine whenever someone speaks under inspiration?

—Are the writings and sermons of Church leaders doctrine?

—Is there room within the Church for differences of opinion on doctrinal principles?

—How serious is the problem when opposing faiths take statements by Latter-day Saints and represent them as being our doctrine, when the statements quoted clearly do not represent the understanding generally held by the Church leadership or general membership?

—What is heresy?

—Where does the line fall between acceptable and unacceptable teaching and belief within the Church?

Yes, Latter-day Saints need to take a careful look at how they define the word "doctrine." This chapter is written to help define the term from a Latter-day Saint perspective. Hopefully, it will clarify some significant points, and will focus on the need for more precise definitions in this crucial area.

Vague Dictionary Definitions of the Term "Doctrine"

"Doctrine" is a difficult word, with a host of meanings. It's often poorly defined, and sometimes roughly abused. It holds different meanings for those of different faiths. In many contexts it doesn't even refer to religion. Dictionaries don't handle it well—their definitions are so vague as to be of little value.[12] One simply says,

> *n.* **1.** what is taught as the belief of a church, nation, etc. **2.** what is taught; teachings.[13]

---

12. See again the comments of Sydney J. Harris, a nationally-known journalist, concerning the problems that occur with dictionary definitions, on p. 28 of this book.

13. Clarence L. Barnhart [Ed.] Thorndike • Barnhart Comprehensive Desk Dictionary (Garden City, N.Y.: Doubleday & Co., Inc., n.d.), Vol. A-K, p. 247.

Another adds other meanings, but is far from definitive, though its synonym explanation adds considerable enlightenment:

n. **1.** something taught; teachings **2.** something taught as the principles or creed of a religion, political party, etc.; tenet or tenets; belief; dogma **3.** a rule, theory, or principle of law ☆**4.** an official statement of a nation's policy, esp. toward other nations *[the Monroe Doctrine]*
SYN.—**doctrine** refers to a theory based on carefully worked out principles and taught or advocated by its adherents *[scientific or social doctrines];* **dogma** refers to a belief or doctrine that is handed down by authority as true and indisputable, and often connotes arbitrariness, arrogance, etc. *[religious dogma];* **tenet** emphasizes the maintenance of defense, rather than the teaching, of a theory or principle *[the tenets of a political party];* **precept** refers to an injunction or dogma intended as a rule of action or conduct *[to teach by example rather than by precept]*[14]

Just as the dictionaries fail to give us adequate definitions of terms such as "prophet," "seer," and "revelator," they also render only vague guidance on the term "doctrine."

What Do The Scriptures Teach About Doctrine?

It is informative to examine what the scriptures say concerning the term doctrine. It can be easily done—the term is only used in about eighty-five different passages. Some verses referring to the term give little insight.[15] Others do not use the word in a definitive sense, yet they link various terms with the word which add an aura of insight and convey a significant general impression—words like "speech,"[16] "pure,"[17] "good,"[18] "law,"[19] "knowledge,"[20] "understanding,"[21] "authority,"[22] "power,"[23] "disciples,"[24] "apostle's,"[25] "new,"[26] "revelation,"[27] "prophesying,"[28] "interpreta-

---

14. Guralnik, David B. [Ed. in Chief], *Websters New World Dictionary of the American Language* (Cleveland, Ohio: William Collins + World Publishing Co., Inc., Second College Edition), p. 414.
15. See, for instance, Jer. 10:8; Mt. 16:12; 22:33; Mk. 11:18; 12:38; Rev. 2:14-15, 24.
16. Deut. 32:2.
17. Job 11:4.
18. Prov. 4:2; I Tim. 4:6.
19. *Ibid.*
20. Is. 28:9; I Cor. 14:6.
21. Is. 29:4.
22. Mt. 7:28-29; Mk. 1:22, 27.
23. Lk. 4:32.
24. Jn. 18:19.
25. Acts 2:42.
26. Acts 17:19.
27. I Cor. 14:6, 26.
28. I Cor. 14:6.

tion,"[29] "sound,"[30] "perfection,"[31] "saved,"[32] "gospel,"[33] "futurity,"[34] "priesthood,"[35] "commanded,"[36] "bold,"[37] and "principle."[38]

But many passages of scripture combine to give significant insights that yield a rich understanding of the nature of doctrine in the religious sense. Let's examine some of those insights:

1. *Doctrine comes from God the Father, through Jesus Christ.* Though the scriptures refer to the "doctrine of the Lord,"[39] and the "doctrine of Christ,"[40] Jesus on several occasions identified his doctrine as coming from God the Father. He said, for instance, that "This is my doctrine, and *it is the doctrine which the Father hath given unto me.*" [41] His comment to the Jews in the Jerusalem temple, who were marveling that he knew how to read, was "My doctrine is not mine, but *his that sent me.*" [42] And Nephi recorded, "This is the doctrine of Christ, and the only and true doctrine of the Father, and of the Son, and of the Holy Ghost, which is one God, without end."[43]

2. *Doctrine is sacred, and represents an attribute of godliness.* Paul, in his first epistle to Timothy, expressed his concern that the saints exercise caution "that the name of God and *his doctrine be not blasphemed.*" [44] He asserted that doctrine *"is according to godliness."* [45]

3. *God's doctrines are revealed statements of eternal truths, saving principles, or aspects of His plan of salvation.* The Lord has revealed that "truth is knowledge of things as they are, and as they were, and as they are to come."[46] We are taught that "the Spirit speaketh the truth and lieth not. Wherefore, it speaketh of things as they really are, and of things as they really will be; wherefore, these things are manifested unto us plainly, for the salvation of our soul."[47] When Christ defined his doctrine, He said,

> Behold, verily, verily, I say unto you, *I will declare unto you my doctrine.* And *this is my doctrine, and it is the doctrine which the Father hath given unto me;* and I bear record of the Father, and the Father beareth record of me, and the Holy Ghost beareth record of the Father and me; and I bear record that *the Father commandeth all men,* everywhere, *to repent* and *believe in me.*
>
> And *whoso believeth in me, and is baptized, the same shall be saved;* and they are they who shall inherit the kingdom of God.
>
> And *whoso believeth not in me, and is not baptized, shall be damned.* Verily, verily, I say unto you, *that this is my doctrine, . . .*[48]

29. I Cor. 14:26.
30. I Tim. 1:10.
31. Heb. 6:1.
32. 1 Ne. 15:14.
33. Jac. 7:6.
34. D&C 101:78.
35. D&C 121:45.
36. D&C 128:7.
37. D&C 128:9.
38. D&C 132:1.
39. Acts 13:12. See Acts 5:28.
40. Heb. 6:1, 2 Ne. 31:2.
41. 3 Ne. 11:32.
42. Jn. 7:16.
43. 2 Ne. 32:21.
44. I Tim. 6:1.
45. I Tim. 6:3.
46. D&C 93:24.
47. Jac. 4:13.
48. 3 Ne. 11:31-35.

Christ has emphasized that His doctrine focuses on the basic principles of the gospel. In this last dispensation He has revealed that parents are to teach their children "the *doctrine* of repentence, faith in Christ the Son of the living God, and of baptism and the gift of the Holy Ghost."[49]

But other precepts are also identified in the scriptures as being doctrine, which shows that doctrine extends beyond the first principles. Paul wrote to the Hebrews of "the doctrine of baptisms, and of laying on of hands, and of *resurrection of the dead,* and of *eternal judgment,*"[50] and wrote to Timothy of "the doctrine which is according to *godliness.*"[51] In modern revelations, the Lord revealed that "the *doctrine of the priesthood* shall distil upon thy soul as the dews from heaven."[52] In another section of the Doctrine and Covenants Joseph Smith wrote of "a very bold doctrine that we talk of—*a power which records or binds on earth and binds in heaven.*"[53] And a revelation to Joseph answering his query concerning several of the ancient prophets spoke of "the principle and *doctrine of their having many wives* and concubines—."[54]

4. *God's doctrines explain man's relationship to Christ.* The theme of man's coming to Christ is a key element in the definition of "doctrine." Doctrine tells man how to be saved through his relationship with Jesus.

The prophet Lehi, for instance, explained that "they shall come to the knowledge of their Redeemer and the very points of his *doctrine,* that they may *know how to come unto him and be saved.*"[55] It was his son, Nephi, who wrote that

> Wherefore, ye must press forward with a steadfastness in Christ, having a perfect brightness of hope, and a love of God and of all men. Wherefore, if ye shall press forward, feasting on the word of Christ, and endure to the end, behold, thus saith the Father: Ye shall have eternal life.
>
> And now, behold, my beloved brethren, this is the way; and *there is none other way nor name given under heaven whereby man can be saved in the kingdom of God. And now, behold, this is the doctrine of Christ,* and the only and true doctrine of the Father, and of the Son, and of the Holy Ghost, which is one God, without end. Amen.[56]

In a modern revelation the Lord proclaimed:

> Behold, *this is my doctrine*—whosoever repenteth and *cometh unto me,* the same is my church.

---

49. D&C 68:25.
50. Heb. 6:2.
51. I Tim. 6:3.
52. D&C 121:45.
53. D&C 128:9.
54. D&C 132:1.
55. 1 Ne. 15:14.
56. 2 Ne. 31:20-21. See also 2 Ne. 32:3-6.

> *Whosoever declareth more or less than this, the same is not of me, but is against me; therefore he is not of my church.*
> And now, behold, whosoever is of my church, and endureth of my church to the end, him will I establish upon my rock, and the gates of héll shall not prevail against them.[57]

5. *Doctrine serves as a standard of conduct.* Intimately related with the concept of coming to Christ is the theme that a doctrine sets forth a standard of conduct which is to be observed by His followers. It is a guide to personal action. The Lord desires "that every man may *act in doctrine and principle pertaining to futurity,* according to the *moral agency* which I have given unto him, . . ."[58]

The prophet Alma admonished his wayward son, Corianton, not to go against the standards that were set forth in doctrine:

> And now behold, my son, *do not risk one more offense against your God upon those points of doctrine,* which ye have hitherto risked to commit sin.[59]

It is by using doctrine as a standard of conduct, and living it, that we can know the truthfulness of Christ's doctrines. As Christ told the Jews in the temple,

> My doctrine is not mine, but his that sent me.
> *If any man will do his will, he shall know of the doctrine,* whether it be of God, or whether I speak of myself.[60]

The second epistle of John contains the warning that

> *Whosoever transgresseth, and abideth not in the doctrine of Christ, hath not God.* He that abideth in the doctrine of Christ, he hath both the Father and the Son.[61]

6. *Doctrine is closely related to the gospel of Christ.* The gospel is a program of commandments and activities that bring man to salvation through Christ. Thus, it is natural that Christ's doctrine would assert that man should live and obey His gospel. On several occasions, the terms "doctrine" and "gospel" are so closely linked as to almost stand as synonyms. In the book of Jacob, for instance, the author speaks of "preaching that which ye call the gospel, or the doctrine of Christ."[62] While speaking of His "other sheep," the Lord said,

---

57. D&C 10:67-69. Concerning the "more or less" aspect of this passage, see also 3 Ne. 11:37-40.
58. D&C 101:78.
59. Al. 41:9.
60. Jn. 7:16-17.
61. II Jn. 9.
62. Jac. 7:6.

Yea, and I will also bring to light *my gospel* which was ministered unto them, and, behold, they shall not deny that which you have received, but they shall build it up, and *shall bring to light the true points of my doctrine, yea, and the only doctrine which is in me.*

And this I do that I may *establish my gospel,* that there may not be so much contention; yea, *Satan doth stir up the hearts of the people to contention concerning the points of my doctrine;* and in these things they do err, for *they do wrest the scriptures and do not understand them.* [63]

In May of 1829, before the Church had been restored, the Lord linked the terms "gospel" and "doctrine" together when He commanded Hyrum Smith to "Wait a little longer, until you shall have my word, my rock, my church, and my *gospel,* that you may *know of a surety my doctrine.* " [64]

Just as 3 Nephi 11:31-35[65] defines Christ's *doctrine* as repentence, belief in Christ, and baptism, various passages define those same precepts as being His *gospel.* Typical is 3 Nephi 27:20-21:

Now this is the commandment: Repent, all ye ends of the earth, and come unto me and be baptized in my name, that ye may be sanctified by the reception of the Holy Ghost, that ye may stand spotless before me at the last day.

Verily, verily, I say unto you, *this is my gospel;* and ye know the things that ye must do in my church; for the works which ye have seen me do that ye shall also do; for that which ye have seen me do even that shall ye do; . . .[66]

Other passages which define the "gospel" in a similar manner to the Lord's definition of His "doctrine" include Doctrine and Covenants 39:6; 33:11-12; and 84:27.

7. *Doctrine is recorded in the scriptures.* A number of passages indicate that the scriptures are the repository for Christ's doctrines. For instance, when the Savior rebuked the Sadducees for their incorrect understanding of life after death, He cited scripture to establish His doctrine: When they asked which of a man's seven wives would be wed to that man in the resurrection,

Jesus answered and said unto them, *Ye do err, not knowing the scriptures, nor the power of God.*

For in the resurrection they neither marry, nor are given in marriage, but are as the angels of God in heaven.

But as touching the resurrection of the dead, *have ye not read that which was spoken unto you by God,* saying,

I am the God of Abraham, and the God of Isaac, and the God of Jacob? God is not the God of the dead, but of the living.

And when the multitude heard this, *they were astonished at his doctrine.* [67]

63. D&C 10:62-63. See Al. 13:20; 41:1.
64. D&C 11:16.
65. See p. 241.
66. 3 Ne. 27:20-27.
67. Mt. 22:29-33.

The scriptures, as seen in this passage, are a compiled record of "that which was spoken unto you by God."

Paul taught Timothy that scripture is the proper source for doctrine when he wrote:

> All *scripture is given by inspiration of God,* and is *profitable for doctrine,* for reproof, for correction, for instruction in righteousness: . . .[68]

Lehi quoted the Lord's revelation to Joseph who was sold into Egypt, and that passage also indicates that scripture is the standard for doctrine. The Lord told Joseph, in a prophecy which foresaw the Book of Mormon and the Bible, that those scriptures would combine to refute false doctrines:

> Wherefore, the fruit of thy loins shall write; and the fruit of the loins of Judah shall write; and that which shall be written by the fruit of thy loins, and also that which shall be written by the fruit of the loins of Judah, *shall grow together, unto_the confounding of false doctrines and laying down of contentions,* and establishing *peace* among the fruit of thy loins, and bringing them to the *knowledge* of their fathers in the latter days, and also to the *knowledge of my covenants,* saith the Lord.[69]

8. *Church workers and leaders sometimes preach incorrect doctrine.* Numerous passages of scripture indicate the constant danger that even faithful Church leaders and members may teach incorrect and false doctrines, thus showing that neither Church membership nor position is a guarantee of doctrinal correctness.

Paul, for instance, left Timothy behind at Ephesus, to admonish the Ephesian saints to preach only correct doctrine:

> As I besought thee to abide still at Ephesus, when I went into Macedonia, that thou mightest charge some that they *teach no other doctrine,*
> Neither give heed to fables and endless genealogies, which minister questions, rather than godly edifying which is in faith: so do.[70]

In the same epistle, Paul reminded Timothy that he had been "nourished up in the words of faith and of *good* doctrine"[71] (which implies that some in his day were not taught *good* doctrine), and instructed him to "Take heed unto thyself, and *unto the doctrine; continue in them:* for in doing this thou shalt both save thyself, and them that hear thee."[72] (Again, the implication is that Timothy could cease to teach *good* doctrine, hence the admonition to *continue* in the doctrine which Paul had taught him.)

---

68. II Tim. 3:16.
69. 2 Ne. 3:12.
70. I Tim. 1:3-4.
71. I Tim. 4:6.
72. I Tim. 4:16.

As he described the qualities which should be found in a bishop, Paul told Titus that a good bishop is one who will be found *"Holding fast the faithful word as he hath been taught,* that he may be able *by sound doctrine* both to exhort and to convince the gainsayers."[73] He cautioned Titus to "speak thou the things which become *sound doctrine,* "[74] and reminded him that he should be showing himself to be living "a pattern of good works: *in doctrine shewing uncorruptness,* gravity, sincerity."[75] All of these admonitions show that they were experiencing doctrinal difficulties within the Church, and that the possibility of the saints being taught incorrect, unsound doctrine, even from faithful members, was very real.

To the saints at Corinth Paul wrote,

> Now I beseech you, brethren, by the name of our Lord Jesus Christ, that *ye all speak the same thing,* and that there *be no divisions among you;* but that ye be perfectly joined together *in the same mind and in the same judgment.*[76]

He recognized that there were doctrinal differences among them, and contentions, and that the people were saying, "I am of Paul; and I of Apollos; and I of Cephas; and I of Christ." His reminder of the need for doctrinal unity was posed in the question, "Is Christ divided?"[77]

The problem of incorrect doctrine being taught within the Church showed up at Galatia also. Paul wrote to the Galatians,

> I marvel that ye are so soon removed from him that called you into the grace of Christ *unto another gospel:*
> *Which is not another; but there be some that trouble you, and would pervert the gospel of Christ.*[78]

He warned that "If any man preach any other gospel unto you than that ye have received, let him be accursed."[79]

As Paul concluded his third missionary journey, he stopped for a day at Ephesus. He warned them of the danger of false doctrine being taught within the Church, saying that *"of your own selves* shall men arise, *speaking perverse things,* to draw away disciples after them."[80]

The fifteenth chapter of Acts records a General Conference of the Church which was called to correct unsound teachings concerning circumcision which were being taught within the Church.

---

73. Tit. 1:9.
74. Tit. 2:1.
75. Tit. 2:7.
76. I Cor. 1:10.
77. I Cor. 1:12-13.
78. Gal. 1:6-7.
79. Gal. 1:9.
80. Acts 20:30.

Differences over doctrines and policies can extend to the highest levels of the Church. Paul, for instance, rebuked Peter, the head of the Church, "to the face," because Peter refused to associate with the Gentile saints when in the presence of Jewish members.[81] And this problem occurred long after Peter had been directed by the Lord in a vision[82] not to exclude the Gentiles from his preaching.

Thus the scriptures show that correct doctrine is a fragile thing, and that no individual, in any position or calling, is immune to the danger of teaching incorrect doctrine or establishing incorrect policies.

9. *Doctrines are to be taught to one another by the saints.* The Lord has commanded His saints to

... *Teach one another the doctrine* of the kingdom.
   Teach ye diligently and my grace shall attend you, that you may be *instructed more perfectly* in theory, in principle, *in doctrine,* in the law of the gospel, in all things that pertain unto the kingdom of God, . . .[83]

It is His expressed desire that "all those who are called to the work" will *"be perfected in the understanding of their ministry,* in theory, in principle, and *in doctrine,* in all things pertaining to the kingdom of God on the earth, . . .[84]

This doctrinal knowledge enables those who labor in the ministry to perform their work properly and thus be deserving of praise. As Paul commented, "Let the elders that rule well be counted worthy of double honour, especially *they who labour in the word and doctrine."* [85] And Paul emphasized that those who teach and "labour in the doctrine" are to have freedom so to do, for he continues by commenting that "the scripture saith, *Thou shalt not muzzle* the ox that treadeth out the corn."[86]

The saints are to gain knowledge of doctrine through a process of continual growth. As Isaiah observed,

   Whom shall he *teach knowledge?* and whom shall he make to *understand doctrine?* them that are weaned from the milk, and drawn from the breasts.
   For precept must be upon precept, precept upon precept; line upon line, line upon line; here a little, and there a little: . . .[87]

10. *Satan seeks to lead men astray through false doctrine.* A final theme that is repeated in the passages which use the word "doctrine" is that Satan

---

81. Gal. 2:11-21.
82. Acts 10:9-16; 11:5-12.
83. D&C 88:77-78. See p. 126.
84. D&C 97:13-14.
85. I Tim. 5:17.
86. I Tim. 5:18.
87. Is. 28:9-10.

seeks to corrupt men, and churches, through false doctrine. This danger was very much present in the Church following Christ's day, as was seen in section number eight of this listing.

The Lord has warned that *"Satan doth stir up the hearts of the people to contend concerning the points of my doctrine."*[88]

The Book of Mormon relates that just before the appearance of Christ in the Americas in the meredian of time,

> ... The people began to forget those signs and wonders which they had heard, and began to be less and less astonished at a sign or a wonder from heaven, insomuch that *they began to be hard in their hearts,* and *blind in their minds,* and *began to disbelieve* all which they had heard and seen—
>
> Imagining up some vain thing in their hearts, that it was wrought by men and by the power of the devil, *to lead away and deceive the hearts of the people;* and *thus did Satan get possession of the hearts of the people again,* insomuch that *he did blind their eyes and lead them away to believe that the doctrine of Christ was a foolish and a vain thing.*[89]

Nephi, when he was prophesying of the last days, warned of those who would advocate the "eat, drink, and be merry" philosophy. He foretold that

> ... There shall be many which shall teach after this manner, *false and vain and foolish doctrines,* and shall be puffed up in their hearts, and shall seek deep to hide their counsels from the Lord; and their works shall be in the dark.[90]

He saw the degenerative effect of false doctrine, and reported that

> Because of pride, and *because of false teachers, and false doctrine,* their churches have become corrupted, and their churches are lifted up; because of pride they are puffed up.[91]

It was Nephi's warning that those who preach false doctrine in the last days shall be "thrust down to hell":

> O the wise, and the learned, and the rich, that are puffed up in the pride of their hearts, and all those *who preach false doctrines,* and all those who commit whoredoms, and pervert the right way of the Lord, wo, wo, wo be unto them, saith the Lord God Almighty, for *they shall be thrust down to hell!*
>
> Wo unto them that turn aside the just for a thing of naught and revile against that which is good, and say that is of no worth![92]

The temptation has long been present for people to preach false doctrines in order to reap riches, honor, and power. To do so is to engage in priestcraft, and the Book of Mormon tells of its spread in olden days. Alma reported that even when the wicked Nehor was put to death,

---

88. D&C 10:63.
89. 3 Ne. 2:1-2.
90. 2 Ne. 28:9.
91. 2 Ne. 28:12.
92. 2 Ne. 28:15-16.

> . . . This did not put an end to the spreading of *priestcraft* through the land; for *there were many who loved the vain things of the world, and they went forth preaching false doctrines;* and this they did for the sake of riches and honor.[93]

Thus ten characteristics of "doctrine" are identified in the scriptures:

1. Doctrine comes from God the Father, through Jesus Christ.
2. Doctrine is sacred, and represents an attribute of godliness.
3. God's doctrines are revealed statements of eternal truths, saving principles, or aspects of His plan of salvation.
4. God's doctrines explain man's relationship to Christ.
5. Doctrine serves as a standard of conduct.
6. Doctrine is closely related to the gospel of Christ.
7. Doctrine is recorded in the scriptures.
8. Church workers and leaders sometimes preach incorrect doctrines.
9. Doctrines are to be taught to one another by the saints.
10. Satan seeks to lead men astray through false doctrine.

When doctrine is correctly taught and universally accepted by the saints, then we will all

> . . . Come in the unity of the faith, and of the knowledge of the Son of God, unto a perfect man, unto the measure of the stature of the fulness of Christ:
> That we henceforth be *no more children, tossed to and fro, and carried about with every wind of doctrine, by the slight of men, and cunning craftiness, whereby they lie in wait to deceive;*
> But speaking the truth in love, may grow up into him in all things, which is the head, even Christ: . . .[94]

The Role and Domain of "Policy" Within the Church

There is a very real difference which should be discerned between Church *policies and/or procedures* and the *doctrines* of the Church. Failure to distinguish between the two can sometimes create difficulties for some Church members.

Church leaders direct the daily affairs of the saints through a variety of ecclesiastical and temporal organizations, delegating authority and responsibility that reaches into many dimensions of Mormon life. Priesthood-led Church units such as stakes, wards, missions and branches function under the supervision of priesthood quorums and committees. They are directed by leaders such as Regional Representatives, Stake Presidents, Bishops, Mission Presidents, and Branch Presidents. Auxiliary organizations such as

---

93. Al. 1:16.
94. Eph. 4:13-15. See Jos. 1:6.

the Sunday School, Relief Society, Primary, the Young Men and Young Women, function under general Church auxiliary leaders. Other organizations and programs also function, such as the Welfare program, the Deseret Industries, LDS Social Services, the Tabernacle Choir, the Genealogical Society, Church purchasing and distribution, the Church legal department, the missionary department, the real estate acquisition department, the building committee, the translation department, and a host of other organizations, committees and departments.

The procedures and immediate objectives of these ecclesiastical units, church-wide committees, auxiliary organizations, departments and other units are constantly changing and adapting to trends and shifts in the Church population, changes in its sociological makeup, and many external events and influences. Letters and directives flow out from Church headquarters in a constant stream which indicate the current procedures to be followed. These directives are statements of *policy*. Policy changes frequently within the Church. Indeed, these policy changes reflect a continual "fine-tuning," as well as occasional "major overhauls," of the Church's methodology and peripheral structures.

Unlike "doctrine," "policy" is not regarded as being a statement of eternal truth. It functions on a lower level. It represents a statement of "this is how we're going to do it at the present time." It rarely is of such significance that it requires the sustaining vote of the Church-wide membership. It is the result of delegated authority, and serves to regulate the affairs of the Church on a level below the system of checks and balances revealed by the Lord.

Some communications from the Church leadership represent policy in another form—that of endorsements of causes and calls to action. Church periodicals will occasionally contain policy statements by Church leaders encouraging the members to support the Red Cross, aid refugees from foreign lands who are settling among the saints, or to exercise their franchise as citizens by participating in upcoming elections. Policy statements also urge the saints to comply with local and national laws. They may treat such mundane matters as thermostat regulation in Church buildings, or the need to comply with copyright laws, local fire codes, and sales tax laws. They generally reflect the Church leadership's desire to comply with such ordinances.

Policy statements sometimes rise to a higher level, where they represent a significant stand on an issue with important moral implications. For instance, while the Church has studiously avoided involvement in political issues, it has, occasionally, issued policy statements in which it takes a stand on political matters involving the general welfare of the saints and/or of the nation. The General Authorities have asserted that the highest quorums hold the right to involve the Church in such issues. For instance, a policy statement issued by the First Presidency in 1979 asserted that

> The many and varied circumstances in which our Church members live . . . make it inadvisable for the Church to involve itself institutionally in every local community issue. These challenges are best responded to by members as they meet their obligations as citizens—preferably in concert with other like-minded individuals. *Only the First Presidency and the Twelve can declare a particular issue to be a moral issue worthy of full institutional involvement.* Absent such a declaration, Church members should exercise great care and caution to distinguish between what they may do as citizens in exercising their constitutional rights and what the Church might do as an institution.[95]

Policies, or changes in policy, which may affect the entire Church membership, are presented for the sustaining vote of the Church assembled in General Conference. This is a rare occurrence, and usually involves matters only of a controversial nature. The two most noteable examples of policy change being presented to the Church through the process of common consent are the Manifesto (issued October 6, 1890, which publicly terminated the practice of plural marriage within the Church)[96] and the announcement concerning the Priesthood (accepted in General Conference, September 30, 1978, which allowed men of all races to be able to receive the priesthood).[97]

Statements of policy sometimes become matters of concern to individual Latter-day Saints if they find that the Church's policy represents a public stand on issues, particularly those of a political nature, which they perceive as infringing on their personal views and tending to compel them to actions they might not otherwise choose to take, thus, in their opinion, limiting their free agency. This has happened on the national scene, for instance, in connection with the Equal Rights Amendment, and in the local Utah area with issues such as liquor-by-the-drink and the picketing of movie theaters which show X-rated films. The dilemma is increased if the Church fails to fully document and disseminate the reasons for its stand, thereby providing members "on the firing line" with adequate evidence with which to answer the queries and comments of friends and associates. To take the stand, without providing a thorough rationale which is acceptable and meaningful to the saints, is to place them in the position of "defender" with no ammunition. The inevitable result is low morale and the danger of defection from the ranks.

---

95. *Church News,* June 29, 1979. See *"The Church and the Proposed Equal Rights Amendment—A Moral Issue,"* (Salt Lake City, Utah: Ensign magazine, 1980), p. 20.

96. "Official Declaration," found in the Doctrine and Covenants, 1948 edition, pp. 256-257.

97. *CR,* September 30, 1978, p. 22.

The inherent question raised when the Church leadership takes a stand on a controversial moral issue is: how far can, and should, the General Authorities or local leaders commit the saints without receiving the prior approval of the general or local Church membership through the principle of common consent? If they go too far, and fail to provide a careful rationale for their action, the result, at best, is a discomforted membership, with questions and concerns about "what's going on at the top;" at the worst, the stand results in much adverse publicity and the apostasy of alienated members, who sometimes form new churches of their own. This, for instance, is what has been experienced in the ERA controversy. Leaders can only lead to the extent that followers will follow.

In American government, the basic understanding is that the government exists by the consent of the people, and to serve the people—the government is the servant; the people are the master. Is it the same in the Church? In situations where Church policies get too far ahead of the people and begin to exert a degree of compulsion so that some members perceive themselves to be compelled to take action they really don't wish to take, the question begins to be raised as to who is to serve whom—is the Church leadership to serve the saints, or are the saints to serve the leaders?[98]

Another question deserves consideration in this context: are statements of policy the most suitable instrument to be used in motivating and influencing the actions of the saints in such highly controversial situations, or is that properly the domain of doctrine—doctrine which has been submitted to the Church through the process of common consent?

There are those who argue that a public stand taken by the Church exerts no pressure nor compulsion upon the saints. Yet those who are in positions "on the firing line"—where member mixes on a daily basis with non-member—would disagree, for they feel the pressure generated by widespread publicity and continual discussion of controversial issues. And if the policy stand starts to be translated into weekly calls in quorum meetings to "take your turn on the picket line" or to "distribute literature in your district," or when daily discussion in one's work environment is

---

98. Jesus told His disciples

> ... Ye know that the princes of the Gentiles exercise dominion over them, and they that are great exercise authority upon them.
> But it shall not be so among you: but whosoever will be great among you, let him be your minister.
> And whosoever will be chief among you, let him be your servant:
> Even as the Son of Man came not to be ministered unto, but to minister, and to give his life as a ransom for many. (Mt. 20:25-28)

See also statements by the Savior concerning the relationship between servants and masters and of serving in the kingdom, such as Mt. 10:24-25; Jn. 12:25-26, 13:16-17; 15:15-16, 20; I Cor. 9:19; Gal. 5:13-15; Heb. 12:28.

continually brought to focus on the issue, then social pressure begins to abridge free agency, and compulsion is felt.

Canonization—The Act of Creating Doctrine

Two significant events in LDS history give information and perspective on the process of establishing an item as the official doctrine of the Church. They are significant because they give a very clear indication of what is and what is not the doctrine of the Church, and reaffirm the pattern found in the scriptures as being the method by which items become doctrine and scripture.

The first of these events occurred in the Saturday-afternoon session of the General Conference of the Church on April 3, 1976. President N. Eldon Tanner presented "the General Authorities, General Officers, and General Auxiliary Officers of the Church"[99] for the sustaining vote of the Church. Then he spoke these words and received the common consent of the Church:

> President Kimball has asked me to read a very important resolution for your sustaining vote.
> At a meeting of the Council of the First Presidency and the Quorum of the Twelve held in the Salt Lake Temple on March 25, 1976, *approval was given to add to the Pearl of Great Price the two following revelations:*
> First, *a vision of the celestial kingdom given to Joseph Smith* the Prophet in the Kirtland Temple, on January 21, 1836, which deals with the salvation of those who die without a knowledge of the Gospel; and second, *a vision given to President Joseph F. Smith* in Salt Lake City, Utah, on October 3, 1918, *showing the visit of the Lord Jesus Christ in the spirit world, and setting forth the doctrine of the redemption of the dead."*
> *It is proposed that we sustain and approve this action and adopt these revelations as part of the standard works of The Church of Jesus Christ of Latter-day Saints.*
> All those in favor manifest it. Those opposed, if any, by the same sign.
> Thank you. President Kimball, the voting seems to be unanimous in the affirmitive.[100]

The second of these significant events occurred in General Conference on Saturday, September 30, 1978. In the afternoon session, just prior to sustaining the authorities of the Church, President N. Eldon Tanner made the following announcement and obtained the vote of the assembled saints, gathered in what he termed a "constituent assembly:"

> In early June of this year, the First Presidency announced that a revelation had been received by President Spencer W. Kimball extending priesthood and temple blessings to all worthy male members of the Church. President Kimball has asked that I advise the conference that after he had received this revelation,

---

99. *CR,* April, 1976, p. 27.
100. *Ibid.,* p. 29.

which came to him after extended meditation and prayer in the sacred rooms of the holy temple, *he presented it to his counselors,* who accepted it and approved it. It was then *presented to the Quorum of the Twelve Apostles,* who unanimously approved it, and was subsequently *presented to all other General Authorities,* who likewise approved it unanimously.

President Kimball has asked that I now read this letter:

"June 8, 1978

"To all general and local priesthood officers of The Church of Jesus Christ of Latter-day Saints throughout the world:

"Dear Brethren:

"As we have witnessed the expansion of the work of the Lord over the earth, we have been grateful that people of many nations have responded to the message of the restored gospel, and have joined the Church in ever-increasing numbers. This, in turn, has inspired us with a desire to extend to every worthy member of the Church all of the privileges and blessings which the gospel affords.

"Aware of the promises made by the prophets and presidents of the Church who have preceded us that at some time, in God's eternal plan, all of our brethren who are worthy may receive the priesthood, and witnessing the faithfulness of those from whom the priesthood has been withheld, we have pleaded long and earnestly in behalf of these, our faithful brethren, spending many hours in the Upper Room of the Temple supplicating the Lord for divine guidance.

"He has heard our prayers, and by revelation has confirmed that the long-promised day has come when every faithful, worthy man in the Church may receive the holy priesthood, with power to exercise its divine authority, and enjoy with his loved ones every blessing that flows therefrom, including the blessings of the temple. Accordingly, all worthy male members of the Church may be ordained to the priesthood without regard for race or color. Priesthood leaders are instructed to follow the policy of carefully interviewing all candidates for ordination to either the Aaronic or the Melchizedek Priesthood to insure that they meet the established standards for worthiness.

"We declare with soberness that the Lord has now made known his will for the blessing of all his children throughout the earth who will hearken to the voice of his authorized servants, and prepare themselves to receive every blessing of the gospel.

"Sincerely yours,

"Spencer W. Kimball

"N. Eldon Tanner

"Marion G. Romney

"The First Presidency"

Recognizing Spencer W. Kimball as a prophet, seer, and revelator, and president of The Church of Jesus Christ of Latter-day Saints, it is proposed that we as *a constituent assembly accept this revelation as the word and will of the Lord.* All in favor please signify by raising your right hand. Any opposed by the same sign.

President Kimball, it appears that the vote has been unanimous in the affirmative, and the motion has carried.[101]

----

101. *CR,* September 30, 1978, p. 22.

These two instances show the Church acting in obedience to the Lord's commandment that *"all things must be done in order, and by common consent* in the Church."[102] (This principle was discussed in detail on pages 82 through 89. Documentation presented there is appropriate in this context.)

These votes of acceptance, by representatives of local ecclesiastical units assembled in what was called in Joseph Smith's day the "Committee of the Whole Church,"[103] constitutes the process which other religious organizations call "canonization."

Since that process has been shown by the above instances to be in active use today, this author suggests that the term is applicable in the Latter-day Saint environment, and proposes that it deserves wider usage among the saints. We've seen the process in action, but many do not associate the process with the word which describes it, though that word conveys meaning worldwide in Christian ecclesiastical circles. This section is an effort to clarify its meaning in an LDS context.

Canonization *authorizes* the acceptance and use of an item as being a prescribed doctrine, law, and belief of the Church. It makes that item *binding upon the saints, and makes their compliance to the item mandatory.* Canonization of an item makes it *scripture,* and adds the item to the Standard Works of the Church. Canonization *asserts the Church's belief and acceptance* that the item is an inspired statement of God's word and will. Canonization makes it *doctrine.*[104]

In the author's view, canonized items stand separate and apart from many items which hold lesser status and importance, such as Church manuals, news conferences and press releases, doctrinal discourses, personal writings which expound gospel teachings, articles in Church periodicals, General Conference addresses, policy letters and bulletins, personal journals and memoirs, etc. All of the above may be true, inspired, important, and relevant, but if they have not been canonized through the process of common consent by the representatives of the entire Church assembled in General Conference, they are not the official, authorized, binding, scriptural doctrine of the Church.

As the author understands the term and process, canonization is the single test by which Church doctrine is to be identified—anything which is not canonized is not doctrine. Oh yes, it may be true, and it may be God's revealed will, but if it is not canonized, it is not doctrine. That is the standard the Lord applied when He commanded that *"all things must be done in order, and by common consent* in the Church." That is the standard the saints have accepted when they voted to accept the Book of Mormon, the

---

102. D&C 28:13. See also D&C 26:2.
103. See for instance, HC 2:509-510, discussed on pp. 86-87 of this book.
104. Or, as termed in some other faiths, *dogma.*

Doctrine and Covenants, and the Pearl of Great Price[105] to be their doctrine. That is the standard applied in 1976 when the Church voted to include the Vision of the Celestial Kingdom and the Vision of the Redemption of the Dead in their scriptures as new doctrine. It is a wise standard, an inspired standard, a safe standard, the only acceptable standard.

No "Almost Doctrine" in the Church

The author has often encountered those who, consciously or unconsciously, have attempted to establish or observe false standards of what is doctrine. Certainly doctrine is not determined by such superficial standards as "was it printed by the Church?" "is it carried in Deseret Book?" "wasn't that book written in the temple?" etc. Doctrine is not determined by when it was said, where it was said, where it was written, who is the author, who published it, who owns the copyright, etc. Eligibility to be classified as doctrine is determined by the one simple question, "Is it canonized?"

By the same token, there is no intermediate level—we have no "almost doctrine" in the Church.

Obviously, the test for "is it doctrine?" is quite different from the test for "is it true?" or "is it revealed from God?" Doctrine is the precise statement of items regarded as eternal truths, the acceptance of which is mandatory for Church members. There is good reason to maintain careful control over that which we designate as binding upon us. Doctrinal additions should be major insights rather than trivial matters, for instance. There is no advantage in adding doctrine upon doctrine, making us like the Pharisees of old—circumscribed by trivial laws in every activity of life.

The canonization process provides the means for distinguishing those writings of a religious nature which are binding upon the Church from the host of personal religious writings which are not binding.

The word "scripture" plays a significant role in this context. When we examine the word in that imperfect instrument, the modern dictionary, we find that the primary meaning of the word is *"act or product of writing."* Secondary meanings include "the sacred writings of a religion" and "a body of writings considered as authoritative." (See *Webster's Seventh New Collegiate Dictionary, op. cit.,* p. 775, under "scripture.")

The Lord, on one occasion, spoke to Orson Hyde, a young convert of less than two months,[106] and to three other new converts: Luke S. Johnson,

---

105. Note that the vote to accept the Articles of Faith in the *Pearl of Great Price* as scripture establishes The Church's doctrine that the Book of Mormon and the Bible are "the word of God." (See A. of F. 8. See also pp. 82-83 concerning the acceptance of the *Pearl of Great Price.*)

106. Orson Hyde was baptized "the first Sunday in October," 1831. (HC 1:217) The revelation was given in November of that year.

Lyman E. Johnson, and William E. M'Lellin.[107] The Lord said His words were to apply to all priesthood holders and missionaries, indicating that "this is an ensample unto *all those who were ordained unto this priesthood,* whose mission is appointed unto them to go forth—"[108] The Lord's instruction unto them was

> . . . This is the ensample unto them, that they shall speak as they are moved upon by the Holy Ghost.
> And whatsoever they shall speak when moved upon by the Holy Ghost *shall be scripture,* shall be the *will of the Lord,* shall be the *mind of the Lord,* shall be the *word of the Lord,* shall be the *voice of the Lord,* and the *power of God unto salvation.*[109]

Confusion occasionally arises over this passage about the phrase "shall be scripture." Is the Lord using the dictionary's primary meaning of the term scripture, "act or product of writing," commanding them to record in their personal journals the impressions they've received through the Holy Ghost and the inspired words they've spoken through that medium? In this sense, the Lord is giving the commandment that whatsoever they shall speak when moved upon by the Holy Ghost *shall be written down.*

Or is it the intent of the passage that the secondary meaning of the word scripture, "a body of writings considered as authoritative," is applicable? If that is the correct interpretation, then the implication is that every inspired word recorded by every LDS missionary and priesthood bearer should be canonized and part of the standard works of the Church. If the latter interpretation were correct, we would now have hundreds of volumes in the standard works, with millions of instructions directing us and binding upon us. Certainly that is not the practice of the Church today. It is obvious that the first interpretation applies here—the passage is telling the saints that when they speak under inspiration they should write it down. But the Lord is by no means asserting that all these historical items should become the canonized doctrine of the Church.

Unfortunately some have abused this passage, using it completely out of context, and in a manner directly opposite to what the Lord apparently intended. They have implied by their usage that the passage had reference to the General Authorities, attempting, by their unwarranted interpretation, to give special status to their words and writings, trying to lift their words to that nonexistent "almost doctrine" level previously mentioned.

---

107. According to the Latter-day Saint *Biographical Encyclopedia,* Lyman was baptized in February, 1831, Luke was baptized May 10, 1831, and William was baptized in the summer of 1831.
108. D&C 68:2.
109. D&C 68:3-4.

This author has no doubt that the writings and statements of Church leaders are of great value—they write with wisdom and inspiration, and usually bring the full scope of their wide experience to bear. Their communications motivate and lift me, and provide guidance for my life, as they do for countless others. I often sense the influence of the Spirit in what I hear and read from them.

But the test of doctrine is *not* whether something is written or spoken by a General Authority. The test of doctrine is canonization—"is it in the standard works of the Church?" President Joseph Fielding Smith expressed the matter succinctly when he wrote:

STANDARD WORKS JUDGE TEACHINGS OF ALL MEN

It makes no difference what is written or what *anyone* has said, if what has been said is in *conflict* with what the Lord has revealed, we can set it aside. *My words, and the teachings of any other member of the Church, high or low, if they do not square with the revelations, we need not accept them.* Let us have this matter clear. We have accepted the four *standard works* as the measuring yardsticks, or balances, by which we *measure every man's doctrine.*

You cannot accept the books written by the authorities of the Church as standards in doctrine, only in so far as they accord with the revealed word in the standard works.

Every man who writes is responsible, not the Church, for what he writes. If Joseph Fielding Smith writes something which is out of harmony with the revelations, then every member of the Church is duty bound to reject it. If he writes that which is in perfect harmony with the revealed word of the Lord, then it should be accepted.[110]

Insights on Doctrinal Formation from New Additions to LDS Scripture

Let's see what insights can be learned from the three items presented for the approval of the general membership of the Church in 1976 and 1978.

Joseph Smith's Vision of the Celestial Kingdom

This vision was given to Joseph Smith the Prophet, in the temple at Kirtland, Ohio, on January 21, 1836. It was a sacred occasion, in which some of the ordinances of the endowment were performed.[111] It was a time of many visions and revelations, given both to Joseph and to others who

---

110. McConkie, Bruce [comp.] *Doctrines of Salvation—Sermons and Writings of Joseph Fielding Smith* (Salt Lake City, Utah: Bookcraft, 1956), Vol. III, pp. 203-204. Italics as printed in *Doctrines of Salvation.*

111. See the heading to the vision, as published in the insert containing the two new revelations (Salt Lake City, Utah: Deseret Book Company, 1976). See also HC 2:379-380.

were present. Some, for instance, "Saw the face of the Savior, and others were ministered unto by holy angels."[112]

We learn a number of things from the canonization of this vision, as follows:

1. *Though prophets and revelators may receive revelations and speak under divine inspiration, their words and revelations are not doctrine until they are canonized.* This becomes clear from an analysis of the canonization process.

Was this revelation a "doctrine" of the Church after it was canonized? Yes.

What made it a "doctrine?" Canonizing it on April 3, 1976.

Was it "doctrine" prior to that time? No, or it wouldn't have been necessary to canonize it.

What was its status prior to canonization? It was an interesting insight, believed by many to be given by revelation from God to a man many believe to be an inspired servant of God. It was information which Latter-day Saints were at liberty to accept and believe, or discard from their personal belief, as they chose to do.

What is its status after canonization? It is a "doctrine" which has been accepted by the Church as being the revealed word of God. Because of its canonization, Latter-day Saints are now committed to accept and uphold it as being a true experience and as being a revealed truth. That acceptance is required for them to be in good standing as members of The Church of Jesus Christ of Latter-day Saints. To reject its validity since it was canonized would be considered an act of heresy.

What is the status of other uncanonized visions, revelations, and preachments received by Joseph Smith and other prophets of the Church? Obviously, not doctrine. Obviously, on a lesser level of Church "status" and "acceptance." While faithful Latter-day Saints believe such experiences and statements are true, quote them frequently, and sometimes receive confirmation of their truthfulness through the witness of the Holy Ghost, they recognize that such items do not constitute the binding "doctrine" of the Church, which becomes the law by which their lives should be oriented, and which becomes the standard by which they should be judged on this earth as well as the standard by which they will be judged before the bar of God at the last day.

2. *The canonization process is selective—it may make some items doctrine while excluding others.* That is particularly evident in this case, for the canonized portion stops right in the middle of Joseph's report of his vision. The remaining portion, which was not canonized, is as follows:

112. HC 2:381-382.

I saw the Twelve Apostles of the Lamb, who are now upon the earth, who hold the keys of this last ministry, in foreign lands, standing together in a circle, much fatigued, with their clothes tattered and feet swollen, with their eyes cast downward, and Jesus standing in their midst, and they did not behold Him. *The Savior looked upon them and wept.*

I also behold Elder M'Lellin in the south, standing upon a hill, surrounded by a vast multitude, preaching to them, and a lame man standing before him supported by his crutches; he threw them down at his word and leaped as a hart, by the mighty power of God. Also, *I saw Elder Brigham Young standing in a strange land, in the far south and west, in a desert place, upon a rock in the midst of about a dozen men of color, who appeared hostile. He was preaching to them in their own tongue,* and *the angel of God standing above his head, with a drawn sword in his hand, protecting him,* but he did not see it. And *I finally saw the Twelve in the celestial kingdom of God. I also beheld the redemption of Zion,* and many things which the tongue of man cannot describe in full.[113]

Critics of the revelation also assert that additional words were deleted out of the portion accepted for canonization.[114]

3. *Items recorded in the accepted histories of the Church are not necessarily doctrine.* This vision, recorded in both the "Documentary" and "Comprehensive" histories of the Church,[115] still was not doctrine until it was canonized, even though it has long been available in these books published under the auspices of the Church.

Joseph F. Smith's Vision of the Redemption of the Dead

This vision was manifested to President Joseph F. Smith in Salt Lake City, Utah, on October 3, 1918. He passed away six weeks later (on November 19, 1918), so it afforded him an opportunity to glimpse the circumstances that lay before him in the spirit world. A significant lesson is to be learned from the canonization of this vision also:

1. *Receiving the acceptance of Church leaders does not make an item doctrine.* Recorded in the book *Gospel Doctrine* is this informative insight, printed immediately following the vision being discussed:

This *Vision of the Redemption of the Dead* was submitted October 31, 1918, to the Counselors in the First Presidency, the Council of the Twelve and the Patriarch, and by them unanimously accepted.—*Improvement Era,* Vol. 22, December, 1918, pp. 166-170.[116]

---

113. HC 2:381. It should be noted that history has not recorded that those other scenes shown to Joseph Smith actually took place.

114. Tanner, *The Changing World . . . , op. cit.,* pp. 62-63.

115. See HC 2:380-381; CHC 2:75.

116. *Gospel Doctrine—Selections from the Sermons and Writings of Joseph F. Smith* (Salt Lake City, Utah: Deseret Book Company, 19th printing, 1978), p. 476.

With this insight in mind, let's again consider the matter with a few probing questions.

Was the Vision of the Redemption of the Dead a binding "doctrine" of the Church prior to 1976? No, or it wouldn't have needed to be canonized.

The General Authorities of the Church had the vision presented to them and it was "by them unanimously accepted" in 1918. What did that acceptance mean? Apparently, their acceptance meant only that they acknowledged its existence, and expressed their personal belief in its truthfulness and validity. We have no indication from history that the vision held further status than that. And what further status is there? There is no such thing as "almost doctrine" in the Church—an item is either doctrine or it isn't. "Has it been canonized?" remains the only valid test of doctrine.

What, then, was the status of the Vision of the Redemption of the Dead prior to 1976? The vision was frequently quoted and widely circulated among the saints, adding further insight and understanding to various scriptural passages,[111] and usually being included, as an example of an interesting private manifestation received, in books and lesson manuals expounding the general subject of life-after-death. Those who quoted it made no assertion that it held the status of doctrine.

The Revelation on Priesthood

This item is more difficult to understand and categorize because it is not clearly definable as either "doctrine" or "policy."

If it's doctrine, how does one apply it in his personal life? It doesn't serve as a standard of conduct; nor explain man's relationship to Christ; nor set forth an eternal truth or saving principle; nor clarify any broad aspect of the plan of salvation. Without the exact wording of the revelation, there are no specific details to ponder nor new insights to gain.

The designation as to whether it is a "doctrinal" or a "policy" change also hinges on the previous status held by the negro people in a doctrinal sense. In the earliest days of the restored Church, some negroes were ordained to the priesthood. This practice then ceased, but no doctrine that would cause the change to be made was ever canonized. Unfortunately, there also is no definitive record of how the non-ordination policy change was decided, if indeed the matter was in the domain of "policy" rather than "doctrine." The very fact that the ordaining of negro members was "on, then off, then on again" seems to place the matter in the realm of "policy," which frequently changes, rather than "doctrine," which states an eternal truth. Therefore, in this brief discussion, the matter is going to be regarded as a policy change rather than as an addition to Church doctrine.

As in the previous examples discussed, there are specific lessons to be learned from the manner in which the revelation was presented to receive the sustaining vote of the Church.

1. *The revelation was first presented to the General Authorities, who approved it unanimously.* When President Tanner presented the revelation to the Church in General Conference, he said,

> President Kimball has asked that I advise the conference that after he had received this revelation, which came to him after extended meditation and prayer in the sacred rooms ef the holy temple, *he presented it to his counselors,* who accepted it and approved it. *It was then presented to the Quorum of the Twelve Apostles,* who unanimously approved it, and was subsequently *presented to all other General Authorities,* who likewise approved it unanimously.[117]

President Kimball later explained that the revelation actually came to him while the Twelve were present, and they together prayed to know the Lord's will on the matter.[118] As would be the usual procedure for any change in Church policy, announcement of the change was made in a letter "To all general and local priesthood officers of The Church of Jesus Christ of Latter-day Saints throughout the world," dated June 8, 1978. Because the change was obviously a news event of major proportions, they also made announcement of the revelation in news conferences with the media.

The difference in their handling of this decision, as opposed to the 1976 canonizing of two revelations as doctrine, should be noted. This revelation was treated as a change in policy, which is appropriately implemented by the General Authorities, rather than as a canonization of doctrine, which requires the acceptance of the general Church membership as required by the law of common consent. They announced the policy and put it into action of their own accord, without seeking prior approval from the membership. Priesthood ordinations of Negro members took place in mid-June, more than three months before the Church voted its approval. In contrast, the doctrinal adoptions of 1976 were not announced nor publicized before they were presented to the "Committee of the Whole Church," or "constituent assembly" for canonization.

2. *The revelation is being classed as an "Official Declaration" in the Doctrine and Covenants.* The visions canonized in 1976 are to be printed as

117. *CR,* September 30, 1978, p. 22.
118. See the *Deseret News,* Church Section, January 6, 1979, p. 4. In a speech entitled "All Are Alike Unto God," given at the Brigham Young University on August 17, 1978, Elder Bruce R. McConkie indicated that each of the Twelve received a direct and personal revelation of his own on the matter at that time, each confirming that received by President Kimball. See Brough, R. Clayton, *His Servants Speak* (Bountiful, Utah: Horizon Publishers, 1980 Revised Edition), pp. 192-196.

sections 137 and 138 in the next printing of the Doctrine and Covenants. In contrast, the revelation on priesthood will be designated differently and reproduced in a different section. It appears that the Manifesto will be classed as Official Declaration Number One and this revelation will be designated Official Declaration Number Two. Again, this indicates that the matter is being treated as a change in policy than as a matter of doctrine.

3. *Church officials had not been in full agreement, over the years, as to whether the Church's position on withholding the priesthood had been a "doctrine" or a "policy." This indicates the need for clarifying the manner in which doctrine is formulated so there is no confusion within the Church.* For instance, a letter from the First Presidency written in 1947 stated,

> From the days of the Prophet Joseph even until now, *it has been the doctrine of the Church,* never questioned by any of the Church leaders, that the Negroes are not entitled to the full blessings of the Gospel.[119]

And an official statement released by the First Presidency in 1951 said,

> The attitude of the Church with reference to the Negroes remains as it has always stood. *It is not a matter of the declaration of a policy but of direct commandment from the Lord, on which is founded the doctrine of the Church* from the days of its organization, to the effect that Negroes may become members of the Church but that they are not entitled to the Priesthood at the present time.[120]

Yet in a conversation in 1954, President David O. McKay stated his personal view that withholding the Priesthood from the Negro *"is a practice, not a doctrine,* and the practice will some day be changed." This view, of course, was substantiated by the alteration of the Church's policy in 1978. President McKay's statement was recorded by Sterling M. McMurrin, who summarized the statement in a letter to President McKay's son Llewelyn as follows:

> At one point in the conversation I introduced the subject of the common belief among the Church membership that Negroes are under a divine curse. I told him that I regarded this doctrine as both false and morally abhorrent and that some weeks earlier, in a class in my own ward, I had made it clear that I did not accept the doctrine and that I wanted to be known as a dissenter to the class instructor's statements about "our beliefs" in this matter.
>
> President McKay replied that he was "glad" that I had taken this stand, as *he also did not believe this teaching.* He stated his position in the matter very forcefully and clearly and said with considerable feeling that *"There is*

---

119. John J. Stewart, *Mormonism and the Negro* (Bountiful, Utah: Horizon Publishers, fourth edition, 1978, p. 47. Letter of the First Presidency to Dr. Lowry Nelson, July 17, 1947.

120. *Ibid.,* pp. 48-49. Statement issued August 17, 1951.

not now, and there never has been, a doctrine in this Church that the Negroes are under a divine curse. He insisted that there is no doctrine of any kind pertaining to the Negro. "We believe," he said, "that we have scriptural precedent for withholding the priesthood from the Negro. *It is a practice, not a doctrine, and the practice will some day be changed.* And that's all there is to it."[121]

And in 1969 President Hugh B. Brown, first counselor to President McKay, stated in a news interview that the Church's policy toward the negro "will change in the not too distant future." A special release to the *Salt Lake Tribune* from San Francisco said,

> The Mormon Church's denial of its priesthood to Negroes of African lineage *"will change in the not too distant future,"* according to Hugh B. Brown, one of the highest ranking officials of the Church of Jesus Christ of Latter-day Saints. Lester Kinsolving, religious columnist for the San Francisco Chronicle reported Wednesday.
>
> Pres. Brown, who is first counselor to Pres. David O. McKay, told Mr. Kinsolving that admission of Negroes to the priesthood will come about *"in the ordinary evolution of things as we go along, since human rights are basic to the church."* [122]

These statements, and others like them, indicate that the term "doctrine" is not used with precision within the Church, and that the meaning of the term, and also the process by which a precept becomes the "doctrine" of the Church, needs to be clarified.

The Need for Greater Precision in the Formulation of Church Doctrine

An objective of this chapter is to propose that the term "doctrine," as used within the Church to refer to official statements of Latter-day belief, be restricted to teachings found in the canonized scriptures contained in the Standard Works. New commandments and revelations, if received, should be canonized through presentation to the Church assembled in General Conference, and accepted by their sustaining vote, in obedience to the Lord's commandment that all things should be done by common consent.

It is the author's observation that many items are represented as being "doctrine" which cannot be substantiated from the scriptures, and which have very weak historicity. Other items alluded to in various Church classes as being "doctrine" clearly represent only the opinion of the person who spoke them, be he a lay member or a general Church officer. To

---

121. Letter from Sterling M. McMurrin to Llewelyn R. McKay dated August 26, 1968, as recorded in Stephen G. Taggart, *Mormonism's Negro Policy: Social and Historical Origins* (Salt Lake City, Utah: University of Utah Press, 1970), pp. 78-79.

122. "LDS Leader Says Curb On Priesthood to Ease," *Salt Lake Tribune,* December 25, 1969.

accept all the many statements and writings made by current and past members and leaders as being "doctrine" is to open a pandora's box with deep and involved implications. In contrast, the test "Is it canonized?" is a test easily applied that avoids almost all of those difficulties. Granted, many things may be true and of value to the Saints which do not come under this definition of "doctrine." Granted, also, that many such things are worthy of careful study and consideration. But there is wisdom in restricting that which is binding upon the Saints to that which is canonized, because the term "doctrine" is used (and abused) so loosely in reference to non-canonized sayings and writings as to be almost meaningless.

An example from Church history shows the problems that exist because the term "doctrine" is too loosely applied. It concerns the physical status of little children following the resurrection—an area where no significant guidance to understanding is given in the scriptures. Joseph Smith is recorded as having expressed his opinion on several occasions that

> *As the child dies, so shall it rise from the dead,* and be forever living in the learning of God. *It will never grow; it will still be the child, in the same precise form* as it appeared before it died out of its mother's arms.[123]

This teaching, it appears, was not particularly popular with parents who had lost children in infancy. The idea that their children would remain infants for all eternity understandably caused them great concern.

The subject became a matter of controversy in 1888-1889, and President Wilford Woodruff stated that

> The Prophet taught subsequently to his King Follett Sermon that children while resurrected to the stature at which they died would develop to the full stature of men and women after the resurrection; and that the contrary impression created by the report of the Prophet's King Follett sermon was due to a misunderstanding of his remarks and erroneous reporting.

Elder B. H. Roberts added a note to that effect in the *History of the Church* as he edited it.[124] He also completely changed the meaning of Joseph's above quoted statement in the King Follett discourse by inserting two phrases in brackets, as follows:

> . . . It will never grow [in the grave]; it will still be the child, in the same precise form [when it rises] as it appeared before it died . . . .[125]

---

123. HC 6:316. King Follett Discourse, April 7, 1844. He expressed the same belief on at least two other occasions. Full documentation for the subject being summarized here is found in the author's book, *Life Everlasting,* pp. 252-256.

124. See Note, HC 4:556.

125. HC 6:316.

The teaching, apparently, was particularly bothersome to Joseph F. Smith. In an *Improvement Era* article which was published in 1918, he told of a different teaching attributed to the prophet Joseph, which was probably uttered between the time of his King Follett sermon quoted above and his martyrdom two months later. President Joseph F. Smith wrote,

> Joseph Smith taught the doctrine that the infant child that was laid away in death would come up in the resurrection as a child; and pointing to the mother[126] of a lifeless child, he said to her: *'You will have the joy, the pleasure, and satisfaction of nurturing this child, after its resurrection, until it reaches the full stature of its spirit. There is restitution, there is growth, there is development, after the resurrection from death.* I love this truth. It speaks volumes of happiness, of joy and gratitude to my soul. Thank the Lord he has revealed these principles to us.'[127]

He then described some data he had collected many years before. He told of a conversation he had in 1854, when he was sixteen years old, with his aunt, who told him this teaching was given by the Prophet Joseph. He then described a conversation with his brother-in-law, Lorin Walker, who happened to remark that he was present at the funeral of his cousin where Joseph supposedly made the statement that the child would be raised by its parents following the resurrection until it was full grown. He questioned Lorin, who also remembered the statement. Then President Smith told how in 1896 he had a conversation with Sister M. Isabella Horne, in which she indicated that she and her husband were at the funeral and heard Joseph's statement. President Smith obtained notarized statements from both the Hornes to that effect. After telling of the collecting of these four testimonies, President Joseph F. Smith wrote,

> Just a little while later, to my joy and satisfaction, *the first man I ever heard mention it in public was Franklin D. Richards; and when he spoke of it, I felt in my soul: the truth has come out.* The truth will prevail. It is mighty, and it will live; for there is no power that can destroy it. *Presidents Woodruff and Cannon approved of the doctrine and after that I preached it.*[128]

He had already set forth the teaching in June, 1904, in an *Improvement Era* article.[129] Elder B. H. Roberts quoted a portion of that article in a

---

126. From the context which follows it appears that this mother was Agnes Coolbrith Smith, who married Joseph Smith's younger brother, Don Carlos Smith, on July 30, 1835 (HC 4:393). The deceased child was Sophronia C. Smith (HC 4:399). The father, Don Carlos, died three years before Joseph made the statement to his widow, his death occurring on August 7, 1841.

127. *Gospel Doctrine, op. cit.,* p. 455.

128. *Ibid.,* pp. 455-457.

129. A reference to the article was made in B. H. Roberts' extensive note on this doctrinal matter in HC 4:556-557.

footnote of the *History of the Church* and represented the teaching as being the Church's doctrine on the subject:

> In the *Improvement Era* for June, 1904, President Joseph F. Smith in an editorial on the Resurrection said:
> 'The body will come forth as it is laid to rest, for there is no growth or development in the grave. As it is laid down, so will it arise, *and changes to perfection will come by the law of restitution.* But the spirit will continue to expand and develop, *and the body, after the resurrection will develop to the full stature of men.*'
> *This may be accepted as the doctrine of the Church in respect to the resurrection of children and their future development to the full stature of men and women;* and it is alike comfortable to that which will be regarded as both reasonable and desirable.[130]

The questions that must be asked are,

—"Is this really the doctrine of the Church?"

—"Is that how doctrine is formed, by gathering affidavits many years after a discourse was given?"

—"Even if there were no conflicting reports of Joseph Smith's teachings, would the fact that he made the statement make it doctrine?"

—"Does a statement by a Church President or other General Authority that the words of a former Church President should be regarded as doctrine actually make those words the binding doctrine of the Church?"

—"Are there such things as "strong" doctrine and "weak" doctrine? Would this shaky historical foundation cause it to be a "weak" doctrine?"

—"Would a member's refusal to accept the above teaching as doctrine constitute grounds for excommunication?"

As can be seen, loose usage of the term "doctrine" truly does open a pandora's box with a host of perplexing questions. Using canonization as the test for determining what is doctrine is a much simpler solution.

Adherence to Doctrine as a Standard of Church Membership

Careful attention to the process of canonization of doctrine is a vital safeguard to the maintaining of doctrinal harmony within the Church. If one is able to determine what is and what is not doctrine by answering the question "Is it canonized?", then serious difficulties and disputes can be averted. Canonization removes the "grey areas"—those fringe areas of opinion which arise and, when blown out of proportion, become the source of serious controversies which affect the lives and testimonies of the saints.

---

130. HC 4:557.

Canonization establishes the rules and regulations of the Church, by making those rules and regulations doctrine and scripture. Canonization becomes the test which enables one to discern whether a policy or practice is a God-directed instruction which is binding upon the saints or a statement or directive representing only private view of a person or group of persons in authority.

An inspired instruction which is accepted by the Church as being the will of the Lord through the canonization process deserves the willing and unqualified support of the members, and clearly stands as a valid criterion for evaluation whether one's conduct and doctrinal belief is in harmony with the Church. But uncanonized statements and practices form that "grey area" where it is sometimes unclear, for instance, whether they should be considered appropriate criteria for the withholding of Church blessings or membership. Partaking of the saving and exalting ordinances of baptism, confirmation, the sacrament, ordination to priesthood office, endowment, eternal marriage, sealings, and other ordinances are vital to one's eternal progress, and should not be denied to anyone without valid doctrinal or moral justification. Just as a testimony of the gospel should be based on eternal principles, the criteria by which fellowship with the saints might be denied to individuals should also be based on sound, scriptural doctrine and nothing less.

Membership and fellowship in The Church of Jesus Christ of Latter-day Saints is a privilege reserved for those (1) who live righteously, and (2) who faithfully accept and obey the doctrines of the Church. Those who fail to meet these two criteria are subject to disciplinary action, either in the form of being disfellowshipped or being excommunicated from the Church.

To be disfellowshipped is to be prohibited, for an indefinite period, from partaking of the sacrament; speaking, praying, or participating in Church meetings; holding any Church office; or attending priesthood meetings or any assembly of Church officers. It is a probationary state, during which the individual is expected to live up to all requirements imposed upon him by the court to regain full fellowship in the Church.

Excommunication is a more serious punishment. It is a complete severance from the Church, with the cancellation of all temple and priesthood blessings and privileges. It is the highest punishment which the Church can impose on its members.[131]

Church courts are held to try persons alleged to have transgressed the moral law, or violated the principles taught by the Church, and to purge iniquity from the Church.

---

131. See D&C 134:10.

Moral transgressions which result in excommunication or disfellow-shipment are clearly defined as including, but not limited to, murder, adultery, fornication, homosexuality, incest, child molesting, advocating or practicing plural marriage, misappropriating or embezzling Church funds, intemperance, cruelty to spouse or children, and unchristianlike conduct in violation of the law and order of the Church. Also, when a member is convicted in a court of the land of a crime involving moral turpitude, it is considered prima facie evidence that excommunication is justified.

Neither inactivity in the Church, nor joining another church (except an apostate breakoff from Mormondom), are considered grounds for excommunication or disfellowshipment.

More difficult to document and define than moral infractions are two other grounds for excommunication. They are

1. open opposition to and deliberate disobedience to the rules and regulations of the Church, and

2. apostasy, the teaching of false doctrines, and advocating the teachings and practices of apostate sects.

It is in these less easily defined areas that difficulties have sometimes arisen in the past. If the rules and regulations of the Church are not those found in the scripture, established through the canonization process, then the statement or directive of any local Church leader becomes the law to those in his jurisdiction. Certainly that leader should function as a guide and counselor to his congregation, but should he have the power to with-hold Church privileges if his personal views are not followed by those of his flock? Is it appropriate, for instance, for a Bishop to refuse to grant a temple recommend to otherwise-worthy parents who are not holding family home evenings, unless that is a regulation accepted and canonized on a Church-wide level? And is it appropriate for an individual to be disciplined for insubordination if the policy or practice he refuses to obey is not an accepted standard required universally of all Church members?

Is there the danger that individuals may attempt to withhold Church privileges and blessings in an effort to establish their own power and supremacy? The Book of Mormon tells of one group, which at that time was within the Church, the Zoramites, which attempted to do so.[132]

The prophet Joseph Smith commented on the tendency of men in authority to overstep the bounds of that authority. He wrote,

---

132. See Alma 31.

> We have learned by sad experience that it is the nature and disposition of *almost all men,* as soon as they get a little authority, as they suppose, *they will immediately begin to exercise unrighteous dominion.*[133]

He warned that

> . . . When we undertake to cover our sins, or to gratify our pride, our vain ambition, or *to exercise control or dominion or compulsion upon the souls of the children of men, in any degree of unrighteousness,* behold, the heavens withdraw themselves; the Spirit of the Lord is grieved; and when it is withdrawn, Amen to the priesthood or the authority of that man.
>
> Behold, ere he is aware, he is left unto himself, to kick against the pricks, *to persecute the saints,* and to fight against God.[134]

When the scriptures are the standard, the only standard, then that which is required of the saints is clearly defined, available to all, and becomes a universal standard. New commandments, if they are received, can be presented for the sustaining vote of the Church assembled in General Conference and thus added to the body of scripture.

It is this universality, based on the canonization process, that prevents individuals from exercising unrighteous dominion, imposing their personal views on others, or requiring compliance from some individuals to vague precepts which are not the standard for the general membership. No individual should be denied Church blessings for actions which are not required of the Church as a whole.

There have been occasional instances when non-doctrinal standards, based on the personal prejudices and antagonisms of a single individual or small group of individuals, have been allowed to substitute for eternal principles as the criteria for which Church fellowship was denied to others. These instances, when seen from the historian's perspective, would cause concern for the validity of the Church's judicial system if they occurred today. One small example from early Church history will demonstrate this point.

In this era when Church units frequently sponsor stake and regional dances, and use those programs as an active tool for friendshipping nonmembers, and when LDS youth by custom attend school proms and other dances, it is somewhat disconcerting to recall that in October, 1837 "The Church in Kirtland disfellowshipped twenty-two brethren and sisters . . . for *uniting with the world in a dance* the Thursday previous." Then, after being disfellowshipped, those who participated in the dance were compelled to confess the activity to the High Council *as being a sin,* being *"required to do so or be cut off from the Church."* [135]

---

133. D&C 121:39.
134. D&C 121:37-38.
135. HC 2:519-520.

Was it really a "sin" for those saints to dance with their Gentile neighbors? Certainly those who preside in a Church judicial proceeding should be prepared to clearly document that the infraction of which an individual stands accused actually is a "sin," a transgression of God's revealed laws,[136] before judgment is imposed or confession required. Revealed, canonized scripture should be the standard, not the opinions or prejudices of the individuals involved.

The teaching of false doctrine and apostasy—the final grounds for excommunication, also require comment.

The individual saints vary widely in their knowledge of the doctrines of the Church. In this era of rapid growth, the Church is experiencing the conversion of many thousands who have been reared in other faiths. They come to Mormonism, in some instances, still clinging to incorrect doctrinal concepts they previously embraced. Others, even those raised in the Church, have personal viewpoints which do not correspond to the teachings of the scriptures. It is not uncommon to hear incorrect doctrines expressed, and occasionally even taught, in Church classrooms and chapels. Our classes are intended to be places of learning, where incorrect concepts are tested, rejected, and exchanged for truth. Incorrect views and personal opinions are generally regarded with considerable tolerance within the Church, and dealt with in a spirit of helpful patience and loving charity.

The saints are commanded to "Teach one another the doctrine of the kingdom." [137] Many times their sermons and lessons reflect only the level of understanding and doctrinal knowledge to which they have attained at that time. As they grow, they discover former beliefs and precepts they have expounded to be incorrect—they had, in fact, been teaching "false doctrine." This is unfortunate, but it is probably experienced by almost all Latter-day Saints—at least those who are growing and progressing. And it happens on all levels, even among the most erudite of our General Authorities—even they have made public apology for erroneous teachings they have promulgated.[138] Doctrinal misconceptions can exist on any level—in any calling; there is no doctrine of infallibility within the Church. Though doctrinal error may exist among the saints, it usually should be dealt with by teaching and counselling, not by public rebuke, Church judicial proceedings, or any other action which would harm the reputation or testimony of the individuals involved.

---

136. See I Jn. 3:4; Ro. 4:15.

137. D&C 88:77.

138. See JD 7:374-376, for instance, in which Orson Pratt apologizes for items he advanced in the *Seer.* See also *Answers to Gospel Questions,* Vol. 1, p. 78, where Joseph Fielding Smith refutes his previous teaching that the Sons of Perdition could be "counted on the fingers of one hand."

But honest mistakes in gospel understanding are not the same as apostasy, and the intentional teaching of false doctrines with the purpose of leading others away from the saving principles and ordinances of the gospel of Jesus Christ.

The sincere believer, thought he may have embraced erroneous doctrinal concepts, remains devoted to the Church and Kingdom. He is anxious to associate with the saints and to labor in the work. He is teachable and pliable, responsive to wise counsel and direction. If others believe his doctrinal understanding incorrect, he will listen as they expound the scriptures to him. Yes, he will probably insist on solid scriptural and/or historical evidence before he will change his view. But he will hunger for truth and will seek to learn and do what is right.

The apostate, in contrast, will turn against the Church, either openly or secretly. He will harden his heart, and cease to be teachable. He will seek to cause strife among the saints, and will embrace false doctrines which conflict with the basic principles of the gospel: the nature and identity of God, the role and mission of Jesus Christ, the necessity and function of the saving ordinances, the manner in which God interacts with man, and the commandments which man must obey to attain his eternal reward. He seeks to harm and to embarrass the Church. He seeks to thwart its growth and progress. He seeks to bring the Church and the saints into disfavor in the eyes of others, and to cause others to reject it. Apostates reject the strait and narrow gate[139] which the Savior holds open to the righteous, and become the thief and robber who attempts to climb over the wall rather than enter through the door, of whom the Savior spoke with disfavor.[140]

In a discourse given over a century ago, President George Q. Cannon attempted to define the difference between a faithful member who differed with the Church on some principle or policy, as contrasted with one who was in apostasy. He said,

> A friend . . . wished to know whether we . . . considered an honest difference of opinion between a member of the Church and the authorities of the Church was apostasy . . . . We replied that we had not stated that an honest difference of opinion between a member of the Church and the authorities constituted apostasy; . . . but *we could not conceive of a man publishing those differences of opinion, and seeking by arguments, sophistry and special pleading to enforce upon the people to produce division and strife, and to place the acts and counsels of the authorities of the Church, if possible, in a wrong light, and not be an apostate, for such conduct was apostasy as we understood the term.* We further said that while a man might honestly differ

139. See Mt. 7:13-14.
140. See Jn. 10:1.

in opinion from the authorities through a want of understanding, *he had to be exceedingly careful how he acted in relation to such differences,* or the adversary would take advantage of him, and he would soon become imbued with the spirit of apostasy, and be found fighting against God and the authority which He had placed here to govern His Church.[141]

Until every Latter-day Saint comes "in the unity of the faith, . . . unto a perfect man," [142] honest differences will probably continue to exist among them. The very spark of the divine which makes every person a distinct individual and personality makes it so. People will perceive situations and issues differently. And within the Church, individuals will perform their callings and assignments with varying degrees of competence. God does not tell his servants how to perform every action. Sometimes mistakes will be made. Honest differences of opinion and belief will occur.

When the news media gave intense coverage to dissenting views held by various Latter-day Saints in the controversy concerning the Equal Rights Amendment, the issue of defining the appropriate limits of religious and doctrinal dissent was cast into a position of nationwide prominence. It appears that the matter is far from resolved as this book goes to press. It is a matter of serious concern, and when the "sifting time" which will so severely try the saints comes,[143] it can take on even more serious dimensions.

How far can members go in expressing their views when they stand in disagreement with their local or general leaders in the Church? An answer, given at least in part, was issued by the Church in connection with the ERA dispute, as follows:

> Membership in the Church has not been threatened nor withdrawn simply because of expressed agreement with the proposed amendment. *In this, as in all other matters, members are free to accept or reject the counsel of the First Presidency. Freedom to discuss the merits of any public issue is a legitimate exercise of citizenship, recognized and encouraged by the Church.* This can be done without indulging in ridicule or attacking those with opposing views.
>
> The mission of the Church is to save, but *when those of its members publicly deride it, demean its leaders, and openly encourage others to interfere with its mission, then it may exercise its right to dissociate itself from them.*[144]

---

141. *Deseret News,* Nov. 3, 1869, p. 457, as quoted in *The Church and the Proposed Equal Rights Amendment—a Moral Issue, op. cit.,* pp. 19-20.

142. Eph. 4:13.

143. See the next chapter for documentation on this subject; also pp. 20-22.

144. *The Church and the Proposed Equal Rights Amendment—a Moral Issue, op. cit.,* p. 17.

The difficulty of defining what is doctrine, if the definition is allowed to extend beyond the canonized scriptures of the Church, can become a major stumbling block to the Church in those difficult times to come which are discussed in the next chapter. If false prophets are to influence the Church, as the Lord clearly revealed in numerous revelations that they will, then canonization becomes an important part of the system of checks and balances. Having to receive the sustaining vote of the Church provides a restraining and moderating influence which can prevent excesses from occurring.

Lessons from Medieval Catholicism—
The Corrupting of Religious Judicial Procedures

But at any time, the test of "Is it canonized?" serves as a necessary standard in determining what is doctrine, especially in the context of Church judicial proceedings. Without that test, there is the danger that individuals can be judged in judicial tribunals in matters of doctrine, with concepts which are not doctrine nor truth used as the standard.

This happened often in early Catholicism, especially during the era of the inquisition, and sometimes shaped the course of history. One such instance involved the case of the great astronomer Galileo. His plight was depicted in this scene from a reader's theatre presentation given several years ago in many stakes of the Church:

Galileo: I've got something for you. Look behind the star charts.
Andrea: What is it?
Galileo: That shows how, according to the ancients, the stars moved round the earth.
Andrea: How?
Galileo: Let's examine it. Begin at the beginning: Description.
Andrea: In the middle is a little stone.
Galileo: That is the earth.
Andrea: Then all around, one outside the other, there are globes.
Galileo: How many?
Andrea: Eight.
Galileo: Those are the crystal spheres.
Andrea: And the globes have little balls fixed on . . .
Galileo: Such as:
Andrea: The lowest ball is the moon, and above it is the sun.
Galileo: And now make the sun move.
Andrea: (Moves the globes) That's beautiful. But we're so shut in.
Galileo: Yes, I felt that too when I saw the thing for the first time. Walls and globes and immobility. *For two thousand years men have believed that the sun and all the stars in heaven revolve about them.*

The pope, the cardinals, the princes, the scholars, captains, merchants, fishwives, and school boys believe themselves to be sitting motionless in the center of this crystal globe.

Andrea: Yes.

Galileo: But now we say: because it was so it will not always remain so. For *everything moves, my boy.*

Andrea: But sir, *isn't that heresy?*

Galileo: *Truth cannot be heresy.* Soon mankind will know the truth about this earth.

Andrea: What do you mean?

Galileo: That it rolls happily around the sun . . . and the fishwives, merchants, princes, and cardinals, and even the pope roll with it.

Andrea: Then overnight the universe has lost it's center.

Galileo: And by morning it has countless ones.

(Lights down on ANDREA up on Cardinals)

Cardinal 1: Keep away from all that Messer Galilei. *This theory contradicts the church.*

Galileo: Monsignor, I know the truth of this cosmology. We can see with the eyes God has given us that the moon is not a celestial sphere without spots. My telescope shows it is a physical body with ridges and craters. My brain—which God has given me—reasons with Copernicus and Kepler. *We on the earth move around the sun.* If I were schooled in theology, I could show Your Excellency that Copernicus and the Holy Bible say the same.

Cardinal 2: Let me turn to you as your spiritual father, as a priest of your faith. *The church will never endorse this theory. And, after all, your salvation should mean a hundred times more to you than any number of learned axioms.*

Galileo: Thank you for your ghostly counsel, but I've thought it over for twenty-five years.

Cardinal 2: (Laughs) Does it matter so much? See how beautiful the spring is with the trees in bloom. Heavens above! What useless things men plague their minds with.

Galileo: *I maintain the earth moves round the sun.*

Cardinal 3: *Messer Galilei, the holy office cannot possibly countenance this doctrine.*

Galileo: Monsignor, may I ask one question?

Cardinal 3: Ask what you please.

Galileo: Is it inconceivable that these teachings can be true?

Cardinal 3: I don't know. *I'm not interested in their truth. For me, the faith of millions of poor people is far more essential.*

Galileo: But why am I forbidden to reveal this truth to learned men?

Cardinal 3: *You must resign yourself to the fact that I can never permit this theory to be expounded as truth. From now on the holy father bids you to cease your arguments and assertions, even among your private friends. The church has spoken!*

Galileo: But I cannot deny what I see, and the time will come when the faith
           of thousands is strong enough to bear the truth of Copernicus.
Cardinal 3:   What makes you defy fate again and again?
Galileo: There is no question of defying fate.
Cardinal 3:   *But you stand alone against the whole of Rome.*
Galileo: *I am not alone, The truth is with me.*[145]

History shows clearly the harmful effects of the excesses of the
Catholic inquisition. That inquisition began within the limits of Church
influence, with excommunication the most serious of the punishments
possible. But the inquisitors allied themselves with secular powers, and
punishment soon extended to imprisonment, confiscation of properties,
torture, death by fire, and the disenterring and burning of the bodies of
those who were condemned after death.

But it is the early practices of the inquisition, while excommunication
remained the supreme punishment, which led to the corruption of the
Catholic judicial system. These practices should be guarded against among
the Latter-day Saints, and never allowed to begin within the Church.

1. Men were appointed to zealously seek out apostates and other
offenders. (Their name, inquisitors, was derived from the Latin verb
inquiro, meaning "to inquire into.") As their influence grew, the truth of
the famous saying became abundantly apparent, that "Power tends to
corrupt, and absolute power corrupts absolutely." [146]

2. Members of the church were required to report suspected apostates
to the inquisition under pain of excommunication. The obligation to report
suspects became an open invitation to denounce personal enemies.

3. The accused individual often was not informed of the identity of
his accusers, nor confronted by them. Valid evidence was frequently lacking, and the charges did not always represent issues of substance.

4. Witnesses for the defense rarely appeared, since this course would
place themselves under suspicion. "Guilt by association" was a widespread
problem.

5. The lawyer of the accused, when he had one, was little more than a
counselor, charged more with getting a confession than with presenting an
adequate defense. He worked against the accused individual.

6. The accused were compelled to confess to things they had not done,
or to actions that were not sins, or to recant statements or beliefs which
were not doctrinal errors.

---

145. Moana B. Bennett, Ronald Q. Frederickson and Joy Sansom, Hi There,
Nobody!—A Readers Theatre Script (Salt Lake City, Utah: The MIA Boards of The
Church of Jesus Christ of Latter-day Saints, 1971), pp. 10-11.

146. Lord Acton, Letter to Mandell Creighton, as quoted in George Seldes
(comp.), *The Great Quotations* (New York, NY: Pocket Books, 1967 paperback
edition), pp. 234-235.

7. Church officials in high positions were able to require the tribunals to excommunicate individuals, even when the tribunals could find no substantial evidence against the accused. Those in the tribunals would render obedience to those in authority over them, rather than render the verdict warranted by the trial procedure.[147]

These practices, and others like them, must never be allowed to find a place within the Church. The judicial system of a church, or of a state or nation, is a prime reflector of the righteousness of the system's leadership. If unrighteousness begins to creep in, judicial irregularities will be an early sign, as potential dissenters are suppressed. It happened to the Catholics, with their inquisitions; it happened to the early Puritans with their witchhunts in Massachusetts; it has happened in many of the governments of modern nations. Freedom from religious oppression can sometimes be more difficult to maintain within a church than outside of it.

Summary

1. An approach frequently used by enemies of the Church in their effort to counteract the rapid spread of the restored gospel has been to quote statements of personal opinions expressed by various early LDS leaders and then attempt to refute them. These opinions are not, and never have been, the "doctrine" of the Church, and do not represent the beliefs held by Church leaders nor members today.

2. Anti-Mormon critics, use this technique to raise "straw men" which they then challenge and attempt to refute, without coming to grips with the actual doctrines and authority of the Church. Their objective is to avoid any discussion of the central doctrines of Mormonism, and instead to "nit-pik" on small items of peripheral significance. They know that the central doctrines of Mormonism have strong scriptural evidence which, when properly presented, provides clear refutation to their views.

3. How the Church authorities of today regard the utterances of former Church leaders is the ultimate answer to the question, "How should the saints regard the statements, discourses, and writings of Church leaders— as statements of infallible truths revealed by God, or as expressions of their own personal insights, counsel, and attitudes?"

4. We can't "have our cake and eat it too"—we can't logically assert that pronouncements made by prophets today are to be accepted as the "mind and will of the Lord," yet discount the unacceptable teachings of former prophets in this dispensation as being only personal views. The same

---

147. These characteristics of the Catholic inquisition, and other abuses, are quite universally recognized, and are commented upon in typical encyclopedia articles under the heading "inquisition."

standard must apply—how we regard the statements of prophets on doctrinal matters today is how we must regard the doctrinal statements of prophets who lived a century ago, and vice versa.

5. "Doctrine" pertains to religious precepts regarded as statements of eternal, unchanging truths. "Policy" refers to instructions as to how particular current situations are to be met or regarded, or how particular tasks are to be accomplished at the present time. It is not regarded as a statement of eternal truth. Policy changes frequently; doctrine remains fixed.

6. We look to current prophets in matters of policy, and their instructions supersede the instructions of former prophets. In matters of doctrine, however, previous doctrine is on a par with newly-revealed doctrine. Truth is eternal and absolute. Something is not more true if revealed today, nor less true if revealed yesterday.

7. The problems caused by anti-Mormon "snipers" today is still in the "irritant" category rather than a major concern. Prophecies of last-days events, however, indicate that the Church must yet endure intense persecution. In the author's view, a careful definition of what is and is not the actual doctrine of the Church will help to stabilize the faith of the saints and help to shield them when persecution and confusion comes upon them.

8. Dictionary definitions of the term "doctrine" are so vague as to be of little value. A better way to define the term is to analyze every scriptural passage that uses the word and draw patterns of understanding which correspond to the Lord's revealed usage of the term.

9. The scriptures reveal ten patterns of understanding which help to define the word "doctrine":

A. Doctrine comes from God the Father, through Jesus Christ.
B. Doctrine is sacred, and represents an attribute of godliness.
C. God's doctrines are revealed statements of eternal truths, saving principles, or aspects of His plan of salvation.
D. God's doctrines explain man's relationship to Christ.
E. Doctrine serves as a standard of conduct.
F. Doctrine is closely related to the gospel of Christ. The gospel is a program of commandments and activities that bring man to salvation through Christ.
G. Doctrine is recorded in the scriptures.
H. Church workers and leaders sometimes preach incorrect doctrine.
I. Doctrines are to be taught to one another by the saints.
J. Satan seeks to lead men astray through false doctrine.

10. When doctrine is correctly taught and universally accepted by the saints, then we will all "come in the unity of the faith, . . . that we henceforth be no more children, tossed to and fro, and carried about with

every wind of doctrine, by the slight of men, and cunning craftiness, whereby they lie in wait to deceive; but speaking the truth in love." (Eph. 4:13-15)

11. There is a significant difference between Church policies and Church doctrine. Policy is not regarded as a statement of eternal truth. It represents a statement of "this is how we're going to do it at the present time." Policy changes frequently, and represents continual "fine-tuning" to accomodate the constant changes in Church population, sociological makeup, and also various external events and influences. Policy serves to regulate the affairs of the Church on a level below the system of checks and balances revealed by the Lord.

12. Policy sometimes takes the form of endorsement of causes or calls to action from Church leaders, inviting Church members to support worthy causes or to exercise their rights and duties as citizens. Policy statements are also issued to demonstrate the Church's intent to comply with various government regulations.

13. Policy statements sometimes represent a significant stand taken by Church leaders on issues which have important moral implications. While the Church avoids most political issues, it does take stands on issues which may seriously affect the well-being of its members or the nation. Church leaders have asserted that only the First Presidency and the Twelve can declare a particular issue to be a moral issue worthy of full institutional involvement.

14. Policies, or changes in policy, which may affect the entire Church membership, are occasionally presented for the sustaining vote of the Church assembled in General Conference. This is a rare occurrence, usually reserved for matters of a highly controversial nature. The two most noteworthy examples are the Manifesto and the announcement concerning the priesthood being available to all races.

14. Statements of Church policy sometimes become matters of personal concern to Latter-day Saints when they find that the Church's policy represents a public stand on issues, particularly those of a political nature, which they perceive as infringing on their personal views and tending to compel them to actions they might not otherwise choose to take, thus limiting their free agency.

16. Stands taken on controversial issues in effect place the Church membership "on the firing line." If the Church fails to provide its members with an acceptable rationale for its actions, the members are placed in the role of "defender" with no ammunition to answer the queries of their associates. The inevitable result is low morale and the danger of defection from the ranks. This is what happened, at first, with the stand taken on the Equal Rights Amendment.

17. When the Church leadership takes a stand on an issue which propels the Church into national controversy, perplexing questions are raised, the answers for which have not been clearly defined. These questions include:

A. How far can, and should, Church authorities commit the saints without receiving the prior approval of the general Church membership through the principle of common consent?

B. Does the Church exist to serve the saints, or do the saints exist to serve the Church? Which has the highest priority, the individual or the group?

C. Are statements of policy the most suitable instrument to be used in motivating and influencing the actions of the saints in such highly controversial situations, or is that properly the domain of doctrine?

18. Canonization of the Vision of the Celestial Kingdom and the Vision of the Redemption of the Dead, and the presentation of the Revelation on Priesthood, show the Church acting in obedience to the Lord's commandment that "all things must be done in order, and by common consent in the church." (D&C 28:13)

19. "Canonization" is a term which is in common usage in the Christian world, but may not be familiar to some Latter-day Saints. Canonization is the process which

A. Authorizes the acceptance and use of an item as being a prescribed doctrine, law, and belief of the Church.

B. Makes an item binding upon the saints, and makes their compliance to the item mandatory.

C. Makes an item scripture, and adds the item to the standard works of the Church.

D. Asserts the Church's belief and acceptance that the item is an eternal truth and an inspired statement of God's word and will.

19. There is no "almost doctrine" in the Church.

20. According to President Joseph Fielding Smith, "You cannot accept the books written by the authorities of the Church as standards in doctrine, only in so far as they accord with the revealed word in the standard works. Every man who writes is responsible, not the Church, for what he writes."

21. An analysis of the three items presented for the approval of the general membership of the Church in 1976 and 1978 yields the following insights:

A. Though prophets and revelators may receive revelations and speak under divine inspiration, their words and revelations are not doctrine until they are canonized.

B. The canonization process is selective—it may make some items doctrine while excluding others.

C. Items recorded in the accepted histories of the Church are not necessarily doctrine.

D. Receiving the acceptance of Church leaders does not make an item doctrine.

E. Policy changes are classed as "official declarations" in the Doctrine and Covenants. Doctrinal items are printed as sections.

F. There has been confusion among Church members as to what is "doctrine" and what is "policy." There is a need to clarify the manner in which doctrine is formulated so there is no confusion within the Church.

22. There has been considerable lack of precision among the saints in the usage of the term "doctrine." Many items have been represented as being "doctrine" which cannot be substantiated from the scriptures, have weak historicity, or clearly represent only personal opinion. To accept all the many statements and writings of current and past members and leaders as being "doctrine" is to open a Pandora's box with deep and involved implications. In contrast, "Is it canonized?" is a test easily applied that avoids almost all of those difficulties.

23. Many things may be true, and of value to the saints, which do not come under this definition of doctrine. They may be worthy of careful study and consideration. But there is wisdom in restricting that which is binding upon the saints to that which is canonized.

24. Changes and weak handling of statements concerning the status of little children after the resurrection make this a prime example of "doctrinal evolution" that really is not worthy of the status of doctrine.

25. Canonization removes the "grey areas"—fringe areas of opinion which arise and, when blown out of proportion, become the source of serious controversies which affect the lives and testimonies of the saints. Canonization establishes the rules and regulations of the Church by making them doctrine and scripture.

26. Participation in the Church, and the partaking of the saving and exalting ordinances, should not be denied to anyone without valid doctrinal or moral justification. The criteria by which fellowship with the saints might be denied to individuals should be based on sound, scriptural doctrine and nothing less.

27. Disfellowshipment is a probationary state in which individuals are prohibited, for an indefinite period, from participating in basic Church activities. Excommunication is a more serious punishment. It is a complete severance from the Church, with the concellation of all temple and priesthood blessings and privileges.

28. Church courts are held to try persons alleged to have transgressed in one of these general areas:

A. Moral transgressions,

B. Open opposition to and deliberate disobedience to the rules and regulations of the Church, and

C. Apostasy, the teaching of false doctrines, and advocating the teachings and practices of apostate sects.

29. The prophet Joseph Smith warned that almost all men, when placed in a position of authority, tend to exercise unrighteous dominion. Recognizing canonized scripture as the standard by which conduct and doctrine is to be evaluated tends to prevent individuals from exercising unrighteous dominion and imposing their personal views upon others.

30. In this day of many converts and rapid Church expansion, it is not uncommon to hear incorrect doctrines expressed in Church classrooms. Many lessons and sermons reflect only the level of understanding and doctrinal knowledge to which the speaker has attained at the time. As Latter-day Saints grow, they may find that they have been teaching some type of "false doctrine." This is unfortunate, but it is probably experienced by most Church members. Doctrinal misconceptions can exist on any level— there is no doctrine of infallibility within the Church.

31. Sincere believers remain devoted to the Church and kingdom. They remain teachable and responsive to wise counsel. Apostates, in contrast, harden their hearts, seek to cause strife, and attempt to harm and embarrass the Church. They attempt to lead others away from the saving principles and ordinances of the gospel.

32. Members are free to accept or reject the counsel of the First Presidency and to discuss their views with others. But if they begin to ridicule or deride the Church, attack those with opposing views, demean the Church leadership, or openly encourage others to interfere with the Church and its mission, they place themselves subject to Church judicial proceedings.

33. The harmful effects of the excesses of the Catholic inquisition show how a church's judicial system can become corrupt. Practices the inquisition embraced, which should be carefully guarded against by Latter-day Saints, included the following:

A. Men were appointed to zealously seek out apostates and other offenders.

B. Church members were required to report suspected apostates or be excommunicated themselves.

C. Accused individuals often were not confronted by their accusers, and those accusers were allowed to remain anonymous.

D. Witnesses for the defense rarely appeared, since that would place them under suspicion.

E. Defense lawyers worked against the accused, rather than preparing an adequate defense.

F. The accused were compelled to confess things they had not done, actions that were not sins, or recant beliefs which were not doctrinal errors.

G. Church officials in high positions were able to order tribunals to excommunicate individuals, even though no substantial evidence existed. The tribunals would obey those in authority over them rather than render the verdict warranted by the trial procedure.

34. The judicial system of a church, state or nation, is a prime reflector of the system's leadership. If unrighteousness begins to creep in, judicial irregularities will be an early sign, as potential dissenters are suppressed.

9

Will Satan Attempt to Deceive the Saints?

This book has been written to accomplish two major objectives, and it is appropriate to review those objectives as this chapter begins.

First, the foremost purpose of this book has been to bear witness that God speaks to His Church and to the world through prophets, seers, and revelators. The major message of the book is that we should trust in His prophets, look to them for inspired direction and revealed counsel, and have faith in the word of God revealed through them. Much has been written about the system of checks and balances God has established so that the proper relationship between prophets and saints is maintained. Other chapters have given guidance from the scriptures designed to increase faith in the prophetic utterances which come to the saints from God's spokesmen—material on the nature of prophecy, how and through whom it is granted, and how it can be verified and tested. Great care has been taken to report the message of the scriptures on these subjects with exactness. It is the messages of the scriptures which have furnished the content of the book—not the author's personal opinions. The overall message of the thousands of passages cited can best be summarized by returning to the words which began the prologue of this work: *"Believe in the Lord your God, so shall ye be established; believe his prophets, so shall ye prosper."* [1]

But there is a second purpose in writing; and that purpose is to raise the warning voice concerning a time yet future. The Lord has revealed warning upon warning that in the last days many people of the earth, including "the very elect," will be deceived and led astray by false prophets. Satan will wage all-out warfare upon the minds and hearts of the righteous, exceeding even the extent of his activities in past dispensations.

The time God has warned about in his revelations concerning false prophets in the last days is drawing nigh, and now is the hour to raise the

---

1. II Chron. 20:20.

283

warning voice. It is better to do so before the problem exists, when the warnings from the scriptures can be considered without undo stress and emotion, than to wait until the problem is upon us.

This warning is raised for the purpose of shielding the saints from future harm, by providing them with foreknowledge of potential danger. It is written with the certain knowledge that it is better to know of coming danger and to be prepared for it than to be caught unaware.

The Lord has revealed that a time of great tribulation lies ahead— *"The day when the wrath of God shall be poured out upon the wicked without measure—,"* [2] when *"Peace shall be taken from the earth, and the devil shall have power over his own dominion."* [3] Concerning that period the Master has said,

> Wherefore the voice of the Lord is unto the ends of the earth, that all that will hear may hear:
> *Prepare ye, prepare ye for that which is to come,* for the Lord is nigh; . . .[4]

As he dedicated the Kirtland temple, the prophet Joseph Smith pled with the Lord to

> . . . *Prepare the hearts of thy saints for all those judgments thou art about to send,* in thy wrath, upon the inhabitants of the earth, because of their transgressions, *that thy people may not faint in the day of trouble.*[5]

The testimony of this chapter is that the Lord has raised His voice with repeated warnings to the saints, and commanded His servants that hold the priesthood to clarify and expound those warnings so they will be understood by all who will give heed. We are commanded to "bind up the law and seal up the testimony, and *to prepare the saints for the hour of judgment which is to come; that their souls may escape the wrath of God,* the desolation of abomination which awaits the wicked, . . ." [6] And then, being properly forewarned, the saints stand admonished by the Lord to "Remember this, which I tell you before, that you may *lay it to heart, and receive that which is to follow "* [7]

This, then, is the second major objective of this book: to give clear warning, from the scriptures and from the Lord's Revelators, that the time draws near when Satan will attempt to deceive the saints and the world through false prophets, as he has done in former dispensations.

This author has observed that there may be those who might twist his words and misrepresent his intent, falsely alledging that this book is written

2. D&C 1:9.
3. D&C 1:35.
4. D&C 1:11-12.
5. D&C 109:38.
6. D&C 88:84-85.
7. D&C 58:5.

to disturb the faith of the saints. I bear solemn witness to those who might attempt to do so that I have carefully quoted what the Lord has revealed, and set forth only what He has set forth, and I issue to those who might misrepresent the message and intent of this book the same warning as did the prophet Nephi, that I will confront them at the judgment bar of God at the last day:

> And if they are not the words of Christ, judge ye—for Christ will show unto you, with power and great glory, that they are his words, at the last day; and *you and I shall stand face to face before his bar; and ye shall know that I have been commanded of him to write these things,* not withstanding my weakness.[8]

Scriptural Warnings of False Prophets Among the Saints

Christ: False Christs and False Prophets Shall Deceive the Very Elect

The 24th chapter of Matthew is generally acknowledged as being one of the Savior's most penetrating prophecies concerning the last days. This prophecy was uttered by the Master during the last week of his mortal ministry. As He sat on the Mount of Olives, his disciples came to him and asked him, "What shall be the sign of thy coming, and of the end of the world?" [9]

As He began his lengthy chronicle of last-days' events, in which He detailed the last-days' challenges to His Church, the theme of warning against Satan's deceptions immediately became apparent, and continued throughout his discourse. The Lord began by saying, *"Take heed that no man deceive you. For many shall come in my name, saying, I am Christ; and shall deceive many."* [10]

He spoke of the suffering and persecution the saints would endure, and foresaw that many false prophets would take a widespread toll among them. Concerning the time when there would be famines, earthquakes, pestilences, and many nations rising up against other nations, he said,

> Then shall they deliver you up to be afflicted, and shall kill you: and *ye shall be hated of all nations* for my name's sake.
> And *then shall many be offended,* and shall *betray one another,* and shall hate one another.
> And *many false prophets shall arise, and shall deceive many.*
> And because iniquity shall abound, the *love of many shall wax cold. But he that shall endure to the end, the same shall be saved.*
> And this gospel of the kingdom *shall be preached in all the world* for a witness unto all nations; and then the end come.[11]

8. 2 Ne. 33:11.
9. Mt. 24:3.
10. Mt. 24:4-5.
11. Mt. 24:9-14.

The author has often marveled at how some saints can read the verses found in Matthew, chapter 24, and not perceive their implications concerning the future course of the Church. Here is a prophecy that speaks of international persecutions against the saints, that warns that many of the saints will be offended and betray one another, and that false prophets will deceive many of them. The prophecy is far-reaching in its scope and its message deserves careful study because of the serious problems it describes. Yet it also tells us that some of the saints will endure to the end and be saved, and proselyting efforts will continue on an international scale.

And when the Savior describes the tribulations we must yet endure as the most severe the world will have ever known, He again warns that false prophets will deceive the very elect:

> For there shall be *great tribulation, such as was not since the beginning of the world to this time, no, nor ever shall be.*
>
> And except those days should be shortened, *there should be no flesh saved;* but for the elect's sake those days shall be shortened.
>
> Then if any man shall say unto you, Lo, here is Christ, or there; believe it not.
>
> For *there shall arise false Christs, and false prophets, and shall shew great signs and wonders;* insomuch that, if it were possible, *they shall deceive the very elect.*[12]

This great prophecy, with its constant allusions to the saints,[13] can only be regarded as a major warning to the Church concerning coming events. Its thrice-repeated message concerning the Church is clear, that false prophets shall rise, and that they shall deceive many, including some of "the very elect." The saints have been clearly forewarned—as the Lord said, "Behold, I have told you before."[14]

Nephi: A False Messiah Shall Deceive the People

The Savior was not the only one who left a revealed warning to beware of false Christs who would attempt to deceive the saints in the end time. Nephi, who had been granted a vision of events down through time to the last days,[15] knew of vital events which will yet influence the Church and shape the destiny of its members. He left his clear warning of "a false Messiah which should deceive the people." The event he warns about should be a major concern to every Latter-day Saint:

12. Mt. 24:21-24. Joseph Smith, in his *Inspired Version* translation of the above passage, indicated that the last verse cited was speaking of the Church: "they shall deceive the very elect, *who are the elect according to the covenant.*" (JS 1:22) Concerning the "covenant" see D&C 66:2; 101:39; 22:1-4; 88:133; 76:101; 132:6.

13. See also verse 15, with its instruction to *"stand in the holy place."* Who would do that except the Lord's people?

14. Mt. 24:25.

15. See I Ne. 11-14.

> And the Lord will set his hand again the second time to restore his people from their lost and fallen state. Wherefore, he will proceed to do a *marvelous work and a wonder* among the children of men.
>
> Wherefore, *he shall bring forth his words unto them, which words shall judge them at the last day,* for they shall be given them for the purpose of *convincing them of the true Messiah,* who was rejected by them; and unto the convincing of them that they need not look forward any more for a Messiah to come, for there should not any come, *save it should be a false Messiah which should deceive the people;* for there is save one Messiah spoken of by the prophets, and that Messiah is he who should be rejected of the Jews.[16]

Here, then, is a specific indication by a prophet of God that the people, or at least a portion of them, will be deceived by the false Christ—a frightening thought!

In his prophecy on the Mount of Olives, the Savior gave guidance for identifying the false Christs that shall come. He said,

> Wherefore if they shall say unto you, Behold, he is in the desert; go not forth: behold, he is in the secret chambers; believe it not.
>
> For as the lightning cometh out of the east, and shineth even unto the west; so shall also the coming of the Son of man be.
>
> For wheresoever the carcase is, there will the eagles be gathered together.[17]

This passage gives understanding for recognizing the Savior's final coming in glory, but will His other appearances prior to His final advent be so visible? Is that how He will come to the New Jerusalem temple, to Adam-ondi-Ahman, or to the Mount of Olives?[18] As will be seen in the remainder of this chapter, the prophesied difficulty concerning the saints being deceived and led astray by false prophets and Christs relates primarily to the first of the above-listed appearances— in the New Jerusalem. It appears the discernment problem will be a difficult one in that period.

Paul: A Son of Perdition Will Cause Them to Believe A Lie

The apostle Paul also prophesied of a false Christ who would attempt to deceive the saints and warned of a future "falling away." His prophecy is one of the most significant last-days' prophecies in all scripture because it deals with a Church-related situation: a son of perdition who will function from within a holy temple.

In his ministry he had taught the saints in Thessalonica about the coming of Christ. Some of them apparently misunderstood and believed that the second coming was imminent. To clarify his teachings, Paul wrote

16. II Ne. 25:17-18.

17. Mt. 24:26-28.

18. The scriptures and prophetic commentaries concerning these appearances are recorded in detail in *Prophecy—Key To The Future,* chapters VII, XI, and XIII. Contrast these with chapter XIV, which describes His final coming in glory.

his epistle to them in which he gave them a sign. He carefully described a last-days' event which would shortly precede Christ's coming, and taught them that the Savior would not appear until the event given as a sign had taken place. This is his prophetic warning:

> *Let no man deceive you by any means:* for that day [Christ's coming in glory] shall not come, except *there come a falling away first,* and that man of sin be revealed, *the son of perdition;*
> Who opposeth and exalteth himself above all that is called God, or that is worshipped; so that *he as God sitteth in the temple of God, shewing himself that he is God.*
> Remember ye not, that, when I was yet with you, I told you these things?
> And now ye know what withholdeth that he might be revealed in his time.
> For the mystery of iniquity doth already work: only he who now letteth will let, until he be taken out of the way.
> And then shall that Wicked be revealed, *whom the Lord shall consume with the spirit of his mouth, and shall destroy with the brightness of his coming:*
> Even him, *whose coming is after the workings of Satan* with all power and signs and lying wonders,
> And with all *deceivableness of unrighteousness* in them that perish, because they received not the love of the truth, that they might be saved.
> And for this cause God shall send them *strong delusion, that they should believe a lie:*
> That all might be damned who believed not the truth, but had pleasure in unrighteousness.[19]

Paul's prophecy has several elements which require detailed comment:

1. There will be a falling away of unrighteous saints who will be deceived, before the coming of Christ (II Thess. 2:3, 10-12).

2. A son of perdition will be revealed whose coming is after the working of Satan (II Thess. 2:3, 9).

3. The son of perdition will sit in the temple of God, representing himself as being God (II Thess. 2:4).

4. Christ will destroy the son of perdition with the brightness of his coming (II Thess. 2:8).

1. *There will be a falling away of unrighteous saints who will be deceived, before the coming of Christ.* Other passages make reference to such an apostasy in the period of the New Jerusalem. Third Nephi 21:20 describes a group of unrepentant individuals who will be cut off from among the Lord's people as the gathering to the New Jerusalem is taking place.[20] Nephi also tells of a group who will be "cut off" because they won't heed the words of Christ, while the righteous "shall not be confounded." This is to happen in the days of the New Jerusalem, for the passage speaks of those who will "fight against Zion" during this time.[21] D&C 64:35 tells

19. II Thess. 2:3-12.
20. See 3 Ne. 21:12-25.
21. 1 Ne. 22:14-22.

how "the rebellious shall be cut off out of the land of Zion,"[22] while D&C 85:11 proclaims that those who "have apostatized" or have been "cut off from the church" will be excluded from the New Jerusalem.[23] D&C 45:57 also alludes to those who will have been "deceived" among the church in the last days.[24] Thus there is a definite pattern of prophecy warning of apostasy and cleansing of the church in the last days, and specifically in the early days of the New Jerusalem period. This prophecy of Paul is a harmonious part of that pattern.

2. *A son of perdition will be revealed whose coming is after the working of Satan.* In the pre-mortal conflict in heaven, Satan stood in opposition to God. He was "thrust down from the presence of God and the Son, And *was called Perdition,* for the heavens wept over him—he was Lucifer, a son of the morning.[25] Members of the Church who succumb to Satan's temptations, after having full preparation and a firm testimony, become "sons of perdition":

. . . We beheld Satan, that old serpent, even the devil, who rebelled against God, and sought to take the kingdom of our God and his Christ—

Wherefore, *he maketh war with the saints of God, and encompasseth them round about.*

And we saw a vision of the sufferings of those with whom he made war and overcame, for thus came the voice of the Lord unto us:

Thus saith the Lord concerning *all those who know my power, and have been made partakers thereof, and suffered themselves through the power of the devil to be overcome, and to deny the truth and defy my power—*

These are they who are the sons of perdition, of whom I say that it had been better for them never to have been born;

For they are vessels of wrath, doomed to suffer the wrath of God, with the devil and his angels in eternity;

Concerning whom I have said there is no forgiveness in this world nor in the world to come—

Having denied the Holy Spirit after having received it, and having denied the Only Begotten Son of the Father, having crucified him unto themselves and put him to an open shame.[26]

Latter-day Saint understanding has been that only members of The Church of Jesus Christ of Latter-day Saints can have sufficient preparation that it becomes possible that they can become sons of perdition if they fall and yield to Satan's wiles.[27] President Joseph Fielding Smith, for instance, taught the following in general conference:

---

22. D&C 64:35. See 64:33-43.

23. D&C 85:11. See 85:3-12.

24. D&C 45:57. See 45:56-75.

25. D&C 76:25-26. Perdition means "Lost."

26. D&C 76:28-35. For further explanation on the sons of perdition—their sin and their fate—see the author's book *Life Everlasting,* pp. 289-308. D&C 76 also indicates that the sons of perdition are those who "deny the Son after the Father has revealed him" (76:43), and that there will be *many* who will suffer this fate (76:45-48).

27. See D&C 76:29, 32.

I think I am safe in saying that *no man can become a Son of Perdition until he has known the light: Those who have never received the light are not to become Sons of Perdition.* They will be punished if they rebel against God. They will have to pay the price of their sinning, but *it is only those who have the light through the priesthood and through the power of God and through their membership in the Church* who will be banished forever from his influence into outer darkness to dwell with the devil and his angels. *That is a punishment that will not come to those who have never known the truth.* Bad as they may suffer, and awful as their punishment may be, they are not among that group which is to suffer the eternal death and banishment from all influence concerning the power of God.[28]

In the same conference, President Stephen L. Richards alluded to President Smith's statement and said,

I wish all of you—perhaps all did not—had heard what President Joseph Fielding Smith told us yesterday, something I have long believed, and I was glad to have sanction for my belief. He said in substance that *there will be no Sons of Perdition who do not hold the Priesthood.* I have believed that for years because I do not think that the Lord in his mercy would ever condemn a man to that indescribable penalty of being put out entirely from the Kingdom and from all grace *unless that man knew that Jesus was the Christ, unless he knew the power of the Christ, and he could only know that, I think, by holding the Priesthood.* I believe that in the main that can be said to be true—*that only men who hold the Priesthood of God stand in danger of that terrible penalty of being classed as outcasts.*[29]

If one must hold Church membership to be a son of perdition, then it becomes obvious that this false Christ cannot be a Catholic pope, nor a Protestant minister, nor some traveling evangelist. He will have to be an apostate Mormon, not some unknown outsider. This would explain how he may be able to "deceive the very elect," and how he will have temple access. He will appear to have priesthood power, and will perform "signs and lying wonders," but his power will be counterfeit, "after the working of Satan."[30]

3. *The son of perdition will sit in the temple of God, presenting himself as being God.* The existence of a temple is an integral part of this pro-

---

28. Joseph Fielding Smith, President of the Council of the Twelve Apostles, *CR,* October, 1958, p. 21.

29. President Stephen L. Richards, First Counselor in the First Presidency, *CR,* October, 1958, p. 86.

30. II Thess. 2:9. Note that the false Christ will not be Satan himself—he will be a "son of perdition" and his power will be *"after the working of Satan."* He will be *"destroyed"* with the brightness of Christ's coming, but Satan will remain on the earth and finally be bound a thousand years. (See Rev. 20:2-3.) Concerning false apostles who function with Satanic power, the apostle Paul wrote:

But what I do, that will I do, that I may cut off occasion from them which desire occasion; that wherein they glory, they may be found even as we.

phetic warning, and the tangible existence of a temple building is a requisite for the literal fulfillment of the prophecy.

Paul visited Thessalonica during his second missionary journey,[31] then journeyed to Athens and on to Corinth. While in Corinth he wrote both his epistles to the Thessalonian saints. Bible scholars place the date of these epistles about 50 or 51 A.D. A temple existed at that time in Jerusalem. This temple, known as the temple of Herod, stood until 70 A.D., when it was destroyed by Roman legions under the command of Titus. No temple was then found on the earth until such sacred temples were again constructed in the last days, beginning with the Kirtland temple in the mid-1830's.

Since the son of perdition must sit in a temple to fulfill the prophecy, he would have to do so in a time when a temple exists upon the earth. This helps to determine the time of fulfillment of the prophecy. If it was fulfilled in ancient times, then the fulfillment would have had to take place in the two decades between the time of Paul's epistle and the fall of the temple, from 50 to 70 A.D.

But those who believe this prophecy was fulfilled in ancient times, as part of the "great apostasy," can offer no historical incident during that period which could be a possible fulfillment. Indeed, 70 A.D. would be an extremely early dating—an untenable dating—for the time of the "great apostasy" to have occurred.

If fulfillment wasn't accomplished before 70 A.D., then it must be in the last days era commencing with the Kirtland temple in 1836. Certainly no fulfillment is known from that date to the present, so it must be concluded that fulfillment is yet future.

The son of perdition will actually represent himself as being the Christ, exalting himself above all that is worshipped. He will occupy a place in God's temple (in the New Jerusalem?) and show himself that he is God, deceiving the unrighteous who lack the spirit of discernment[32] through lying wonders, and causing their downfall.[33]

4. *Christ will destroy the son of perdition with the brightness of his coming.* Again, an element of the prophecy aids in its interpretation. Did Christ come in ancient times and destroy an apostate representing himself to be God, or is that event still future? The answer is obvious—history

---

For such are *false apostles, deceitful workers, transforming themselves into the apostles of Christ.*

And no marvel; *for Satan himself is transformed into an angel of light. Therefore it is no great thing if his ministers also be transformed as the ministers of righteousness;* whose end shall be according to their works. (II Cor. 11:12-15. See also Al. 30:53.)

31. See Acts 17:1-14.
32. See D&C 50:1-34; 45:56-57.
33. II Thess. 2:9-12.

records no event that would fulfill the prophetic warning.[34] The event is yet future.

Here, then, is a prophecy of extreme importance to Latter-day Saints. It warns of a false Christ who will have profound influence upon the course of the Church in a future era, and will be able to deceive an unrighteous faction, leading them away into strong delusion and damnation. He must be a Church member to be able to be a son of perdition, and one who enjoys ready access to a temple in the last days. The ultimate message to future Church members concerning this individual was aptly stated by Paul: "Let no man deceive you by any means. . . ."[35]

Christ: They Who Are Not Apostles and Prophets Shall Be Known

This chapter has spoken at length of the future influence of false prophets upon the saints. The various prophecies are like the pieces of a jigsaw puzzle which are very similar—it is extremely difficult to put them into their proper place and perspective until the pattern is clearly understood. Previously quoted in this chapter are a number of prophecies which clearly allude to the danger of false prophets within the Church at a time yet future. Others, yet to be cited, appear to have reference to false prophets outside the Church—functioning in Israel, or in the worldwide arena of international affairs. The relationship of these various prophets, if any, is yet unclear, and cannot be determined until the situation begins to unfold and more pieces of the puzzle are available.

But let us return to the prophecies of false prophets who will function among the saints in the last days. It should be recalled that the Church has had to contend with false prophets and apostles in other dispensations. John the Revelator wrote to the saints in Ephesus, for instance, and commented that "I know thy works, and thy labour, and thy patience, and how thou canst not bear them which are evil: and *thou hast tried them which say they are apostles, and are not, and hast found them liars.*"[36] King Mosiah, in the Book of Mormon, alluded to prophets which had "fallen into transgression."[37] And many Old Testament passages tell of problems caused by false prophets who, despite their false revelations which

---

34. If there are those who would persist in the assertion that this prophecy was fulfilled long ago as part of the "great apostasy," they should be prepared to explain:
    1. Who was the son of perdition?
    2. In what temple did he manifest himself as God?
    3. When and how Christ destroyed him by the brightness of his coming?
    4. What historical records lend credence to such an interpretation?
35. II Thess. 2:3.
36. Rev. 2:2.
37. Mos. 15:13.

were leading the people astray, were the accepted leaders of the Church in their day.[38]

A warning from the Lord in section 64 of the Doctrine and Covenants indicates that the spirit of deception may reach into the highest councils of the Church in the early days of the New Jerusalem. The prophecy speaks of the period when the glory of the Lord will be upon the New Jerusalem in Jackson County, Missouri,[39] the era when people will gather out of all nations to the city and the nations of the earth will fear her.[40] He revealed that in that era liars and hypocrites will be judged by the saints, and warned that in that era when the rebellious shall be "plucked out," a situation will occur when *"they who are not apostles and prophets shall be known."* These are the words of the revelation:

> . . . *The rebellious shall be cut off out of the land of Zion, and shall be sent away, and shall not inherit the land.*
>
> For, verily I say that the rebellious are not of the blood of Ephraim, wherefore *they shall be plucked out.*
>
> Behold, I, the Lord, have made my church in these last days like unto a judge sitting on a hill, or in a high place, to judge the nations.
>
> For it shall come to pass that *the inhabitants of Zion shall judge all things pertaining to Zion.*
>
> *And liars and hypocrites shall be proved by them, and they who are not apostles and prophets shall be known.*
>
> And even the bishop, who is a judge, and his counselors, if they are not faithful in their stewardships *shall be condemned, and others shall be planted in their stead.*[41]

Those are strong words! Yet can a revelation from the Lord be ignored? Why did He cause it to be placed in the scripture, unless it was His intention to forewarn the saints so they would be alert to the difficulty as the time drew near? Note His specific warning—that in the early days of the New Jerusalem period when a rebellious faction will be cut off from the saints, that cleansing will reach even some who will be rejected as apostles and prophets because they will have influenced the people with lies and hypocrisy. Surely no one in the Church stands immune from God's justice.

Paul: Some Shall Give Heed to Seducing Spirits

Are those false apostles and prophets who will speak lies in hypocrisy in that era the same individuals that Paul foresaw when he wrote his prophetic warning to Timothy?

38. See, for instance, Zeph. 3:4; Jer. 2:8; 5:31; 10:21; 12:10-11; 14:13-16; 23:1-2, 11, 13, 16-17, 21-22, 25-40; 27:9-10, 14-18; 29:8-9; Ezek. 13:2-4; 22:25-28; 34:2-4; Zech. 10:2; Mal. 2:7-8; etc.

39. See D&C 64:41-43, which indicates that the time of fulfillment for this passage is yet future, and not during the brief interlude in the first decade of the Church's existence when the saints lived in Jackson County, Missouri.

40. *Ibid.*

41. D&C 64:35-40.

> Now the Spirit speaketh expressly, that *in the latter times* some shall
> *depart from the faith, giving heed to seducing spirits, and doctrines of devils;*
> *Speaking lies in hypocrisy;* having their conscience seared with a hot iron;
> Forbidding to marry, and commanding to abstain from meats, . . .[42]

The "lies" and "hypocrisy" parallel between Doctrine and Covenants
64:39, in the preceding section, and I Timothy 4:2, quoted in this section, is
of more than passing interest!

Christ: Be Not Deceived by Those Forbidding to Marry and Commanding to Abstain from Meats

But another set of scriptural parallels is of even greater importance.
In the Doctrine and Covenants, Section 49, there is a passage which explains
a variety of last-days' situations while discussing a sect called the "Shakers."
Like Paul's warning to Timothy, this passage comments on men who will

1. Forbid to marry (compare D&C 49:15-17 with I Tim. 4:3)

2. Command to abstain from meats (compare D&C 49:18-21 with
I Tim. 4:3)

3. Be deceived (compare D&C 49:23 with I Tim. 4:1)

But Doctrine and Covenants 49 places the situation in a time context, linking it to the time when "Zion shall flourish . . . and be assembled together
unto the place which I have appointed,"[43] just prior to the day when the
heavens will be shaken and the earth is "to tremble and to reel to and fro
as a drunken man," and the valleys are to be exalted.[44]

The Lord sees fit to warn, in this context, that the "Son of man cometh
not in the form of a woman, neither of a man traveling on the earth,"[45]
and warns the saints to "be not deceived" on this point. It is interesting
that the Lord would link all these concepts together, relate them to the
time when Zion is to be established, and carefully identify that those who
forbid to marry and command to abstain from meats in this period are
"not ordained of God."[46] This is the passage in Section 49:

> And again, verily I say unto you, that whoso forbiddeth to marry is not
> ordained of God, for *marriage is ordained of God unto man.*
> Wherefore, it is lawful that *he should have one wife, and they twain shall
> be one flesh,* and all this that the earth might answer the end of its creation;
> And that it might be filled with the *measure of man,* according to his
> creation before the world was made.
> And *whoso forbiddeth to abstain from meats, that man should not eat
> the same, is not ordained of God;*

42. I Tim. 4:1-3.
43. D&C 49:25.
44. D&C 49:23.
45. D&C 49:22.
46. D&C 49:15, 18.

For, behold, *the beasts of the field and the fowls of the air, and that which cometh of the earth, is ordained for the use of man for food* and for raiment, and that he might have in abundance.

But it is not given that one man should possess that which is above another, wherefore the world lieth in sin.

And *wo be unto man that sheddeth blood or that wasteth flesh and hath no need.*

And again, verily I say unto you, that *the Son of Man cometh not in the form of a woman, neither of a man traveling on the earth.*

Wherefore, *be not deceived,* but continue in steadfastness, looking forth for the heavens to be shaken, and the *earth to tremble and to reel to and fro* as a drunken man, and for the valleys to be exalted, and for the mountains to be made low, and for the rough places to become smooth—and all this *when the angel shall sound* his trumpet.

But *before the great day of the Lord shall come, Jacob shall flourish in the wilderness, and the Lamanites shall blossom as the rose.*

Zion shall flourish upon the hills and rejoice upon the mountains, and shall be assembled together unto the place which I have appointed.

Behold, I say unto you, go forth as I have commanded you; repent of all your sins; ask and ye shall receive; knock and it shall be opened unto you.

Behold, *I will go before you and be your rearward; and I will be in your midst, and you shall not be confounded.*[47]

Nephi: All Who Fight Against Zion and Won't Hear the Prophet Will Be Cut Off; The Righteous Shall Not Be Confounded

Several prophecies in the scriptures warn that when Christ comes to His Zion,[48] there will be many who will have been deceived and confounded—they will refuse to hear and obey Him, and will choose to fight against Zion.

Nephi, for instance, prophesied of a time when

1. Christ, the Holy One of Israel, will be raised up.

2. Some will be confounded, and will not hear that prophet.

3. Those that will not hear Him, and that fight against Zion, shall be cut off.

4. The righteous shall not perish, and they shall not be confounded. His prophecy, like others, portrays the conflict which will rage in the early days of the New Jerusalem, as an apostate faction struggles with the faithful. Note the seriousness of the problem: people are fearing, and fighting, and perishing. The context of the passage[49] shows the chaotic world-wide

_____

47. D&C 49:15-27. Note that the final verse cited (verse 27) alludes to travel, asserting that the Lord "will go before you and be your rearward." Could this have reference to the saints' return to Jackson County? Could the prohibition on marriage and the directive to not eat meat pertain to the travel instructions for that journey?

48. See *Prophecy—Key To The Future,* pp. 112-117 for details on this event.

49. I Ne. 22:11-18.

conditions of the period: the great and abominable church has persecuted the saints and brought nations to war against the Lord's people, only to have those nations turn and war among themselves; the Lord is preserving the righteous, while destroying their enemies. These will be perilous times, indeed.

This is Nephi's prophecy:

> For behold, *the righteous shall not perish;* for the time surely must come that *all they who fight against Zion shall be cut off.*
> And the Lord will surely prepare a way for his people, unto the fulfilling of the words of Moses, which he spake, saying: *A prophet shall the Lord your God raise up unto you, like unto me;* him shall ye hear in all things whatsoever he shall say unto you. And it shall come to pass that *all those who will not hear that prophet shall be cut off from among the people.*
> And now I, Nephi, declare unto you, that *this prophet of whom Moses spake was the Holy One of Israel;* wherefore, he shall execute judgment in righteousness.
> And *the righteous need not fear,* for *they are those who shall not be confounded.* But it is the kingdom of the devil, which shall be built up among the children of men, which kingdom is established among them which are in the flesh—[50]

Is this, then, the key to Satan's plan to deceive the saints? He will confuse them through false Christs and false prophets so they won't recognize and accept the true Christ when He comes among them!

Christ: Whosoever Shall Not Believe My Word Shall Be Cut Off; Deceivings and Priestcrafts Shall Be Done Away

A prophecy made by Christ when He appeared in the Americas also warns that many will refuse to believe His words and will be cut off from the people in the early New Jerusalem period. He also foretells "lyings, and deceivings, and envyings, and strifes, and priestcrafts, and whoredoms" which shall exist among the gentiles in that day, which "shall be done away." In the context to the verses cited below, it is shown that at the time this prophecy is to be fulfilled, many of the gentiles will have been baptized and learned Christ's doctrine, and the gathering of Israel will have already progressed to the point that it will be a source of amazement to kings and world leaders.[51] In that day the Lord will do his "great and marvelous work" which will separate those "gentiles" who believe Christ's words from those who will reject them and be cut off from the covenant people. Note that the term "gentiles" in this passage refers to members of

---

50. I Ne. 22:19-22. Concerning the identity of the prophet to be raised up, see Acts 3:22-23, 3 Ne. 20:23, 3 Ne. 21:11, Deut. 18:15-22, and JS 2:40, which together indicate that the prophet is Christ.

51. 3 Ne. 21:6-9.

the Church, for they are "people who are of the covenant" (3 Nephi 21:11) and of the "house of Israel" (3 Nephi 21:20). These are the Savior's words:

> For in that day, for my sake shall the Father work a work, which shall be a *great and a marvelous work* among them; and *there shall be among them those who will not believe it,* although a man shall declare it unto them.
>
> But behold, the life of my servant shall be in my hand; therefore they shall not hurt him, although he shall be marred because of them. Yet I will heal him, for I will show unto them that *my wisdom is greater than the cunning of the devil.*
>
> Therefore it shall come to pass that *whosoever will not believe in my words, who am Jesus Christ,* which the Father shall cause him to bring forth unto the Gentiles, and shall give unto him power that *he shall bring them forth unto the Gentiles,* (it shall be done even as Moses said) *they shall be cut off from among my people who are of the covenant.*
>
> And my people who are a *remnant of Jacob shall be among the Gentiles,* yea, in the midst of them as a lion among the beasts of the forest, as a young lion among the flocks of sheep, who, if he go through both *treadeth down and teareth in pieces, and none can deliver.*
>
> Their hand shall be lifted up upon their adversaries, and *all their enemies shall be cut off.*
>
> *Yea, wo be unto the Gentiles except they repent;* for it shall come to pass in that day, saith the Father, that I will *cut off thy horses* out of the midst of thee, and I will *destroy thy chariots;*
>
> And I will *cut off the cities* of thy land, and *throw down all thy strongholds;*
>
> And I will *cut off witchcrafts* out of thy land, and thou shalt have no more soothsayers;
>
> Thy graven images I will also cut off, and thy standing images out of the midst of thee, and thou shalt no more worship the works of thy hands;
>
> And I will *pluck up thy groves* out of the midst of thee; so will I *destroy thy cities.*
>
> And it shall come to pass that *all lyings, and deceivings, and envyings, and strifes, and priestcrafts,* and whoredoms, shall be done away.
>
> For it shall come to pass, saith the Father, that at that day whosoever will not repent and come unto my Beloved Son, them will I *cut off from among my people, O house of Israel;*
>
> And *I will execute vengeance and fury upon them, even as upon the heathen, such as they have not heard.*
>
> But if they will *repent and hearken unto my words,* and harden not their hearts, I will establish my church among them, and they shall come in unto the covenant and be numbered among this the *remnant of Jacob, unto whom I have given this land for their inheritance;*
>
> And they shall assist my people, and remnant of Jacob, and also as many of the house of Israel as shall come, that they may *build a city, which shall be called the New Jerusalem.* [52]

This, then, will be a situation in which the Lord will match His wisdom against Satan's cunning,[53] and will overcome the lyings and deceivings and

---

52. 3 Ne. 21:9-23.
53. See again 3 Ne. 21:10.

priestcrafts[54] the devil will have engendered. Note, also, that it will be in the same period when the Lamanites, or "remnant of Jacob" will go through the land and bring great destruction, as part of the Lord's cleansing judgments.[55]

Christ: The Gentiles Will Sin Against My Gospel and Be Filled With Deceits

The Savior had previously made a similar prophecy about the saints in the last days, which pertained to the same era when a portion of Israel (the Lamanite remnant of Jacob) will go through and tread down the gentiles. He focused on a faction of "Gentiles" who would be members of the Church, for they "shall sin against my gospel,"[56] (how could they sin against the gospel unless they had it?) and shall "reject the fulness of my gospel"[57] (how could they reject it unless they first had it?). He warned that this group will "be filled with all manner of lyings, and of deceits, and of mischiefs, and all manner of hypocrisy, and murders, and priestcrafts, and whoredoms, and of secret abominations."[58] This is the Savior's prophetic warning:

> And thus commandeth the Father that I should say unto you: *At that day when the Gentiles shall sin against my gospel,* and shall be lifted up in the pride of their hearts above all nations, and above all the people of the whole earth, and *shall be filled with all manner of lyings, and of deceits, and of mischiefs,* and all manner of hypocrisy, and murders, and priestcrafts, and whoredoms, and of *secret abominations;* and if *they shall do all those things, and shall reject the fulness of my gospel,* behold, saith the Father, *I will bring the fulness of my gospel from among them.*
>
> And then will I remember my covenant which I have made unto my people, O house of Israel, and I will bring my gospel unto them.
>
> And I will show unto thee, O house of Israel, that *the Gentiles shall not have power over you;* but I will remember my covenant unto you, O house of Israel, and ye shall come unto the knowledge of the fulness of my gospel.
>
> But *if the Gentiles will repent and return unto me,* saith the Father, behold they shall be numbered among my people, O house of Israel.
>
> And I will not suffer my people, who are of the house of Israel, to go through among them, and tread them down, saith the Father.

---

54. See again 3 Ne. 21:19. Nephi's definition is informative in this context: "Priestcrafts are that men preach and set themselves up for a light unto the world, that they may get gain and praise of the world; but they seek not the welfare of Zion. Behold, the Lord hath forbidden this thing." (2 Ne. 27:29-30). In Alma's account of the difficulty with Nehor, it was observed that "were priestcraft to be enforced among this people it would prove their entire destruction." (Al. 1:12) An attempt to enforce priestcraft by force may be part of the problem which will arise in the early New Jerusalem period.

55. See again 3 Ne. 21:12-21.

56. 3 Ne. 16:10.

57. *Ibid.*

58. *Ibid.*

But if they will not turn unto me, and hearken unto my voice, I will suffer them, yea, *I will suffer my people, O house of Israel, that they shall go through among them, and shall tread them down,* and they shall be as *salt that hath lost its savor,* which is thenceforth good for nothing but to be cast out, and to be trodden under foot of my people, O house of Israel.[59]

Thus this wicked faction, *if* it sins against the gospel and rejects it, will be tread down and cut off. Those fallen saints will truly be as salt that has lost its savor.[60] Again, in this prophecy, there is indication of lying and deceits, and of people being led away from the true gospel in the New Jerusalem era.

Christ: Every Soul That Will Not Hear Me Shall Be Cut Off

In yet another prophecy the Lord warned that when He will appear in the New Jerusalem there will be those who will refuse to hear and accept Him. He told once again how the remnant of Jacob will ravage the land. He then said that He "will gather my people together" and will "establish in this land . . . a New Jerusalem." He promised that "I will be in the midst of you," but warned that "every soul who will not hear" will be "cut off from among the people" when He appears.

Again, His implication is clear: some of the saints will reject Him when He comes among them in the New Jerusalem. This is His prophecy:

And I say unto you, that if the Gentiles do not repent after the blessing which they shall receive, after they have scattered my people—

Then shall ye, who are a *remnant of the house of Jacob, go forth among them;* and ye shall be in the midst of them who shall be many; and ye shall be among them as a lion among the beasts of the forest, and as a young lion among the flocks of sheep, who, if he goeth through both *treadeth down and teareth in pieces, and none can deliver.*

Thy hand shall be lifted up upon thine adversaries, and *all thine enemies shall be cut off.*

And *I will gather my people together* as a man gathereth his sheaves into the floor.

For I will make my people with whom the Father hath covenanted, yea, I will make thy horn iron, and I will make thy hoofs brass. And *thou shalt beat in pieces many people;* and I will consecrate their gain unto the Lord, and their substance unto the Lord of the whole earth. And behold, I am he who doeth it.

And it shall come to pass, saith the Father, that *the sword of my justice shall hang over them at that day;* and *except they repent it shall fall upon them,* saith the Father, yea, even upon *all the nations of the Gentiles.*

---

59. 3 Ne. 16:10-15.

60. 3 Ne. 16:15. "Salt that has lost its savor" is used by the Lord in several instances as a reference to Church members who have not functioned righteously and valiantly. See 3 Ne. 12:13; D&C 101:39-41; 103:8-10; Mt. 5:13-16; Mk. 9:50; Lk. 14:34-35.

And it shall come to pass that I will establish my people, O house of Israel.

And behold, *this people will I establish in this land,* unto the fulfilling of the covenant which I made with your father Jacob; and it shall be a *New Jerusalem.* And the powers of heaven shall be in the midst of this people; yea, even *I will be in the midst of you.*

Behold, *I am he of whom Moses spake, saying: A prophet shall the Lord your God raise up unto you of your brethren, like unto me;* him shall ye hear in all things whatsoever he shall say unto you. And it shall come to pass that *every soul who will not hear that prophet shall be cut off from among the people.*[61]

And as His prophecy continued, He warned that when the Gentiles *"shall have received the fulness of my gospel,* then if they shall *harden their hearts against me* I will return their iniquities upon their own heads, saith the Father."[62] His prophecy, like the others in Third Nephi, focuses on an apostate faction which will refuse to hear and accept the Savior when He comes among them in the New Jerusalem. Having been deceived and led astray by Satan's cunning, they will harden their hearts and turn away from the Lord, bringing His justice and judgments upon themselves.

Christ: Prepare for the Day When They Who Won't Hear the Voice of the Lord Shall Be Cut Off

Modern revelations speak of the same period in the future when a wicked faction of the Church will refuse to hear the word of the Lord, or give heed to His servants, the prophets and apostles. The Master warns that this faction will "have strayed from mine ordinances, and have broken mine everlasting covenant."

In this passage, the Lord commands the saints to do exactly what this book is attempting to accomplish. The Savior says to *"Prepare ye, prepare ye for that which is to come, . . . "* And how do we prepare? First and foremost, by acknowledging that a broad pattern of scriptural prophecies are warning that in the early New Jerusalem era, many of the saints will be confused and deceived by false Christs and false prophets. They won't recognize the true Messiah when He comes into their midst, and will be unable to discern between false and true prophets.

This is the Lord's warning:

Prepare ye, prepare ye for that which is to come, for the Lord is nigh;

And the anger of the Lord is kindled, and his sword is bathed in heaven, and it shall fall upon the inhabitants of the earth.

And the arm of the Lord shall be revealed; and *the day cometh that they who will not hear the voice of the Lord,* neither the voice of his servants,

---

61. 3 Ne. 20:15-23.
62. 3 Ne. 20:28.

neither give heed to the words of the prophets and apostles, *shall be cut off from among the people;*

For they have strayed from mine ordinances, and have broken mine everlasting covenant;

They seek not the Lord to establish his righteousness, but every man walketh in his own way, and after the image of his own God, whose image is in the likeness of the world, and whose substance is that of an idol, which waxeth old and shall perish in Babylon, even Babylon the great, which shall fall.[63]

Note the extent of their wickedness: they will stray from the ordinances and break the everlasting covenant. It appears that the righteous saints will have real need for the Spirit of discernment in this era, so that they will be able to recognize that these changes will be unauthorized of God. What kind of leadership will this faction have, that has sufficient power to enact a change in sacred ordinances and have it accepted by many of the people?

Isaiah: The Earth To Be Desolate Because Inhabitants Will Transgress and Change the Ordinances

The prophet Isaiah also foresaw this period and the wicked faction of which Christ spoke. He warned that the changing of the ordinances and the breaking of the everlasting covenant would lead to the desolation of the earth:

The earth also is defiled under the inhabitants thereof; because they have *transgressed the laws, changed the ordinance, broken the everlasting covenant.*

Therefore hath the curse devoured the earth, and they that dwell therein are desolate; therefore the inhabitants of the earth are burned, and few men left.[64]

As was seen in Doctrine and Covenants 1:12-16 above, it will be an unrighteous faction of the saints who will transgress the laws and break the everlasting covenant. Could this be done by people outside of the Church? The answer appears to be no. Can someone break a covenant if he has not first made it? Can someone transgress laws if those laws are not binding upon him? Can someone change ordinances unless he first has those ordinances? To do those things, and thus to fulfill this prophecy, the perpetrators must be Church members—partakers of the covenant.

And note how serious will be the implications of their deeds. Because they defile the earth, it will be burned and left desolate—a sobering thought indeed!

---

63. D&C 1:12-16.
64. Is. 24:5-6.

Christ: Mine Anger Is Kindled Against the Rebellious

Yet another warning from the Lord alludes to a rebellious faction which will refuse to obey a commandment from the Lord in this same period, "the day of visitation and of wrath upon the nations." The Savior spoke of the period in the last days when His wrath would come upon the nations, and said that those who professed His name but would not obey His commandments would be cut off:

> Hearken, *O ye people who profess my name,* saith the Lord your God; for behold, *mine anger is kindled against the rebellious, and they shall know mine arm and mine indignation, in the day of visitation and of wrath upon the nations.*
>
> And he that will not take up his cross and follow me, and keep my commandments, the same shall not be saved.
>
> *Behold, I, the Lord, command; and he that will not obey shall be cut off in mine own due time, after I have commanded and the commandment is broken.*
>
> Wherefore I, the Lord, command and revoke, as it seemeth me good; and *all this to be answered upon the heads of the rebellious,* saith the Lord.[65]

To be cut off apparently means to be sent away from the saints as well as to be removed from Church membership, in that future era. A revelation in 1831 stated:

> Behold, the Lord requireth the heart and a willing mind; and the willing and obedient shall eat the good of the land of Zion in these last days.
>
> *And the rebellious shall be cut off out of the land of Zion and shall be sent away, and shall not inherit the land.*
>
> For, verily I say that the rebellious are not of the blood of Ephraim, wherefore *they shall be plucked out.*[66]

Christ: The Five Wise Virgins—Those That Have Not Been Deceived

Another prophecy, the Savior's parable of the ten virgins,[67] which has reference to the Church in the last days,[68] indicates that only half of the saints will be prepared for the coming of the Savior. The Lord has described them as "they that are wise and have received the truth, and have taken the Holy Spirit for their guide, and *have not been deceived.*"[69] The inescapable implication of the passage is that the other half of the saints will have been unwise, will have been without the guidance of the Holy Spirit, and will have been deceived. Notice, in passage after passage quoted in this

65. D&C 56:1-4.
66. D&C 64:34-36.
67. Mt. 25:1-13.
68. See its context: Mt. 24 and Mt. 25:31-46.
69. D&C 45:56-57; 63:53-54.

chapter, how the Lord emphasizes the theme that many will succumb to Satan's deceptions in this future era.

Isaiah: Prophets Shall Err in Vision and Stumble in Judgment

Another prophecy by Isaiah focuses on future events and warns of priests and a prophet who are "out of the way," saying that "they err in vision, they stumble in judgment." This prophecy alludes to often-prophesied last-days people and events, making reference to the Lord's "mighty and strong one," the "overflowing scourge [which] shall pass through," and the Lord's "consumption, even determined upon the whole earth." It shall be fulfilled in the era when the Lord will "lay in Zion for a foundation a stone, a tried stone, a precious corner stone, a sure foundation," and when the Lord will "do his work, his strange work; and bring to pass his act, his strange act." At that time there will be those who have been led astray, who will say, "We have made lies our refuge, and under falsehood have we hid ourselves." At that time, according to Isaiah's prophecy, the wicked shall "fall backward, and be broken, and snared, and taken," and "hail shall sweep away the refuge of lies." Again, all of these time clues are related to the early New Jerusalem period as the American "Zion" is being established. It also alludes to events in the land of Israel.

This is Isaiah's prophecy:

Woe to the crown of pride, to the drunkards of Ephraim whose glorious beauty is a fading flower, which are on the head of the fat valleys of them that are overcome with wine!

Behold, the Lord hath a mighty and strong one, which as a tempest of hail and a destroying storm, as a flood of mighty waters overflowing, shall cast down to the earth with the hand.

The crown of pride, *the drunkards of Ephraim, shall be trodden under feet:*

And the glorious beauty, which is on the head of the fat valley, shall be a fading flower, and as the hasty fruit before the summer: which when he that looketh upon it seeth, while it is yet in his hand he eateth it up.

In that day shall the Lord of hosts be for a crown of glory, and for a diadem of beauty, unto the residue of his people.

And for a spirit of judgment to him that sitteth in judgment, and for strength to them that turn the battle to the gate.

But they also have erred through wine, and through strong drink are out of the way; *the priest and the prophet have erred through strong drink, they are swallowed up of wine, they are out of the way through strong drink; they err in vision, they stumble in judgment.*

For all tables are full of vomit and filthiness, so that there is no place clean.

Whom shall he teach knowledge? and whom shall he make to understand doctrine? them that are weaned from the milk, and drawn from the breasts.

For precept must be upon precept, precept upon precept; line upon line, line upon line; here a little, and there a little:

For with stammering lips and another tongue will he speak to this people.

To whom he said, This is the rest wherewith ye may cause the weary to rest; and this is the refreshing: *yet they would not hear.*

But the word of the Lord was unto them precept upon precept, precept upon precept; line upon line, line upon line; here a little, and there a little; that they might go, and fall backward, and be broken, and snared, and taken.

Wherewith hear the word of the Lord, ye scornful men, that rule this people which is in Jerusalem.

Because ye have said, We have made a covenant with death, and with hell are we at agreement; *when the overflowing scourge shall pass through, it shall not come unto us: for we have made lies our refuge, and under falsehood have we hid ourselves:*

Therefore thus saith the Lord God, *Behold, I lay in Zion for a foundation a stone, a tried stone, a precious corner stone, a sure foundation: he that believeth shall not make haste.*

Judgment also will I lay to the line, and righteousness to the plummet: and the *hail shall sweep away the refuge of lies, and the waters shall overflow the hiding place.*

And your covenant with death shall be disannulled, and your agreement with hell shall not stand; *when the overflowing scourge shall pass through, then ye shall be trodden down by it.*

From the time that it goeth forth it shall take you: for morning by morning shall it pass over, by day and by night: and it shall be a vexation only to understand the report.

For the bed is shorter than that a man can stretch himself on it: and the covering narrower than that he can wrap himself in it.

For the Lord shall rise up as in mount Perazim, he shall be wroth as in the valley of Gibeon, *that he may do his work, his strange work; and bring to pass his act, his strange act.*

Now therefore be ye not mockers, lest your bands be made strong: for I have heard from the Lord God of hosts *a consumption, even determined upon the whole earth.*[70]

The key phrases deserve special comment:

1. *"The Lord hath a mighty and Strong One"* (Isaiah 28:2). Note the relationship with D&C 85:7, which foretells the coming of "one mighty and strong" to set in order the house of God and to arrange the inheritance of the saints in the New Jerusalem. His appearance is described as being accompanied by hail, a destroying storm, and a flood.[71] Does verse 5 ("In that day shall the Lord of hosts be for a crown of glory . . .") and verse 16 ("Behold, I lay in Zion for a foundation a stone, a tried stone, a precious corner stone,[72] a sure foundation . . .") indicate that Christ himself is the "mighty and strong one"?

---

70. Is. 28:1-22. Compare verses 17-19 with D&C 97:22-26.

71. Is. 28:2, 17. Is this prophecy linked to D&C 29:14-21, which associates a hailstorm, a terrible disease, and the fall of the great and abominable church?

72. Christ is the cornerstone and foundation. See Eph. 2:20, I Cor. 3:11, Ps. 118:22 and Mt. 21:42-44.

2. In that day the Lord will be a *"spirit of judgment to him that sitteth in judgment and for strength to them that turn the battle to the gate"* (Isaiah 28:6). This will be the era when the Church will judge the nations (D&C 64:37-38) and during the period when those in Zion will be the only ones not as war (D&C 45:66-71).

3. *"The overflowing scourge shall pass through"* (Isaiah 28:15, 18-19). Though the people think they will be able to escape this terrible last-days plague (through a false "covenant with death"[73]), it will still come upon them. They will be "trodden down by it,"[74] and "it shall be a vexation only to understand the report."[75] This scourge is also prophesied in D&C 84:58, 96-97; 97:22-26; 5:19; and 45:31. Isaiah warns that there will be *"a consumption, even determined upon the whole earth"* (Isaiah 28:22).

4. The Lord will *"do his work, his strange work; and bring to pass his act, his strange act"* (Isaiah 28:21). As prophesied in D&C 95:89-95, the Lord will vex the nation, and perform a strange act "that men may discern between the righteous and the wicked."[76] (The relationship of this "strange act" and the "marvellous work and a wonder" have been previously discussed by the author in his book, *Prophetic Warnings to Modern America.*[77])

Yet the prophecy of Isaiah 28 does not appear to be directed only to the saints in America, but also to "scornful men, that rule this people which is in Jerusalem."[78] It is not stated where these men will be functioning—whether they will be in the old Jerusalem or based in the New Jerusalem in Missouri. One place or the other, they are depicted as "the drunkards of Ephraim, whose glorious beauty is a fading flower,"[79] and they are described by Isaiah as erring in vision and being troubled by drunkenness:

> But they also have erred through wine, and through strong drink are out of the way; *the priest and the prophet have erred through strong drink, they are swallowed up of wine, they are out of the way through strong drink; they err in vision, they stumble in judgment.*[80]

It is obvious that this prophecy makes pointed reference to key phrases found in modern scripture which can only be understood in a future context, and that this prophecy warns of prophets who will "err in vision."

---

73. Is. 28:15, 18.
74. Is. 28:18.
75. Compare with D&C 97:23.
76. D&C 101:95.
77. See *Prophetic Warnings to Modern America* (Bountiful, Utah: Horizon Publishers, 1977), pp. 175-183. Note also the close proximity of Is. 28:21 and Is. 29:14, which links the two terms together. Both chapters of Isaiah are showing last-days' relationships between America and Israel.
78. Is. 28:14.
79. Is. 28:1.
80. Is. 28:7.

Nephi: Satan Will Cheat Those in Zion and Lead Them Down to Hell

Nephi, in a prophecy couched in the last-days' era when the judgments of God are about to come upon the great and abominable church,[81] warns that a portion of the saints—those who are "at ease in Zion"—will be cheated by Satan. He will lead them astray, carefully guiding them down to hell. How does Nephi identify these people? They will

1. Be passified and lulled into carnal security, believing that "all is well in Zion . . . Zion prospereth."
2. They will hearken unto the precepts of men, and deny the power of God and the gift of the Holy Ghost.
3. They will refuse to receive new revelations, saying "we need no more of the word of God, for we have enough."
4. They will put their trust in man, rather than in the power of the Holy Ghost.

In other words, they will follow leaders who will lead them astray, by causing them to reject new revelation and inspiration from God. This is Nephi's prophecy:

> For behold, at that day shall he rage in the hearts of the children of men, and *stir them up to anger against that which is good.*
> And others will he pacify and lull them away into carnal security, that they will say: *All is well in Zion; yea, Zion prospereth, all is well—and thus the devil cheateth their souls, and leadeth them away carefully down to hell. . . . Therefore, wo be unto him that is at ease in Zion!*
> Wo be unto him that crieth: All is well!
> Yea, wo be unto him that *hearkeneth unto the precepts of men, and denieth the power of God, and the gift of the Holy Ghost!*
> Yea, wo be unto him that saith: *We have received, and we need no more!*
> And in fine, wo unto all those who tremble, and *are angry because of the truth of God!* For behold, he that is built upon the rock receiveth it with gladness; and he that is built upon a sandy foundation trembleth lest he shall fall.
> Wo be unto him that shall say: *We have received the word of God, and we need no more of the word of God, for we have enough!*
> For behold, thus saith the Lord God: I will give unto the children of men line upon line, precept upon precept, here a little and there a little; and blessed are those who hearken unto my precepts, and lend an ear unto my counsel, for they shall learn wisdom; for unto him that receiveth I will give more; and *from them that shall say, We have enough, from them shall be taken away that which they have.*

---

81. Again, this is the early New Jerusalem period. See the other prophecies concerning the great and abominable church: 1 Ne. 13:4-9, 24-29, 32, 34; 14:6-17; 22:7-23; 2 Ne. 6:12-18; 10:10-16; 28:15-20; D&C 18:20; 29:21; 86:1-7 & Mt. 13:24-30; Rev. 17 & 18.

> *Cursed is he that putteth his trust in man, or maketh flesh his arm, or shall hearken unto the precepts of men, save their precepts shall be given by the power of the Holy Ghost.*[82]

Note the constantly-recurring theme found in a number of passages cited in this chapter—that in that period, some of the saints will refuse to hear and accept new revelation when it is given to them. The Prophet Joseph Smith, on one occasion, commented on how difficult it was for some of the saints to accept new revelation. He said,

> Many men . . . will say, "I will never forsake you, but will stand by you at all times." *But the moment you teach them some of the mysteries of the kingdom of God that are retained in the heavens, and are to be revealed to the children of men when they are prepared for them, they will be the first to stone you and put you to death.*
>
> It was this same principle that crucified the Lord Jesus Christ, and will cause the people to kill the prophets in this generation. . . .
>
> Would to God, brethren, I could tell you who I am! Would to God I could tell you what I know! But you would call it blasphemy, and there are men upon this stand who would want to take my life.
>
> If the Church . . . *knew all the commandments, one-half they would reject through prejudice and ignorance.* . . .
>
> *When God offers a blessing, or knowledge to a man, and he refuses to receive it, he will be damned.*[83]

Christ: No Man Among You Received Me; Ye Obeyed Not My Voice

Another prophetic warning by the Lord speaks specifically of a time when He will come among "his own" and a portion of them will not accept Him. He warns that those who will be cut off are those who

1. "Obeyed not my voice when I called to you out of the heavens. . . ."
2. "Believed not my servants, and when they were sent unto you ye received them not." He also observed that
3. "No man among you received me."
4. "When I called again there was none of you to answer."

He proclaims that those who will reject Him will be "driven out," they "shall lie down in sorrow," and "they shall go away into outer darkness."

Isn't the scene He portrays the same as the other passages previously cited in this chapter—a portion of the saints will refuse to hear and accept Him when He comes among them in the New Jerusalem? This is His warning:

> And upon them that *hearken not to the voice of the Lord* shall be fulfilled that which was written by the prophet Moses, that they should be *cut off from among the people.*
>
> And also that which was written by the prophet Malachi: For, behold, the day cometh that shall burn as an oven, and *all the proud, yea, and all that*

82. 2 Ne. 28:20-21, 24-31.
83. *Life of Heber C. Kimball, op. cit.,* pp. 322-323.

do wickedly, shall be stubble; and the day that cometh shall burn them up, saith the Lord of hosts, that it shall leave them neither root nor branch.

Wherefore, this shall be the answer of the Lord unto them:

In that day when I came unto mine own, no man among you received me, and *you were driven out.*

When I called again there was none of you to answer; yet my arm was not shortened at all that I could not redeem, neither my power to deliver.

Behold, at my rebuke *I dry up the sea. I make the rivers a wilderness;* their fish stink, and die for thirst.

I clothe the heavens with blackness, and make sackcloth their covering. And this shall ye have of my hand—*ye shall lie down in sorrow.*

Behold, and lo, there are none to deliver you; for *ye obeyed not my voice when I called to you out of the heavens; ye believed not my servants, and when they were sent unto you ye received them not.*

Wherefore, they sealed up the testimony and bound up the law, and *ye were delivered over unto darkness.*

These shall go away into outer darkness, where there is weeping, and wailing, and gnashing of teeth.

Behold the Lord your God hath spoken it. Amen.[84]

This, then, is a reporting of many of the key scriptural passages which warn that a portion of the saints will be deceived and led astray by Satan, through false Christs and false prophets, during the early New Jerusalem period. Whether the problem will precede that era is not known. But the message of the scriptures is clear: the saints are to prepare for that which is to come, being alert to the prophesied danger and being forewarned of those who would put aside the revealed system of checks and balances God has revealed to prevent the deception from occurring.

Modern Prophets Have Warned of Division and Deception

Have modern-day prophets spoken of this era, and foretold the impact of false prophets upon the Church? Yes, they too have cautioned us of the difficulties which must yet be overcome. These are some of their words.

Brigham Young: The People Will Receive False Spirits

Brigham Young warned that the fate of the saints, if they did not receive revelation from the Holy Ghost, would be to receive promptings from false spirits to the extent that it would damn the whole nation:

It was revealed to me in the commencement of this Church, that the Church would spread, prosper, grow and extend, and that in *proportion to the spread of the Gospel among the nations of the earth, so would the power of Satan rise.* It was told you here that Brother Joseph warned the Elders of Israel against false spirits. It was revealed to me that *if the people did not*

---

84. D&C 133:63-74.

receive the spirit of revelation that God had sent for the salvation of the world, they would receive false spirits, and would have revelation. Men would have revelation, women would have revelation, the priest in the pulpit and the deacon under the pulpit would have revelation and the people would have revelation enough to damn the whole nation, and nations of them, unless they would hearken to the voice of God. It was not only revealed to Joseph, but to your humble servant, that *false spirits would be as prevalent and as common among the inhabitants of the earth as we now see them.*[85]

Joseph Smith: They Shall Deceive Almost the Very Chosen Ones

Joseph Smith anticipated that false prophets would take a terrible toll among the Lord's people in the last days. On May 12, 1844, he said:

> *The scripture is ready to be fulfilled when great wars, famines, pestilence, great distress, judgments, &c., are ready to be poured out on the inhabitants of the earth.* John saw the angel having the holy priesthood, who should preach the everlasting Gospel to all nations. God had an angel—a special messenger— ordained and prepared for that purpose in the last days. *Woe, woe be to that man or set of men who lift up their hands against God and His witness in these last days: for they shall deceive almost the very chosen ones!* [86]

Joseph Smith: My Concern—The Saints Will Be Divided

In a discourse on temple work five months earlier, Joseph Smith had already voiced his fear that "there are as many fools in the world for the devil to operate on" that the "Saints will be divided, broken up, and scattered":

> The Saints have not too much time to save and redeem their dead, and gather together their living relatives, that they may be saved also, *before the earth will be smitten, and the consumption decreed falls upon the world.*
> I would advise all the Saints to go to with their might and gather together all their living relatives to this place, that they may be *sealed and saved, that they may be prepared against the day that the destroying angel goes forth;* and if the whole Church should go to with all their might to save their dead, seal their posterity, and gather their living friends, and spend none of their time in behalf of the world, they would hardly get through before night would come, when no man can work; and *my only trouble at the present time is concerning ourselves, that the Saints will be divided, broken up, and scattered, before we get our salvation secure; for there are so many fools in the world for the devil to operate upon, it gives him the advantage oftentimes.*[87]

85. JD 13:280-281. October 30, 1870.
86. HC 6:364.
87. HC 6:184.

Joseph Smith: Men in Power Will Put Down the Friends of the Savior

Mosiah Hancock recorded the prophecy of Joseph Smith that

You will live to see[88] men arise in power in the Church *who will seek to put down your friends and the friends of our Lord and Savior, Jesus Christ.* Many will be *hoisted because of their money and the worldly learning* which they seem to be in possession of; and many who are the true followers of our Lord and Savior will be cast down because of their poverty.[89]

In addition to the prophetic warnings by early Church leaders which warn that the saints may be influenced and/or led astray by false prophets, there are numerous other prophetic statements which foretell future strife and apostasy within the Church. A number of Church leaders have made statements which reveal their anticipation of such an event.

Brigham Young: Those Who Call Themselves Saints Will Hunt Priesthood Holders

For instance, the report of an address given by Brigham Young, in late 1846, contains his warning that:

Unless the people humble themselves and quit their wickedness, *God would not give them more teachings* and that they would continue to slide off. *The time would come when those who hold the priesthood will be hunted by those who now call themselves Saints.*[90]

Heber C. Kimball, in the same meeting, warned that "Unless there is a reformation among us I am afraid that God will send a plague among us. I want the Saints to begin a new reformation, have the Holy Ghost in our midst, and *not have the twelve driven from our midst, for if they are it would be the greatest curse that possibly can befall us.*"[91]

Heber C. Kimball: Look Out for the Great Sieve—A Test Is Coming

Other statements by President Kimball contain his prophetic warning of a future time of strife and apostasy. In 1856, he said,

We think we are secure here in the chambers of the everlasting hills, where we can close those few doors of the canyons against mobs and persecutors,

88. Concerning this phrase, see pp. 211-212.
89. Mosiah Lyman Hancock, *Life Story of Mosiah Lyman Hancock,* (typewritten original), p. 29.
90. Stout, Wayne, *Hosea Stout—Utah's Pioneer Statesman,* p. 89. In a speech he made on April 14, 1848, Brigham Young raised the possibility of insurrection among the saints, which could cause them to be driven from the Rocky Mountains, though he said he had no fear of that. (See, Cowley, *Wilford Woodruff, op. cit.,* p. 330.)
91. *Ibid.*

the wicked and the vile, who have always beset us with violence and robbery, but I want to say to you, my brethren, *the time is coming when we will be mixed up in these now peaceful valleys to that extent that it will be difficult to tell the face of a Saint from the face of an enemy to the people of God. Then, brethren, look out for the great sieve, for there will be a great sifting time, and many will fall; for I say unto you there is a test, a Test, a TEST coming, and who will be able to stand?* [92]

---

92. Whitney, *Life of Heber C. Kimball, op. cit.,* p. 446. Statement of Edward Stevenson. Another witness, President A. F. McDonald, testified that Elder Kimball "clearly foreshadowed the time of trial the Saints are now passing through, *and to a period still before us. He often used the language, 'A test, a test is coming.' "* (p. 447.)

Heber C. Kimball made a similar statement in 1869, in which he referred to future trials of the saints. A difficulty exists in determining, in some instances, whether he had reference to the trials the Church endured during the 1880's or whether he was speaking of the period of persecution and strife which lies ahead.

This statement was reported by Elder John Nicholson. As it begins, Heber is referring to those who wished they had been associated with the prophet Joseph:

> You imagine, . . . that you would have stood by him when persecution raged and he was assailed by foes within and without. You would have defended him and been true to him in the midst of every trial. You think you would have been delighted to have shown your integrity in the days of mobs and traitors.
>
> Let me say to you, that many of you will see the time when you will have all the trouble, trial and persecution that you can stand, and *plenty of opportunities to show that you are true to God and his work. This Church has before it many close places through which it will have to pass before the work of God is crowned with victory. To meet the difficulties that are coming it will be necessary for you to have a knowledge of the truth of this work for yourselves. The difficulties will be of such a character that the man or woman who does not possess this personal knowledge or witness will fall.* If you have not got the testimony, live right and call upon the Lord and cease not till you obtain it. If you do not you will not stand.
>
> Remember these sayings, for many of you will live to see them fulfilled. *The time will come when no man nor woman will be able to endure on borrowed light. Each will have to be guided by the light within himself.* If you do not have it, how can you stand? Do you believe it?
>
> How is it now? You have the First Presidency, from whom you can get counsel to guide you, and you rely on them. *The time will come when they will not be with you. Why? Because they will have to flee and hide up to keep out of the hands of their enemies. You have the Twelve now. You will not always have them, for they too will be hunted and will have to keep out of the way of their enemies.* You have other men to whom you look for counsel and advice. Many of them will not be amongst you, for the same reason. *You will be left to the light within yourselves. If you don't have it you will not stand; therefore seek for the testimony of Jesus and cleave to it, that when the trying time comes you may not stumble and fall. . . . You will have all the persecution you want and more too, and all the opportunity to show your integrity to God and truth that you could desire.* (*Life of Heber C. Kimball, op. cit.,* pp. 449-451.)

Heber C. Kimball: Persecution Will Cause Many to Apostatize

Heber C. Kimball spoke on this theme and raised the warning voice on several occasions. In May, 1868, he warned,

> An army of elders will be sent to the four quarters of the earth to search out the righteous and warn the wicked of what is coming. *All kinds of religions will be started and miracles performed that will deceive the very elect if such a thing is possible. Our sons and daughters must live pure lives so as to be prepared for what is coming.*
>
> After a while the Gentiles will gather to this place by the thousands, and *Salt Lake will be classed among the wicked cities of the world.* A spirit of *speculation and extravagance* will take possession of the Saints, and the result will be *financial bondage.*
>
> *Persecution comes next, and all true Latter-day Saints will be tested to the limit. Many will apostatize, and others will stand still, not knowing what to do. Darkness will cover the earth and gross darkness the minds of the people.*
>
> The judgments of God will be poured out upon the wicked to the extent that *our elders from far and near will be called home.* Or in other words, the gospel will be taken from the Gentiles and later on will be carried to the Jews.
>
> The western boundaries of the State of Missouri will be swept so clean of its inhabitants that, as President Young tells us, when we return to that place, 'There will not be left so much as a yellow dog to wag his tail.'
>
> *Before that day comes, however, the Saints will be put to a test that will try the integrity of the best of them. The pressure will become so great that the more righteous among them will cry unto the Lord day and night until deliverance comes.*
>
> *Then* the Prophet Joseph and others will make their appearance and those who will have remained faithful will be selected to *return to Jackson County,* Missouri, and take part in the upbuilding of that beautiful city, the New Jerusalem.[93]

Joseph Fielding Smith: Those Who Won't Keep the Lord's Laws Will Deny the Faith

More recent statements by General Authorities also warn of a future falling away within the Church. Elder Joseph Fielding Smith, for instance, made this statement:

> The time will come, just as sure as we live, that there will be a separation between the righteous and the unrighteous. *Those who will not keep the law of*

---

93. *Prophetic Sayings of Heber C. Kimball to Amanda H. Wilcox.* A copy of this prophecy is available in the Brigham Young University library. The earlier context, together with the portion quoted, serve to indicate the time of fulfillment. It follows "after a while" the completion of the Salt Lake City temple and the gathering of thousands of Gentiles to the area, but precedes the pouring out of the judgments, the recall of the missionaries, and the return to Jackson County, Missouri. What are the implications of his phrase, "Many will apostatize and others will stand still, not knowing what to do"? Does this indicate division in leadership? unavailability of leadership? or merely confusion because of the persecution?

the Lord will deny the faith, for he will withdraw his Spirit from them if they do not repent after laboring with them and doing all that is possible to keep them in the line of duty. He will withdraw his Spirit from them and they will be left unto themselves. They must take one side or the other, for *this separation must surely come.* [94]

President Smith on another occasion, expressed an optimistic statement concerning the faithfulness of the saints, which should be compared with his statement above. He expressed his belief that those who will fall away will not constitute the majority of the saints:

> I have the assurance in my heart through the teachings I have received from the Spirit of the Lord, and *from the inspiration that has come to me* from the revelations of the Lord through his servants, *that the majority of this people will always remain true . . .* [95]

Scriptural Warnings of False Prophets Influencing World Affairs in the Last Days

Just as a host of prophecies warn of the danger of a portion of the saints being led astray, there are also scriptural prophecies which warn of false prophets and Satanic powers which will influence world affairs. According to Biblical prophecies, the power and control of these individuals will be of world-wide scope, and a matter of major international concern. Central to their method of operation will be the practice of deceiving people through the performance of miraculous deeds.

John: The Beast Will Deceive by Means of Miracles

John the Revelator foretold the great world-wide scope of a Satanic influence which will function in a last-days setting. In the future era when Satan's forces will do open battle with the Lord's true followers,[96] this evil power will deceive them that dwell on the earth by the means of great miracles which are to be performed. This Satanic force will gain great power, both economic and actual power over life and death, as people are compelled to yield obedience:

> And I beheld another beast coming up out of the earth; and he had two horns like a lamb, and he spake as a dragon.

---

94. McConkie, *Doctrines of Salvation, op. cit.,* Vol. 3, p. 16.

95. *Ibid.,* Vol. 1, p. 240. This statement is from the April, 1927, *Conference Report,* p. 108. See also p. 244 for the basis of his belief.

96. See Rev. 12:17: "The dragon was wroth with the woman, and went to make war with the remnant of her seed, which keep the commandments of God, and have the testimony of Jesus Christ."

And *he exerciseth all the power of the first beast* before him, and *causeth the earth and them which dwell therein to worship the first beast,* whose deadly wound was healed.

And he doeth great wonders, so that he maketh fire come down from heaven on the earth in the sight of men.

And deceiveth them that dwell on the earth by the means of those miracles which he had power to do in the sight of the beast; saying to them that dwell on the earth, that they should make an image to the beast, which had the wound by a sword, and did live.

And *he had power to give life unto the image of the beast,* that the image of the beast should both speak, and *cause that as many as would not worship the image of the beast should be killed.*

And he causeth *all,* both small and great, rich and poor, free and bond, *to receive a mark in their right hand, or in their foreheads:*

And *that no man might buy or sell, save he that had the mark,* or the name of the beast, or the number of his name.

Here is wisdom. Let him that hath understanding count the number of the beast: for it is the number of a man; and *his number is Six hundred threescore and six.*[97]

As God counteracts the influence of this evil power, an angel will proclaim this terrible warning to the people of earth, telling them not to worship the beast nor his image:

And there followed another angel, saying, Babylon is fallen, is fallen, that great city, because she made all nations drink of the wine of the wrath of her fornication.

And the third angel followed them, saying with a loud voice, *If any man worship the beast and his image, and receive his mark in his forehead, or in his hand,*

The same shall drink of the wine of the wrath of God, which is poured out without mixture into the cup of his indignation; and he shall be tormented with fire and brimstone in the presence of the holy angels, and in the presence of the Lamb:

And the smoke of their torment ascendeth up for ever and ever: and *they have no rest day nor night, who worship the beast and his image, and whosoever receiveth the mark of his name.*[98]

Many books have been written setting forth theories concerning the identity of this beast, and the consideration of this prophecy and its ramifications is too broad for this context. Suffice it to here recognize that this prophecy indicates that Satan will be able to deceive people on a world-wide scale, to the extent that this "beast" will hold both extensive economic power and actual power over life and death for a major segment of the world's inhabitants.

---

97. Rev. 13:11-18.

98. Rev. 14:8-11. John also foretold the eventual glory to be inherited by those "that had gotten the victory over the beast, and over his image, and over his mark, and over the number of his name, . . ." See Rev. 15:2-4.

John: Unclean Spirits Working Miracles Will Gather Nations to Armageddon

In another part of his great vision, John saw that the influence of this evil power will be so great that it will bring the nations of the earth into the great last-days conflict known as the Battle of Armageddon:

> And the sixth angel poured out his vial upon the great river Euphrates; and the water thereof was dried up, that the way of the kings of the east might be prepared.
>
> And *I saw three unclean spirits like frogs come out of the mouth of the dragon, and out of the mouth of the beast, and out of the mouth of the false prophet.*
>
> *For they are the spirits of devils, working miracles,* which go forth unto the kings of the earth and of the whole world, *to gather them to the battle of that great day of God Almighty. . . .*
>
> And he *gathered them together into a place called in the Hebrew tongue Armageddon.* [99]

Again, examination of the implications of John's prophecies is beyond the scope of this work. But it should be noted that he again foretells the extensive influence of an evil power, in the last days, which with the aid of a false prophet will deceive the people of the earth as it gains international power and influence. That influence will lead to the most prophesied of all last-days events: the Battle of Armageddon.

Daniel: The Horn Will Speak Great Words Against the Most High

The prophet Daniel also made reference to an evil power which shall make war against the saints and shall prevail against them until the Council at Adam-ondi-Ahman is held.[100] He saw that this evil power would "make war with the saints, and prevail against them; until the Ancient of days came," that he would "speak great words against the most High," and that he shall "wear out the saints of the most High, and think to change times and laws." Speaking of this evil power, or "horn," Daniel said,

> Then I would know the truth of the fourth beast, which was diverse from all the others, exceeding dreadful, whose teeth were of iron, and his nails of brass; which devoured, brake in pieces, and stamped the residue with his feet;
>
> And of the ten horns that were in his head, and of the other which came up, and before whom three fell; even of that horn that had eyes, and a mouth that spake very great things, whose look was more stout than his fellows.
>
> *I beheld, and the same horn made war with the saints, and prevailed against them;*
>
> *Until the Ancient of days came, and judgment was given to the saints of the most High;* and the time came that the saints possessed the kingdom.

---

99. Rev. 16:12-14, 16.
100. See Dan. 7:13-14.

THUS SAITH THE LORD

Thus he said, The fourth beast shall be the fourth kingdom upon earth, which shall be diverse from all kingdoms, and shall devour the whole earth, and shall tread it down, and break it in pieces.

And the ten horns out of this kingdom are ten kings that shall arise: and *another shall rise after them; and he shall be diverse from the first, and he shall subdue three kings.*

And he shall speak great words against the most High, and shall wear out the saints of the most High, and think to change times and laws: and they shall be given into his hand until a time and times and the dividing of time.

But the judgment shall sit, and *they shall take away his dominion, to consume and to destroy it unto the end.* [101]

This prophecy links events within the Church with the international influence of an evil last-days power that will oppose the saints. Again, detailed examination of this prophecy is beyond the scope of this book, but it should be noted that

1. The "horn" is a political entity, with sufficient power that he "shall subdue three kings."

2. The horn not only makes war with the saints, but prevails against them.

3. The horn will speak great words against the Most High.

4. The horn shall "wear out the saints."

5. The horn will "think to change times and laws."[102]

6. The saints will be given into the horn's hand until "a time and times and the dividing of time."[103]

7. When the Ancient of Days[104] shall come, judgment will be given to the saints. They shall take away the horn's dominion.

8. The horn's dominion will be consumed and destroyed unto the end.

It is clear that the above prophecy deals with a major trial which the saints must endure. While the absolute interpretation is not clear, many believe that the "horn" of Daniel's prophecy is the "beast" of John's Revelation, and thus is involved in the great false miracles and deceptions which John foretold.

---

101. Dan. 7:19-26.

102. Is it pressure from the "horn" to change times and laws that will cause some of the saints to transgress the laws, change the ordinances, and break the everlasting covenant, as is prophesied in Is. 24:5-6?

103. In prophetic dating a "time" is usually interpreted to be a year, "times" equals two years, and "the dividing of time" to be a half year. If this interpretation is correct in this instance, the prophecy is saying that the horn will oppress the saints for 3½ years.

104. The Ancient of Days is Adam. See D&C 27:11; 116:1.

God's Kingdom Shall Never Be Destroyed

Many prophecies have been cited in this chapter, from the scriptures and from modern prophets, which warn that Satan will make a determined effort to deceive mankind and seal them as his in the last days. He will focus particularly on the saints, bringing persecution and the work of false prophets upon them from outside, and the challenge of false Christs and false prophets from inside the Church. The warning has been given repeatedly to "be not deceived," and to "prepare for that which is to come."

Certainly I find no pleasure in these prophecies of future difficulties within the Church. Nor do I want to see them come to pass, for I recognize the problems, sorrow, strife and confusion their fulfillment would inevitably bring. I write to avert or soften their fulfillment, in the spirit of a priesthood bearer functioning in the universal calling to "watch over the church always, and be with and strengthen them; and see there is no iniquity in the church."[105]

These prophetic warnings should be viewed, I believe, in the context of what God has revealed concerning His kingdom and authority in this last dispensation. Daniel prophesied of the permanent nature of the restored kingdom of God as he interpreted the prophetic dream received by the Babylonian king, Nebuchadnezzar. He foresaw that the God of heaven would

> . . .set up a kingdom, which *shall never be destroyed:* and the *kingdom shall not be left to other people,* but it shall break in pieces and consume all these kingdoms, and *it shall stand for ever.*[106]

A modern revelation alludes to Daniel's interpretation of Nebuchadnezzar's vision, proclaiming that "the keys of the kingdom of God are committed unto man on the earth, and from thence shall the gospel roll forth unto the ends of the earth, as the stone which is cut out of the mountain without hands shall roll forth, *until it has filled the whole earth.*"[107]

That this kingdom will endure was repeatedly emphasized by the Savior, who revealed to the Church in the days of Joseph Smith that "the kingdom is yours, and *the enemy shall not overcome,*"[108] and "Fear not, little flock, *the kingdom is yours until I come.*"[109] It was revealed to the saints that "the kingdom is given you of the Father, and *power to overcome all things which are not ordained of him—*"[110] The prophet Joseph was

---

105. D&C 20:53-54.

106. Dan. 2:44. For a discussion of Nebuchadnezzar's dream see the author's book, *The Prophecies of Joseph Smith,* pp. 197-199. Concerning other interpretational views of a political nature, see *Prophecy—Key to the Future,* pp. 67-81.

107. D&C 65:2.

108. D&C 38:9.

109. D&C 35:27. See also 62:9; 64:4; 78:18; 82:24.

110. D&C 50:35.

318 THUS SAITH THE LORD

told by revelation that the "kingdom is coming forth *for the last time*" [111] and the saints believe that the Savior "shall deliver up the kingdom, and present it unto the Father, spotless," when "Christ shall have subdued all enemies under his feet, and shall have perfected his work." [112]

The priesthood power restored in the last days is also established with permanence, for John the Baptist proclaimed that the priesthood of Aaron *"shall never be taken again from the earth,* until the sons of Levi do offer again an offering unto the Lord in righteousness." [113] And the Lord has revealed that "the power of this priesthood [is] given, *for the last days and for the last time,* in the which is the dispensation of the fulness of times." [114]

Thus, though deception, apostasy and strife may come among the saints in fulfillment of the prophecies, it is expected that the Church and priesthood will remain and fulfill the roles to which they have been called and appointed.

Though scriptural prophecies warn of difficult times ahead for the Lord's Church, the message of the scriptures is that the Church will survive the problems it must endure and will eventually come off victorious in the latter-days panorama.

Summary

1. This book is written to accomplish two major objectives:
A. To bear witness that God speaks to His Church and to the world through prophets, seers and revelators, and to testify that we should trust them, look to them for inspired direction and revealed counsel, and have faith in the word of God revealed through them.
B. To show that numerous revelations from God warn that in the last days many people of the earth, including members of the Church, will be deceived and led astray by false prophets. It is intended to give clear warning that the time of Satan's attempted deceptions draws perilously near.
2. The time to raise the warning voice about the danger of false prophets is before the problem exists. It is better that the saints be thoroughly familiar with the warnings given in the scriptures now, when they can examine them without undo stress and emotion, than to wait till the problem is upon us. It is better to know of coming danger and to be prepared for it than to be caught unaware.

---

111. D&C 90:2.
112. D&C 76:106-107.
113. D&C 13:1. See D&C 84:18.
114. D&C 112:30.

3. This warning is raised for the purpose of shielding the saints from future harm, by providing them with foreknowledge of potential danger. The saints are to prepare for the judgments that are to come so that they will not "faint in the day of trouble."

4. The Lord has commanded priesthood holders to clarify and expound the warnings He has given so they will be clearly understood by all. They are to "prepare the saints for the hour of judgment which is to come, that their souls my escape the wrath of God."

5. The author gave clear warning, as did Nephi of old, that if individuals attempt in any way to misrepresent his intent or motive in presenting these warnings from that which is summarized above, he most certainly will confront those individuals at the judgment bar of God at the last day.

6. The scriptures contain numerous warnings that many of the saints will be deceived by false prophets in the last days. From all indications given in the scriptures, the conclusion is inescapable that these false prophets will function both within and without the Church.

7. Christ, in his discourse on the Mt. of Olives recorded in Matthew, chapter 24, spoke specifically of the saints in the last days. He warned that

A. The saints would be hated of all nations,
B. Many saints will be offended and will betray one another,
C. Many false prophets shall arise, and shall deceive many,
D. The love of many shall wax cold because iniquity shall abound,
E. There shall be greater tribulation than the world has ever known,
F. False Christs and false prophets shall show great signs and wonders; if it is possible, they shall deceive the very elect.

But in spite of these frightening conditions, the Lord foresaw that

G. He that shall endure to the end shall be saved, and
H. In this era the gospel shall be preached in all the world for a witness unto all nations.

8. Nephi (2 Ne. 25:17-18) warned that in the last-days period when the Lord "will set His hand to restore his people from their lost and fallen state" and He will "do a marvelous work and a wonder," there "should be a false Messiah which should deceive the people."

9. One of the most significant prophecies of the last days is Paul's warning of the son of perdition who will sit in the temple and deceive many (II Thess. 2:3-12). His prophecy indicates that

A. There will be a "falling away" shortly before the second coming of Christ,
B. During that falling away a "son of perdition" who is a "man of sin" will be revealed,
C. (It was shown that a son of perdition is not Satan himself, and that by definition he must be a member of the Church),

D. The son of perdition will oppose all that is called God or that is worshipped, and will exalt himself above such,

E. The son of perdition will sit in the temple of God, and represent himself as being God,

F. (It was shown that the existence of a temple was a vital element in the interpretation of the prophecy; since it was not fulfilled in the days of the ancient Jerusalem temple nor in the early history of the restored church, fulfillment is yet future,)

G. The son of perdition will show signs and lying wonders, and will function with the "deceivableness of unrighteousness" so that "they should believe a lie,"

H. The Lord will destroy the son of perdition with the brightness of His coming, and

I. (It was shown that the destruction of the son of perdition at Christ's coming clearly fixes the future time of the prophecy and shows that the prophecy does not relate to the "great apostasy" of medieval times).

10. In D&C 64:35-40, the Lord warns of difficulties which will exist within the Church in the early days of the New Jerusalem in Missouri, and indicates that the problems will extend to the highest levels of Church government. He reveals that in that day there will be a rebellious faction among the saints who "shall be cut off out of the land of Zion, and shall be sent away, and shall not inherit the land . . . they shall be plucked out." Then, as the inhabitants of Zion "shall judge all things pertaining to Zion," they will purge out the unrighteous from their ranks, even including people in the highest levels of Church government: "liars and hypocrites shall be proved by them, and they who are not apostles and prophets shall be known." If Church leaders are not "faithful in their stewardships," they "shall be condemned, and others shall be planted in their stead."

11. Paul (I Tim. 4:1-3) also warned that "in the latter times some shall depart from the faith, giving heed to seducing spirits, and doctrines of devils; speaking lies in hypocrisy." This passage has important parallels with D&C 64:39 and with D&C 49:15-27.

12. D&C 49:15-27 relates to I Tim. 4:1-3, but clearly places the prophesied situation in a latter-days context. In the time when "Zion shall flourish . . . and be assembled," just before the earth is to "reel to and fro," will come a time when

A. Men, not ordained of God, will forbid to marry.

B. Men, not ordained of God, will command to abstain from meats.

C. The Lord warns those of that time to "be not deceived"—He won't come in the form of a woman nor as a man traveling on the earth.

13. Nephi (1 Ne. 22:19-22) warned that all they who fight against Zion shall be cut off. All those who will not hear that prophet [Christ] shall be

cut off. The righteous need not fear, for they are those who shall not be confounded.

14. Christ (3 Ne. 21:9-23) warned that among the "Gentile" members of the Church in the early New Jerusalem period there shall be those "who will not believe" my work, though a man shall declare it. He shall be marred, yet I will heal him to show "my wisdom is greater than the cunning of the devil." Whosoever will not believe my words "shall be cut off from among my people."

15. Christ (3 Ne. 16:10-15) warned that at the day when the gentiles will sin against my gospel and shall be filled with lyings and deceits, "I will bring the fulness of my gospel from among them."

16. Christ (3 Ne. 20:15-23), in another prophecy of the New Jerusalem period, taught that He would appear "in the midst of you," and warned that "every soul who will not hear . . . shall be cut off from among the people."

17. Christ (D&C 1:14-15) warned the saints to "prepare ye for that which is to come," then warned that they who won't give heed to the words of the prophets and apostles shall be cut off from the people, for they have strayed from the ordinances and broken the everlasting covenant.

18. Isaiah (Is. 24:5-6) warned that the earth will be burned and left desolate because people will have "transgressed the laws, changed the ordinance, broken the everlasting covenant." It was observed that those spoken of must be Church members, because one cannot violate a covenant unless he has first made it.

19. Christ (D&C 56:1-4) proclaimed that "mine anger is kindled against the rebellious," and "he that will not obey shall be cut off in mine own due time." In D&C 64:34-36, Christ warned that the rebellious shall be cut off out of the land of Zion and shall be sent away. The rebellious shall be plucked out.

20. Christ's parable of the ten virgins, found in Matthew 25, indicates that only half of the saints will be prepared for the coming of the Savior. D&C 45:56-57 indicates that the half which will be prepared will be those who "have not been deceived," implying that the other half will have succumbed to Satan's deceptions and temptations.

21. Isaiah (Is. 28:1-22) warned of the future era when "the priest and the prophet . . . err in vision, they stumble in judgment." They will "go, and fall backward, and be broken, and snared, and taken." It will be in a time when the people will doubt that God's judgments will come upon them; they will have said, "we have made lies our refuge, and under falsehood have we hid ourselves." This will happen in the last-days period when

A. The "mighty and strong one" shall "cast down to the earth with the hand,"

B. The Lord of hosts shall be "a crown of glory . . . unto the residue of his people,"

C. His people will sit in judgment, but still do battle,

D. The priests and prophets err through strong drink, and "there is no place clean,"

E. The people will be taught "precept upon precept, line upon line,"

F. An overflowing scourge shall pass through; it shall be a consumption upon the whole earth,

G. The Lord will do "his strange work," and bring to pass "his strange act," and

H. Zion will be "a precious corner stone, a sure foundation."

22. Nephi (2 Ne. 28:20-21, 24-31) spoke of the same last-days period, identifying it as the era when the judgments of God are about to come upon the great and abominable church. He warned that in that day

A. Some saints will be lulled into carnal security, believing "All is well in Zion."

B. They will hearken unto the precepts of men and deny the power of the Holy Ghost.

C. They will refuse to receive new revelations, saying "we need no more of the word of God, for we have enough!"

D. They will put their trust in men, rather than in the power of the Holy Ghost.

E. If they do the above, the devil will cheat their souls and lead them down to hell.

23. Joseph Smith warned that the saints are not yet prepared to receive the revelations God has prepared for them. He said that "if the Church . . . knew all the commandments, one-half they would reject through prejudice and ignorance. Then he warned, "when God offers a blessing, or knowledge to a man, and he refuses to receive it, he will be damned.

24. Christ (D&C 133:63-74) foretells of the time when He will come among "his own" and a portion of them will not accept them. They will be those who "obeyed not my voice when I called to you out of the heavens," and who "believed not my servants." He warned that the proud and all that do wickedly "shall be stubble," and that they shall be "delivered over unto darkness." This will be in the era when he will "dry up the seas, . . . make the rivers a wilderness," and "clothe the heavens with blackness."

25. Modern prophets have also warned of the future era when the danger of deception among the saints would be great. Brigham Young warned that the power of Satan would rise as the gospel spread among the nations of the earth. He warned of a revelation he had received that "if the people did not receive the spirit of revelation God had sent . . . , they would receive false spirits, and would have . . . revelation enough to damn the

whole nation." He said that "false spirits" would be prevalent and common among the inhabitants of the earth.

26. Joseph Smith warned that a man or set of men will "lift up their hands against God and his witness in these last days," and that "they shall deceive almost the very chosen ones!" In another discourse he expressed his fear "that the Saints will be divided, broken up, and scattered, before we get our salvation secure." In another statement he warned that men will "arise in power in the Church who will seek to put down your friends and the friends of our Lord and Savior, Jesus Christ. Many will be hoisted because of their money. . . ."

27. Brigham Young warned that "unless the people humble themselves and quit their wickedness, God would not give them more teachings." He said, "The time would come when those who hold the priesthood will be hunted by those who now call themselves Saints."

28. Heber C. Kimball warned that "the time is coming when we will be mixed up in these now peaceful valleys to that extent that it will be difficult to tell the face of a Saint from the face of an enemy to the people of God." He said that then would be when they will have to "look out for the great sieve, for there will be a great sifting time, and many will fall."

29. In another statement, Heber C. Kimball warned that there will come a time when there will be "miracles performed that will deceive the very elect if such a thing is possible." He warned of other future events also:

A. The gentiles will gather to Salt Lake City by the thousands, and it will be classed among the wicked cities of the world,

B. The saints will indulge in speculation and extravagance, and the result will be financial bondage.

C. "Persecution comes next, and all true Latter-day Saints will be tested to the limit."

D. "Many will apostatize, and others will stand still, not knowing what to do."

E. "Darkness will cover the earth and gross darkness the minds of the people."

F. The judgments of God will be poured out and the elders will be called home.

G. "The Saints will be put to a test that will try the integrity of the best of them. The pressure will become so great that the more righteous among them will cry unto the Lord day and night until deliverance comes."

H. Then the saints will return to build the New Jerusalem in Jackson County, Missouri.

30. Joseph Fielding Smith warned that there will come a separation between the righteous and the unrighteous. "Those who will not keep the

law of the Lord will deny the faith, for he will withdraw his Spirit from them if they do not repent. . . . They must take one side or the other."

31. John the Revelator (Rev. 13:11-18) foretells a great Satanic power which will hold tremendous influence in the last days:

   A. He will do great wonders, making fire come down from heaven,
   B. He will deceive them that dwell on the earth by means of his miracles,
   C. He will have power to put to death those who will not worship "the image of the beast,"
   D. He will cause all to receive a mark in their right hand or in their foreheads, and
   E. His number will be 666.

32. Daniel (Dan. 7:19-26) saw the evil influence a "horn," or power, will exercise over the saints at a period just prior to the Council at Adam-ondi-Ahman. This "horn" will

   A. Make war with the saints, and prevail against them until the "Ancient of days" comes, and judgment will be given to the saints,
   B. Speak great words against the most High,
   C. Wear out the saints of the most High,
   D. Think to change times and laws.

Daniel says that the saints

   E. Shall be given into his hand until a time and times and the dividing of time," and
   F. "They shall take away his dominion, to consume and to destroy it unto the end."

33. Though there is abundant scriptural evidence that Satan will be able to deceive many of the saints, and there are serious challenges which lie ahead, numerous passages indicate that the Church and kingdom will remain intact through it all. As the Lord revealed through Daniel, this kingdom "shall never be destroyed, . . . it shall stand forever."

Epilogue

Insights for the Future

Much has been written in this volume about many facets of the principle of revelation. My intent has been to assemble sufficient evidence to show the broad doctrinal patterns which exist in the scriptures and in Latter-day Saint history. These patterns clearly show how God has chosen to reveal His word. They provide concise examples which demonstrate what has actually taken place in days gone by. They are carefully documented and are reported with accuracy. Hopefully, they have expanded the understanding of many who have read this book.

Detailed summaries at the end of each chapter have drawn attention to the major messages presented. Further summary is not the intent of this final section. The purpose of this epilogue is to draw what I feel to be the most significant conclusions which emanate from the documentation assembled in the book. There are four:

1. The preservation and well-being of the saints is dependent upon their obedience to the words of future revelation and guidance to be revealed through God's appointed Revelators.

2. God governs His communication to His spokesmen and to His Church through a precise set of checks and balances. The well-being of the Church will be directly proportional to the degree these checks and balances are used or abused by the saints and their leaders.

3. The Church has yet to pass through the most severe trials of its existence. During the future era of "great tribulation" which the Lord has foretold, it will be buffeted by strife and persecution resulting from the actions of false prophets and their followers, within and without the Church.

4. The severity of the trials to be caused by Satan's deceptions can be greatly reduced if members of the Church heed the Lord's prophetic warnings of that future period. If the saints accept the warnings and are prepared, Satan will be effectively thwarted. But if they reject the prophetic warnings, and fail to prepare and anticipate the danger, their suffering will be greatly increased.

Render Obedience to God's Future Instructions
Through His Revelators

We must return once again to the opening words of the Prologue:

Believe in the Lord your God, so shall ye be established; believe his prophets, so shall ye prosper. [1]

The most dominant theme of all scripture is the prophetic anticipation of the cataclysmic events of the last days. More words have been revealed on that subject than on any other! We stand in the "Saturday night" of time, knowing that these trials are about to be poured out upon the world. And we know that they are to be more severe than this world has ever known. If ever there is to be a time when the saints will need divine guidance, that rapidly-approaching era of tribulation is the time!

The scriptures have been quoted in the other chapters. My responsibility here is to convey my personal witness—that the path of survival and safety lies in the righteous saints remaining firmly united, ready and willing to be guided from the heavens. We must place our faith in God's word, and in His chosen servants. We must be personally prepared to receive inspired counsel and to render obedience to it. We must look to the "Prophets, Seers, and Revelators" for guidance, receive their inspired instructions, receive our personal confirmation that the words spoken are God's will, and then we must obey! And if my perception of those future events is correct, we will not be able to function as stumbling recruits, but must be seasoned and trained. We will have to recognize without question who speaks for the Master, and render unwavering obedience and allegiance to His words revealed through them. And as the battle lines are drawn between the righteous and the wicked, we will have to discern, through every avenue of guidance open to us, what our personal role will be, and what cross we will be required to bear.

Maintain the System of Checks and Balances Which
Establish the Proper Relationship Between Spokesmen and Saints

As was expounded at length in chapters two and three, the Lord has placed responsibilities on both the saints and upon His Revelators. The careful observance of these principles will be vital to the well-being of the Church in the day of future trials.

If the leaders fail to observe the revealed guidelines, they will foster doubts and concerns among the saints which will open the way to Satan's

---

1. II Chron. 20:20.

onslaughts. If the saints fail to maintain their obedience to the revealed guidelines, and cease to recognize the necessity of the checks and balances system functioning smoothly, then God will withhold His word from them.

The system is God's inspired plan. It cannot be ignored or circumvented. It is what keeps the Church healthy, allowing it to receive a proper "spiritual diet." Just as our bodily defenses are weakened if we fail to eat good food and adopt poor health habits, if we fail to keep the system of checks and balances working effectively within the Church we will lower our resistance to spiritual disease and the onslaughts of the evil one.

Or, to use another comparison, the system of checks and balances is a "quality control" system. If the system fails to function properly, defects will soon appear, on either or both sides of the equation. The checks and balances relationship between spokesmen and saints is the Church's first line of defense against error.

Those who know the scriptures should react with real concern if individuals, no matter what their calling, attempt to circumvent or eliminate those safeguards the Lord has established with painstaking care. The future well-being of the Church will be directly proportional to the degree these checks and balances are used or abused by the saints and their leaders.

Accept the Lord's Warnings—
False Prophets Will Deceive Many Saints

The Bible contains many warnings of an apostasy which was to occur shortly after the days of the apostles in the meridian of time. Catholicism has steadfastly refused to accept the reality that those passages referred to it.

Latter-day scriptures, and the Bible also, warn of false prophets and extensive apostasy to come in the approaching era of great tribulation. The saints can either assume the undignified stance of the ostrich and disregard the existance of these inspired warnings (as most have apparently managed to do), or they can accept the future danger as a grave reality and prepare before the darkness falls. Ignoring the prophecies will not help us, just as ignoring the prophecies prevented Catholicism from correcting its errors and averting its continual slide into further apostasy.

Yes, the thought of such difficulties is extremely unpleasant—I don't want them to happen any more than any other Latter-day Saint. But the Lord has told us repeatedly, heaping warning upon warning. Doesn't He want us to recognize the approaching danger and to prepare for it?

In a dilemma of such gigantic proportions, with potential to bring both great temporal and tremendous spiritual harm to the saints, it is vital that we recognize the threat, accept the gravity of the situation, and make adequate preparations. Just as one cannot ignore a hurricane when it approaches his home, this time of trial cannot be ignored. It will come! The

Lord has told us so! Acknowledge it! And be afraid of false prophets and ostrich-oriented saints who deny it and cry "peace," or who attempt to portray those who are aware of the Lord's warnings as "worry mongers"— it is they who are without knowledge!

Prepare to Resist Satan's Deceptions

Sound knowledge of the gospel, a firm testimony that God is directing his people, freedom from sin, true receptivity to personal inspiration, a thorough understanding of the prophesied events of the last days, family unity, an awareness of impending danger—all these are vital ingredients to the personal preparation which will be needed of every faithful Latter-day Saint.[2] Such preparation requires *time,* and it doesn't come easily. The saints need to study and pray, provide for their temporal needs, increase their spirituality. They need to warn and prepare their children, and unite their families into a solid, cohesive unit that can withstand the trials which lie ahead. They need to prayerfully determine what God will require of them—what role will be theirs to enact. And they need to be ready to report for duty when God calls, and willingly serve to turn the tide and win the victory.

May we prepare well, be ready when our Master calls, and faithfully perform all that is to be required of us, I humbly pray—

Duane S. Crowther

---

2. For a comprehensive outline of what preparations need to be made, see the author's book, *Prophetic Warnings to Modern America,* pp. 355-403.

List of Quotations

Index

to non-leaders, 15-16; Only when acting as such, 66, 97; Can fall and be removed, 67-79; Some envy for the sake of the prophet, 101-102; Those not prophets to be known, 292-293.

Prophetic Warnings to Modern America, 24; Cross references to, 20, 305.

Prophets and Prophecies of the Old Testament: Cross references to, 159, 174-175, 202-203.

Q

Quorum of Twelve Apostles, 131-132, 260; Hold keys jointly, 39; Authority of, 40; Can be tried for transgression, 71; Apostasies from, 75-76.

R

Records: Of Revelations, 81.

Responsibilities: Of revelators, 52-53, 92; Of Church members, 52-54, 56, 76, 97.

Revelation, 120, 121; Thou shalt have, 125; Not all acts of leaders inspired, 58, 103, 108-110; Examples of r. to saints which influenced the Church, 104-110; To be shared with the saints, 113-119.

Revelator: Definition of the term, 35-36; President of the Church, 36-37; Blessings promised to, 89-91.

Revelation on Priesthood, 251-252, 259-262.

Richards, Stephen L.: Statement by, 290.

Richards, Willard: Prophecy concerning, 110-111.

Rigdon, Sidney, 85, 86, 87; Secretary of Kirtland Safety Society, 46; Sins forgiven, 69; Joseph objects to, 88-89.

Roberts, Brigham H.: Statements by, 58, 128-129, 134, 263, 264-265.

Rogers, Aurelia S.: Establishment of Primary Association, 107.

S

Sacred, 158, 142.

Salt, 299.

Satan, 226-227; Teaches false doctrine, 246-247; Will attempt to deceive the saints, 283-318.

Scripture: Words of those moved upon by Holy Ghost, 115-116; Canonization, 116, 253, 254; Define doctrine, 238-247; Term means "act or product of writing," 254-256; The test of doctrine, 256.

Secondary Sources, 194-195.

Secrecy, 142; Don't keep revelations secret, 117-119; commanded to share revelations, 155-159.

Seer: Definition of the term, 31-35; Is a prophet also, 31; Listed, 33, 34; President of the Church, 36-37.

Seer Stones, 32-34.

Smith, Joseph, 35, 36; Kirtland Safety Society, 46-47; Calling conditioned on obedience, 67-69; Sins forgiven, 67, 69; Statements by, 38, 40, 47, 70, 97, 103-104, 120, 131-132, 145, 148-149, 156-157, 162, 258, 263, 307, 309, 310.

Smith, Joseph Fielding: Statements by, 38-41, 256, 264, 265, 312-313; Standard works the measure of doctrine, 256; Refutes previous doctrinal error, 269; Only priesthood holders can be sons of perdition, 290.

Son of Perdition: To sit in temple and deceive the saints, 287-292.

Sunday School: Established, 106-107.

Sustaining Vote of Members, 37, 82, 85-88; Definition, 37, 42-43; Does not make leader a prophet, 37.

T

Testimony, 123-124; Personal revelation essential for, 120-121.

Tests for Revelation, 97, 189-216; Church Covenants, 79-80; Checklist for evaluating validity, 200-202.

Thoughtful Disciples: Crying need for, 128-129.

Thus Saith the Lord, 59-66.

U

Urim and Thummim, 33-34.

U.S. Constitution: God established, 19.

V

Vision of the Celestial Kingdom, 251, 256-258.

Vision of the Redemption of the Dead, 251, 258-259.

W

Watchman, 23-25, 56, 64-65, 283-285.

Widtsoe, John A.: Statements by, 36, 37, 57, 122.

Williams, Frederick G.: Dropped from First Presidency, 87-88.

Woodruff, Wilford: Statements by, 73, 136, 138, 155, 161-162, 263; Visions of, 105.

Women: Can prophesy, 162-164.